I0797678

PLAY-
MAKERS

ALSO BY
MICHAEL KIMMEL

Roads Not Taken: Progressive Populism in Historical Perspective

Healing from Hate: How Young Men Get Into—and Out Of—Violent Extremism

Angry White Men: American Masculinity at the End of an Era

The Guy's Guide to Feminism (with Michael Kaufman)

Misframing Men: The Politics of Contemporary Masculinities

Guyland: The Perilous World Where Boys Become Men

The History of Men: Essays on American and British Masculinities

The Gender of Desire: Essays on Male Sexuality

The Gendered Society

Manhood in America: A Cultural History

Against the Tide: Pro-Feminist Men in the United States, 1776–1990 (with Tom Mosmiller)

Revolution: A Sociological Perspective

Absolutism and Its Discontents: State and Society in Seventeenth Century France and England

* * *

The Jewish Entrepreneurs
Who Created the
Toy Industry in America

MICHAEL KIMMEL

W. W. NORTON & COMPANY
Independent Publishers Since 1923

Printed in the United States of America
First Edition

For information about special discounts for bulk purchases, please contact W. W. Norton Special Sales at specialsales@wwnorton.com or 800-233-4830

Manufacturing by Lakeside Book Company
Book design by Lewelin Polanco
Title page art (Teddy Bear): AlsuSh / Shutterstock
Production manager: Anna Oler

ISBN: 978-1-324-10528-2

W. W. Norton & Company, Inc., 500 Fifth Avenue, New York, NY 10110
www.wwnorton.com

W. W. Norton & Company Ltd., 15 Carlisle Street, London W1D 3BS

Authorized EU representative: EAS, Mustamäe tee 50, 10621 Tallinn, Estonia

10 9 8 7 6 5 4 3 2 1

For Sandi

And those ideal Saturday mornings

The Russian Jewish element defies analysis. . . .
But to say what the Russian Jew is and can be in America is to prophesy the course of the twentieth century.

***THE RUSSIAN JEW IN AMERICA*, 1906**

Men may change their clothes, their politics, their wives, their religions, their philosophies, to a greater or lesser extent: they cannot change their grandfathers.

HORACE KALLEN, 1915

It's fun to have fun, but you have to know how.

DR. SEUSS, 1957

Contents

PART IV
Creating Childhood

PLAY-MAKERS

INTRODUCTION

Photo of Morris Michtom and Shirley Temple (photographer unknown).

Like so many journeys, this one starts with a photograph.

When I was growing up, a framed photograph of Shirley Temple stood on my family's Knabe piano. Shirley is about ten, her hair is curled perfectly, her eyes are bright and wide, and her lips are puckered in that adorable faux-surprised look she made famous. She sits on the lap of an older man, with little hair and a full mustache, who is wearing a suit and glasses. He looks serious, a bit sad, but in a kindly grandfatherly way. The photograph was autographed by someone named Morris, obviously the man in the photo, as if he were also famous. "To Barbara," it read. "Love from Shirley Temple and Uncle Morris."

Who was this Uncle Morris? And what was he doing with America's most popular child actor sitting on his knee?

He was, my mother told me, her great-uncle Morris, my great-great-uncle, the brother of my great-grandfather. I knew only the sketchiest of stories about him, passed to my sister and me from my mother and her father, but only sporadically and with little enthusiasm. My mother's side of the family spoke of him the way many of us speak of the distant past, a past with no present.

It turns out that my great-great-uncle *was* famous: He had invented the Shirley Temple doll and founded the Ideal Toy Corporation. His most important invention, the one that started it all, was the Teddy Bear, which he and his wife, Rose, created in the back room of their Brooklyn candy store in 1902.

The story of how Morris Michtom invented a soft little bear made from clothing scraps, stuffed with sawdust, with button eyes and an expression of sad longing—a certain head-tilted yearning that only the love of a child could assuage—began my journey into the history of eastern European Jewish immigrants in the early twentieth century as well as the history of the American toy industry. The story morphed into one of the first-generation Jewish immigrants who remade America—and in particular, American childhood—not in their own image but in the image of what they wanted it to be.

Morris and Rose weren't the only poor immigrants to find their way, make their mark, and ultimately succeed in America. Morris wasn't even the only Jewish *toymaker* to follow such a path. In fact, it's astonishing, and not coincidental, that there were so many others, like the Hassenfeld brothers—Henry, Hillel, and Herman—in Providence; Ruth Moskowicz and her husband Elliot Handler in Los Angeles; and Louis Marx and Joshua Lionel Cowan, both in New York City—though you may be more familiar with the names of the toy companies they founded: Hasbro, Mattel, Marx, Lionel Trains.

In fact, the entire toy industry in America was largely Jewish, from the company founders and executives to the designers and factory workers, from the wholesale distributors, the army of salesmen, to the retail outlets and the large department stores that sold them.

I started this research thinking I was writing a family memoir, a story of my own distant relatives who played an important role in the lives of children for over a century. But I always came across another story to be told, another thread of this rich tapestry to be uncovered. Not just the Michtoms and the Ideal Toy Company, but the Hassenfelds and Hasbro, the Handlers and Mattel, Lionel Cowan, Louis Marx, down to Eddy Goldfarb and his Yakity Yak Talking Teeth and Lewis Glaser and those plastic model airplanes that so dominated my childhood.

Around another corner I found the inspirations for many modern toys and later action figures: comic book characters like Li'l Abner, Popeye, and Joe Palooka, comic book heroes like Superman, Batman, Spiderman, and the entire Marvel Universe, and even Archie and his Riverdale pals, as well as those *Classics Illustrated* comics that gave kids like me our first taste of Cliff Notes.

Open another door, and so many of the best-known children's authors appeared, from Ezra Jack Keats, Kay Thompson, and Ruth Krauss to Maurice Sendak and the Reys. Yes, Curious George, Peter, Eloise, and Max—all were created by first-generation Jews.

Another turn, and I was suddenly surrounded by parenting magazines and advice books, and the legions of parenting experts and child psychologists who taught Americans how to raise their children.

For a while, it felt like everywhere I looked, I saw first-generation Jews—they created so many of the toys, games, books, TV shows, and comic books that composed my own childhood. Spanning the entire twentieth century, nearly all these men and women had stories similar to Morris's: For the most part, they were first-generation Jews or, if not, immigrants who came to America as young children. Virtually that entire first wave experienced the depravity and deprivation of the slums of the East Coast cities, went to work at an early age, and struggled to find their way in America, a land of both unimaginable riches and entirely familiar bigotries. Yet in spite of—and because of—these struggles, they shared a clear vision for what childhood *might* look like, a vision borne out in the toys they made, the stores they ran, the comics they drew, and the books they wrote. It was a vision that ended up shaping the future of not just their own children but all children in twentieth-century America and beyond.

I decided not only to try to tell the bigger story about all those creators and entrepreneurs and the world they made, but also to ask why: Why them? Why then? Why here?

Playmakers is the story of the creation of the idealized childhood that these poor, often Yiddish-speaking, tenement-dwelling children of immigrants from Russia and eastern Europe never got to live for themselves. They imagined a world where other children could have the experiences they lacked—and, in so doing, they transformed America. They didn't just transform the way we understand childhood. They invented twentieth-century American childhood.*

* * *

Children weren't always "children" in the sense we understand today. Since long before the founding of the United States, the offspring of all but the uppermost echelons of American society were apprenticed out or worked the family farm before their age hit double digits. Both boys and girls had work to do on the farm. Urban daughters learned the skills they would need to be mothers and wives, even if they also ended up working for wages. Boys could ship out on a whaler, join the army, or learn a trade. Everyone had a job. Childhood was about work, not play. Children were economic assets; their value in labor offset the costs of housing and feeding them.

But around the time when Morris Michtom and his contemporaries began arriving in America, then inventing and selling their toys, a sea change was starting to coalesce. Economic and social shifts—declining birth rates, urbanization, educational reforms, labor relations—were

---

* A word about terminology. I use the term *first-generation* to refer to those people who were the first in their family to be born in the United States. Some have referred to these as *second-generation*, assuming that their immigrant parents were the first generation. I think it's both linguistically and culturally preferable to use *first generation* to denote the first ones born in America.

under way that would lead to changes in our ideas about child-rearing, child development, and proper parenting. These changes, in turn, opened up opportunities for entrepreneurs to create a new material culture, to provide toys, games, and books to entertain and educate children for a new century, *their* century, the "century of the child."

This new childhood didn't just happen. It was created. My task here is to tell the story of those men and women who channeled the promise of the American Dream into a new way of thinking about childhood, even as they were haunted by the privations of their own pasts. In the process, they secured the financial success that guaranteed that their own children would enjoy the fruits of their creations.

Histories of American childhood have been written before, as have a few academic histories of American toys. Some of these books describe the cutthroat toy business or offer a biography or memoir of one of the pioneers in these collective industries of childhood. A few more scholarly tomes address the ways that child-rearing experts used magazine columns and parenting books to popularize medical and psychological advice. There's even been a Pulitzer Prize–winning novel about the world of the early superhero comic books and their creators.

But here I want to pose a question about this phenomenon: Why were so many of these inventors, marketers, toymakers, sellers, artists, writers, and scholars—the cultural and professional arbiters of the new childhood—Jews? And not just any Jews but first-generation Jews? Why in America but not in England or continental Europe? What, if anything, did being Jewish have to do with any of this?

This is not a Hollywood fairy tale—although most of the Hollywood films with those happy endings were *also* produced by first-generation Jews, as Neal Gabler's *An Empire of Their Own* so ably details. Instead, it's a story of both triumph and ambitions thwarted and unrealized. As much as these men and women climbed the ladder of success, they were never fully accepted into the elite circles they yearned to enter. As Jews, they were always outsiders, no matter how close they got to the hallowed inside. Thus, this is a quintessentially *American* story, a story of men who devoted themselves earnestly to the American Dream, only to find that it was a fiction—comfortable but ultimately, often, devoid of meaning. What could be more American than that?

I don't intend this book to be a triumphalist parade of famous and not-so-famous first-generation Jews that attributes their success to some cultural, ethnic, or even biological gift. Not in the least. Nor am I claiming that *every* great creator of the new American childhood was a first-generation Jew. Benjamin Spock, Walt Disney, Charles Schulz, and Theodore Geisel had as much to do with the creation of American childhood as any other quartet I can think of—and none of them was Jewish. (Disney, in fact, was rumored to be anti-Semitic, or at the very least, an ally to known anti-Semites of his day.) Like the Jews whose stories I will tell here, these men, too, saw childhood as a world unto itself, enchanted, inhabited by wild creatures, animated by the eternal struggles between good and evil, in which the good guys inevitably triumphed (except for dear, sweet, pathetic Charlie Brown, the loser as Everyman). They too imagined a reality that might magically transport children to realms of beauty and safety.

However, I will argue that Spock, Disney, Schulz, and Geisel were collaborators in the creation of something that was overwhelmingly shaped by first-generation Jews, in numbers far out of proportion to Jews in the overall population. Moreover, I won't simply enumerate the individual Jews who dominated the industries (although they held virtual monopolies over the toy and comic book sectors); rather, I'll probe the deeper affinity between first-generation Jews and the new vision of childhood—which might never have come to exist without their contributions.

Nor will I claim that Jews, as such, invented American childhood. On the contrary, the German Jews who had immigrated in the mid-nineteenth century were as European in their outlook about children, and often as strictly authoritarian, as any good Protestant family. Those German immigrants created other things—the modern system of investment banking (Schiff, Lehman, Loeb, Goldman, Sachs) that funded the railroads that unified the nation after the Civil War, and the large retail department stores (Gimbels, Abraham & Straus, and eventually Macy's) on which the new turn-of-the-century arrivals would depend for the distribution of their goods.

It was, rather, the second wave of Jews, the eastern European shtetl Jews, the *Yiddishkeit* Jews like Isaac Bashevis Singer, who saw in children's precocity and wonder the miracle of life itself. It was the Yiddish-speaking Jews from the Pale of Settlement who fled pogroms, only to live in squalid tenements on the Lower East Side and other ghettos, who gave contemporary American childhood both its form and its content.

There is, I will argue, a confluence among the experiences of being a Jew, an immigrant, and a child. All three are outsiders; all look into a world that they cannot enter but into which they want desperately to fit. The child looks at the adult world with wonder and fear, as the newcomer to America looks at a world of unparalleled opportunity as well as discrimination and violence by the nativist majority. The connection among these experiences is not preordained, but it is not mere coincidence either.

Taken together, the toymakers, artists, writers, psychologists, and others whose stories I will tell created both the idea and the material reality of childhood that came to dominate—indeed, to *define*—the world of American children for the rest of the twentieth century. Their legacies carry through to today, when seven of the top-ten toy companies in the world are either Mattel and Hasbro proper or their wholly owned subsidiaries like Barbie, Fisher-Price, Nerf, and Hot Wheels.

In the pages that follow, you'll meet the toymakers and follow them from the shtetl to the Lower East Side, the Bronx, and Brooklyn. You'll watch Morris Michtom create the Teddy Bear and almost single-handedly start the modern American toy company. You'll read of how a clever young engineer, Joshua Lionel Cohen, changed his name and invented the world's most successful electric train set. You'll listen as African American celebrities, urged on by Eleanor Roosevelt, finally persuade Ideal's executives to create the first mass-produced and nationally-marketed Black doll. You'll sit with a group of wide-eyed young men who drew comic strips and comic books, creating the superheroes whose exploits dominated youthful imaginations and whose namesake toys animated so many childhoods. You'll meet the "toy king" who copied other toymakers' designs, then undersold them. You'll encounter an artist fleeing the Nazis with a portfolio full of sketches for *Curious George*. You'll follow along as three brothers took their scrap material business and branched out into doctor and nurse kits and eventually Mr. Potato Head. And you'll see how Ruth Handler took a rather risqué German "adult" model doll and created Barbie, the best-selling doll in history—and how every other company kept trying, and failing, to imitate her success.

A few of the stories in this book will be familiar; others less so. What I hope will be original is that I try to tie together these disparate stories that collectively constitute the "century of the child" and look at them through the prism of ethnicity and immigration. If it works, you will never again be able to look at a comic book or a toy or a parenting manual without wondering if it, too, was created by a first-generation Jew. Moreover, beyond offering a simple tally of those cultural artifacts and their creators, I'll explain *why* it was those first-generation Jews who created so many of our childhoods—and why it matters that they did.

PART I

The World of Our Great-Grandfathers

1

TEDDY'S BEAR

* * *

The story of the Teddy Bear begins with a labor strike. In the spring of 1902, the United Mine Workers were on strike throughout the United States. The mineworkers wanted shorter working days and higher wages, but the coal industry was suffering from low profits and an oversupply. The mine owners were therefore happy to have their workers strike and saw no profit in coming to the table, because stalling would lead to a decline in production, letting the supply stabilize and prices rise.

Neither side would budge, and winter seemed about to set in with a national coal shortage, at a time when most homes were heated by coal. President Theodore Roosevelt decided to intervene and even threatened to send troops to Pennsylvania to take over the anthracite mines if the two sides didn't come to the table and start negotiating. All through the fall, Roosevelt met with both sides, trying to persuade them to yield at least a little. Finally, in late October, as temperatures dropped, the two sides came to the table and reached an agreement.

Roosevelt was exhausted. He declared he needed a vacation and accepted the invitation of Mississippi governor Andrew Longino to come south for a hunting trip.

Longino was the first governor in Mississippi elected after the Civil War who was not a Confederate veteran. A southern Democrat, he wasn't exactly a liberal on race relations, but he wasn't a notorious racist either. He was facing a difficult reelection challenge from James Vardaman, an avowedly racist Democrat who had declared on the campaign trail, "If it is necessary every Negro in the state will be lynched; it will be done to maintain white supremacy." Vardaman had called Roosevelt the "coon-flavored miscegenist in the White House."*[1]

Never one to miss an opportunity to combine political business with a little R&R, Roosevelt agreed to meet Governor Longino in Onward, Mississippi, a town about thirty miles north of Vicksburg, near the Louisiana state line. The location was strategic: Louisiana and Mississippi were then locked in a boundary dispute, and both governors had earlier asked Roosevelt to intervene.

Mississippi and Louisiana both claimed control of the oyster beds along the Pearl River, which meanders along the historically fluid border between the two states. (Even today the river wanders between them.) Both governors sought to make their case to Roosevelt, but from the outset he clearly sided with Mississippi—a position that would be upheld in 1906 by the U.S. Supreme Court.[2]

Roosevelt tacked on a ten-day bear hunt in the Delta Forest, and for the first four days, newspapers reported not only on his success in arbitrating the boundary dispute but also on his failure to find a bear. To help with the latter, Roosevelt's aides engaged the services of Holt Collier, a former slave who had served in the Confederate Army and

---

* Vardaman defeated Longino in that 1904 gubernatorial race and went on to become a virulently racist U.S. senator. In 2017 the University of Mississippi removed his name from a prominent building on campus.

had seen action as a cavalryman under General Nathan Bedford Forrest (an eventual founder of the Ku Klux Klan).

Collier was a well-known and well-respected bear tracker; it was estimated that he had killed more than three thousand bears in his lifetime. When he was interviewed in the 1930s by the Federal Writers Project, he noted that the president had been pretty impatient. " 'I must see a live bear the first day,' he said. I told him he would if I had to tie one and bring it to him."[3]

On the second day of the hunt, Collier's hounds picked up the scent of a bear. TR and Collier tracked it for a few hours, paused for lunch, and eventually spotted a fat old 235-pound black bear near a watering hole. Cornered, the bear swiped at several of the dogs with its paws, crushing one to death. Collier bugled for TR to join, then saw that his dogs were in danger, so he smashed the bear in the skull with his rifle butt. He tied it to a nearby tree and waited for TR.

When the president caught up with the hunting party, he came upon a "horrific" scene: "a bloody bear tied to a tree, gasping for breath, surrounded by dead and injured dogs, and a crowd of hunters shouting to 'let the President shoot the bear!' "[4]

Faced with what biographer Edmund Morris described as "a stunned, bloody, mud-caked runt," TR refused to draw his gun, saying that killing the bear would be unsportsmanlike. "I only kill prey that have a sporting chance of defending itself," he said. "Put it out of its misery." Collier killed the bear with a knife, slung the animal over his horse, and brought it back to camp.[5]

This episode in the private life of a public figure might easily have been forgotten had not Clifford Berryman been along on the hunt. Berryman was a well-known illustrator and cartoonist, working mostly for *The Washington Post*. The next day, November 16, 1902, he published a cartoon showing TR, dressed in full Rough Rider regalia, turning his back to a ruffled and frightened bear. The title of the cartoon, "Drawing the Line in Mississippi," had a double meaning, given TR's efforts to adjudicate the boundary dispute.

The next day Berryman revised the cartoon slightly. and it was published a second time. It was then that the bear passed from a

"Drawing the Line in Mississippi" by Clifford Berryman in the *Washington Post*, November 16, 1902.

momentary blip on the presidential radar to the beginning of a national, and later global, obsession. In the second cartoon, Berryman depicted the bear as a smaller, cuter, and cuddlier little critter. (Somehow, overnight, Collier had been transformed into a bejowled older white man holding the bear's tether.)

That cartoon, as we might say today, went viral. Berryman knew he had a winner and went on to draw many more bear cartoons; indeed they became his trademark, while this bear became TR's doppelgänger and constant companion. As Berryman continued to draw the bear, it got smaller, rounder, and cuter—"a poor measly little cub with most of its fur rubbed off, and big ears like prickly pears."[6]

The cartoon caught the attention of Morris Michtom, a recent immigrant whose candy store in Brooklyn sold newspapers that reprinted it, including *The New York Herald.* He was smitten, as much by the cuddly little bear as by the apparent compassion of the president. "The Czar was never that humanitarian," he said later. He hung the cartoon in the candy store window.

Morris was captivated by the story—and by the cartoon. He

couldn't let go of the image of a national leader refusing to kill a bear that had been specially prepared just for him. Who was this man? A night or two later Morris suggested to his wife, Rose, that she fashion a small replica of the bear out of whatever she could find in the store's basement. She used some mohair and stuffed the model with "excelsior," wood shavings used as packing material. Morris loved it, and the next morning he put it in the window of the candy store, labeled TEDDY'S BEAR.[7]

Soon customers came by and asked about it. Could they buy one?

Morris and Rose were puzzled but also flattered by the attention their store window display was causing. Rose seemed especially pleased, and the two of them set out to make some replicas for the neighbors who stopped by.

The "official" family story has it that Morris sent one of the first ones to Roosevelt himself and asked the president for his blessing to call the creature Teddy's Bear. As the story goes—and as it was told to me as a child—Roosevelt wrote back a handwritten note on White House stationery, giving Morris and Rose permission to name the bear after him. "Dear Mr. Michtom, I don't think my name is likely to be worth much in the bear business, but you are welcome to use it." He signed it with his initials, "T.R." (The letter has never been found, though an original teddy bear, made by the Michtoms, now sits in an exhibit of the presidents at the National Museum of American History.)*

Who knows what prompts someone to make a fateful decision, risk everything, and just hope for the best? Mostly we know about the success stories, the stories of those who had an idea, then, importantly, recognized that it was a good idea, even a great idea, and ran with it, throwing their entire life savings after it. We never hear of those whose eyes grew bright and wide at the prospect of making it

---

* Some of the elements of this official story have recently been questioned, citing dates that don't completely align or some alternate claims of invention. Based on family papers, letters, and stories handed down over several generations, my telling hews closely to the family's and the Smithsonian's rendition.

big but whose idea never really catches on, whose dream evaporates in the cold light of morning. History, it is said, is written by the winners, and they leave out the losers. That's equally true in the land of invention. How many patents sit in the U.S. Patent Office, having never become the game-changing product their creators foresaw?

Morris saw this chance, and he took it. At first, he invited a few local yeshiva boys to help him keep up with demand in the neighborhood. What Jewish boy at the time didn't know a little tailoring? Jews dominated the garment industry, the *schmatta* trade, as it was more colloquially known. Slowly, Morris and Rose realized that there would be more profit in selling these little teddy bears than in selling newspapers, even if you carried all the Yiddish ones.

Morris took that letter and a prototype of the Teddy Bear (the possessive was dropped in the process) to Butler Brothers, a textile manufacturing concern that could turn out the bear in quantity. A couple of months later, on February 15, 1903, the first manufactured Teddy Bears went on sale at the candy store.

They were an immediate hit, "the first sensational fad of the twentieth century."[8] Within a few months, ads for stuffed bears graced every issue of *Playthings*, the trade journal of the burgeoning toy industry. By late 1906, at least seven importers and domestic manufacturers were advertising their wares, and all the ads—whether for Tingue Manufacturing, which boasted bears of different color plush, or Strobel & Wilken bears with movable joints, to Strauss's self-whistling bears, Kahn & Mossbacher's bears with outfits, or A. S. Ferguson's Uncle Remus line—were for companies in Lower Manhattan, which was, without question, the center of this new industry.[9]

As even the most casual observer could easily tell you today, teddy bears never lost their popularity. Today there are hundreds of teddy bear manufacturers (Morris refused to patent his original design), and the teddy bear has become a global icon of childhood.

Is it hyperbolic to call the teddy bear an icon? I don't think so. After all, if childhood could be captured in microcosm, represented by one item, the teddy bear would likely rate pretty high. If you ask

Google what toy best represents childhood, the first entries are of teddy bears. The name *teddy bear* is a touchstone for stuffed animals, a synonym for cuteness and a happy reminder of childhood. In 1957, in his first starring role, in *Loving You*, Elvis Presley sang "(Let Me Be Your) Teddy Bear"; the song reached the top ten that year. In 1950 a survey of eleven hundred Ohio State University women found that more of them snuggled up to a teddy bear at night (16 percent) than slept in the nude (9 percent). During World War I, *teddy bear* was the term given to the one-piece fur-lined overalls worn by American flyers of open-cockpit planes and also to the shaggy goatskin coats worn by British soldiers in the trenches.[10]

More recently, in 2016, the artist Ydessa Hendeles unveiled *Partners (The Teddy Bear Project)*, a two-room installation at the New Museum in New York, consisting of more than three thousand black and white photographs that include the presence of a teddy bear. The photographs were bought on eBay during a two-year hunt, as Hendeles collected photos from family albums and personal collections, showing people dressed as teddy bears, sports teams holding bears, live animals posed with teddy bears, and menacingly, Nazi soldiers posing with the toys.[11]

At the time of its birth, though, not everyone was so enamored of this little stuffed bear. No one predicted in 1903 that it would become the iconic toy of the entire century. Nor did everyone immediately hail Morris and Rose Michtom (who, don't forget, actually made that first bear) as its proud parents.

For one thing, others claimed credit for creating the teddy bear, or at least for naming it.

For example, although Seymour Eaton didn't coin the name *teddy bear*, he certainly was one of the most important popularizers of the moniker. Writing under the name Paul Piper, Eaton wrote in verse about the adventures of the Roosevelt Bears, aptly named Teddy B. and Teddy G., in the pages of *The New York Times*, which erroneously noted upon his death in 1916 that he was "widely known as the creator of the 'Teddy Bear.'"[12]

Eaton's bears were a playful pair, rollicking in the pastimes of the day, from playing baseball to going to the zoo, fishing, and playing with fireworks (and injuring themselves!) on the Fourth of July.[13]

No sooner did the teddy bear debut in New York than it appeared at the annual 1903 toy trade fair in Leipzig, Germany. These world-wide but largely European affairs were testimony to European prominence in the toy industry in general, at a time when American toys remained mostly handmade rag dolls and home-crafted metal and wood playthings. The European toy industry was far more advanced, and pretty much every commercial enterprise displayed its wares at the Leipzig toy fair. American buyers were always on hand to order these European imports.

The Michtoms and the Butler Brothers exhibited "Teddy's Bear" there, a mere three months after its launch in Brooklyn, where it was a huge success. At the same fair, the Steiff company also exhibited a stuffed toy bear.

The Steiff bears were the brainchild of Richard Steiff, the nephew of the German toy company's founder, Margarete. He'd joined the Steiff company in 1897 and soon took over the design work. In the late summer of 1902, he visited the Stuttgart Zoo and made sketches of animals. He thought they'd make an interesting variation on the stuffed dolls that were Margarete's well-established fare. Later that year he made a prototype of one or two stuffed animals, but they garnered little attention. In the spring of 1903 he took three thousand prototypes to the Leipzig toy fair, where the bears were, again, not especially popular. Nonetheless an American, Hermann Berg, bought the entire lot for his American company, George Borgfeldt & Company.

Though produced simultaneously, the two bears were very different in appearance. Morris and Rose's bear was similar to the Berryman cartoon version, with large eyes and a small snout. Standing about thirty inches high, it weighed about three pounds and was lean rather than plump. It had a large rounded head and black wooden buttons for eyes.

Steiff's bear looked more lifelike, with a humped back and long snout. It stood upright; the Michtoms' bear sat. And the Michtoms'

The original Teddy Bears. *Left*: An original Teddy Bear, made by Morris and Rose Michtom, and given to Kermit Roosevelt. This one sits in a display case in the Smithsonian Institution. Museum of American History. *Right*: A replica Steiff model 55PB displayed at the Steiff-Museum, Gienegen, Germany, 2006

looked a bit sadder, its mouth turned down, its face and paws somewhat plaintive. It's tempting to say the Michtom bear looked more Jewish.

The Steiff bear was an immediate hit in the United States, due in large part to the company's massive and well-oiled distribution network. Since the Michtom bear was being produced by a small cottage industry, it was initially far less visible. Besides, and let's be honest, the Steiff bear was quite adorable, too.

The Teddy Bear Is "Idealized"

Rose Michtom may have actually created the teddy bear, but Morris took the credit and applied his organizational moxie toward producing it. He was no more or less patriarchal than other families at the turn of the century. Women were often creators or co-creators, equally entrepreneurial, and equally as organizationally savvy as their spouses, but they rarely if ever received the credit for their work. In fact, as we'll see, women were central to the stories of several other iconic toys and games, though their contributions are rarely as celebrated as their husbands', who retained naming rights to the toys and thus achieved that elusive association between man and toy.

Morris, with or without Rose, saw potential in teddy bears. Producing them was certain to be more lucrative than selling newspapers, penny candies, and egg creams to local customers. He decided to go all in. So in the back room of the candy store, at 404 Tompkins Avenue, he began producing the bears immediately. Later, in 1907, he founded and incorporated the Ideal Novelty and Toy Company.

By the time Richard Steiff came to the 1904 World's Fair in St. Louis, the country was in full grip of a teddy bear craze. The Steiff and Michtom bears were both popular. The Steiff bear won a grand prize at the fair, and Richard and his aunt won gold medals. The Steiff bear rode the gargantuan wave created by the Michtom bear, especially its connection to the very popular president. The Michtom bear had come first, at least chronologically, but the Steiff bear was initially more popular.[14]

When Steiff toys were displayed at Alice Roosevelt's wedding reception in February 1906, the president was asked what the bears were, and he answered "teddy bears." (The Steiff company never used the name *teddy bear.*) If this apocryphal story is true, it means that Teddy Roosevelt already knew their name.

Perhaps the best and most judicious arbitration of the Great Teddy Bear Controversy comes from Richard Gehman who, in 1961, went searching for the truth. After conversing with Ideal executives in New York and making a trip to the Steiff factory in Germany, he came away unconvinced that anyone could ever find the single true story of its origins. Eventually, he asked a young girl, a relative, who was just over two years old. She owned both bears and lugged them around together all the time. When he asked her which came first, she answered, "Both of them."

The official story, though, comes from the Smithsonian Institution in Washington—collector, legitimator, and arbiter of all things American. Its gift shop showcases racks of teddy bear paraphernalia: stuffed bears, outfits, coloring books, chapter books, and even a machine that squashes a penny with an image of a Teddy Bear. Alongside is a small card that reads, in its entirety:

> The name "Teddy Bear" did not become synonymous with stuffed bears until 1902, when Morris Michtom contacted President Roosevelt requesting his permission to use his name for the stuffed bears he had created. One of Michtom's [soft-stuffed] "teddy bears" is in the National Museum of American History's collection. The bear in this collection was donated to the Smithsonian in 1964 by Kermit Roosevelt.[15]

* * *

For the first three years, 1903–6, Michtom's sales were good, but after 1906 they went through the roof. Since Morris had not patented the bear, there were instant knockoffs. "Teddy is all the rage in the cities," proclaimed one ad for a knockoff bear. "The children carry him to school and even the grown up ladies carry him with them when they go out for a walk or ride, or to the theatre."

Fashionable society ladies took to having themselves photographed with their teddy bears. A note in *Playthings* in 1909 commented that plenty of "fashionable women" had purchased dozens of bears, and wardrobes for them, for their seaside cottages. One woman "always has a bear with her in her carriage or automobile." A salesman in one department store noted that "a great many buy jewelry for the bears, too, real jewelry. Absurd?" he asked the journalist. "Oh, I don't know," he mused. "Fashionable women, you know."[16]

The craze produced plenty of smug dismissals. "The entire country is in the clutches, or rather the embrace, of the plush bear," wrote *The San Francisco Sunday Call* in November 1906. "Even pet dogs and dolls have had to step down and out." It was, they concluded, an "astonishingly silly fad."

Others were incensed. Clergymen complained that the bear would discourage girls from playing with human dolls, which would discourage them from wanting to become mothers. On July 8, 1907, *The Telegraph Herald*, from Dubuque, Iowa, reported that a Catholic priest from St. Joseph, Michigan, Reverend Michael Esper, had delivered a sermon titled "Teddy Bear Dooms Race" that inveighed against this new "fad": It was "supplanting the good old dolls of our childhood with the horrible monstrosity known as the teddy bear." Teddy's chief sin was its "blunting" a girl's innate instincts for motherhood; at the national level, this little stuffed animal was an instrument of "race suicide":

> There is something natural in the care of a doll by a little girl. It is the first manifestation of the feeling of motherhood. In the development of those motherly instincts is the hope of all nations. It is a monstrous crime to do anything that will tend to destroy these instincts. That is what the "teddy bear" is doing and that is why it is going to be a factor in the race suicide problem if the custom is not suppressed. It is terrible enough that the present generation of parents in this country is leading us into grave danger by the practice of race suicide. If we cannot awaken the present generation let us at least save the future ones.[17]

In defense, the September 12, 1907, issue of *The Nation* took a different tack, focusing on what the bear did represent, not what it didn't. "The bear which waits around the corner to devour naughty little boys and girls loses its terrors when the child knows by experience what an amiable, comfortable beast it is. Thus the toy may have robbed childhood of one of its terrors."

Teachers in the New York University sewing department put a ban on making teddy bears because they "breed idleness among

Early ad for Ideal Toy Company Teddy Bear, ca. 1920.

children." But making teddy bears may have become a lucrative sideline for some students, who were likely to be enticed away from college and go directly into the garment industry.

One indicator of the dramatic success of the teddy bear was that even the normally staid and hardly effusive *New York Times* jumped on board. Departing from a tradition that had distinguished the newspaper from its more commercially entertaining competitors, the *Times* ran this announcement on January 4, 1906:

> I beg to announce to the public, and particularly to boys and girls of New York and the suburbs, that the *Sunday New York Times* had secured the exclusive rights to publish reports and pictures of the "doings" of the Roosevelt Bears, beginning next Sunday, January 7. These Bears are good and wholesome fellows brought up in the mountain countryside of Colorado.

Yes, for the first time in its history, *The New York Times* was publishing a Sunday comic strip. The first episode appeared on a full page in the paper's magazine. The text was by Paul Piper (pseudonym of Seymour Eaton), and the drawings were by V. Floyd Campbell. The strip lasted for six months, and the weekly installments followed the bears as they traveled east to Washington, where they met the president.

On July 22 an editorial in the *Times* gushed that the paper "feels entitled to exult that under its guidance their appearance before the public has been so successful and left such a right and pleasant train of ursine remembrances."

Actually, wrote former *Times* columnist Harold Faber, the bears were a "failure" as a comic strip; they were too polite and too good to be true. Definitely not the sort for the funnies. "I dutifully tried reading them," Iphigene Sulzberger, publisher Adolph's daughter, recalled, "but it was too boring and I gave up." Curiously, the newspaper continued to claim it had never published a comic strip, even in its centennial *Magazine* (April 14, 1996). Faber subsequently corrected it in a letter to the editor later.[18]

The *Times* dared not admit its failure. Instead, the bears themselves must be to blame, a flash in the pan that would soon disappear. In 1907 the paper assured readers who might have been expecting the continuation of the comic strip that "the Teddy Bear is merely one of the humors of the day," and "it will soon pass, however, to the limbo of Uncle Sam dolls, the walking and talking dolls, and the other toys of the past, now forgotten."

After the amazing success of the teddy bear, it made sense that TR's successors would try to duplicate it. William Howard Taft's well-known gluttony offered an opportunity. At a banquet in Atlanta, the president requested "possum and taters." His hosts obliged him handsomely with an eighteen-pound opossum surrounded by sweet potatoes. Almost immediately Billy Possum made its appearance, its manufacturers hoping to displace the teddy bear. It lasted a year and went nowhere.

In 1912 when Senator James Beauchamp Clark of Missouri was running against Woodrow Wilson in the Democratic primary, a young girl named Helen Orr created a mascot for him that she called a "hound dog." Clark's supporters penned a theme song, "The Hound Dog Song." The Missouri delegation to the Democratic convention arrived in Baltimore in what they called the Hound Dog Express. They rented some actual hound dogs and paraded them through the streets outside the convention site. Wilson and Roosevelt's supporters threw mud at the dogs. Clark lost, and hound dogs faded into obscurity.

No, it was only the teddy bear that Americans wanted. "No other toy has the therapeutic value of the teddy bear," writes Linda Mullins. "It's the only software that's never going to be obsolete."[19]

Why Bears?

But why bears? Why did teddy bears grab our imaginations so instantly and never let go? And why did the Berryman cartoon grab Morris? What if TR had been hunting gators in a Louisiana bayou? Or elk in Montana? Or a plain old deer in upstate New York? Would Morris have been so captivated by the story of an aging alligator that had been trapped for him to shoot? And, closer to home, why not stuffed animals representing dogs or cats?

Perhaps the Berryman cartoon connected Morris to his own childhood. After all, bears are very prominent in the mental landscape of the Russian countryside. They figure prominently in Russian children's literature, and while we don't know whether Morris had ever read them (he spoke Yiddish and only some Russian), many a child in the old tsarist world would have known and loved the stories of Mishka.

Perhaps the soft cuddly ursiform creature was a way to tame the wild but still keep it familiar, to render it harmonious with the increasingly urban landscape. The most frightening icon of wildness was transformed into a cute and cuddly toy for children. Tethering him somehow made the world symbolically safer.

The safety was not just symbolic. Psychologists latched onto the bear as a way to facilitate easier sleeping for children: something to hug, something warm, for a child sleeping alone in his or her own bed. (With more children in middle-class families, children were no longer sleeping several to a bed.) The association with TR, the Rough Rider, didn't hurt either. Later on, psychologists preoccupied with boyhood feminization championed teddy bears as a way to ease the separation from "overdominant" mothers.

Perhaps the bears were a way to make fathers less frightening. In her 1936 book *The Ego and the Mechanisms of Defense*, Anna Freud, daughter of Sigmund and keeper of the Freudian flame, discussed teddy bears as an example of "denial in fantasy." Father is huge and potentially violent, constantly threatening explosive anger. In their imagination, the child transforms the evil and terrifying father into a loving teddy bear, rendering him harmless.[20]

One type of psychotherapy even uses a teddy bear as a substitute therapist: The child tells it all their secrets, hidden fantasies, and the like. A writer who is no fan of the talking cure writes that "Teddy Bears have done more for children than every child psychologist, child therapist, children's support group, or parenting 'expert' who ever opened a case file."[21]

Perhaps the teddy bear's supposed age is what renders it so appealing. After all, the teddy bear is not a grown-up bear. It's a cub, a baby, and it stands up and sits down just like a baby human. It's safe and familiar, the wild tamed.

Whatever the reason—cultural, psychological, or just accidental—the teddy bear caught on in 1903, and not just with one plush toy—it has held on in the popular imagination ever since.

Not many children manage to avoid the story of Goldilocks and the Three Bears, where the bear family finds clues of an intruder (porridge gone, chairs sat in, even beds lain on), but the situation resolves into a happy family story. (The original Three Bears story, by Robert Southey in 1837, was decidedly less familial and pleasant: An old woman breaks into the lair of three bachelor bears of different sizes and, when caught, jumps through a window and is never seen again.)

Comic book bears include Barnstable Bear and P. T. Bridgeport (both characters in *Pogo*), while Pooky showed that even comic book cats like Garfield want and need teddy bears. Huge polar bears sell us Coca-Cola in advertisements, and in Britain, they sell beer. And don't forget Winnie-the-Pooh, who made his appearance in 1926 in England, the sunny and optimistic antidote to the depressive Eeyore as the two sides of Christopher Robin's childhood. Pooh was based on a teddy bear owned by A. A. Milne's son, Christopher Robin Milne.

What of that friendly bear Paddington, created in 1958 by Michael Bond? Sweet Paddington, always polite, always minding his manners, especially around grown-ups, is first found in a London railway station with a little sign around his neck that reads PLEASE LOOK AFTER THIS BEAR. THANK YOU. Bond was inspired by the trains of Jewish refugee children arriving at that London train station with name cards tied around their necks. Although Paddington was said to be from Peru, perhaps he was actually Jewish!

Let us not forget the perfect marriage of an iconic historical toy with contemporary selfie culture in which we, not the toy, are the star. In 1997 the first Build-a-Bear Workshop opened in a St. Louis mall. Now people young and old can design their own teddy bears themed to whatever they may want.

One of the teddy bear's great achievements was that it was a unisex toy, embraced by both girls and boys. It's both a girl-toy and a boy-toy, able to simultaneously evoke natural wildness and domesticate it. Today there are pink and blue teddy bears, and even though they're not gender neutral, somehow they still manage to feel at home at both ends of the gender binary. Or perhaps the bears transcend the binary entirely. That unity of opposites may help explain their enduring grip on the imaginations of Americans, young and old alike.

They're unisex, sure, but the enduring success of teddy bears may still have more to do with boys than with girls. Yes, girls and boys loved them equally, held them tight, and rubbed their snout and forehead fur. Ben Michtom, Morris's son, believed that the teddy bear was a way for a boy to play with a doll without any questioning of his "manhood." "If you gave a boy a doll, he would be subject to ridicule," Benjamin Michtom told a journalist in 1977, on the occasion of the bear's seventy-fifth anniversary. "But he needs to have something to cuddle, and there's no disgrace in his hugging a teddy bear."[22]

* * *

The teddy bear has given much joy to hundreds of millions of children. It was one of the first mass-produced toys, the beginning of a multibillion-dollar industry that has become one of the defining features of childhood, not only in the United States but around the world. It was the fulcrum, on which the entire modern idea of childhood would pivot. And the people who created that teddy bear were soon joined by hundreds of other creators, artists, writers, and thinkers who developed not only new toys but a new American childhood for the twentieth century.

You might even say that that American childhood began with the Michtom's Teddy Bear. It signaled the end of the era of childhood that had prevailed since the nation's founding, and it set America on course to enter "the century of the child," as the social reformer Ellen Key put it in 1900. During the twentieth century, the lives of children would be transformed. What they wore, what they read, what they played with and why, what they learned in school, even what they ate—not to mention what adults thought about children and how to raise them—all took the shape that we might easily recognize today as belonging to the realm of childhood.

This transformation of both the idea of childhood and the lived experience of children was, in large part, the collective, if uncoordinated, work of a group of men and women who didn't particularly set out to change the culture. Rather, they were trying to find a place where they might fit in. They were the sons (and a few daughters) of Yiddish-speaking Jewish immigrants from Russia and eastern Europe. Born into depraved poverty on the Lower East Side, they grew up enormously fast, without the material culture that defines contemporary childhood. Caught between the traditionalism of their immigrant parents and a largely anti-Semitic society that was resistant to their entry, they determined to find a place for themselves in this new world of opportunity, a niche of their own, a place they could call home. Together, the first generation of American-born Yiddish Jews generated a cultural, economic, and social wave so powerful that it changed the very direction of the tides.*

---

* Another word about terminology. Oy, the politics of names! What, exactly to call these Jewish immigrants? Since they didn't speak or read Russian, and since so many came from Poland and other lands, calling them "Russian Jews" would be inaccurate. Calling them "eastern European Jews" would be more accurate perhaps, but there were Russians among them also. The German Jews often called them *Ostjuden*—Eastern Jews—but this was derogatory, used to distinguish themselves from these new arrivals. And "Russian and eastern European Jews" is just too clunky. If there were an adjective for "Jews from inside the Pale"—say "Pallic"—that might work. I've decided to call them Yiddish Jews, since among all their reminders of home, they carried their cultural memories stored in their language.

2

COMING TO AMERICA

* * *

The first "modern" pogrom was scheduled for April 15, 1881, in Yelisavetgrad, a village in what is now Ukraine, barely a month after the assassination of Tsar Alexander II. Yes, it was scheduled. Planned. Everyone knew it was coming. Everyone, that is, who could read the Cyrillic alphabet. Alexander needed to be avenged. Of the revolutionary nihilists who bombed his carriage that March morning in St. Petersburg, two were rumored to have been Jews. That was all the pogromists needed—the match to start the fire. The tinder—a long history of Russian anti-Semitism and particular resentment of any sign of Jewish prosperity—was already well-seasoned.

Alexander II had been a serious reformer of a regime that was both corrupt and cruel. He'd curtailed some aristocratic privileges, ended corporal punishment, reformed the judiciary, and instituted a new system of local administration, *zemstvo*, that granted greater local autonomy. But of all his reforms, he was best known for emancipating the serfs in 1861. This edict alone may have earned him the nickname "Alexander the Liberator."

On the other hand, life under Alexander wasn't exactly liberatory for the Jews in the Pale of Settlement, that giant ghetto established in 1791 as the exclusive zone where Jews could live. Newly emancipated serfs could now own land—and the Jews, clustered in small towns, thriving villages and shtetls, had some. "The breakup of Russia's semi-feudal agricultural economy did the Jews no favors," writes the historian John Klier. In fact, in both the short and the middle term, the emancipation of the serfs was "catastrophic" for the Jews of the Russian Empire, in many cases dissolving the few niches that Jews had carved out for themselves economically, and heightening competition in already impoverished Jewish communities.[1]

Not only was shtetl life threated from without, but it was also dissolving from within. Modern ideas about individual liberty, a search for identity, a rational foundation for collective life—all strained the communal bonds that had bound the Jewish community together for centuries. In the Sholem Aleichem story "Tevye the Dairyman" (on which the Broadway musical *Fiddler on the Roof* was based), Tevye witnesses this erosion firsthand as each of his three daughters seeks marital fulfillment further and further from what the family (and the matchmaker) would have chosen. Sholem Aleichem's characters saw the ominous handwriting on the wall. Repression was coming.[2]

According to the 1906 *Jewish Encyclopedia*, the pretext for the first modern pogrom was the recitation of the age-old anti-Semitic blood libel that accused Jews of kidnapping Christian babies and using their blood in religious ceremonies. (It later formed a foundational accusation in the *Protocols of the Elders of Zion*, the fabricated anti-Semitic screed originally published in Russia in 1903.) I'll let the contemporaneous encyclopedists describe the pogrom. The rioters:

> proceeded to the Jewish quarter and commenced a systematic destruction of Jewish shops and warehouses. At first the Jews attempted to protect their property; but, seeing that this only served to increase the violence of the mob, and that the soldiers, who were called to protect

> them, took part in the pillage, they barricaded themselves in their houses. For two days the rioters perpetrated, under the very eyes of the officials, and with the cooperation of the soldiers, the most barbarous and hideous deeds. Synagogues were wrecked and Jewesses outraged. Two young girls, in dread of violation, threw themselves from windows. An old man named Pelikov, who attempted to save his daughter, was thrown from the roof by the enraged soldiery. Many persons were killed; 500 houses and 100 shops were demolished; and 2,000,000 rubles' worth of property was stolen or destroyed.[3]

The year after Alexander's death, conditions in the shtetl deteriorated significantly. Alexander III may have inherited his father's name, but he had none of the elder Alexander's reformist zeal. The May Laws of 1882 drove many Jews off the land; as a sop to landless freed peasants, Jews were no longer allowed to settle in rural areas or to own or lease properties in the countryside. Jews were prohibited from doing business on Sundays and Christian holidays; added to the prohibition on Saturdays and Jewish holidays, this made commerce extremely difficult. Entrance to schools was severely curtailed, but conscription was more rigorously enforced.

The May Laws sounded like a declaration of "open season" on the Jews, and over the next two years, hundreds of Jews were murdered, and hundreds more women and girls were raped—or, as the 1906 encyclopedists put it more delicately, "outraged." According to one estimate, more than twenty thousand homes were destroyed and 100,000 more were damaged.[4] As the newly emancipated serfs poured onto lands that had been owned by Jews, the uprooted Jews swarmed into the shtetls and cities.

Surrounded by sycophants and anti-Semites, Alexander III was eager to find a solution to what he saw as the "Jewish problem." One adviser, Konstantin Petrovich Pobedonostev, the procurator of the Holy Russian Synod, came up with a novel scheme: One-third of the

Jews would be forced to emigrate, one-third would be converted, and the remaining third would die off. Carrying out such a plan for ethnic cleansing on such a mass scale would require violence. Lots of it.[5]

In truth, for Jews inside the Pale of Settlement, life hadn't exactly been happy even before the assassination. Jews had been dispersed throughout the Pale, that stretch of land between the Baltic and Black seas in twenty-five western provinces that had been Poland before that nation was dismembered at the end of the eighteenth century. Russia inherited the Polish Jews, who stayed where they were, did not move to other areas, and lived behind a locked fence, the "pale" of settlement. Close to 95 percent of Russian and formerly Polish Jews lived in the Pale.[6]

Before the nineteenth century, shtetl life was more prosperous, hardly the desiccated collection of decrepit hovels of the popular imagination. It resembled the Jeffersonian small town or market-sized hamlet more than muddy near-serfdom. Most shtetls were market towns, ranging in size between one and five thousand residents.[7]

But over the second half of the nineteenth century, life got worse. The tsar's edict in 1861 to emancipate the serfs had the twin effects of industrializing the cities and "ruralizing" the countryside, causing massive rural displacement and ushering in an era of hardship and famine across the land.

Jews were especially hard hit, squeezed in the cities between restrictive laws that regulated Jewish opportunities in commerce, industry, and civil service and in the countryside by landless freed peasants searching for a way to scratch out a living in fertile areas. According to Mark Zborowski and Elizabeth Herzog's classic ethnography-by-memory of shtetl life, *Life Is with People* (1952), the shtetl fused the "teeming market place, the unpaved streets, the shabby wooden buildings" with the memory of more prosperous times and the promise of increasing misery. Hasidism was a response to the extreme misery of the Ukrainian and Polish Jews. As the shtetls fell on harder times than ever before, they became, in effect, "islands of unadulterated Yiddishkayt," all "piety and poverty."[8]

Whatever détente had existed between the hapless Jews and their increasingly restive neighbors collapsed with Alexander II's assassination. The pogroms started soon afterward.

Pogrom is a Russian word, derived from "to break, to smash, to conquer." After the assassination, rumors abounded. One was that the new tsar, Alexander III, had issued a *ukaz* or ukase (decree) instructing people to beat Jews. Newspapers warned of pogroms to come, with dates fixed weeks in advance. (Of course, most Russian Jews did not read or speak Russian.)

In that sense, the pogroms most closely resembled lynchings throughout the Jim Crow South in the late nineteenth- and early twentieth-century United States. Choreographed and ritualized while seeming spontaneous and emotion-driven, these mass events were intended instrumentally to dispossess the Jews of their land and to terrorize the entire Jewish population with fears of murder, looting, and rape. There was a well-known code for the onset of the pogrom: An item in the newspaper that the "red cock is about to crow" in a particular village meant that the town would be deliberately set on fire, according to a contemporaneous account, *The Persecution of the Jews in Russia*.[9]

For many years, historians assumed that the pogroms were elaborately organized and well-coordinated from the top, with the full complicity of the government, and that the "anti-Jewish movement was not engendered and did not rise among the people, but, on the contrary, the people were deceived, confused and led into error by inspirers and leaders." As the pogroms progressed, local authorities "stood by with folded arms, doing little or nothing to prevent their occurrence or recurrence, and allowing the ignorant peasantry to remain up to this day under the impression that a ukase existed ordering the property of the Jews to be handed over to their fellow-Russians."[10]

All true, no doubt, but should we let the Russian peasants off so easily? No, writes the historian Michael Aronson. Just as Daniel Goldhagen's description of the German citizenry under National Socialism as "willing executioners" challenged the prevailing idea that they were only passive frightened spectators, Aronson argues that these pogroms spontaneously channeled existing anti-Semitic feelings among the rural peasantry. The Russian peasantry's gleeful complicity and often-sadistic pleasure in the pogroms dispelled any illusions that Russians Jews may have harbored that they were "Russian." They were Jews, pure and simple. Which meant, essentially, that they were nothing, worthless.[11]

Both sides are right. Pogroms had to be well coordinated from the top, since they were planned and even announced in advance by the local press. At the same time, both instrumentally and expressively, the peasantry were "willing executioners," appropriating countless Jewish-owned farms and unleashing long-smoldering passions.

The savage cruelty of the pogroms shattered the Jews' worldview that enlightenment and modernization, especially after the 1861 emancipation of the serfs, had finally come to Russia. Life had become even more precarious, survival more tenuous, than during their meager survival for the previous hundreds of years. In a 1982 children's book based on historical documents, Barbara Cohen describes this new reality:

> But winter came and war. We put feather pillows around the walls of the rooms so if bullets hit our house they wouldn't hurt us. Soldiers in steel helmets searched every corner, looking for boys to take away to the army. They tore mezuzah off the door jambs because they thought gold was hidden inside. There was no gold inside the mezuzah, only a little scroll inscribed with words from the Bible.[12]

Here's how the contemporaneous *Persecution of the Jews in Russia* described these years of pogroms:

> In short, it seems to be the intention to make Russia an impossible home for the Jews, or perhaps even to doom them to complete extinction. The Russo-Jewish question may, therefore, be summed up in these words: Are three

> and a half millions of human beings to perish because they are Jews?[13]

An increasingly large number didn't want to know the answer—or rather, they feared they already did know. The plan to terrorize the Jews worked. A "traumatized" people had few options. The community was "beleaguered" and on the "verge of disintegration."[14]

It was these pogroms that launched the mass migration of Russian and eastern European Jews to the United States and other lands.

But first, they had to get out. Earthly possessions, whatever they might have been, were sold, bribes were paid, and families separated, hoping to rejoin one another when the money could be found. Smugglers and profiteers offered help to get people over the border; only sometimes were they honest enough to actually fulfill their part of the bargain. Travel was perilous, uncertain, yet necessary.

Imagine their bitterness, their anger at betrayal and humiliation, as they left. "It is impossible and unthinkable that a Jew should regret leaving Russia," one émigré wrote in 1882 as he left the land of his forefathers. "Be thou cursed forever, my wicked homeland, because you remind me of the Inquisition."[15]

Betrayed, bewildered, and embittered, they left. Between 1881 and 1914, more than 2 million Jews fled the Russian Empire. The vast majority spoke Yiddish, not Russian, and nearly a third of the males and virtually all the females were illiterate.[16]

From Moshe to Morris

One of them was Morris Michtom. Not that he had much choice in the matter. It was either that or become cannon fodder for the tsarist army. The brutal conscription laws exempted the firstborn sons of peasant families, as they were needed to tend the farm, but all second-born Jewish boys were liable for conscription—and that included Morris.

Born Moshe Michael Charmatz in September 1869, he was the

only son of his father, Yaakov's second marriage. (His older half-brother, Harris, was born in 1855 in Kovno.) The family lived in a relatively poor shtetl in the Minsk district of the Russian Empire, in what is now Belarus. It's a dark, fetid land of thick forests where it always feels like rain, snow, and near-permanent dampness. In fact, if you want to get a picture of that life, Anatevka, the fictional shtetl of that Sholem Aleichem story that formed the basis of *Fiddler on the Roof*, would be a pretty good image.

Yaakov was very much like Tevye the dairyman—a *luftmensch* in both the positive and negative sense—a man of ideas, yes, but also a spacey, ethereal dreamer. He knew many trades: He'd been a *melamed* (nonrabbinical Torah teacher) for a few seasons, working with a group of tailors on Sabbath afternoons. He would trade at the weekly market, bringing flax and the occasional calf to sell. He sold vodka. He was a night watchman for a nobleman's orchard. His wife delivered eggs and fish, kneaded dough in a bakery, and sold bagels.

Even with all these activities, the family barely scraped by. They lived in a house without a chimney and had only enough money for secondhand shoes. Yet every Saturday, Yaakov would bring a guest for Sabbath dinner, and he tried to support a Torah student with free meals one day a week. They eked out a living, and they made a life.[17]

Moshe received a traditional Jewish education for a poor peasant. A bookish boy, he loved reading and often spent hours at the local library in Minsk, reading to a group of eager little children. In short, he was a perfect candidate to become a rabbi.

It may have been a tragic time for Jews inside the Pale, but it was also a heady time. Political agitators moved through the towns, and Moshe was surrounded by, and eventually immersed in, the progressive politics of the Russian and eastern European ferment: socialism, anarchism, nihilism, populism. Sympathetic to anarchism, Moshe became a Freethinker, a member of a relatively secular social justice group that believed that only through nonviolent political means could revolutionary change be accomplished. Freethinkers were rationalists, believing in the secular power of reason over superstition. They made up their own minds, freed from the constraints of theology—weighing evidence, seeking empirical verification. The Enlightenment's bulb was dim in those dank forests and small villages, among a peasantry both illiterate and superstitious, but for the People of the Book, it was a balm and an inspiration, all they needed to imagine a better life.

All this made Moshe a likely target. Not only was he eligible for conscription, he was visible as a potential troublemaker, a possible subversive. The Russian army command seemed to take particular delight in sending such political progressives right to the front. The less training they got the better, as far as they were concerned.

The family huddled. If Moshe ran away, the family would be prosecuted for evasion and would be subjected to fines and possible harassment. There was only one solution, Moshe believed. He had to "die." It was the only way he could stay alive.

The family announced to the community, which was no doubt in on the deception, that Moshe had contracted typhus. Three days later they mourned his death, with all the traditional rituals. They held a solemn funeral and buried a coffin filled with just enough rocks to mimic a dead body, followed by the traditional shiva period of mourning. Meanwhile Moshe Charmatz quietly slipped over the border into Lithuania and ceased to exist.

Six months later in Vilna, 150 miles from home, Moshe felt safe enough to reemerge. Moshe Charmatz was dead. He was now named Moshe Michtom.

No one in my family has ever been able to figure out why Moshe chose the name Michtom. Virtually everyone seems to assume it was derived from Moshe's Talmudic studies. There are six Psalms of David known collectively as the Miktam. Collectively, Psalms 16 and 56–60 are known as the Wisdom Psalms—pious, sullen, even a bit dour; they are public expressions of devotion to God and prayers for deliverance from harm. Some in my family believe that since every rabbinical student must specialize in some portion of the Talmud, the Miktam must have been the section that Moshe chose; others think that he chose the name to reflect his gratitude for getting out of Minsk alive.*

Once he settled in Vilna, Moshe Michtom enrolled in a local yeshiva to study to become a rabbi. No one particularly asked about his origin story; shtetl Jews were streaming into cities like Vilna and Minsk from the increasingly dangerous and impoverished countryside. He understood that being a rabbi might condemn him to a life of eternal poverty, so he also attended an ORT school. (ORT stood for Russian Obstchestuo Resemes Lenovo Truda, or Society for the Encouragement of Handicraft, founded in 1880 to help poor Jews beyond the Pale learn a trade or craft.) Morris trained as a machinist and learned how to build and repair industrial machines. This would serve him well later, in his transition to American life.

As was the custom for young rabbinical students, young Moshe lived *af kest*, receiving free room and board with a local family. Living the home of Reb. Shabtai Joseph Katz, he noticed the rebbe's daughter, Rachel Malka. (This was likely another custom for rabbinical students: to receive room and board in a home with a marriageable young Jewish woman.) Rachel was a trained seamstress, three years older than Moshe. He liked her.

She also had an eye for him, and her parents noticed. He was a poor yeshiva boy, a rabbi in training, such a good catch, and such an obvious one-way ticket to a life of poverty. He was respectable, to be sure, and poor.

But Moshe had tasted life outside the shtetl, city life, literate life, political life. He had no interest in staying in Vilna, and he certainly wasn't going back to the Minsk district, where the local authorities assumed he was dead. He set his sights on America, a land where he

---

* The origin story of the Michtom name also explains its pronunciation. Michtom is pronounced with a hard *ch* as in Mik-tum, not the guttural German-Yiddish *ch*, nor the softer-sounding *sh*, as in Hebrew Psalms. For several generations, my family clarified its pronunciation in a revealing way when we would introduce ourselves: "The name is Michtom, it rhymes with victim."

could really start over, really reinvent himself. He saved up and make plans to emigrate.

The great blizzard of 1888 provided his chance, and Moshe took it. The night before he left Vilna, he and Rachel married under a chuppah at her sister's home. The next morning he crossed the border from Lithuania into Prussia on foot and made his way eventually to Rotterdam, the most popular port of embarkation for steamships bound for America. Rachel remained in Vilna for the time being, earning enough money so that she could emigrate, too.

The next year Rachel made her way from Vilna to Hamburg where she boarded the SS *Rhaetia*. She arrived at the Castle Garden immigration center in Lower Manhattan on August 19, 1889. Moshe, outfitted with new clothes and a new American name, Morris, met her at the processing center and brought her to his new home in Newark. Following her husband, she changed her name from Rachel to Rose.

Harris, Morris's older half-brother, arrived in 1890. He joined Morris right away; Morris signed his older brother's application for citizenship in 1893. The brothers were reunited, and Harris changed his name to Michtom, also.

America offered hope and opportunity. The land of the do-over, the reboot, America was a place, but it was also an idea, where one could make one's mark and hope that such a mark could be indelible. It was a land of dreams and a land for dreamers, where, in the words of the twentieth century's most famous song, "the dreams that you dare to dream really do come true."[18]

That song is "Over the Rainbow." And who else could have channeled such dreams but two sons of Jewish immigrants? Harold Arlen (Hyman Arluck) was born in 1905 in Buffalo, New York, to a Lithuanian-born cantor and his wife, and Yip Harburg (Isidore Hochberg) was born in 1896 on the Lower East Side to poor Russian immigrants. To them, America was literally the world "over the rainbow," and their song aches with the longing of every wide-eyed, naïve, and impoverished new arrival.

Who Else Arrived

There were, literally, millions of such stories. In the rural areas of eastern and southern Europe, conditions were deteriorating. Following the emancipation of the serfs in 1861, Russia and Poland pushed people off the land in record numbers. Between Russia's first pogrom in 1881 and the closing of the U.S. immigration doors in 1924, over 2.5 million Jewish immigrants from the Pale of Settlement, the Kingdom of Poland, Hapsburg Galicia, and Romania arrived in the United States. Within one generation, nearly one-third of all the Jews of eastern Europe migrated. "What we are witnessing," wrote one observer in 1914, "is a Jewish migration of a kind and degree almost without parallel in the history of the Jewish people." Well, he did say *almost.* Let's not forget the exodus from Egypt.[19]

In 1920 there were 3.6 million Jews in the United States, of whom more than two-thirds had settled in New York, making the city "the largest Jewish urban community in world history." Jews weren't the only immigrants—Italians and residents of Austria-Hungary followed suit, especially after Italy's unification. Between 1881 and 1890, about 925,000 immigrants arrived from these lands; between 1891 and 1900 the number was about 1.8 million; and between 1901 and 1910, roughly 5.8 million flooded into the United States. From the 1880s to the first decades of the 1900s, wave upon wave of immigrants—13 million of them—streamed into the country. By 1900, the majority of men in Manhattan over age twenty-one were foreign born.[20]

In 1903 Hillel, Herman, and Henry Hassenfeld's father, Osiras, heard that a new round of pogroms was coming in Kishinev (in what is now Moldova) and gave his sons what little money he had and a piece of paper with the name of an uncle in New York. Once settled, they found their way to Providence, Rhode Island, where they started out in the rag trade, lining pencil boxes with cloth. Then they branched off, one brother making the pencils and the others making the boxes, which eventually morphed into doctor and nurse bags, which became toys, which in turn became Hasbro.

Three years after the Hassenfeld boys crossed the Atlantic, sixteen-year-old Jacob Moskowicz of Warsaw deserted the Russian army, found his way to Ellis Island, and eventually arrived in Denver. His daughter Ruth met Izzy Handler at a local dance, and they moved to Los Angeles to make a life together in the postwar economic boom. At first, they made picture frames from plastics, and eventually they established a toy company named Mattel that produced toy guns and a doll that changed the world.

A few more examples:

Louis Marx, born in 1896 in Brooklyn to Austrian Jewish parents, founded the toy company that bore his name in 1921. By the 1950s, it was the nation's largest toy company. Dubbed "the Henry Ford of the toy industry," Marx succeeded largely by copying toys already on the market and then selling at prices below the competition.

Joshua Lionel Cohen, born on Henry Street on the Lower East Side in 1877 to immigrants from the Polish-Lithuanian border town of Suvalk, was a precocious boy and a born tinkerer. His invention of an electric-powered model train set married new technologies to boyhood fantasies and created Lionel Trains, still the largest toy train manufacturer in the world.

Jack Pressman's father, Abe, fled the pogroms in the Pale and settled in Yorkville, on the Upper East Side, and opened a variety store in Harlem. A local jobber named Nathan Liebowitz took a shine to young Jack, working in his father's store, and taught him about marketing and selling toys. Returning from the First World War, Pressman launched himself full time into Pressman Toys, and after a few modest hits, the company acquired the rights to a German game that used marbles and a star-shaped board. They called it Chinese Checkers or Hop Ching Checkers, although the game had absolutely no connection to China.[21]

Creating the comic strips that often provided the characters for children's dolls and toys were men like Ham (Hammond Edward) Fisher, born in 1900 in Wilkes-Barre, Pennsylvania, the son a Jewish scrapyard dealer. His character, Joe Palooka, was a simple-minded scrapper with a heart of gold who by accident became heavyweight champion of the world.

Fisher's former apprentice, and later his rival, was Al Capp—born Alfred Gerald Caplin in 1909 in New Haven to eastern European Jewish parents. Capp began America's most beloved and longest-running comic strip, *Li'l Abner*, imagining a world that Jews never entered and could never enter: the white rural South.

Or Mell (Melvin) Lazarus, born in 1927 in Brooklyn to Jewish immigrant parents. He created of *Miss Peach*, which ran for half a century after its debut in 1957. And don't forget Rube Goldberg, creator of that eponymous series of contraptions attributed to Professor Lucifer Gorgonzola Butts. Goldberg was born in 1883 to Jewish immigrant parents in San Francisco.

The world of comic book creators reads like the attendance list at a local yeshiva: Maxwell Charles Ginzberg (who became Max Gaines), Stanley Martin Lieber (Stan Lee), Jacob Kurtzberg (Jack Kirby), Robert Kahn (Bob Kane), Joe Kubert, Lee (Leopold) Elias, Harry Lampert, Sam Glanzman, and Jerry Siegel and Joe Shuster, creators of the first "Jewish" superhero, Superman. Even John Goldwater, creator of the utterly middle-American Archie, was born Max Leonard Goldwasser, to Jewish immigrants.

What children read when they weren't disobeying their parents by clandestinely sneaking a look at comic books were children's books, by authors like Eleanor Estes (born Eleanor Rosenfeld), Louis Slobodkin, Esphyr Slobodkina, Arnold Lobel, and Hans and Margarete Rey.

William Steig, born in 1907 in the Bronx to Polish Jewish immigrants, created more than 2,600 cartoons and more than one hundred covers for *The New Yorker* before he created Shrek at age eighty-three. Kay Thompson, born Catherine Louise Fink in 1909 in St. Louis to an Austrian Jewish immigrant father and American-born mother, created the precocious, entitled, and utterly assimilated Eloise. Ezra Jack Keats (Katz), born in 1916 in Brooklyn to poor immigrant Jewish parents, created *The Snowy Day*, the first mainstream children's book to feature an African American protagonist. And finally Maurice Sendak, born in 1928, the youngest child of Jewish immigrant parents who fled the shtetls outside Warsaw after the First World War, created the hero, Max, who knew where the wild things were.

Some worked with children more directly: Reformers like Sidonie Gruenberg, who was born in 1881 in Austria, and arrived in New York as a young child, wrote a best-selling parenting book and served as director of the Child Study Association. George Hecht, the man credited with creating the parenting advice genre, was born in New York City in 1895 to immigrant parents, and was the founding editor of *Parents' Magazine*, and eventual owner of FAO Schwarz.

Last but not least are the theorists, the academics and clinicians who tried to make sense of it all and who provided a psychological road map for the emerging view of American childhood. Take, for example, Erik Erikson, the dean of developmental psychologists, whose landmark books *Childhood and Society* (1950) and *Identity: Youth and Crisis* (1968) defined the academic study of childhood in the postwar era. Born out of wedlock in 1902 in Copenhagen as Erik Salomonsen to a Jewish mother, he took the name of his stepfather, Homberger, in 1911. Later he changed it again, symbolically giving birth to himself in the land of the self-made man. His interest in his own identity led to a lifelong preoccupation with the question of identity itself. Abraham Maslow, one of the pioneers of humanistic psychology, was born in 1908 in Brooklyn to parents who had emigrated from Kiev; Maslow proposed a "hierarchy of needs" on a journey toward what he called "self-actualization."

Finally, in the postwar era, there were the producers, directors, and creators of the television shows that animated the lives of America's children (not to mention men like Mark Goodson, Bill Todman, Dan Enright, and Jack Barry, whose lineup of television game shows entertained their parents). I'm thinking of Jack Chertok, a first-generation Jew, born in 1906 in New York, who took over producing *Our Gang* from Hal Roach before going on to produce both *The Lone Ranger* and *Sky King*. And Herbert Leonard, the younger child of two New York Jewish immigrants, who produced both *Circus Boy* and *The Adventures of Rin-Tin-Tin*. And Sidney Salkow, who created *Fury*. Or Jay Ward, born in 1920 to an Orthodox Jewish immigrant family, who created *Crusader Rabbit*, *The Adventures of Rocky and Bullwinkle and Friends*, "Dudley Do-Right of the Mounties," and *George of the Jungle*, among others.

But let's not get too far ahead of ourselves. All these people were either very young immigrants who arrived in America with parents who were penniless dreamers, or the sons and daughters of those poor shtetl immigrants. Most lived in the squalid tenements of the Lower East Side, and their parents were peddlers and seamstresses and tailors, eking out just enough to survive, hoping for enough to propel their upward mobility to Brooklyn or Queens. Dark, dirty, and dangerous, the Lower East Side, the "symbolic home of Jewishness," was, as Jack Kirby, the great comic book artist and creator of Captain America, put it, "not a pleasant place to live in." Hardly. You became a "toreador at an early age, just dodging the ice wagons," he recalled.[22]

They had nothing, this first generation of American-born Jews—no dolls, no toys. They had hardly anything resembling a childhood. They had to create it. "You must be alert, my son, alert and ready to fight," a Polish Jew wrote to his son on the eve of the Holocaust. "You can never really be a child in such turmoil."

Such turmoil, indeed. After seeing so much human depravity and cruelty, it is impossible to be an innocent child. Even after they and their families reached America, what kind of "childhood" could these immigrants have had in impoverished tenements, settlement houses, and on the clogged and dangerous streets of the city? What kind of "childhood" can any child have when they are uprooted, impoverished, and surrounded by such privation and despair?

What They Found

These unwashed but literate peasants were not exactly universally embraced. They encountered few welcome mats and far more NO JEWS

ALLOWED signs. For Woodrow Wilson, then a professor at Princeton, his well-known racism was matched only by his anti-immigrant sentiments. As early as 1902, he claimed European countries "were disburdening themselves of the more sordid and hapless elements of their population." As a result, the "sturdy stocks of the north of Europe" were being overtaken by "multitudes of men of the lowest class from the south of Italy and men of meaner sort out of Hungary and Poland, men out of the ranks where there was neither skill nor energy nor any initiative of quick intelligence."[23]

Yiddish Jews were regarded with particular scorn by many of the German Jews who had arrived in the mid-to-late nineteenth century and had already found a foothold in the new world. The German Jewish immigrants were more likely to have been from middle-class families than this new horde of unwashed, penniless peasants; many were bankers, professionals, merchants, and small businessmen. The last thing they wanted was to be dragged down by any association, especially a religious one, with these huddled masses. The new immigrants "transformed a middle-class acculturated and politically conservative Jewish community into one large working class, Yiddish-speaking, and committed to a mix of ideologies including socialism, Zionism, and religious orthodoxy."[24] Class and cultures divided them, as did geography. The worlds of the Upper East Side and the Lower East Side, of Madison Avenue and Mott Street, were more than a streetcar ride apart; they were entirely separate worlds.

So religion ought not to lump them together. The novelist Jakob Wasserman, a German Jew, recalled that as a young man, "if I spoke with a Polish or Galician Jew and tried to understand his way of life and thinking, I could stir myself to feel compassion or sadness, but never a sense of brotherhood. He was entirely strange and, when individual human sympathy is lacking, even repulsive." Another prominent German Jew, Jacob Voorsanger, made clear that by their "illiteracy, physique, criminality, immorality, speech, [and] demeanor," these new immigrants were not to be confused with his Americanized, middle-class friends. The Yiddish Jews were too much, "gregarious," "legalistic and tradition-bound." In the end, he declared, "I believe in immigration restriction."[25] As the historian Stephen Birmingham writes:

> The Jewish immigrants who came to America between 1881 and 1915 seemed, at first glance, to be culturally unadaptable: poor, hungry, ill-clothed, often sickly, speaking no English and in some cases illiterate, they were also steeped in a religious tradition that even America's old-established Jews considered barbaric and bordering upon fanaticism.[26]

In his classic 1962 work on Lower East Side Jews, Moses Rischin quotes one contemporaneous writer who explained the difference:

> I think I know what constitutes a normal Jew in New York. A normal Jew . . . is one who either himself or whose father speaks English with a German accent. An abnormal . . . Jew . . . is one who speaks English with a Russian accent. . . . A man who speaks English with a German accent is a native, but a man who speaks English with a Russian accent is a foreigner.[27]

On the other hand, the author Carey McWilliams offered a more nuanced view in his insightful *A Mask for Privilege* in 1948. German and Yiddish Jews often shared a background, he argued, and even a figurative backyard, in the old country, and German Jews offered both assistance and contempt for the new arrivals:

> While the Orthodox East European Jews were culturally more sharply set apart from the native-born population than the German Jews, what really distinguished the two groups was the fact that the German Jews had settled here fifty years earlier, under far more favorable circumstances, and were already "Americanized." Actually many of the German Jews were from Posen, Moravia,

> and other provinces right on the frontier of Eastern Europe and might well have been regarded as Eastern Jews themselves. Fearful of their hard-won and already threatened status, the German Jews at first looked down upon their eastern brothers "as a grotesque species of ill-bred savages," although at a later date external pressures forced them to come to the aid of their "unprepossessing co-religionists."[28]

This is not a unique phenomenon: Every wave of Jewish immigrants was treated with contempt and disavowal by those who had previously arrived and staked their claim for assimilation. Each ethnic wave was seen as somehow less than, poorer, less cultivated. The historian Paula Hyman has documented this same phenomenon in France from the mid-nineteenth century through the 1970s.[29] First, German Jews struggled to gain a foothold, and they did so at the expense of Russian and eastern European Jews. "We're the real French people," they seemed to say, "not like these raggedy poor 'other' Jews!" Later those same Russian Jews teamed up with the older German Jews to say the very same thing about the Sephardic Jews migrating from North Africa.

So, too, in New York at the turn of the century, the proportion of Jewish immigrants shifted dramatically. In 1880 only about one-fifth of all Jews in the United States were of eastern European origin. About 150,000 German Jews had arrived before 1880, but as German industrial and military power expanded, the number of German Jews who emigrated shrank. In that next decade, between 1890 and 1899, only a third of that number, less than 50,000, came to the United States. Compare that to the numbers of Russian and eastern European Jews.[30]

Of course, one should be careful in drawing too large a distinction between the earlier German-speaking immigrants and the later Yiddish-speaking Russians and eastern Europeans. The "German" Jews were a diverse lot as well, and many came from the eastern parts of Germany; some even spoke Yiddish.[31]

Yet their differences were broad and telling. For one thing, the German Jews were a lot fewer, perhaps only about 35,000 in 1860, and they were often young unmarried men searching for a future. The Yiddish Jews came as families, often spanning three generations. Nor were the German Jews fleeing from particularly repressive conditions; in midcentury Germany, anti-Semitism was at a "relatively low point." Arriving at midcentury, at the moment of America's greatest expansion, many German Jews went west or south, even if they tended to settle in cities. At the turn of the century, Yiddish Jews crowded into eastern cities, especially New York.

The German Jews tended to identify as Germans who happened to be Jewish, rather than as Jews who happened to be German. Rabbi Bernhard Felsenthal, for example, wrote of his identity that he was "spiritually" and culturally German, an heir to the great German intellectual traditions of Schiller, Goethe, and Kant. Rabbi Isaac Wise's newspaper, *The American Israelite*, promoted German identity, and sermons in Cincinnati's synagogues were frequently delivered in German.[32] The German Jews had found their place, carved out a life, built a community, and been relatively successful in moving into the middle class. They'd done it by downplaying their Jewishness and playing up their Germanness. They had arrived with a leg up: many were urban, educated, and comfortable in a more cosmopolitan urban setting. Most of them spoke German, not Yiddish, and moved more easily into American society.

By contrast, these timorous new Jews, poor, uneducated, and unwashed, were a threat to the German Jews' sense of accomplishment for having made it. They feared being dragged down, through guilt by association—a general fear of downward mobility. So they shunned these new arrivals, claiming that they, immigrants themselves only one generation ago, were "true" Americans compared with these huddled masses. Writes Jeremiah Berman:

> The German Jews considered the Talmud Torah [orthodox, Yiddish-speaking Jews, following eastern European religious practices] to be the antithesis of everything they

> were striving to achieve. To them the foreign speech and what they considered uncouth manners and the fanatical religious customs of the Russian Jews were things better discarded as quickly as possible, certainly not cultivated.[33]

Just as it would be inaccurate to assert categorical and unbridgeable differences between the German and Russian Jews, it would also be unfair to say that all German Jews held Yiddish Jews in contempt. German Jews also provided lots of assistance, founded charity organizations, and assisted with assimilation. They evinced a "mixture of pity, horror, and dismay, but ultimately with compassion," writes the historian Stephan Brumberg.[34]

Jacob Schiff, a German immigrant who had become one of the country's wealthiest bankers, founded and funded many of the

"A Happy New Year." German Jews welcoming Russian Jews to America. Hebrew Publishing Company, postcard, circa 1910. (Alfred and Elizabeth Bendiner Collection, Library of Congress)

charitable organizations like the American Fund in Aid of Russian Emigrants that welcomed the Yiddish Jews and helped them find housing, jobs, and meals and get settled. "In spite of Jacob Schiff's efforts," though, "the Russian Jews of downtown and the German Jews of uptown lived in completely different spheres. What linked them together were the charitable aid groups that were funded by the German Jews and patronized by the Russian Jews."[35]

One wedge driven between these two groups was the reaction of gentile society to them. More "civilized" New Yorkers, who represented polite society, were disgusted by what they saw on the Lower East Side. "The Jew makes me creep," wrote Henry Adams, who winced at "the furtive Yacoob or Ysaac, still reeking of the ghetto, snarling a weird Yiddish." Henry James was equally distressed by these "swarming" hordes, who reminded him of "small, strange animals . . . snakes or worms."[36]

The turn of the century witnessed a marked increase in anti-Semitism. Clubs and hotels began to restrict Jews, just as they barred Blacks and Irish. For many German Jews, the arrival of Russian Jews was a horrifying setback: They were suddenly seen as Jews, not as Americans, not even as German immigrants. Many opposed further Jewish immigration, and some went so far as to advocate the legal restriction of all immigration to the country. *The Hebrew Standard*, a major organ of more established Jews, declared "the thoroughly acclimated American Jew" to be "closer to the Christian sentiment around him than to the Judaism of these miserable darkened Hebrews."*[37]

---

* Stephen Birmingham even goes as far as to argue that it was the German Jews who came up with the slur *kike* to refer to Jews. He suggests that so many Yiddish Jews were from Russia, and had a *ki* at the end of their names, that German Jews started referring to them as "ki-kes." To be honest, this seems less plausible than Leo Rosten's theory that the word originated from Yiddish Jews' entry at Ellis Island or Castle Garden. When the processors told these illiterate peasants to sign their names on entry documents, they could barely understand what was being asked, and so they were instructed to sign with an

An anti-Semitic cartoon from *Judge* magazine. *Right*: Russian Jewish immigrants flee persecution to New York. At the center is a stereotypical Jewish businessman. Behind him is "Broadway in 1892," with Jewish names on every building. *Left*: the elegantly dressed upper class heads west. (*Judge* magazine, January 23, 1892)

Thus the earlier-arriving German Jews became "white," by identifying with gentile culture and lumping the new arrivals in with other marginalized groups, while the eastern Jews were seen as "nonwhite."

But this racial classification is only to blame the victim. How could it have been otherwise for these newly arrived penniless hordes?

X for their name. Horrified at being asked to write the sign of the Christian cross, they instead put a circle, an *O*. In Yiddish, the word for "circle" is *kikel* [pronounced KY-kel], and those who signed like this became known as *kikele*. Either way, the word bears an origin in anti-Semitism. Stephen Birmingham, *The Rest of Us: The Rise of America's Eastern European Jews* (New York: Berkley Books, 1985), 24.

Where They Lived

Life on the Lower East Side was a tumult, a frenzy of sweatshop labor, crowded and filthy tenements, routine violence, and relentless misery. "Nowhere in the world are so many people crowded together on a square mile as here," noted Jacob Riis in his classic *How the Other Half Lives* (1890). With about 335,000 people per square mile, it was the most densely populated place on earth: "Life here means the hardest kind of work almost from the cradle." If they had dreamed of a land where the streets were paved with gold, they were rudely surprised to find, instead, rough-hewn cobblestones run over with fetid water, raw sewage, and the blood and guts of animals slaughtered in the markets. They lived in cramped tenements, dirty, poor, and frightened. Crime was rampant, both against the newly arrived and among them, for survival. The streets were filled with kids who snatched an item, a piece of fruit, or a wallet; pushcarts and stalls; prostitutes who slunk in darkened doorways; and countless middlemen and procurers who ripped your last pennies from you to secure for themselves a decent place to live. Life in this "state of nature," as Thomas Hobbes might have seen it, was exactly as he described it in *Leviathan*: "nasty, brutish and short."[38]

"I suppose there are and have been worse conditions of life, but if I stopped short of savage life, I found it hard to imagine them," William Dean Howells wrote after an 1896 trip to the Lower East Side. Here's how *The New York Times* described it:

> This neighborhood, peopled almost entirely by the people who claim to have been driven from Poland and Russia, is the eyesore of New York and perhaps the filthiest place on the western continent. It is impossible for a Christian to live there because he will be driven out, either by blows or the dirt and stench. Cleanliness is an unknown quantity to these people. They cannot be lifted up to a higher plane because they do not want to be.[39]

Residents chronicled this world in barely fictionalized stories of depravity and dignity. Mike Gold called the neighborhood "a great carnival of catastrophe" in his unsparing novel, *Jews Without Money* (1930). (Gold was born Itzhok Granich in 1893, the son of impoverished Romanian and Hungarian immigrants. His pseudonym was ironic in its assimilationist impulse; Gold remained a Communist all his life, refusing to renounce Stalin's alliance with Hitler or even the gulag.)

And here's how Abraham Cahan, the celebrated author of, among other works, *The Rise of David Levinsky* and the founding editor of *The Jewish Daily Forward*, the foremost Yiddish newspaper in New York City, described life in the teeming ghetto of the Lower East Side:

> Hardly a block but shelters Jews from every nook and corner of Russia, Poland, Galicia, Hungary, Roumania; Lithuanian Jews, Volhynian Jews, south Russian Jews, Bessarabian Jews; Jews crowded out of the Pale of Jewish settlement; Russified Jews expelled from Moscow, St. Petersburg, Kieff, or Saratoff; Jewish runaways from justice; Jewish refugees from crying political and economic injustice; people torn from a hardgained foothold in life and from deep-rooted attachments by the caprice of intolerance or the wiles of demagoguery—innocent scapegoats of a guilty Government for its outraged populace to misspend its blind fury upon; students shut out of Russian universities, and come to these shores in quest of learning; artisans, merchants, teachers, rabbis, artists, beggars—all come in search of a fortune.[40]

Those children lived largely on the street, at least when they weren't working in the family's tenement apartment. If home life was miserable, cramped, and dirty, they could hang out with their mates, roaming in packs, socializing with each other in this bewildering new world. Their lives began to diverge from the world of their parents:

They spoke English in public and Yiddish at home. "Where did you learn to speak English?" asks one mother in Anzia Yezierska's *Bread Givers* (1925), a novel of tenement life, standing in for hundreds of thousands of such mothers, clinging to the last of their old familiar world. "On the street. With my friends."[41]

Bread Givers is more than a simple coming-of-age story; it's also the story of that first native-born generation wrestling with the weight of the past and the promise of the future. Think *Fiddler on the Roof*, but from the point of view of the three daughters. Sara strives to become an independent woman. "I'm going to live my own life," she declares. "Nobody can stop me. I'm not from the old country. I'm American!" Yet even as she makes her way in this new world, she feels the pull of the old. The book's last lines underscore the dilemma of these first-generation Jews: "But I felt the shadow still there, over me. It wasn't just my father, but the generations who made my father whose weight was still upon me."[42]

Or take David Levinsky, the poor *yeshiva bocher* hero of Abraham Cahan's epic 1917 saga of the Russian Jewish immigrant experience, *The Rise of David Levinsky*. Levinsky arrived in New York penniless and alone, a man who had "no acquaintance with the face of a coin." In this new world, David finds a constant hustle, a "riot of prosperity," tense with danger, frenzied and jostling, yet open to those who might seize the moment.[43]

Cahan tells the story of Levinsky's rise as a Gatsby-esque saga; a young immigrant, abject and virtually without skills, rises to the very top of the garment trade, only to find it empty and meaningless, even a fraud. For so many other immigrants, whether the fictional Gatsby himself, or the fictionalized Charles Foster Kane, or real-life characters, the American Dream, as Levinsky says, was comprised of "sham ecstasy, sham sympathy, sham smiles, sham laughter."[44]

David Levinsky might well have been a composite of thousands of Jewish immigrants at the turn of the twentieth century, each of whom built a fortune in the new world that was simply unimaginable in the world of their fathers. And Cahan might just as well have been writing about Levinsky's compatriot and Cahan's eventual friend,

Morris Michtom. But while Levinsky's story reveals the emptiness of the American Dream, Michtom's is one in which that emptiness takes several generations to work itself out. But it will, eventually; it is inevitable.

Morris and Rose

Into this strange new world stepped Morris and Rose Michtom, and also Harris, Morris's older brother, and his wife, Lena. They all disembarked at Castle Garden, a huge, hulking structure built in 1807 as a fort on a small island just off the Battery. (After Ellis Island opened in 1892, it was connected to the island of Manhattan by landfill.) Arrival there was frenzied; thousands sat around waiting to be processed. Castle Garden was crowded, noisy, and foul-smelling. Leeches and scoundrels abounded. Those with medical problems were quickly shunted off to Ward's Island. It was a museum of despair. "Who can depict the feeling of desolation, homesickness, uncertainty and anxiety with which an emigrant makes his first voyage across the ocean?" wrote Abraham Cahan of newly arrived immigrants like the fictional David Levinsky.[45]

Morris arrived before the others in the family, with a grand total of fifty cents in his pocket, no place to live, no job, and no prospects. And as he left Castle Garden, he encountered unscrupulous "benefactors" who would gladly have relieved him of his pocket change.

Politicians were indifferent, and locals were distrustful—official sources of assistance were scarce. But Jewish charities rushed into the vacuum to offer honest help. Begging for resources from local congregations, and from the city and the state, they sought to assist the teeming throngs who were disembarking daily. These aid societies were one way German Jews recognized their eastern European cousins and sought to help.*

---

* In 1881 the Hebrew Emigrant Aid Society (HEAS) was formed to ease the settlement of Russian and Galician Jews, and it worked to send Jews off to the

The newly formed Hebrew Sheltering House Association—which later became the Hebrew Immigrant Aid Society (HIAS)—found Morris before he even wandered off from the pier. After interviewing him about his skills and interests, they found a job for him in Newark, New Jersey, at the Eberhard Faber Company, the pencil manufacturer. His ORT training served him well; he got the job as a mechanic.

Off he went to Newark. Morris didn't much like factory work, but he did observe how well management at the company treated its employees. Perhaps, he thought, class struggle was not inevitable. Perhaps this American system could make everyone happy.

Morris became an American citizen on March 17, 1890. Possessing little respect for official authority, he had a wicked sense of humor. All aspiring citizens had to renounce forever any allegiance and fidelity to foreign princes. When Morris declared his intention to become a citizen, he did happily renounced his affiliation, as he said, to the "Sultan of Turkey, of whom I am a subject."

Life in Newark was stable, particularly after Rose arrived the next year. (Their first child, Joseph, was born in 1891.) By 1892, Morris's naturalization papers came through, and the Eberhard Faber factory closed. The family decamped first to the Lower East Side, where Morris ran a newsstand, and then to the Bedford-Stuyvesant neighborhood of Brooklyn.

Most young arrivals eventually found their way into the garment trade. Close to half of all Jewish immigrants sewed clothing in hundreds of small-scale sweatshops, tenement sitting rooms, and larger-scale loft-factories, working between sixty and seventy hours a week, barely scraping by on meager wages. "There is no doubt that the neatly dressed American public is indebted to the tattered, sometimes,

---

countryside in addition to helping them settle in big eastern cities like Philadelphia and New York. (Disbanded in 1883, HEAS was absorbed into the United Hebrew Charities.) It was not uncommon for New York City's United Hebrew Charities to interview ten thousand people a year.

soiled Jewish masses," Isaac Rubinow wrote in 1903. Indeed, echoed Abraham Cahan, "the Russian Jews had made the average American girl a tailor-made girl."[46]

Though Morris could be an adequate tailor, Rose was the seamstress in the family. Morris wasn't particularly interested in the garment industry, the *schmatta* trade, as the relatives called it. He didn't want to work in a factory or to be one more cog in a machine. A small, independent shopkeeper's life was more his style, a place where he could be the master of his fate, the king of the hill, even if it was the tiniest of anthills.

So Morris and Rose opened a small candy store at 404 Tompkins Avenue in Bedford-Stuyvesant. The front of the house was the store, where they sold newspapers, cigars, candy, and occasionally small stuffed dolls. Rose would make them in the evenings, and they displayed them in the glass front window of the store. Their other four children were all born in the back of the store, where the couple lived in a large single room. Benjamin Franklin Michtom was born in 1901, nine years after his older sister Emily. (She eventually married David Rosenstein, who would run the Ideal Toy Company with Ben.) Two other children died young, Henry at age five and Fred at three.

It's hard to overestimate the centrality of the candy store in the immigrant Jewish community. Standing next to the synagogue, it was the center of community life, the "informal social center on the immigrant streets," according to the author Irving Howe. Candy stores were "gathering spaces, centers of the community," and a "meeting place for the local kibitzers." There were more candy stores than saloons in New York's working-class neighborhoods. "If the saloon was the workingman's club," writes David Nasaw in his history of urban childhood, "the candy shop was the youngster's."[47]

Children were drawn to candy stores "like bees to blossoms," Nasaw writes. A candy store was more than just a shop to sell sweets; it was, in the words of a later report from the Russell Sage Foundation, "something still more attractive—a place to meet friends, to chat, sometimes to play games—always to talk and skylark a little

404 Tompkins Avenue today. Morris and Rose lived in a room at the back of their candy store.

amid light and warmth, protected alike from the distractions of the tenement home and the inconveniences of the street corner."[48]

For slightly older boys, it was a "clubhouse," a "haven of refuge and a safe retreat from the 'persecution' of the corner policeman," according to a report of the University Settlement Society of New York, a Jewish charity. While it was generally a safe haven, the candy store had a darker side, much like a pool parlor, the report's author warned. "The boys congregating in these stores are of an age to be susceptible to either good or evil influences," wrote Benjamin Reich in 1899. A candy store, he insisted, was like a gateway drug; an adolescent might "graduate" from it to a pool room, and pretty soon he'd be hanging out in saloons and dance halls (unless a watchful and clever candy store owner could find a useful occupation for him, like sewing stuffed animals).[49]

Think of the candy store as playing a role like the barbershop in the contemporary African American community; next to the church, the barbershop was the community's social center. The candy store offered cheap sweets for kids, but more important, it also offered a wide array of newspapers in both Yiddish and English (and more than a dozen other languages), which enabled browsers to stay in touch with what was happening in their homelands and also to begin to feel part of this new community. As Howe put it in *World of Our Fathers*:

> It attracted adolescents who found their parents' apartment too stifling and dreamed of moving on to the glamour of Broadway, or the big money of uptown business, prize fights, and rackets. It served a purpose somewhat like that of the barbershop in small-town America, harboring the gritty wisdom of street people, the undeluded "realism"—prey neither to social ideologies nor the mystiques of learning—that would flourish among Jewish cab drivers, fight managers, ward heelers, and the like. In the candy store these men could find coziness, gossip, tips about the big time; they could assert the commonplaces of human nature, talking about baseball instead of socialism, boasting about Jewish middleweights instead of philosophers, looking for tips at the races rather than paths to utopia.[50]

To cement their importance in the neighborhood, candy stores, along with pharmacies, were often the only places that had a telephone. When Abe Kent was first hired at Ideal in the mailroom (he would eventually rise to various senior vice-president positions in sales and merchandising), his tenement apartment in the Bronx didn't have a phone. In fact, no one in the building had a phone. At his initial interview with Ideal, he had given them the phone number of the candy store on the corner of the next block over, and when they wanted to offer Abe the job, they called the candy store, and an employee walked over to Abe's apartment building, walked up the five flights of stairs, knocked on the door, and told Abe there was a phone call for him at the store. Abe walked over the candy store, picked up the phone perhaps ten minutes later, and was offered the job.[51]

Nor is it possible to overstate the importance of the Yiddish press in the maintenance of the immigrant community. While New York alone had more than one hundred foreign-language newspapers at the turn of the century, none were more important to the community than the Yiddish newspapers and magazines. There were more than 150 of them launched between 1872, when the first one appeared, and 1917. (Many, naturally, failed and disappeared.) By the time of the U.S. entry into the World War, the five daily Yiddish-language newspapers had a combined circulation of over 300,000. They were smaller than the mainstream English-language papers, and they published only in the afternoons, when they could pirate the morning news and add some stories of local interest, as the great reformer Hutchins Hapgood noted in his landmark 1902 study, *The Spirit of the Ghetto.* And they had no sports sections, "the Jew being utterly indifferent to exercise of any kind," he continued. As the eminent sociologist Robert Park summed it up two decades later, "No other foreign language press succeeded in reflecting so much of the intimate life of the people which it represents, or reacted so powerfully upon the opinion, thought, and aspiration of the public for which it exists."[52]

Morris and Rose's candy store, offering both candy and newspapers, put the couple at the center of the neighborhood—and they relished it. Gradually, and without much effort, they embedded themselves in the political life of progressive Jewish Brooklyn. Always drawn to anarchism, Morris drifted toward anarchists in the neighborhood and helped post handbills that called on people (in Yiddish) "to rise and fight landlords, priests, and officials." (One such group included the Vilna immigrant anarchist Emma Goldman.)

One night in a local bar, after an evening of drinking and singing with his anarchist comrades, the group burst into a set of anti-Semitic songs. That was it. Morris walked out of the bar and severed his association with the anarchist movement. Anarchism, to his mind, was not synonymous with anti-Semitism. He'd had enough of that in the old world; he didn't need to revisit it in the new one.

Instead, Morris became a socialist and a follower of Eugene Debs's Socialist Party. He was concerned with the plight of poor working Jews like himself. Forget revolution; he supported electoral candidates who would bring about democratic changes. In Brooklyn, he cofounded Branch 3 of the Workmen's Circle (Arbeiter Ring), a fraternal organization founded by Jewish socialists. The Workmen's Circle offered funeral benefits, health insurance, credit assistance, and a fraternal community dedicated to self-help and social change. It supported Jewish labor unions and maintained strong ties to the Yiddish labor movement and press. It promoted Yiddish culture through singing and drama clubs and operated an educational system for both children and adults.

Morris befriended Abraham Cahan and worked to popularize Yiddish rather than archaic Hebrew. Cahan was the founder and editor of *The Jewish Daily Forward*, the most prominent Yiddish-language newspaper in New York (and the longest-surviving, publishing its last online issue in 2019). In its pages, generations of Yiddish-speaking Jews, immigrants and their descendants alike, saw both leftist politics and capitalist upward mobility. Here protection of Jewishness and celebration of a deracinated universalistic class politics slid almost effortlessly into one another. *The Forward* would treat the community of Jews as victims of anti-Semitic discrimination and violence, and it would also celebrate Jewish entrepreneurialism and the inevitable move uptown. News of the old country warmed New York Jews' nostalgia while simultaneously assuring them that they had made the right decision to come to America's shores—even before Hitler's rise to power in Germany.

Brooklyn was rapidly becoming the largest Jewish community in the world. By 1907, it was home to at least ninety synagogues, most of them Orthodox, as well as dozens of Hebrew schools, lodges, Zionist societies, and charities. In 1920 New York City had 1.6 million Jews, making up nearly 30 percent of its population. In 1940 Brooklyn was the largest Jewish city in the world, with over 1 million Jews in that borough alone.[53]

They were well served by the press, more than just *The Forward*. At the turn of the twentieth century, New York alone had more than a dozen Yiddish and Jewish-oriented newspapers, sometimes publishing multiple editions throughout the day to capture as many readers as possible—on their way to work, during lunch break, on their way home from work, and in the evening. In 1900 the city also had at least fifteen daily English-language newspapers. One could define oneself by the newspaper one read, in what language, in the morning or the evening.

Morris assiduously read them all, sitting in the candy store. He was known to try to keep up with everything that was going on. So it was no surprise that he knew all about that famous 1902 hunting trip of President Theodore Roosevelt and his refusal to shoot that adorable bear cub.

What Else They Brought

The teeming masses of Russian and eastern European Jewish immigrants had two things on their minds: first survival, then, mobility. How to fit in, how to become American, how to assimilate. Like virtually all other immigrants, they were outsiders, wanting desperately to be accepted. They wanted to start over, fresh and clean, yet hold fast to those cultural memories that linked them to their pasts.

In a short story by Anzia Yezierska (a Polish immigrant who arrived in 1890 at age ten), in her aptly titled 1923 collection, *Children of Loneliness*, a college-educated daughter confronts her Yiddish-speaking parents: "I can't live with the old world, and I'm yet too green for the new. I don't belong to those who gave me birth or to those with whom I was educated."[54] What a familiar plaint, captured so eloquently in lines by the English poet Matthew Arnold a century earlier:

> *Wandering between two worlds, one dead,*
> *The other powerless to be born,*
> *With nowhere yet to rest my head.*[55]

Here is how the journalist Hutchins Hapgood understood the specificity of the Jewish dilemma of assimilation in 1902:

> The ideal situation for this young Jew would be that where he could become an integral part of American life without losing the seriousness of nature developed by Hebraic tradition and education. At present he feels a conflict between these two influences: his youthful ardor and ambition lead him to prefer the progressive, if chaotic and uncentered, American life; but his conscience does not allow him entire peace in a situation which involves a chasm between him and his parents and their ideals. If he could find along the line of his more exciting interests—the American—something that would fill the deeper need of his nature, his problem would receive a happy solution.[56]

These poor immigrant Jews, outsiders, were entering a world where insiders spoke a language they didn't share and blocked their path at every turn, yet they became the masters of making lemonade out of those proverbial lemons. The price of being on the cutting edge is chronic restlessness. Maybe, after all, wrote the sociologist Charles Hirschman, this outsider status was "an asset that sparked creativity," offering "new possibilities for entrepreneurship."[57] If a door closed in your face, look for an open window.

Morris Michtom was only one of many young Jewish immigrants, especially their first-generation children, who shared a particular vision of America as the land where they might create for others the life they had never been able to live themselves. These few hundred young Jewish men idealized this new America that afforded so much promise, so much opportunity, so much potential wealth—if only they could find how to penetrate its outer skin of gentile and genteel privilege.

They brought with them the same dreams and desires that have motivated so many millions of seekers and escapees, adventurers and refugees. But perhaps they brought something else too, in those worn satchels and cardboard suitcases held together by string—something tucked away between the pages of their prayer books, wrapped in oily cloths with the menorahs, or inscribed in the mezuzahs they nailed to their doors. That something would change the land they had entered, as much as, if not more than, it changed them: a new idea about childhood.

Taking childhood as a stage of life, they sought to create a perfect version of it, the one that had been denied them by poverty, anti-Semitism, violence, and murder. The one that had been denied them by having to work at such an early age, or to care for aging or sick relatives. The one that could be had by anyone, as long as they consumed the right products. These largely first-generation American Jews invented an idealized childhood that they hadn't had by creating childhood as a stage of consumption. If they themselves "could not ever be a child in such turmoil," as that Polish father wrote to his son, then they would create a childhood that one could have, in a turmoil-free world where one could—and should—have it: America.

3

A NEW IDEAL OF CHILDHOOD

* * *

In her international best-selling book *The Century of the Child*, Ellen Key, the famed Swedish reformer proclaimed that the twentieth century would be "the century of the child." (It was first published in Swedish in 1900 and translated into English nine years later.) As far as Key could tell, Americans had been going about raising children all wrong: straitjacketing them, locking them in charmless classrooms, and forcing them to memorize and recite multiplication tables in schools built more for "soul murder" than for self-exploration. Even kindergarten had become a "factory"; homework was soul-crushing, and spanking was barbaric. Instead, she argued, we should leave children alone to explore, to create, to wonder. Her idea was not to mold children to fit their environment, but to control the environment so as to allow children to express themselves within it. Such a view coincided with Progressivism generally and was amplified by many American educational reformers like G. Stanley Hall, John Dewey, and later Erik Erikson, who, breaking with prevailing orthodoxies, sought to create the conditions for children to create themselves, instead of molding them to fit preconceived ideas.*

Key's best-selling pronouncement heralded a new idea of childhood that began to take hold at the turn of the twentieth century. Gradually, at least among the urban, and later suburban, middle classes, an idea of childhood as a specific stage of development emerged. Play replaced work. School became the dominant institutional feature of children's lives.

On the nation's farms, children still did chores before they went to school, but schooldays began to last longer. In 1900 most American children attended school until age twelve. Progressive reformers started promoting a "sheltered" childhood, a stage of life in which children would be removed from the labor force, protected from adult concerns, and cared for by experts and expertly trained mothers. No longer valued for their instrumental potential as family workers, children became instead, as the sociologist Viviana Zelizer argues, "priceless."[1]

Indeed, before the twentieth century, childhood, as we now know it, barely existed. Then as now, children needed to be socialized into the world they would someday inhabit. It's just that they had to be able to inhabit it far more quickly than they do today. The idea of child*hood* is a relatively modern phenomenon. As the historian Paula Fass writes in *The Routledge History of Childhood in the Western World*:

> The "modern" perspective on children as sexually innocent, economically dependent, and emotionally fragile, whose lives are supposed to be dominated by play, school and family nurture, provides a very limited view of children's lives in the modern western past. While some

---

* Key took her title from a little-known play, *The Lion's Whelp*, in which an older man says to a younger man, "The next century will be the century of the child, just as this century has been the woman's century." Key, *Century of the Child*, 45.

> children did experience this kind of childhood, for the vast majority, it is quite literally only in the twentieth century that these have been enforced as both preferred and dominant.[2]

The historian Steven Mintz notes that "modern childhood was invented" in these first years of the twentieth century. As one man, recalling his own childhood, put it rather succinctly, "Childhood, I didn't have much."[3]

A century ago children enjoyed little parental attention or warmth, had little free time for play, and received little encouragement to express themselves. Childhood as a separate and distinct stage of life, one that required special attention, emerged as the product of economic and social shifts—declining birth rates, urbanization, educational reforms, labor relations—that led to shifts in our ideas about child-rearing, child development, and proper parenting. These shifts, in turn, opened up opportunities for entrepreneurs to create the material culture of the twentieth-century child, providing the toys, games, and books that entertained and educated children for a new century, *their* century, the "century of the child."

The Prehistory of Childhood

In 1962 the celebrated French historian Philippe Ariès propounded the surprising notion that childhood was a relatively modern idea and depended on changing demographic and material factors. By scouring through French parish church records of births and deaths through the Middle Ages, he discovered that "in medieval society, the idea of childhood did not exist." "Of all the characteristics in which the medieval age differs from the modern," echoed the celebrated British historian Barbara Tuchman, "none is more striking as the comparative absence of interest in children."[4]

For example, the idea that a child's name adhered to one—and only one—child, an idea taken for granted today, was a relatively modern invention. In eras when the infant mortality rate hovered around half of all births, Ariès surmised, families might have considered a child's name to be their property rather than the infant's identity. Back then, if my wife and I wanted a "Michael Jr.," we'd have kept naming our sons Michael Jr. until one survived past age three. We might get lucky with the first, but there was no guarantee, and continuing the family line was more important than identifying any specific infant. Here's Tuchman, echoing Ariès:

> Owing to the high infant mortality of the times, estimated at one or two in three, the investment of love in a young child may have been so unrewarding that by some ruse of nature, as when overcrowded rodents in captivity will not breed, it was suppressed. Perhaps also the frequent childbearing put less value on the product. A child was born and died and another took its place.[5]

Ariès, Tuchman, and other historians noticed the absence of childhood because children were not permitted a separate existence as children; rather, they were valued for their economic utility, whether as potential workers or as more mouths to feed. From the earliest times, girls were seen as less economically valuable as workers; therefore fathers would pay to enhance their daughters' marriageability and to ensure that their family of origin would no longer be responsible for feeding and caring for them.*

Because life itself was initially tenuous, and because children had value only as economic actors, they were perceived to be what Ariès called "little adults." Ariès noticed that portraits painted of children, from medieval Europe through the seventeenth century, depicted children as miniature adults, wearing adult clothing, and bearing expressions as dour and unfriendly as those of their parents.

---

* The idea of dowries can take root only where the "value" of children is calculable in economic terms and gender inequality ranks boys as much more "valuable" than girls.

Other historians have roundly and largely-convincingly challenged this view, arguing, for example, that while children might have been dressed for formal portraits as little adults, that was not necessarily what they would have been wearing when they weren't sitting for portraits. Besides, everyone looked dour and unfriendly in portraits, perhaps because they took so damned long to paint! Even in family photographs from the nineteenth century, entire families would put on their most serious facial expressions because they had to hold them for quite some time. More centrally, the historians Shulamith Shahar and Barbara Hanawalt used different types of evidence to show that medieval parents did invest emotionally in their children, mourned them when they died young, and saw childhood as a distinct and separate stage of development.[6]

Despite these and other criticisms, Ariès provided the starting point for the history of childhood. He'd argued that children were regarded less for their intrinsic value as children than for their potential contribution to the family's economic survival. If nothing else, older views of children were markedly different than our views today.

These views were rooted in Catholic Europe, then were uprooted and replanted on American shores. By that time, the Puritans saw children less as a pleasure than as a responsibility, since a family or a community's failure to align a child with God was among the surest signs of its damnation. Puritan—and what we now affectionately call "puritanical"—ideas about child-rearing held that children were little devils, unsocialized and wild, and that the task of the devout parent was to "break" the child's will and "mold" them toward a devout and obedient adulthood. Children, in this sense, had to be tamed; they were feral outsiders who had to be brought into society through a ruthless socialization. In the more "enlightened" early twentieth century, Lothrop Stoddard, the notorious eugenicist and purveyor of race suicide, looked back at Puritan New England and bemoaned that there, as in old England, children "were subjected to a discipline calculated to crush the spirit and terrorize the mind."[7]

A core idea of Puritan child-rearing was infant damnation. Children were born in sin, and infant baptism did not absolve the child of original sin. "The Devil has been with them already," said the New England minister Cotton Mather. "They go astray as soon as they are born."[8] The goal of parenting was to restrain evil in their children by breaking them from their sinful wills. They didn't see this necessarily as cruelty; discipline was love.

Here is the seventeenth-century English minister Richard Baxter:

> Train them up in exact obedience to yourselves, and break them of their own wills. To that end, suffer them not to carry themselves unreverently or contemptuously towards you; but to keep their distance. For too much familiarity breedeth contempt, and imboldeneth disobedience.[9]

Perhaps the best-known purveyor of these ideas was the early seventeenth-century minister who became the Pilgrims' first pastor, John Robinson, who wrote that "there is in all children . . . a stubbornness and stoutness of mind arising from natural pride, which must, in the first place, be broken and beaten down". He continued: :

> For beating, and keeping down of this stubbornness parents must provide carefully for two things: first that children's wills and willfulness be restrained and repressed, and that, in time; lest sooner than they imagine, the tender sprigs grow to that stiffness, that they would rather break than bow. Children should not know, if it could be kept from them, that they have a will in their own, but in their parents' keeping: neither should these words be heard from them, save by way of consent, "I will" or "I will not."[10]

It's not that Puritans hated or even disliked their children—far from it. They saw the discipline they inflicted on them as an expression of love, both for their children and for God. It was their responsibility. Puritans regarded childhood "as a time of deficiency, associating an infantile inability to walk or talk with animality." Even newborn infants were seen as "potential sinners who contained aggressive and willful impulses that needed to be suppressed," writes the historian Hugh Cunningham. Crawling was considered bestial, and play was frivolous and frightening, "a sinful waste of time, a 'snare of the Old Deluder, Satan.' "[11]

To the colonists, "a baby represented a miniature adult," writes the historian Geoffrey Wilson, "who would soon help out on the farm or in a trade." Parents "treated [babies] severely."[12] Excessive affectionate smothering, or "doting," of their children was frowned upon. Eighteenth- and nineteenth-century parents wanted to be not cold toward their children but judicious and impartial. Play was "the devil's workshop," and corporal punishment was meted out not just by parents but by teachers and Sunday school teachers. At best, in the words of Reverend Samuel Willard, children were "innocent vipers," prone "to commit evil at an early age but not to be held responsible for their acts until they had achieved the age of reason."[13] In their 1869 handbook of advice for mothers, Catharine Beecher and Harriet Beecher Stowe complained of the "deficiency of the free expression of kindly feelings and sympathetic emotions" in middle-class New England homes.[14]

From that era we inherited some of the cruel aphorisms that still, today, shadow contemporary child-rearing: "Spare the rod and spoil the child." "Children should be seen and not heard." And when spanking the child, the declaration that "this will hurt me more than it hurts you"—which surely every child who has ever lived knows to be untrue.

By the turn of the century, the fading Puritan views on original sin found a new voice in the influx of Freudian theories of child development, especially among the middle and upper classes. Freud dispensed with theology (original sin) but replaced it with a notion that people are biological creatures driven by sexual urges and that their libidinal energies must be redirected away from the objects of their desires toward more useful and productive ends. In Freud's argument, a person's self, or personality, develops through a series of shocks and disappointments to their biologically driven aspect, which he called the id. The id was pure desire, wanting gratification, aggressive and untamed.

In the Freudian outlook, children came to be seen, in Geoffrey Wilson's words, as "obstinate angels."[15] Children needn't be broken, exactly, but their libidinal energies had to be, if not repressed, then sublimated from their immediate objects and redirected by moral instruction. The entire civilizing project was to take creatures who were outside the social order—children—and bring them into it by instilling it into them internally as a sense of morality. Or as Freud put it in his *New Introductory Lectures on Psychoanalysis,* "Where id was, there ego shall be. It is a work of culture." The Puritan and psychoanalytic perspectives alike saw childhood as a threat to the social order; children had to be tamed.

Many of these ideas took a distinctly American turn. Neither Puritan theology nor Freudian psychoanalysis proposed that the goal of life should be happiness. The Puritan acceptance of duty may have been superseded by the Freudian adjustment of an individual to a world that would not, and could not, satisfy its craving; but any notion of joy or exuberance remained at least suspect, if not potentially toxic. "The notion of shielding the young from knowledge of violence, wickedness, or sex would have astonished a Puritan parent, who reasoned that the more they heard about such things, the better; it would make them consider their own wickedness and try to correct it," wrote Mary Cable in her 1975 history of American child-rearing practices.[16]

Still, the inquisitive child, the precocious child, was a source of anxiety and concern, hardly someone to be celebrated. Precocity was perhaps a danger sign that, if unchecked, might lead to feeblemindedness. Beecher and Stowe believed that intellectual precocity was a brain disorder and recommended that the precocious child be forbidden the use of all books and encouraged to play outdoors. One nineteenth-century doctor, Frances Emily White, advised parents to prevent the precocious child from engaging in any kind of mental activity whatsoever lest brain inflammation develop. He should not be allowed to learn to read and should spend his early years in a rural area playing outdoors.[17] It was as if childhood precocity were part of the growing problem of mental and physical decline, particularly for boys, who were losing their hardy sense of rough-and-tumble manhood in favor of nerdy book-learning. (This would have come as a bit of a shock, I imagine, to those Yiddish immigrant boys, for whom the highest expression of manhood was a burning desire to sit and read the Talmud all day. But that's part of our story.)

If precocity was to be suppressed, so too was any manifestation of anxiety or distress. Crying, particularly, was to be met with decisive discouragement. William and Lena Sadler's parental advice book, *The Mother and Her Child*, published in 1915, put it this way:

> We run into many snags when we undertake to discipline the nervous baby. The first is that it will sometimes cry so hard that it will get black in the face and may even have a convulsion; occasionally a small blood vessel may be ruptured on some part of the body, usually the face. When you see the little one approaching this point, turn it over and administer a sound spanking and it will instantly catch its breath. This will not have to be repeated many times until that particular difficulty will be largely under control.[18]

This advice was to be repeated if the child awakened in the night and cried. If gently explaining to him that there was no need to cry proved ineffective, parents were to "turn him over and administer a good spanking—and repeat, if necessary, to get results."[19]

Influenced by eugenics, several best-selling child-rearing books were so concerned about the possible ways that parents could ruin their children that they advised pregnant mothers to "avoid thinking of ugly people, or those marked by any deformity or disease," lest they inflict grievous harm on the "little stranger" growing inside them.[20]

But a kinder and gentler discourse was also emerging. Increasingly, parents were counseled against adhering to the puritanical notion of inherent wickedness, animality, or sinfulness. "Children are not cherubs, nor always such as we imagine those the Savior blessed," wrote John F. W. Ware in his best-selling *Home Life*, published in 1863. "They, too, are a bundle of wants—troubles that want soothing, tears that want wiping, effort that wants encouraging, hunger that wants appeasing, clothes that want patching, and mischief and disobedience that want the closet or the rod."[21]

It no longer seemed necessary to break the child's will. Perhaps one needed only to bend it toward obedience, through what one child development expert, Jacob Abbott, called "gentle measures." "Gentle measures are those which tend to exert a calming, quieting, and soothing influence on the mind, or to produce only such excitements as are pleasurable in their character, as means of repressing wrong and encouraging right action. Ungentle measures are those which tend to inflame and irritate the mind, or to agitate it with *painful* excitements."

To be sure, instilling obedience to authority was still paramount. "The first duty which devolves upon the mother in the training of her child is the establishment of her *authority* over him," he wrote, "that is the forming in him of the habit of immediate, implicit, and unquestioning obedience to all her commands."[22]

The early twentieth century witnessed a "more involved" parenthood, at least among the educated middle classes, that seemed to leave physical punishment behind: "Whipping, beating, and the like gave way to explaining to the child why it is in their best interest to do something." Ironically, among the working class, as the historian Christine Stansell tells us, the persistent "absence" of a specific stage of childhood provided children with a wider latitude of freedom. "In contrast to their middle- and upper-class contemporaries," she writes, "the working poor did not think of childhood as a separate stage of life in which girls and boys were free from burdens, nor did poor women consider mothering to be a full-time task of supervision. Women of the laboring classes condoned for their offspring an early independence—within bounds—on the streets."[23]

Thus did the "American century" and the "century of the child" begin to converge. Widespread prosperity, rapid industrialization, and the emergence of a distinct urban middle class meant for many that, at last, the third item on the Jeffersonian list of inalienable rights—the pursuit of happiness—might be more than just a pipe dream. One could, and perhaps even should, be happy. Or at least try.

A key change in gender roles accompanied these economic changes. At the very moment when large numbers of women began to agitate to leave their homes—to work, join unions, vote, and participate in public life—and demanded recognition that many women already worked outside the home, the persistence of the nineteenth-century ideology of separate spheres consigned them to the world of home and family, particularly the world of children. Motherhood wasn't simply a biological fact, nor even a social reality: It was to be seen as a calling, a profession. Women needn't leave their homes to find fulfillment; it was right in front of them.

The three institutions that encompassed children's lives—family, church, school—were increasingly dominated by women. The ranks not only of mothers but of teachers and Sunday school teachers were filled by women. What the historian Ann Douglas called "the feminization of American culture" was more than simply a demographic shift—the dramatic exit of men from classrooms and church pews; it also signaled a cultural shift to a "softer" Protestant theology. The nation's pulpits were more likely to offer a kinder, gentler savior, whose emphasis on love and compassion was gradually displacing his angrier and more vindictive father.

For them, infant damnation was too cold and heartless a doctrine for the increasing warmth of the turn-of-the-century family. Children were born neither bad nor good; they were born innocent. They needed to be raised in a nurturing environment. In this modernized version of John Locke's idea of the mind as a "blank slate," children could basically go either way, depending on their environment.[24]

The feminization of American culture inevitably produced a backlash, particularly among those who worried that boys were becoming softer and less manly. Organizations like the Boone and Crockett Club and, most notably, the Boy Scouts of America promised to wrest boys from the feminizing clutches of mothers and teachers and bring them into a hardier manhood, comfortable in the wild, able to tame nature. Dude ranches in the countryside and gymnasiums in the cities helped fathers man up from their emasculating office jobs. And with significant promotion from President Theodore Roosevelt, high schools and colleges introduced massive sports programs, proclaiming that a healthy mind required a healthy body, while the urban working and middle classes flocked to stadium bleachers to watch baseball games.*

In large part, the established German Jewish community embraced this idea of childhood innocence. As assimilated Americans, they were comfortable with a view of the German father as somewhat softer than the stereotypic domestic authoritarian, and they gave a much larger role to mothers, especially in the maintenance of the family and household. Many German Jewish immigrants had been influenced by the kindergarten movement, which had begun in Germany in the early nineteenth century. Though the Prussian government banned kindergartens in 1851, many German Jews living in the United States remained dedicated to its principles.

The historian Marion Kaplan describes how easily these German and Jewish ideas coincided to create the dominant American Jewish culture:

> In addition to promoting cleanliness, refinement, and order, German Jewish women were intent on inculcating in their children the habits of duty, obedience, thrift, industriousness, and respect. The adoption of those values and their incorporation into existing Jewish traditions resulted in a set of beliefs and mores particular to

---

* That this masculine emphasis offered a new opportunity for man-making toys and games should be obvious, from Morris Michtom's own Teddy Bears to athletic gear and the Erector Set, created in 1913, one of the first, and most gendered, toys of the century.

> Jews at this time. Through German Jewish immigration to the United States, those values came to be identified with American Jewish culture. Having arrived earlier than the masses of Russian and Eastern European Jewish immigrants, German Jews in America provided a model of success for later immigrants, exemplifying a desirable social pattern.[25]

The notion of innate childhood innocence was an important, indeed necessary intermediate position between the Puritans and the ideas of childhood articulated at the turn of the twentieth century.

From Puritans to Progressives

Few movements in American history have been as optimistic as Progressivism. In a world dominated by archaic monarchies, authoritarian rulers, and hereditary fiefdoms, Americans believed that they were a nation capable of self-governance. Progressives trusted the individual and the community to bend toward greater democracy. By relying on scientific principles, rational modes of organization, and an education for democracy, the country could become a better version of itself, fulfilling the promise of becoming a "shining city on a hill," a beacon of hope and light to the world. The Statue of Liberty may have been a gift from the French, but Americans—native born and immigrant alike—saw in it a mirror of who they thought they were.

Children, in this view, were not outsiders but important central characters, capable of reason, creativity, and morality. In 1922 Rabbi Stephen Wise remarked on the deepening "consciousness of children" and affirmed the sense that "they have the unchallengeable right to live their own lives, under freedom to develop their own personalities. Revolting against the superimposition of parental personality . . . they have begun to hearken to Emerson's counsel to insist upon themselves." Children were individual moral agents. No wonder that central to the Progressive ideal was what the great pragmatist philosopher and progressive educational reformer John Dewey called "democratic education" or, more accurately, an education for democracy.*

Dewey believed that only by experiencing democracy could one become an effective democratic citizen. Thus he believed that schools must become more democratic. Instead of an authority figure standing over them, instilling knowledge into them as one fills a vessel, children should have a greater say in their own education. "Each of us at birth has special potentialities which are slowly crushed and destroyed by a standardized and mechanical method of teaching," was how the writer and critic Malcolm Cowley later put it.[26]

In the first decades of the twentieth century, the dominant culture began to embrace these views, adopting them as part of the larger Progressive movement and changing the circumstances in which children grew up. A group of developmental psychologists and parental advisers proposed a positive notion of childhood that cast children as happy, curious, and playful beings who entered the adult world by passing through a series of predictable stages. Each stage poses a specific challenge to the developing child, whose mastery of it enables them to function better in society. Child development was a process, not of taming the wild child, but of gradually integrating the child into the world.

Progressives wanted to establish a new view of childhood, based on scientific principles of biology and psychology. Children, in this view, were to be shielded from the labor force, protected from adult concerns, age-segregated, and cared for by specialized experts and expertly trained mothers. Children were precious and valuable in their own right, and child-rearing was too important a task to be left to amateurs (i.e., untrained mothers).

This reinvention of childhood as a separate, happy, and carefree

---

* As if to illustrate the case made by Ariès about children's names, Dewey was born in 1859, a mere forty weeks after his older brother John died in an accident. The second John survived.

stage was contingent on the political economy of childhood. For one thing, the birth rate had declined rapidly during the nineteenth century, partly due to access to improved medical care. In 1800 American mothers bore an average of 7.04 children. By 1851 it was 5.42, and by 1900 it was 3.56. By 1930, partly as a result of access to birth control, it further declined to below 3 (2.9). (Ironically, the decline of the number of children may have contributed to an increased need for toys, since children had fewer peers to play with and parents had more disposable income to spend.)

Ironically, while the average number of babies born to a particular mother may have been declining, the actual number of babies was rising, fueled by the immigrants streaming into the country. In 1890 children under five years old constituted nearly 15 percent of the U.S. population. (By contrast, in 1950, when the baby boom took off, it was only 11 percent.) Fully one-quarter of those children were immigrants, and in the Northeast and the mid-Atlantic states, the percentage hovered between one-third and one-half.[27]

Expanded schooling, regulating child labor, and the rise of an urban middle class combined to transform American thinking about childhood. One pioneer reformer was Felix Adler, founder of the Ethical Culture Society in 1877. Born in Germany, Adler had come to New York City at age six, when his father became the chief rabbi at Temple Emanu-El. In 1901 Felix issued a revised edition of a widely popular child-rearing manual, *The Moral Instruction of Children*. As he later wrote, childhood "shall be sacred."[28] In 1904 Adler became the founding chairman of the National Child Labor Committee (NCLC), which campaigned to end child labor in the United States. He hired photographer Lewis Hine to document the conditions of child labor in America in 1908, which would propel the campaign toward its eventual, if uneven, path to success.

* * *

The emerging conception of these creatures called children required a progressive understanding of the stages of their development. At the turn of the century, childhood got not only a lot larger but also a lot longer. In the developmental sequence, after childhood came, not adulthood, but an entirely new stage of development: adolescence.

The psychologist G. Stanley Hall's massive treatise *Adolescence* (1904) placed the term—and the stage of development—into the national understanding of development. As president of Clark University, Hall argued that in the nineteenth century children had gone directly to being adults: after they graduated from high school, they went to work on the family farm or in a trade, got married, and started families. Empirically, he was right: The average age of marriage in 1900, when he wrote, was about twenty-two years for women and twenty-six for men. But by the turn of the century, Hall argued, a new developmental stage had appeared, a passage between childhood and adulthood, a period of conflict, or inner searching for identity, of testing out new freedoms of adulthood while still being constrained by childhood.

In an odd way, the notion of the adolescent further "infantilized" the child. After all, the characterization of adolescence as rebellious and agitated period reimagined childhood as a more bucolic time, without care or responsibility. The rebelling adolescent had to be rebelling against something, shedding the security and pleasures of childhood while moving toward the indeterminate and unknown world of adulthood. Adolescence was a molting season.

As adolescence was demarcated from childhood, it established childhood as a stage different from adolescence, a stage characterized by play and the lack of responsibility or consequences. With adolescence as an intermediate stage, adulthood and childhood became further opposed. Indeed, at the turn of the twentieth century, the word *manhood* was the opposite of *childhood*, and *virility* was the opposite of *puerility*. A mere twenty or thirty years later *masculinity*'s opposite was *femininity*.

As a result, a veritable cult of childhood emerged in the early twentieth century—and, let's face it, continues to this day. A study of Chinese and American child-rearing in 1963 observed: "No other country accords so much attention to infancy or so many privileges to childhood as does the United States."[29] In one child-rearing advice manual, *Infant Care* (published by the Children's Bureau of the U.S. Department of Labor in 1929), Martha Eliot discerned a notable shift in ideas about children's impulses, especially around the idea of play. In the first half of the century, children's impulses were seen as "enjoyable," but in a bad way, as dangerous and almost certainly erotic. That which gave pleasure to children might become harmful and wicked. But by the midcentury, play was more about obligation and duty—that is, preparation for adult responsibility.

Having a child came to be seen as less about responsibility for the parents than about fun for them, too. *Enjoy! Enjoy!* counseled the child-rearing literature. It was, we learned, sort of politically important. A "child-centered home is the key to a future society of well-adjusted individuals" was the way historian Gary Cross summarized the results of White House Conference on Child Health and Protection in 1930.[30] That conference produced "The Children's Charter" which enumerated the "rights" of every child, including a healthy birth, adequate nutrition, medical care, and education and the right to grow up in a family environment of love and understanding.

Those Yiddish Jews

These emerging notions of childhood fit easily with the ideas held by the masses of Yiddish Jews streaming into East Coast cities. Whereas the Jews of the nineteenth century had largely assimilated into American patterns of family life and child-rearing, the massive numbers of Yiddish Jews were unassimilated, and they carried with them some ideas about childhood that were traditional for them, yet in the American context sounded like Progressivist mantras.

Yiddish Jews were something like Yiddish itself—a tongue without a home or, rather, a home-land. There is no "Yidland" where Yiddish is the official language. "Jews were a team without a ballpark, always the visitors," observes the comic book historian Danny Fingeroth. Nationless, but not exactly homeless, uncomfortable everywhere they went, they picked up scraps of other cultures when they were allowed to interact with them.[31]

Yet the Yiddish Jewish immigrant was not a blank slate. Over centuries, both insular and homogenous, and both itinerant and mingling assimilationist, Yiddish Jews had developed well-formed cultural ideas and practices, mixtures of hardship, marginalization, and tradition. Here is how Marcus Ravage put it in his 1917 book, *An American in the Making*:

> The alien who comes here from Europe is not the raw material that Americans suppose him to be. He is not a blank sheet to be written on as you see fit. He has not sprung out of nowhere. Quite the contrary. He brings with him a deep-rooted tradition, a system of culture and tastes and habits—a point of view which is as ancient as his national experience and which has been engendered in him by his race and his environment. And it is this thing—this entire Old World soul of his—that comes in conflict with America as soon as he has landed.[32]

But for Yiddish Jews, what wasn't in much conflict was their view of children. In fact, it was conveniently prescient.

One shouldn't draw too fine a distinction between Yiddish Jews and their Protestant peers. Jewish homes were—or at least were supposed to be—also patriarchal, with the father as the unquestioned authority. But that view of family life is that of parents. Seen from the point of view of their children, both parents provided warmth and a belief in their natural curiosity, precocity, and creativity.

In that sense, the Yiddish family was "child centered," writes Nathalie Joffe in her somewhat gauzy gloss on *The American Jewish Family* (1954). Children were seen as pure and wondrous, "a garland of roses," according to the Talmud. Yiddish Jews believed the "child is a blessing to the family," just as the people are children to God. According to the historian Jenna Weissman Joselit, they valued children "not for their material contributions to the family economy but for the emotional satisfaction—the *yidishe nachas*—they provided." Indeed, it was a Yiddish expression that "children are their parents' *nachas.*" Biblical child-rearing required a loving and trusting atmosphere, not a fearful one.[33] And what was true in content was equally true in form. The cultural tradition of Talmudic debate and discussion was playful, playing with ideas; indeed, we'd say "toying" with them.

Entirely absent was any notion of infant damnation. Instead, as one rabbi put it, children's "very breath is free of sin." "The child who comes to bless a household is regarded as an individual from the moment of conception," write Mark Zborowski and Elizabeth Herzog in their classic ethnographic reconstruction of the shtetl, *Life Is with People.* As a result, every child was to be accorded love, compassion, and respect.[34]

In her study of Jewish mothers, Zena Smith Blau noted:

> Jewish mothers seemed singularly unconcerned with "discipline" and "independence training." They allowed their children a greater degree of latitude in acting out at home . . . and readily acknowledged that their children were "*zelosen*"—pampered, demanding, spoiled, not well-behaved. The Anglo-Saxon code of stoic endurance and suppressed emotion was alien to Eastern European Jews.[35]

Perhaps one origin of the stereotype of the smothering Jewish mother was that anything other than callous indifference was regarded with suspicion.

Actually, Jewish child-rearing was an indicator of a much larger worldview. In his expansive 1916 treatise *The Child in Human Progress*, the reformer G. H. Payne went so far as to claim that it was the Jewish "nation," or people, who first introduced humanitarianism into the world precisely through their attitudes toward children. The key departure was in the condemnation of child sacrifice in the story of Abraham and Isaac. While many readers consider this story to be about Abraham's obedience to God, with the father willing, in fact, to sacrifice his only son to a God whose ways could not be fathomed by mere mortals, Payne wrote that Jews saw this story as meaning something else. Abraham's obedience to the singular God is the origin point of monotheism; God's response, sparing Isaac, is thus the origin of humanitarianism. The God of Abraham does not need blood sacrifice, doesn't need that level of obedience. The monotheistic moment is a moment of compassion, not judgment.[36]

It's true that Puritans and late nineteenth-century immigrants alike regarded education as essential, a commandment, an obligation. Deuteronomy 6:7 commands "And you shall teach them [the words of God] diligently to your children and speak of them when you sit at home and when you walk along the road and when you lie down and when you rise up." And it's true that Yiddish Jews expected discipline and obedience, but it was to be nurtured in them, not extracted from them through force or threat. "Hillel was the forerunner of Montessori," as one contemporary historian put it.[37]

Thus it is no surprise that one of the three pillars of the new childhood of the twentieth century—"the century of the child"—was education. Indeed, it was the necessary connective tissue between the other pillars, work (or rather the absence of it) and play. Making changes in these three domains would ensure that each person had claimed, as the Progressives put it, a "right to childhood."

School

In 1850 half of all American young people aged five to nineteen attended grammar school; this percentage increased to nearly 60 percent by 1870. Between 1870 and 1915, the number of children in schools increased from 7 million to 20 million, and expenditures rose from $63 million to $605 million.[38]

The central theme of Progressive education was that children had a stake in their education, and hence their childishness was a resource to be cultivated, not a problem to be remedied. Progressive schooling should also, as John Dewey put it, serve "the whole child," seeking to "preserve rather than tame the child's uncivilized impulses."[39] Certainly one purpose of school was to socialize the young, to buttress the lessons of home and church, but another was to let children remain children as long as possible.

This vision of the "natural" untamed child rippled throughout the culture. Some articulations of it sounded downright Rousseauean, extolling the innocent but noble savage. In a somewhat romantic inversion, children were the real grown-ups, untainted by the corruptions of civilization. Floyd Dell, a bohemian radical of Greenwich Village, wrote that "the object of genuine democratic education is to enable [the child] to remain always a child." Education was to highlight the child's imagination in reaction to "the numbing effects of modern civilization," added the celebrated poet and novelist (and first-generation American, born in 1883 to immigrant Jewish parents) Alfred Kreymborg.[40]

By the 1920s, this romanticized antimodernist regression had seeped into other cultural forms. Childhood impulses were seen not as aggressive urges in need of control and repression but rather as a form of resistance to that repression itself. Rationality had brought us the trenches of World War I, poison gas, and the slaughter of many innocent boys, so perhaps a regression to childhood, a return to the "natural," before socialization, held a key to our liberation. In European art, the primitivists, Picasso's cubist reductions to geometrics, Dubuffet's intentional efforts to paint like a child, Dada and Surrealist happenings—these were the forerunners of the 1960s be-ins and today's poetry slams.

Progressive ideas changed both the form and the content of education. School started earlier in a child's life, and it lasted longer. The first seed of kindergartens was planted by Friedrich Froebel in Germany in the 1830s. A follower of Rousseau, Froebel embraced the French philosopher's view of childhood innocence as articulated in his treatise on education, *Émile*. We are born good, innocent, and noble, and then we are corrupted by society as we grow into it. The purpose of education, Rousseau argued, was to enable children to sustain that innate goodness as long as possible. Children were not miniature adults: "Nature wants children to be children before they are men," he wrote. For Froebel, the kindergarten was to be, literally, a garden *of* and *for* children, who would, with careful cultivation, grow into beautiful flowers. Kindergartens were imported into the United States in the 1870s, connecting with the Progressive ideas about children advocated by the educational luminary John Dewey, who began a kindergarten program at the University of Chicago in the 1890s.[41]

Meanwhile Maria Montessori, an Italian doctor, opened her first Casa dei Bambini in 1907, suggesting a similar idea of child development through creative interaction with the environment. By 1912 the movement had begun to take off in the United States when Frank Vanderlip, an esteemed banker who became a social reformer, founded the Scarborough School outside New York City.[42]

Educational reforms like these also resonated with Progressive ideas about class and ethnicity, especially as it pertained to the assimilation of immigrants. In the United States, kindergartens were initially a social reform initiated to relieve working-class families—where mothers worked, unlike mothers in more affluent middle-class families—from the double burden of work and childcare. In 1860 Elizabeth Peabody funded four private kindergartens in Boston for the children of immigrant factory workers. In 1873 St. Louis became the first municipality to provide free kindergartens throughout the public school system. By 1880, there were more than four hundred kindergartens in thirty states and kindergarten training schools in every major city. The kindergarten movement wasn't simply glorified babysitting; Peabody and others believed that children's play had an intrinsic educational value, whether they played with other children or alone, or perhaps with a doll. Indeed, the idea of the American kindergarten, said Froebel, was "organized play."[43]

* * *

At the other end of the developmental spectrum, children were staying in school far longer than in the past. This change was driven from below, as urbanization and industrialization freed up children later and later in their development, and from above, as laws requiring schooling through high school took hold across the country. In 1918 Mississippi was the last state to enact compulsory education laws for children aged six to seventeen.

The development of the comprehensive high school was among the most important social reforms of the turn of the century. In 1900 the number of Americans attending high school was just over 110,000; by 1930, it was up to 4.4 million. Between 1890 and 1918, high school attendance rose by over 700 percent, from 200,000 to 1.6 million. In 1915 about one-fifth of all young people were in high schools; by 1928, half of American children were attending. For the first thirty years of the twentieth century, a new high school opened on average every day.[44]

Perhaps no one embodied these new ideas about school better than Margaret Naumburg. Born in New York to German Jewish immigrants in 1890, Naumburg became involved with Ethical Culture early on, and after attending both Vassar and Barnard, she studied with John Dewey at Columbia. Convinced that traditional schooling focused on all the wrong things, she was determined to recenter education on the child itself, or as she put it in an article in 1922, to move away from "the barren field of the curriculum to the fertile field of the child." A year after founding the first Montessori school in New York in 1914, she founded the Children's School, soon renamed the Walden School, where the entire day allowed children to explore, create and set their own interaction patterns based on how they felt. How long a child studied any particular subject was, she wrote, "fitted to the needs of the children and not to a mechanical school program."[45]

In her major work, *The Child and the World* (1928), Naumburg elaborated this view. In a series of fictional dialogues, she critiqued behaviorist education for so separating work and play that it stripped children of their natural curiosity and inquisitiveness and induced them to try to get the best grades for the least effort so they could go play. Instead, Naumburg, deriving ideas from Locke, Rousseau,

Freud, and Whitehead, proposed that school be a place where work and play were united, and where the whole child was educated and allowed to develop in their own way, not according to a predetermined pattern. A school, in other words, was a place where children's growth determined the curriculum, not the other way around.

The behaviorist system, Naumberg argued, "kills the spirit of our best teachers and presses the life out of our keenest children." The Walden system, by encouraging "spontaneity and freedom" among the children, could attend to their physical and emotional needs, as well as their need for information. "The problem is no longer how much cut-and-dried information can be crammed into a class of children," she wrote, "but how many well-rounded individuals, genuine personalities, can be brought to fulfillment in such a school."[46] (Eventually, Naumberg left the Walden school movement and used the techniques she had developed there to work with mentally ill patients. It was she who created the field of art therapy.)

The American education system did have regional and class differences. Fewer than half of all Southern children attended schools, while percentages in the Northeast and Far West approached 70 percent. Poor families, rural families, and Black families were much less likely to send their children to school than were white, affluent, and/or urban families. In the cities, immigrant children made up the large majority of students in the nation's largest schools. In New York City, immigrant children were so numerous that classes would swell to sixty or even seventy pupils.

Which meant that teachers often had to be more concerned with keeping order than with educating. And they didn't have much time to pay attention to specific learning styles or linguistic differences. An "English first" program really meant "English only," and children who grew up speaking another language were often disciplined for behavioral problems. English as the language of instruction tended to drive a wedge between English-speaking (and -reading and -writing) children and their native-language-speaking parents. Some educators seemed to relish the socializing function of the schools while caring not at all about those differences. In New York City schools, Jewish students were sometimes punished for disobedience—or for not speaking English—by having their mouths washed out with nonkosher soap.[47]

Ethnic groups tended to vary significantly in their responses to American education. Italian immigrants, for example, were likely to subordinate education to maximizing income for the family, largely because the family expected to go back to Italy. (Between 1900 and 1910, approximately 53 percent of Italian immigrants eventually returned to Italy. By the 1910s, this had increased to 63 percent—nearly two of three.)[48]

Jews, by contrast, leaped at the chance to get an education, in part because they had nowhere to "return to," and so they "used public schools to a greater extent than any other immigrant group."[49] To their eyes, families needed both school and *shul* as institutional supports to sustain their culture and to propel their children into successful American lives.

Jewish children tended to stay in school longer than other ethnic groups, and they saw education as a vehicle both for individual mobility and for collective assimilation. Attending school became a way for that first generation, especially, to toggle between the two worlds, old and new, traditional and modern, sacred and secular—a navigation of both insider and outsider that is common to many immigrant groups and yet, in turn-of-the century schools, was specific at that time to first-generation Jews.

In fact, *The Jewish Daily Forward* reported with pride: "To the list of Jewish holidays should be added another immigrant important holiday, graduation day." In fact, "to the proud Jew, reflecting somewhat partially on the splendid representation of Jewish children in the commonwealth rituals, it seems as if commencement day is an institution for the exhibition of Jewish love for knowledge."[50]

School reformers saw education as the key socializing agent enabling the children of immigrants to become successful Americans. In school they would learn English, lose their accents, become quiescent and disciplined workers, and shed their old-world trappings. The only way for them to move up in American society was to reject the world of their parents.*

Such assimilationist fantasies were ripe for ridicule, and the Marx Brothers tried their best. Their vaudeville sketch *Fun in Hi Skule* (1910), the prototype of what became known as "the school act," was wildly popular and would become the basis for their first feature film, *Horse Feathers* (1932). Transposed onto a college campus, *Horse Feathers* skewers the pretensions of faculty as a bunch of pompous fools without a lick of common sense among them.

In so doing, as the theater historian Rick DesRochers writes, the Marx Brothers "destabilized the authority of the classroom, aesthetic hierarchies, and loyalty to American nationalism through their version of the school act." The Marx Brothers pulled back the curtain on pompous blowhards and oh-so-earnest reformers, revealing their hubris and incompetence, beginning a trend that would dominate movies about schools and college life in the century to come. No wonder kids still love their movies![51]

The heirs to the school act were the "angels with dirty faces" featured as the Dead End Kids in various film series (fronted by Leo and David Gorcey, sons of Russian Jewish immigrants), and in the Our Gang comedy series, which featured the Little Rascals, children who were on their own, irreverent, defiant of authority, cheerful, and resourceful.

Work

If children were going to claim their right to be children, or at least to be freed up from other activities in order to go to school, they first had to stop working. Campaigns against child labor converged with

* Let me be clear, I am not criticizing this strategy, only describing what remains today one of the most resilient assumptions about the socializing function of our educational system.

policies to promote education to begin to move large numbers of children from the workplace to the schools.

It was a long struggle. In 1900, according to the U.S. Census, 186,358 children, or one out of every six between the ages of ten and fifteen, were gainfully employed. And that was likely an undercount, since it didn't include the routine work that children did on farms and in homes. The formal economy of gainful employment was supplemented by an informal economy. "On farms," writes the historian Steven Mintz, "children as young as five or six pulled weeds and chased birds and cattle away from crops. By the time they reached eight, many tended livestock, milked cows, churned butter, fed chickens, collected eggs, hauled water, scrubbed laundry, and harvested crops." In cities, children ran errands, scavenged, and took part in outwork, or forms of manufacturing that took place in the home. Some worked in factories and even in bars![52]

One might have thought that prohibiting, or at least controlling and curtailing, child labor would have been an easy lift. After all, public sentiment was strongly in favor of regulation. Unions, allied with women's organizations and consumer groups, all lobbied to end child labor. In 1881 the newly formed American Federation of Labor passed a resolution calling on states to prohibit all children under fourteen from participating in gainful employment.

In 1903 about ten thousand children walked out during a strike at a Kensington, Pennsylvania, mill. Mary Harris "Mother" Jones organized two hundred of them (she deliberately chose children who had been injured, "with their fingers off, and hands crushed and maimed") to march from Pennsylvania all the way to President Theodore Roosevelt's home in Oyster Bay, New York, to press their case. (He refused to meet with them, citing state purview over labor issues.)[53] The next year the National Child Labor Committee was formed to promote a national strategy to eliminate child labor.[54]

Many of the era's foremost Progressive reformers jumped in to support the effort. In 1914 the poet Edwin Markham, Judge Ben Lindsey (who was primarily responsible for developing the juvenile justice system), and the crusading journalist George Creel combined to document the injustice and miseries of child labor. Their *Children in Bondage* bemoaned that children were being "mangled, mind, body, and soul, and aborted into a maturity robbed of power and promise." To drive home their point, they compared child labor to slavery.[55]

But efforts to end child labor faced concerted opposition, not only from manufacturers and mine owners but also from parents, who argued that they needed the income from their children. That parental opposition was often well funded and carefully orchestrated, primarily by owners of textile mills in the South. David Clark, a wealthy mill owner and editor of the *Southern Textile Bulletin*, for example, organized a campaign that used testimony from farmers who worried that any child labor amendment would prohibit farm kids from doing their chores and deprive farmers of their children's wages. The Supreme Court struck down the law as unconstitutional, as it would do three years later with the 1919 Child Labor Tax Law.[56]

Failing to gain traction in the Congress or through the courts, in 1924 campaigners proposed a new constitutional amendment, the Child Labor Amendment, that would give Congress the power to regulate child labor. All the presidential candidates in the campaign of 1924—Democrat John Davis, Republican Calvin Coolidge, and Progressive Robert LaFollette—endorsed it, and yet the anti-amendment campaign managed to stall ratification in enough states to doom it.

It wasn't until 1938, when Franklin Roosevelt pushed through the Fair Labor Standards Act, that Congress established minimum ages for employment and regulated the number of hours that children could work. By the 1930s, the number of children who were gainfully employed (excluding farm chores) had already shrunk to fewer than thirty thousand.[57] Even among the working class, the child went from being "a component of the labor force to a subject of education."[58]

It turned out that wresting children from the factories to the classrooms required a change in the cultural view of children. Since parents often opposed curtailing child labor because they needed the money, the prevailing idea of children's value needed to move from economic to emotional. This required a shift in consciousness. As the sociologist Viviana Zelizer explains, children's "worth" rose as their "value" declined. Their economic contribution was in direct opposition to their emotional and moral worth to the family and to society. "The price of a useful wage-earning child was directly counterposed to the moral value of an economically useless but emotionally priceless child," she writes. Children "belong in a domesticated, unproductive world of lessons, games and token money." If parents truly loved their children, they would shield them from the marketplace, not force them into it. "True parental love could only exist if the child was defined exclusively as an object of sentiment and not as an agent of production."[59]

This new attitude toward children became visible in patterns of adoption. The historian Gary Cross observes that before 1900, families wanted to adopt older boys, who could be put to work on the farm right away or trained in the family business. That is, the adopted child was an economic investment. By the first decades of the twentieth century, prospective parents increasingly wanted to adopt newborns: Those adoptions rose from 20 percent of adoptees in 1930 to 48 percent by 1950 and to 68 percent in 1960. By the end of the 1970s, newborns accounted for 98 percent of all adoptions. A newborn was a familial investment, a desire on the part of the parents to fulfill their own emotional needs, accompanied by the belief that children were innocent and pliable.[60]

First-generation Yiddish Jews were immediately active in the campaigns against child labor, propelled in part by their labor militancy in the trade unions, particularly after the horror of the 1911 fire at the Triangle Shirtwaist Factory. In this large New York City factory, more than seven hundred girls and women, most of them Jewish, worked in the building's cold, dimly lit upper floors, breathing the "filthy air" and the "cloth dust" for twelve hours a day. When fire broke out on the eighth, ninth, and tenth floors, the panicked workers ran to the fire doors but found them locked. (Managers had feared the women would steal the clothing and sneak out through those doors.) Many leaped to their deaths. In all, 146 girls and women died.[61]

Jewish children protesting child labor with signs in Yiddish and English, 1909.

Felix Adler and the organization he founded and chaired, the National Child Labor Committee, became especially active. Gertrude Folks Zimand edited the NCLC's magazine *American Child* from its founding. She was not Jewish (her father was the celebrated social reformer Homer Folks), but she married into the faith when she wed Romanian immigrant Savel Zimand, a well-known journalist for *The New York Times* and the *New York Evening Post*, in addition to being an ardent social reformer and public health advocate.[62]

The campaign didn't really resonate with people until they could see child labor's dismal effects. That was where Lewis Hine came in. In 1908 Felix Adler hired the photographer on a temporary basis to document the lives of working children; he later became a permanent NCLC staff member. His more than five thousand images of dirty, overworked, underfed children shook the sensibilities of Americans, who were also captivated, indeed shocked, because the children looked so serious, so old before their time, and so sad. Their demeanor was not, per Ariès's analysis of Renaissance portraits, because their poses made them look serious. Many of the children

Left: Lewis Hine, "Seven-year-old Rosie. Regular oyster shucker. Her second year at it. Illiterate. Works all day. Shucks only a few pots a day." February 1913. *Right*: Lewis Hine, "Rosie with her doll." February 1913.

appeared stern and stoic, but even those who were smiling seemed strained, as if smiling were a heroic effort. The public was touched. Children should not be so sad so soon in life.

A pair of Hine's photographs from 1913 bracket the costs of child labor. In one photo, Rose Berdych of Bluffton, South Carolina, a coastal town near Hilton Head, grimaces as she shucks oysters for the Varn and Platt Canning Company. Her hands are rough and cut, her dress and apron soiled, her life obviously hard and unsparing. A second photo shows Rose playfully holding her doll, her face almost smiling, as if she was caught doing something untoward.

Play

Rose Berdych was, perhaps, the only child Hine photographed a second time. Three years later, when Rose was ten, he returned to Bluffton to find her well-dressed and no longer working at the canning company. (He didn't photograph her then.) She was in school (in part because her mother feared the law).[63] Perhaps she also had more time to play with her doll.

She would have received a lot of support from the cultural arbiters and critics who were concerned about child labor. For example, in the book *Children in Bondage*, after offering graphic descriptions of the shrimp-shucking factories of the Gulf Coast, the coal mines of Pennsylvania, the cotton mills across the South, and the glass factories of New England, the authors ask, "Is it not a cruel civilization that allows these little hearts and little shoulders to strain under these grown-up responsibilities?"[64]

If work made children into "little adults," then play would set them free. Play was no longer simply characterized by absence—the empty space between school, meals, and sleep. It was a positive time, a real space—a space of leisure, yes, but also a space where children could fantasize and create. Play replaced work, and the payoff was far greater than mere money. It was a place to grow. Playtime and work time were mutually exclusive. Indeed, as Maria Montessori put it, "Play is the work of the child."

Progressive reformers had to wrest the idea of play from the traditionalists, who adhered to the old proverb about idle hands being the devil's workshop. The reformers sought to recast children's play as essential to healthy development. Luther Gulick pioneered the formation of the Playground Association of America in 1906, then helped establish the Camp Fire Girls in 1912, two years after Ernest Thompson Seton (author of *The Biography of a Grizzly*) founded the Boy Scouts of America. The U.S. government created a Children's Bureau in 1912. Sidonie Gruenberg, director of the Child Study Association of America, provided a critique of the "arbitrary Puritanism" of American parents in her book *Your Child Today and Tomorrow* (1912) and claimed that playing with toys had many benefits for children.

The playground movement advanced Progressive ideas about children with a reformer's zeal about social control and the problem of immigration. Playgrounds were necessary for the healthy development of children, yes, but they were also a vehicle for social order, as they would keep children off the streets, where life was more dangerous and temptations abounded, and they would also ensure that parents—that is, grown-ups—were practicing informal neighborhood surveillance. Playgrounds created neighborhoods; they were essential means of social integration for different groups of people into the community. (This idea persisted throughout the century. During his years as New York City's chief urban planner, Robert Moses constructed more than 650 playgrounds there.)

The dramatic expansion of public libraries served a similar function of ministering to the needs of children and promoting social integration as a form of social control over the new arrivals. "The new view of childhood went along with the expansion of library services to children and growth of public education around the turn of the century," writes the historian Julia Mickenberg.[65]

G. Stanley Hall, who coined the term *adolescence*, wasn't Jewish, but many of the developmental psychologists who followed him were, mapping out the contours of healthy child development. Hall's theory of adolescence posited a break with childhood, a transference of a boy's identification from mother to father, and a confused, often troubled period of searching and exploration.

In 1897, a few years before Hall wrote his treatise on adolescence, he conducted a short empirical study of children's play with dolls. He engaged dozens of teachers throughout the country to generate data from their students about their engagement with dolls, cataloging the dimensions of what the children liked, what they did, and how they interacted with dolls. In analyzing data from about eight hundred children, he amassed all sorts of interesting findings. Some of them were curious but unimportant, like the fact that children preferred curly-haired dolls to straight-haired ones, but some of it revealed the life cycle of doll play. Girls, Hall found, played with dolls until age thirteen or fourteen, at which point "it is realized more distinctly than before that dolls have absolutely no inner life or feeling."[66]

It was "unfortunate," Hall thought, that playing with dolls was considered girl play. He found abundant evidence that "boys are naturally fond of and should play with dolls," but many boys "abandon it early or never play, partly because it is thought girlish." Hall also thought boys would prefer rougher and wilder activities and that one must always be on guard against turning these boys into "milliners"—that is, into wimps. But the effect of doll play was extremely positive and would "tend to make them more sympathetic with girls as children, if not more tender with their wives and with women later."

Hall's advocacy of doll play in 1897 was perfectly timed, as dolls and toys were just about to explode into American consciousness, when Americans would have more disposable income to spend on their children. Fueling this explosion were the many developmental psychologists charting the new course of American childhood.

Many of the twentieth century's most prominent developmental psychologists were first-generation Jews. Their theories grounded the individual person's search for identity within society, instead of opposed to it, just as "their" people searched for a collective identity within society and not opposed to it. Many embraced Jean Piaget's constructivist theory of cognitive development, a far more sanguine view of children's conceptual understanding. Piaget held that young children learn through experience, deciphering meaning and decoding themes by manipulating physical objects, like toys. Teachers in this framework are not disciplinarians but guides and mentors. One can easily see the symbiotic relationship with toymakers.

Before the twentieth century, children received few store-bought presents. Girls may have had homemade rag dolls, but most boys and girls also played with toys that were designed for group play, like marbles, kites, hoops, jump ropes, and balls. "Life for children was simple in the extreme [as] there were no array[s] of costly toys," wrote one nineteenth-century New England woman in her autobiography. Added another, "I had no toys, but a single doll."[67]

Toys became a material expression of the new idea of childhood. In an 1892 essay entitled "Children's Rights," Kate Douglas Wiggin, the author of *Rebecca of Sunnybrook Farm*, proclaimed a set of rights for children—"a right to a place of his own, to things of his own, to surroundings which have some relation to his size, his desires, and his capabilities."[68] Childhood was a realm apart, a safe space, so to speak, and toys were an essential part of that. Toys were the literal means by which the child gave voice to imagination.

> At this period the well-beloved toy, the dumb sharer of the child's joys and sorrows, becomes the nucleus of a thousand enterprises, each rendered more fascinating by its presence and sympathy. If the toy be a horse, they take imaginary journeys together, and the road is doubly delightful because never traveled alone. If it be a house, the child lives therein a different life for every day in the week; for no monarch alive is so all-powerful as he whose throne is the imagination. Little tin soldier, Shem, Ham, and Japhet from the Noah's Ark, the hornless cow, the tailless dog, and the elephant that won't stand up, these play their allotted parts in his innocent comedies, and meanwhile he grows steadily in sympathy and in comprehension of the ever-widening circle of human relationships.

Thus, Wiggin counseled parents to "choose his toys wisely and then leave him alone with them."[69]

Dolls, toys, children's books, playgrounds—all these signaled the explosion of this new idea about children onto the national stage. And what accompanied that idea was the institutional and organizational infrastructure to implement it and make it permanent.

Just as childhood became a separate space, child-rearing became a more exact "science." The increased efforts to tie family life to science propelled the child study movement. The National Congress of Mothers, a national network of mothers' clubs, was organized in 1897; in 1908 the organization voted to change its name to the Parent-Teacher Association. Baby Week was launched in Chicago and New York City in 1914, designed to apply scientific principles to more rational and "progressive" baby care and, not coincidentally, to create a more "national" template for baby and child development than the simple agglomeration of the various national and cultural practices of the new immigrant masses.

New educational reformers and developmental psychologists challenged prevailing orthodoxies and promoted the "century of the child." A new type of children's book appeared, shifting away from heavily didactic and moralistic stories to those purely for the amusement. The first Children's Book Week was held in 1919; the Newbery Medal was first awarded in 1922, the Caldecott Medal in 1937.

In 1928 Jesse and Percy Straus at Macy's organized an extensive "toy exposition" to display thousands of toys and to show parents the importance of playing with toys for a child's healthy development. The store invited experts like Sidonie Gruenberg (director of the Child Study Association of America) and George Hecht (founding editor of *Parents' Magazine*) to speak on the subject "why children should have toys." In that moment, with the Great Depression just over the horizon, child development experts partnered with the city's most prominent department store to promote toys. It was a match to make any yenta proud, and it set in motion efforts by toymakers to find innovative ways to convince parents to buy toys for their children.

Another speaker at the exposition was Joseph Jastrow, an eminent lecturer in psychology at the New School for Social Research and author of *Character and Temperament* (1915). Born in Poland in 1863, Jastrow emigrated to New York at age three with his parents; his father was a well-known Talmudic scholar. Among the founders of the American Psychological Association, Jastrow had been the organization's ninth president in 1900. In his presidential address, he raised the idea of giving children "graded" toys, suitable for building from success to success, since "failure is one of the most serious distractions for children."

Few reformers were more connected to these developments than Hecht and Gruenberg. Both were products of the Ethical Culture Society and were believers in Felix Adler's secular humanism. Perhaps it was their connection to Adler that brought them face-to-face with turn-of-the-century anti-Semitism. Gruenberg was born Sidonie Matsner in Austria in 1881 and came to New York as a teenager. After the birth of her first child in 1907, she joined the Federation of Child Study, a small group of Ethical Culture mothers that Adler had organized in 1888 under the auspicious name Society for the Study of Child Nature. (A total of five mothers were involved.) She'd found her calling.

As a young educator, Gruenberg sought to advance a notion of children's innate creativity and reserved her deepest animus for puritanical notions of children as willful, sinful, and wicked. Children, she argued, had a right to "imaginative play" and "individual expression," and should not suffer from "an arbitrary Puritanism which suggests every desire and impulse of being Satanic." In her view, it wasn't children who were wicked and Satanic; it was strict parents who were. Her book, *Your Child Today and Tomorrow* (1912), promoted "flexible, permissive care for children," anticipating Benjamin Spock's *The Common Sense Book of Baby and Child Care* (1946) by more than thirty years. It was among the most popular child-rearing works of the first half of the century.[70]

The Federation of Child Study expanded nationally, with study groups in nearly a dozen cities by 1923. Its success caught the eye of the Laura Spelman Rockefeller Memorial (LSRM), a foundation that had been organized to promote child welfare. But here the Jewishness of the entire field of child study became a cause for some anti-Semitic anxiety.

The LSRM wanted to issue a grant to the Federation of Child Study, but before releasing the funds, it instituted an undercover investigation into the federation's "Jewish leadership." So concerned were they that they insisted that the federation change its public image as a condition for receiving the funding. So the federation, hitherto associated with the Ethical Culture Society, became the stand-alone Child Study Association of America (CSAA). While Gruenberg would not step down as the CSAA's first director, the organization hired a non-Jewish field director outside New York City.[71]

Perhaps no one was more entrepreneurial about child development than George Hecht, for whom children were both a mission and a profession.

Born to relatively affluent German Jewish parents in 1895—his Victorian brownstone was built by his grandfather on the site where Radio City Music Hall stands today—Hecht attended the Ethical

Culture High School and then Cornell University. His mother was active in reform and welfare organizations. When the First World War broke out, he became head of the Bureau of Cartoons, where he encouraged cartoonists to harness their talents to support the war effort and produce patriotic cartoons. (A year after the war ended, he published a collection of the best ones in *The War in Cartoons*.)

After the war, Hecht jumped into the parenting and child-rearing world in a big way. Following the path set by Adler and Gruenberg, Hecht approached Lawrence Frank and Beardsley Ruml, program officers at the LSRM, and persuaded the foundation to support a commercial mass-circulation magazine devoted to popularizing the new science of child study.

The magazine, Hecht later wrote, was inspired by a chance encounter on a ship returning from Europe. He had been talking to a woman whose greatest disappointment was her children—for which she blamed herself. "'I have failed,' she said, 'where every woman wants to succeed—as a mother. As parents, both of us meant well, but we didn't know how to bring up our children.'" This led to the conclusion that "the most productive and the most long-lasting work would be work with children and work with parents in teaching them how to bring up their children."[72]

The LSRM board was uneasy. Hecht was a man on a mission, as much a cheerleader as a businessman, and he was hard to dissuade. "Promotion and advertising may have been his true loves," writes the historian Steven Schlossman, and this ran counter to the staid board. They were suspicious that it might simply be a money-grubbing scheme, so they imposed counterweights—Otis Caldwell, acting director of the Institute of Child Welfare Research, and James Earl Russell, president of Teachers College at Columbia University—as Hecht's partners. Russell, particularly, was concerned that Hecht might run off with the foundation's money and wanted guardrails against such financial exploitation.

What seems clear is that at the very moment of the emergence of serious child research, these serious educators feared that a loud, pushy, mercenary booster might sully their reputation. In his notes about one meeting, in fact, Lawrence Frank, the LSRM's program officer, wrote that Russell worried that Hecht's possibly "undesirable conduct" could reflect back badly on Teachers College.[73]

Maneuvering around these possibly anti-Semitic qualms, Hecht proposed that the LSRM give the money not to him but to the child study programs at four major universities: Yale, Iowa State, the University of Minnesota, and Teachers College. These four programs would then provide the academic advisory board for the magazine, as well as the academic legitimacy that they felt Hecht alone could not provide.

Once the compromises were grudgingly made and funding finally secured, the magazine, originally called *Children—A Magazine for Parents*, was launched in 1926 and soon changed its name to *Parents' Magazine*. It quickly became the most widely circulated parenting magazine in the world and was "the only commercial periodical whose circulation and advertising revenues climbed steadily upward" during the Great Depression. It's said that George Hecht "helped to raise 137,000,000 children during its half-century of publication."[74]

From that start, Hecht built a veritable childhood publishing empire, launching other magazines like *Children's Digest* (founded in 1950, with a monthly circulation of up to 600,000); *Humpty Dumpty* (for children 3 to 7), with a circulation of 1.1 million, making it the largest circulation of any magazine for children; *Young Miss* (for preteen girls, 9 to 14); and *Children's Playcraft* (with crafts activities for boys and girls 7 to 14), each of which had a circulation of 350,000.

Hecht's passion for child development was matched only by his entrepreneurial talents. He eventually bought out the shares of *Parents' Magazine* held by those four universities, and the magazine became a fully stand-alone (and wildly profitable) operation. In 1963 he engineered by *Parents' Magazine*'s purchase of FAO Schwarz toy stores, which he expanded to sixteen branches. He even sponsored a training course for Santa Claus impersonators at the stores.

* * *

By the time of America's entry into World War I, the new concept of childhood had become well established, both in cultural ideas about child development and in organizational structures to minister to them.

It was a group of first-generation Jews, almost all sons of immigrants, who created the material culture of the childhoods they never got to have and, in so doing, gave flight to the fantasies of American children. They made the toys, drew the comic strips, imagined the superheroes, played the music, and produced the movies that came to express American childhood.

Their parents may have suffered the privations of the pogroms of Russia, the miseries of the teeming tenements, the grinding poverty of the Lower East Side sidewalk peddlers and sweatshops, and the daily humiliations of marginality, but their children were born in America and grew up going to public schools, even college. The first generation escaped the tenements for working-class row houses in Brooklyn and the Bronx, creating not ghettoes but Jewish neighborhoods. They had staked a claim for their share of the American Dream.

PART II

The Material Culture of Childhood, 1920–1950

4

FURNISHING THE NEW IDEAL CHILDHOOD

* * *

In 1850, according to the U.S. Census, there were only forty-seven professional toymakers in the United States. Most of the toys they made available were sort of training wheels for adulthood—corn husk or hand-sewn dolls, wagons, peg-based solitaire, and mechanical banks. Virtually all were homemade. Victor Hugo made such a point in his 1887 novel, *Les Misérables*: "As birds make nests out of everything, so children make a doll out of anything which comes to hand."[1] Some experts and clergy disapproved of even these vocation-oriented toys. There were no mass-produced dolls.

Throughout the nineteenth century, most commercial toys and dolls (those not made locally) were imported from Germany. Wooden toys from Saxony, metal toys and tin soldiers from Nuremberg, and dolls from Sonneberg were so well made and so popular that at the end of the century, Germany controlled about 60 percent of the world's market for dolls and dollhouses. In 1910 alone Germany exported 40 million dolls; its metal factories produced 100,000 tin soldiers a day. Toys were so ubiquitous that they "helped Germans define themselves as good middle-class citizens in much the same way that cars do people in the United States."[2]

So refined and productive was the German toy industry that some critics said the toys were leaving too little to the child's imagination in the context of middle-class competition. One critic had it:

> The colorful, inartistic trash [and] the insubstantial, unsolid doodads that lend their signatures to the show windows of our department stores at Christmastime are not merely entirely valueless for the development of the child; they are often well-nigh damaging. They destroy the healthy sense for the useful and solid, transmit to the child totally false ideas of the form and quality of things.

And another argued that "The automaton with clockwork in its belly, the dollhouse with all its furniture copied in painful detail, the toy train that runs figure eights on its tracks . . . they suck the blood out of the minds of children." Still another extolled the virtues of the more authentic "primitive" doll: "As a mother loves a sick child more deeply, so may the child be more fond of a primitive doll. Her fantasy is excited most powerfully."[3]

Most commentators noted that this industry's promotion of the domestication of play was politically purposive. Children who played with such well-designed and well-made toys would construct more sensible fantasies and so would become more productive citizens.[4]

Some of the German toymakers found American distributors, especially among German immigrants. George Borgfeldt, Henry Schnibbe, and Hamburger & Sons all imported toys and train sets; Strobel & Wilken, Louis Wolf, and Louis Amberg (not to be confused with the notorious Jewish gangster who was part of Meyer Lansky's Murder Incorporated) all imported German-made dolls.[5]

And some German immigrants founded their own companies. The A. Schoenhut Company, established in 1872 in Philadelphia, began producing toy boats, guns, and swords early. Louis Amberg had begun as an importer but later manufactured dolls, using imported bisque for the heads. (Bisque, or biscuit porcelain, had a more realistic matte finish than that of the shinier "china" porcelain.) A few years later the Philadelphia Tin Toy Manufactory began producing tin pistols, and Charles Crandall made lithographed blocks until he earned enough money to turn to toys and games. His ball-in-a-maze puzzle, a "dexterity game," was called Pigs in Clover and was enough of a hit that several U.S. senators were caught playing competitively in a Capitol cloakroom instead of sitting in legislative session.[6]

At the turn of the century, the toy world took off. "In former years, Germany and France had almost a monopoly of the toy making business," observed *Playthings* magazine in 1903, "but to-day the United States is their formidable rival."[7] The new idea of childhood unleashed, or created, a new demand for toys and dolls—and for anything else that could reasonably be marketed for children. New materials made mass production easier, and toys were more durable. The new science of advertising, and new media like radio, could put ads for products in every middle-class home. The seeds were sown for the transformation from marketing products *for* children into marketing products *to* children. During the Great War, the embargo on German-made goods greatly spurred the massive expansion of the American toy industry.

That first generation of Jewish toymakers—Morris Michtom, Louis Marx, Joshua Lionel Cohen, and many others—might not have had the invention of childhood on their minds when they started their toy companies, but they knew they wanted to break into what had been, until recently, a small, relatively genteel, and almost entirely Protestant cottage industry. They saw opportunities, given the new attitudes about child-rearing that arose after 1900.

The Lives of Children

The dramatic expansion of the toy industry perfectly coincided with massive social changes at the turn of the century, and nowhere were those changes greater than in gender relations among adults. This transformation couldn't help but ripple downward to the world of boys and girls. The separation of spheres that had been asserted so vigorously in the antebellum era began to break down, and adherents frantically sought to build it back up. In fact, the separation of spheres had been a historical novelty, as women and men often worked side by side in workshops and on farms.*

As we've seen, the separation of work and home, the perceived "feminization" of American life (and the attendant fears of the emasculation of American manhood), combined to create an anxious and restive nation, as Americans were alternately, or perhaps even simultaneously, thrilled by new opportunities and frightened by the blurring of traditional boundaries.

If the genders were becoming more similar—that is, if the things that women and men did were becoming increasingly similar—then the ideology of separation had to be more vigorously enforced. And what better way to ameliorate this crisis than by training boys and girls separately from the get-go? Part of the new separation of spheres, the children's version, was the separation of boys and girls—at school, at home, and at play.

Take school first. The turn of the century witnessed a fierce battle over coeducation. Before the mid-nineteenth century, boys and girls were educated separately—which is to say that boys were educated in schools, often through high school, while girls, when their education continued beyond learning to read and write, were educated separately, often at home in conjunction with learning domestic tasks. But the push for mass compulsory education meant that boys and girls would end up in the same classrooms.

Many Victorian opponents of girls' education, especially of

* There were more female store owners and businesspeople in the 1780s, the historian Gerda Lerner found, than in the 1830s, which meant that the ideology of separate spheres pushed women out of the workforce, much as they were pushed out of the workplace following the Second World War. "Women were," as Lerner put it, "excluded from the new democracy." Gerda Lerner, "The Lady and the Mill Girl: Changes in the Status of Women in the Age of Jackson," *American Studies Journal* 10, no. 1 (Spring 1969): 7, 9.

women's higher education, believed that women could not withstand, and would not wish to subject themselves to, the rigors that education demanded. Opponents of coeducation also believed that bringing boys and girls together would have disastrous effects on both sexes—feminizing the boys and masculinizing the girls. (The former was far more worrisome.)

The opponents invoked biology first. Since the "minds of men and women are radically different," as one editorialist wrote in the UC Berkeley *Daily Californian* in the 1890s, they must be taught separately. And when appeals to biology didn't work, the opponents tried homophobia, suggesting that coeducation would lead to gender inversion. So when the University of Michigan first debated coeducation, its president opposed it because "men will lose as women advance, we shall have a community of defeminated women and demasculated men." A local paper applauded the trustees' decision, arguing that to educate women would "unwoman the woman and unman the man."[8]

Some worried that educating women and men together would "emasculate" the curriculum, watering it down by forcing the inclusion of subjects and temperaments better omitted, slowing down the pace, or otherwise reducing standards to allow women to keep up. In his influential treatise on adolescence, G. Stanley Hall warned against coeducation because it "harms girls by assimilating them to boys' ways and work and robbing them of their sense of feminine character," while it harms boys "by feminizing them when they need to be working off their brute animal element." By making boys and girls more alike, he warned, coeducation would "dilute" the mysterious attraction of the opposite sex—that is, it could result in homosexuality for both boys and girls.

School buildings were built with separate entrances for boys and girls—though one entrance was often labeled for "boys" and the other for "girls and infants," in case girls weren't already insulted enough by the separation. Just passing through the same doorways might cause one sex to contaminate the other.

At home, boys and girls were differentiated at earlier and earlier ages. Prior to the 1880s, little boys and little girls of the middle classes would have been dressed similarly. Both wore outfits similar to white christening gowns during infancy, then short, loose-fitting dresses in early childhood. This was equally true on the nation's farms until ages four or five, when the boys would switch to breeches and suspenders and the girls would remain in dresses. But all that changed in the late 1880s as parents began to dress their toddlers in more "gender-appropriate" clothing: knickerbockers and trousers made their first appearance for little boys.[9]

Not until the first decade of the twentieth century did clothing generally become gendered. The first question was which color would be appropriate for girls and which for boys. In a 1918 editorial entitled "Pink or Blue," a magazine called *The Infants' Department* explained:

> There has been a great deal of diversity of opinion on the subject, but the generally accepted rule is pink for the boy and blue for the girl. The reason is that pink being a more decided and stronger color is more suitable for the boy; while blue, which is more delicate and dainty, is prettier for the girl.[10]

That's right: Boys wore red or pink because those colors were considered more manly, suggesting determination and strength. Blue, particularly light blue or sky blue, was deemed more ethereal, flightier, and thus more appropriate for girls. It's not clear when the colors were reversed, but parents continued to debate the question through the 1920s and '30s. Indeed, in 1939 an article in *Parents' Magazine*, entitled "What Color for Your Baby?" still held that "red symbolizes zeal and courage, while blue is symbolic of faith and constancy."

By the first decades of the new century, boy and girls were not only wearing different clothes but also playing with different toys. It was through toys that the separation of the sexes could be most firmly established and made to appear most natural. If children played with different toys, they must be different, right? Toys, then, both differentiated the sexes and legitimated that differentiation at the same time, normalizing it as the natural and inevitable outcome of different maturation. The world of girl-toys and boy-toys opened a new era in toy making and thus in the development of the twentieth-century child.

Dolls

The manufactured dolls of this period were nothing like what we have today. They were made of porcelain, mostly with a bisque finish. Their elaborate outfits were sewn onto their fabric bodies. Usually they were placed on pedestals or in glass cases, kept on high shelves and bookcases, out of the reach of children. Virtually all were of little girls with curly hair, rosy cheeks, and perpetually open eyes, staring vacantly from a breakfront shelf. They were not to be "toyed" with.

Of course, other homemade dolls were made of rags, carved wood, or corn husks—pretty much anything that was at hand. "Life for children was simple in the extreme [as] there were no array[s] of costly toys," wrote one New England woman in her autobiography. She and her sister "had the regulation rag doll with long curls and club feet, very ugly but dear to our hearts." Another wrote that she had "no toys, except a few homemade articles of our own. I had but a single doll, a wooden jointed thing, with red cheeks and staring black eyes."[11]

But mass production made dolls and toys cheaper and brought them within reach of most everybody, and new materials made the dolls less precious and fragile. Everyone could have them and, what's more, *should* have them. The new doll makers saw an opportunity to drive a wedge between these fragile figurines and the rough-hewn homemade versions.

At the end of the nineteenth century, a new material changed everything. So-called "composition" dolls were made from a combination of sawdust and glue, with additives like resin, cornstarch, and wood flour (finely pulverized wood), developed through the 1890s by Solomon D. Hoffman. New toy companies began to produce composition dolls almost immediately. E. I. Horsman, for example, started out in the late 1860s as a doll importer, but by 1904 he'd created

Stella, a rag doll, and by 1909, he'd switched to making and distributing composition dolls. His game Nobat baseball appeared in 1903, in which players toss a ball into a target several yards away, similar to Cornhole.[12]

The toy and doll business was in perpetual dialogue with new materials and technologies that enabled exciting possibilities. The ability to manufacture an unbreakable doll transformed the industry from those precious figurines that sat on shelves to small people whom children did not have to just stare at and admire but whom they could hold, feed, and play with.

No sooner did one company invent a new material, or find a new character for a doll, than another technique would emerge, and another company would create another character. The pressure to innovate followed the classic formula: The manufacturer with a competitive advantage reaped large profits; other firms caught up and innovated and took the lead; the first manufacturer had to either reduce its prices or come up with a new product. The competition was constant, relentless, and not at all for the faint of heart.

Trains, Cranes, and Automobiles

A few entrepreneurs seemed to specialize in toys for boys. Not all the boy-toy pioneers were first-generation Jews. A. C. Gilbert, for one, was a magician, and his business of making the materials for magic shows supplied his profession. He and his partner operated the Mysto Manufacturing Company of New Haven, Connecticut. In 1910, while riding on the New York, New Haven, & Hartford Railroad, he was mesmerized by the girders that the rail company was installing to electrify the railroad. He and his wife made a few cardboard cutouts of the girders and realized they could construct models of the cranes and girders if they manufactured the parts and added some plain screws and bolts. They launched the Erector Set in 1913. "Hey boys!!" was the opening line of the first instruction booklet. "I know what boys like," Gilbert said. (He continued to know what boys liked: the Mysto Manufacturing Company became the A.C. Gilbert Company, and it turned out hit toys for older boys like chemistry sets. In the late 1930s it acquired American Flyer sleds and launched Gilbert HO electric trains.)[13]

Trains also figure in the story of Charles Hamilton Pajeau and the creation of Tinker Toys. A stonecutter who worked for a tombstone company, Pajeau one day in 1914 saw a child playing with an empty spool of thread and a pencil and thought that a toy based on a series of spools and sticks might be fun. He built some prototypes and had the clever idea of selling the component parts in a can rather than a box. Few buyers were interested until he traveled to New York and set up a window display at Grand Central Station. A buyer for Macy's saw the Tinker Toy windmill, powered by an electric fan, and created its own window display of the toys in Macy's flagship store. Tinker Toys was launched.[14]

No toy effort was more successful, though, than bringing those mesmerizing trains themselves into people's homes. That was the work of Joshua Lionel Cohen.

Cohen's grandparents came from Suvalk, a small village near the border of Poland and Lithuania. After Russian soldiers pillaged it, Hyman Cohen and Rebecca Kantrowitz married and moved to London, where they started a cap business. Their first children were born there; one of them, Rachel, became the maternal grandmother of the infamous attorney Roy Cohn.[15]

By the late 1860s, the family had moved to New York, where Joshua Lionel Cohen was born in 1877 in a brownstone on Henry Street, on the Lower East Side. A precocious boy, Joshua was fascinated by engineering and science. In high school at the Peter Cooper Institute, he experimented with storing electrical energy in batteries. He claimed to have invented the world's first electric doorbell there, but he was discouraged from pursuing it, he later said, by his teacher, who said nothing would ever replace the doorknocker. Later, he maintained that he'd invented the electric fan, the flashlight, and the dry cell battery.

While the provenance of those inventions may be debated, it is indisputable that Cohen created the first popular electric toy train. Its brand name derived from his middle name—chosen, again, because it sounded less Jewish. In 1910 he changed his last name from Cohen to Cowen in order to Americanize it. By then, he had already founded the company that would make him famous, Lionel Trains. His first train wasn't intended as a toy at all: It was commissioned by the Ingersoll Company as a sale come-on in the large display window of their Manhattan store. But Lionel trains soon became the industry standard and the best-selling electric trains in the world.[16] The great child development expert Benjamin Spock even noted that toy trains were "a particularly exciting symbol of masculinity because they represent enormous power that is nevertheless under complete control, from a distance, as if by magic."[17]

For more than a century, these model trains have captivated the imaginations of American boys—and their fathers! Promoted as a bonding opportunity for fathers and sons, model freight trains, winding their way through imaginary prairies and a newly tamed West, enabled these urban, and later suburban, children to imagine the world beyond, to fantasize escape, wilderness, adventure far beyond their playrooms. The clattering sounds on the tracks, the fake smoke puffing from the engine, provided a way for them to experience that glorious freedom of the open road (before cars took over), the virilizing power of the train—Superman's power would be even "more powerful than a locomotive"—all from the safely confined space of home.

More than that, model passenger trains may have offered an additional pleasure: on board a passenger train, at least in the North, everyone could ride, find a seat, and even rub elbows with their "equal" neighbors. Here was a space of successful assimilation, of acceptance at last, if only in fantasy.

Lionel trains may have been the gold standard, but they were ripe for cheaper knockoffs. That was how Louis Marx made his fortune. Not long after Ideal's launch in 1907 and not far from Morris and Rose Michtom's candy store in Brooklyn, Louis Marx began to make a name for himself in the toy business. Born in Brooklyn in 1896 to Austrian Jewish parents, he quit high school at fifteen to go to work for Ferdinand Strauss, a mechanical toy manufacturer who was himself a German immigrant. His first creations were little racist metal acrobats, like Zippo the Climbing Monkey and the Alabama Minstrel Dancer. Louis and his brother eventually bought Strauss out and created a simple business model: Copy other manufacturers' products, mass-produce them more cheaply, and undersell their competitors. "Give the customer more toy for less money" was his motto. For example, after Donald F. Duncan introduced the yo-yo in 1928, Marx immediately marketed a cheaper version. Marx electric trains were a cheaper version of Lionel's. It was a brilliant strategy, earning Marx a reputation as a "toycoon," the "Henry Ford of the toy industry."

By the 1950s, Louis Marx would grow the business into the world's largest toy company. In a 1955 profile, *Time* magazine described the "toy king" or the "little king" as a "roly-poly, melon-bald little man with the berry bright eyes and beneficent smile of St. Nick touching down on a familiar rooftop." But this "little" man understood something big about capitalist competition: One way to win was to sell cheaper than everyone else, and to sell a lot.[18]

Even as they became wealthy enough to stand out, these early Jewish entrepreneurs sought to fit into their newly adopted country. They shed their original names, Americanized their identities, and in a further assimilationist impulse, cemented their American-ness with their children. In their efforts to fit into their new adoptive country, Morris and Rose Michtom reached back a bit further. Benjamin Franklin Michtom was born in the back room of the Tompkins Avenue candy store in Brooklyn in 1901, just a couple of years before his very famous older brother, the teddy bear. Not to be outdone, Morris's brother Harris named his oldest son Daniel Webster Michtom. It's fascinating that both brothers named their children after famous Americans, as if to cement their ties to their adopted country.

Ideal Novelty and Toy

Soon after both the teddy bear and their son were born, Morris and Rose outgrew their storefront. The family moved to a ramshackle loft in the Brownsville section of Brooklyn, where they lived upstairs and produced the bears downstairs. In 1907 Morris entered into a partnership with another Russian Jewish immigrant, Aaron Cone. They established the Ideal Novelty Company, later renamed the Ideal Novelty and Toy Company, and finally the Ideal Toy Company.

From the beginning, Ideal was family-owned, and company shares were distributed only to the family and friends who were part of Morris's inner circle. Morris was loyal to his family—that is, until he wasn't. Harris, my great-grandfather, never worked for the company; nor was he invited to join the inner circle and become an executive. When my grandfather, Lew Michtom, returned from the war (he'd fought in the Battle of the Somme in 1918), he was hired to work at the factory briefly, but Morris made it clear that he had no plans to bring him in. But Harris's son Daniel Webster Michtom worked at Ideal for most of his life, starting at the lowest level and rising eventually to become the head of production.

Still, Dan's dream of being brought into the inner circle of owners and executives was never fulfilled, even though he was part of the family. He eventually left Ideal to start his own company. The Dandee Doll Company created some impressive dolls, but it lacked the financing and marketing experience necessary to make a dent in the already well-developed toy industry. Eventually, humiliated, he returned to Ideal, at a far lower position, which remained a source of resentment for the rest of his life. In fact, Dan's son, Jay, has only the bitterest of memories of his father's stories: The family felt insular yet didn't include him. Nor were Harris's children part of the inner circle, although one could marry into the family.

Morris did better by his own family, and he also became a benefactor to all the local Jewish boys in the neighborhood. The old anarchist leftist was now an employer, determined to do right by his workers. Well, apparently, not *that* right. Initially, Morris hired local boys to work as tailors and produce teddy bears at his loft factory. No sooner did he start to succeed than the workers decided to organize a union. That decision would sorely test Morris's commitment to the labor movement—a test he surely and spectacularly failed.

According to the independent historian Peter Jensen Brown,

Morris's first small manufacturing firm had just started operations in 1907 when his workers went on strike.[19] Why? The stuffers and cutters wanted to join a union with other workers in the country's growing toy industry. Morris wasn't happy about it, not at all. He fired the young woman who was organizing the union—he said it was because she wasn't a very good worker, a claim that seems to have been backed up by others. He hired some strikebreakers. Fights broke out, *The Brooklyn Eagle* reported. One hundred and twenty men and women walked out of the factory.[20]

Two weeks later Morris capitulated, and in late November his workers joined the Teddy Bearmakers Union. According to *The Wichita Beacon*, the union prevailed because of the requirement that the teddy bears have that inscrutable, half-human smile, which apparently took considerable skill to create. "According to the union, it requires workmen of an artistic temperament to make Teddy Bears with the half-human expression on their faces that they are supposed to wear, and the strike breakers missed the expression."[21]

The strike shook Morris and may have led him, embittered, to branch out. While the factory continued to make the bears, and the contract with the Teddy Bearmakers Union remained in force, he decided to create other kinds of dolls. Eight years later he told a

Teddy Bear stuffer, circa 1912.

reporter that he had been in the "unbreakable doll business" for "the past eight years." He made no mention of teddy bears.[22]

Whether it was teddy bears or dolls, Morris Michtom was determined to make toys for children, not for adults. If parents fretted that their children would break the precious shelf-bound dolls, then he would create unbreakable dolls. It was a radical idea, and most other toymakers thought it terrible. From their perspective, a broken doll meant another sale. But Morris was convinced that a sturdier doll would create a much bigger and better market. He was right. He seized on the composition construction and never looked back.

Then came the next question: How to dress the dolls? Instead of sewing the outfit onto the doll's body, Morris believed that if the child could change the outfit, he or she would enjoy the doll far more—and that removable outfits would create an after-sale market for doll accessories. This proved among his most revolutionary ideas.

Finally, what sex should the doll be? Hitherto dolls had virtually always been little girls or babies of indeterminate sex (though most girls played with them as baby girls). But Morris had a novel idea. He was a fan of Richard Outcault's comic strip *The Yellow Kid*, which ran in Hearst newspapers starting in 1896. (Outcault was also the creator of *Buster Brown*.) The lead character, a buck-toothed, bald-headed, baby-faced denizen of Hogan's Alley, embodied "the spirit of the streets, an energetic, crude, beady-eyed, carnivalesque symbol of a raw and wild urban America." He was mischievous, with an ingratiating style that would later be incarnated in the Bowery Boys, those "angels with dirty faces," and the Little Rascals, and even later in middle-class Bart Simpson. (Baldness wasn't entirely unknown at the time, as many poor children had their heads shaved to prevent lice.)[23]

Mickey Dugan was the street urchin's official name, and the bright yellow coat that bore his written-out dialogue transported him from Hogan's Alley onto the stage as a cultural icon. Dugan, a streetwise smart aleck, embodied the "spirit of the streets, an energetic, crude, beady-eyed carnivalesque symbol of raw and wild urban America," writes the historian Jeremy Dauber. Soon branded the Yellow Kid,

Left: The Yellow Kid by Richard Felton Outcault.
Right: Original Yellow Kid doll. (Photo courtesy of hakes.com).

his oversize yellow nightshirt became a talisman, especially as the coat coincided, in 1896, with the first widespread use of color by Joseph Pulitzer's *New York World*.

Color had been introduced into newspapers a few months earlier by the *Chicago Inter Ocean*, but Pulitzer made it de rigueur for the tabloid press. It caught on immediately, and the Yellow Kid soon lent his moniker to the brand of journalism practiced by William Randolph Hearst. Hearst, Pulitzer's rival, lured Outcault away from the *World*, and so for a time both papers published the comic. The strip was technically owned by the newspaper, not by the artist, so the *World* published it as *Hogan's Alley* and Hearst's *New York Journal* published it as *The Yellow Kid*. The rivalry became so heated, so war-mongeringly scandal-ridden, that critics called it "Yellow Kid journalism," almost immediately shortened to "yellow journalism."

As a comic strip character, the Yellow Kid was followed by millions of Americans, most of them boys. And so Morris's first doll was a durable, unbreakable Yellow Kid. Yup, a boy doll. Well, maybe not a boy doll, exactly. Think of the Yellow Kid as the country's first action figure.

The Yellow Kid doll was an instant hit with adults and children, boys and girls. It was a boon to merchandising—pretty soon there were Yellow Kid playing cards, pins, ice cream, bottle openers, and cigarettes.

Morris believed the toy industry's future—or at least the future of his own fledgling company—lay in dolls, including generic baby dolls. But he also set out to produce more dolls like the Yellow Kid, replicas of well-known characters from movies and comics. He could count on such dolls playing off the popularity of celebrities.

In 1912 the couple's nephew, Abe Katz, joined Morris "to help out." His mission was to make dolls that were as realistic as possible. This meant that he constantly moved between material engineering and marketing. Katz became the creative force that drove the new lines of dolls.

The success of the Yellow Kid led to other tie-ins. Ideal tried a Naughty Marietta (from the Victor Herbert operetta of the same name) and Admiral Dot. In fact, following the Yellow Kid, its major successes were dolls that were based on male characters—hardly the cuddly babies that we might imagine today as beginning the twentieth-century doll era. The company produced doll babies as well, geared to the little girl market. But the dolls of male characters were embraced by both boy and girls.

Their tie-ins to products or patriotism brought adults, not their children alone, into the consumer market. For example, the Uneeda Kid, released in 1914, was a generic doll dressed in the costume of the emblem of Uneeda brand of the National Biscuit Company. Despite his rouged cheeks and red-glossed lips, the Uneeda Kid was a boy who stood, as did the product's mascot, for safety in unsettled and stormy weather.

The tie-in dolls also tracked historical developments, seeking to both capture the moment and to advance it. As America lurched toward World War I, Ideal launched Liberty Boy, a doughboy in uniform. Liberty Boy, the first patriotic doll, appealed as much to adults as to children. For any given product, there was probably a tie-in doll licensed to one of the big toy companies. Aunt Jemima, Buster

Brown and his dog Tige—all had jingles and dolls tied in to products that could be consumed by a wholesome healthy family: shoes, foods, and clothing, but not cigarettes and alcohol.

By the eve of America's entry into the First World War, Morris was predicting a bonanza for the American toy market, especially as embargoes on German goods would dull the competition from the higher-priced but better-quality German toys. "This war is giving us the chance we need," Morris told *The Brooklyn Eagle* in 1915, "not so much in cutting off the supply of German dolls, for there is still an ample supply in the country, with more coming that were held up at the beginning of the war, but in making the doll buyers realize that before the end of the war their foreign supply will be gone, and that they had better discount that event by taking advantage of the domestic supply.

"Our dolls are better than the foreign ones, anyway," he continued, ever the booster for domestic products. "You can't break these doll heads with anything short of a sledge hammer. . . . And you know how fragile the German and Austrian bisque dolls are. You can't give one to a baby."[24]

Postwar Doll Competition

World War I provided a fortuitous opportunity for the American toy industry, especially the doll industry. The boycotts of German products and the official embargoes on many German goods cleared the playing field of the competition, and in rushed domestic manufacturers.

Of course, as those manufacturers entered the market, their workers sensed their increased power. To establish himself in the doll-making business, Morris had to first get past the unions.

In June 1916, according to *The Brooklyn Eagle*, two hundred employees walked out of the factory in Brownsville, demanding recognition of their newly formed Stuffed Toy and Doll Makers Union. Morris Michtom said "he would close up the shop rather than concede" to the union's demands.[25] The next day it launched a general strike. As *The New York Times* reported:

> With the season for making Christmas dolls approaching and with few dolls coming from Europe to stock Santa Claus's pack, the 1,800 members of the Stuffed Toy and Doll Makers' Union went on strike yesterday. The workers, more than half of whom are women, quit work at 10 o'clock yesterday morning and went to Astoria Hall . . . and spent the afternoon dancing. They demand shorter hours, longer luncheon time, and more pay, as well as recognition of the union.[26]

At a standoff, the two sides, unwilling to yield yet uninterested in simply walking away, called in Paul Abelson, the foremost labor arbitrator in New York. A Jewish childhood immigrant from Kovno, Lithuania, Abelson had honed his skills in the fur, millinery, men's hat, Jewish baking, and jewelry trades. The two sides eventually came to a resolution. The union was established, and Morris shifted his political attention to Jewish causes, never again supporting or engaging with labor.

Ideal was hardly alone in facing labor trouble, as both immigration and the expansion of industry fueled a dramatic increase in the power of organized labor. The doll industry, too, was expanding. Indeed, it was getting pretty crowded, which only further increased labor's negotiating power, as doll assembly was a highly skilled occupation.

Ideal was the industry leader in developing—and transcending—the gendering of dolls. Whether the dolls were commercial tie-in "action figures" or imaginary newborn babies, the company was committed to introducing them at a feverish pace. And it paid off. "By 1925," noted *Fortune* magazine, "dolls made in America had collectively established themselves."

Naturally, this success attracted others to the fertile commercial venture. In 1910 two young enterprising first-generation Jewish businessmen, Bernard Fleischaker and Hugo Baum, began to sell dolls along the Atlantic City boardwalk. Within a couple of years, they commissioned others to make doll heads especially for them, and by 1920, they were making all the composition parts. The company name, Fleischaker & Baum, was a bit cumbersome, so they adopted a trademark using the initials their last names, which in 1915 morphed into the new name Effanbee.

Effanbee snagged the rights to manufacture a few dolls based on popular comic strips. Little Orphan Annie, launched in 1924, was immensely popular. The company's most famous doll was Patsy, launched in 1926. Designed by Bernard Lipfert, a German immigrant, she was rather plain, not at all glamorous. She stood thirteen and a half inches tall, and her head was made of composition, with painted eyes and a closed mouth. She was marketed as the first "doll that looked like a real girl," a "loveable imp," and she came with a wardrobe of changeable dresses and accessories. Patsy was a game changer for the company: It relied for its profit margins more on wardrobe sales for the doll and her "family" than on the dolls themselves. Outfits were far easier to create and market than doll identities. One little girl in Arkansas, Helen Gurley, loved her Patsy, but since her family couldn't afford the wardrobe, her mother made replicas of her outfits, which little Helen carried in an old suitcase.[27] (Helen Gurley would grow up to have quite an impact on young women as Helen Gurley Brown, the editor of *Cosmopolitan*.)

Another cleverly named company, the Arranbee (R&B) Doll Company, was founded just after the war in the back room of a candy store on the Lower East Side. William Rothstein was born in Poland, around 1900, and emigrated to New York at age three. His younger brother, Morris, followed two years later. They named the company Rothstein and Brother (R&B), which immediately became Arranbee. After 1919, when the World War I embargo was lifted, Arranbee imported doll parts from Germany, and the company assembled the dolls in its factory. The company prospered, in part because of the dynamic salesman Joe Ardbaum, but after Mike Emerson (originally Epstein) married one of Rothstein's daughters and took over the company, it floundered.[28]

Bernard Lipfert was a legend among doll designers—the designs for the era's most famous dolls were produced in his Brooklyn basement. His designs were incredibly lifelike for the time; indeed, William

Rothstein's son-in-law compared Lipfert to the Della Robbia sculptors of Renaissance Florence, whose cherubic babies set an artistic standard for centuries. He created the composition models for the Shirley Temple doll, Toni, and for many others.

Equally legendary was Bertha Alexander Behrman. She was born in 1895 on the Lower East Side to an Austrian Jewish mother and a Russian-born father, who died when she was a toddler. Her mother's new husband, Moritz Alexander, was a pushcart peddler selling toys who sidelined as a "doll doctor" working in a "doll hospital." It was a common sideline, since the dolls, you'll remember, tended to be expensive porcelain imports from Germany.

Bertha thought dolls should be played with, not admired from afar, and World War I offered her a chance to transform her thought into reality. The embargo on German goods nearly put doll hospitals out of business, as there were fewer dolls to break and therefore fewer in need of repair. In an effort to save the doll hospitals from going out of business, Bertha and her sisters sewed a series of Red Cross nurse dolls, inspired by the war effort, and sold them through the doll hospitals. In today's language, the nurse dolls went viral.

In 1923, at twenty-eight, Bertha founded, the Alexander Doll Company, where she reimagined dolls and also rebranded herself. As company president, she was now known as Madame Beatrice Alexander Behrman. It was not only an assimilationist shedding of her Jewish identity; adding the aristocratic-sounding Madame implied a certain stateliness and elegance to both herself and her dolls. By the 1930s, the Alexander Doll Company was the nation's third-largest-grossing doll company and was competing successfully with Ideal and others.[29]

Alexander was an advocate for a child-centered childhood in which play was central. "Dolls should contribute to a child's understanding of people, other times and other places," she would write. Dolls were not just for girls, she believed—boys should play with them too. "After all, the paternal instinct in men is as important as the maternal instinct in women," she said.[30] In a male-dominated business, Alexander was the queen of dolls.

The Pressman Toy Company made dolls too, but it was far more polyglot, also producing games and mechanical toys. A first-generation Jew, Jack Pressman grew up working in his immigrant father's variety store, selling school supplies, sporting goods, and toys, which sparked his interest in them. In 1925, with his partner Max Elbitz, he opened the company headquarters in Brooklyn, where the Pressman Toy Company produced novelties and toys, often based on movies. In 1937 it made an Orphan Annie–branded bubble pipe, a small pipe that was fitted with a bowl of soapy water that created bubbles when you blew gently into it. The next year, after the success of *Snow White and the Seven Dwarves*, it made dolls of all seven dwarves, licensed from the Walt Disney Studios. That successful licensing partnership would lead, in 1955, to Pressman's early sponsorship and licensing arrangements with the Disney company for *The Mickey Mouse Club*.

Pressman was known as "the Marble King" because of his ability to market children's marbles even during World War I. On a trip to Colorado, he saw a game marketed as Hop Ching Checkers. In 1928 he bought the rights and rebranded it as Chinese Checkers, though the game had no connection to China at all. Chinese Checkers was the first hit toy for Pressman, which went on to create home-based bingo, cap pistols, police uniforms, and later the G-Man Detective Set as a tie-in with Dick Tracy. Often its games were junior-size versions of adult games like Lotto; Tricky Sticks was a knockoff of the popular game pickup sticks.[31]

When it came to games as toys, though, Transogram gave Pressman a run for his money. In 1915 Charles Raizen, son of poor Jewish immigrants, developed a method of using friction to transfer images to paper—and children really enjoyed it. Raizen developed the Toy Research Institute at 200 Fifth Avenue and hired a child psychologist to run focus groups with the kids to help develop new toys. The groups were a revolutionary innovation—Transogram toys came with the tagline "Kid Tested." In 1934 Transogram launched the Little Country Doctor and Little Country Nurse kits, which began craze for doctor and nurse kits. But the company's bestseller was

Tiddledy Winks, a small set of plastic chips on a felt mat that players flip toward a cup in the mat's center. (It's currently marketed as Tiddlywinks.) The game was a sensation and made a fortune. Regardless of whether a company marketed marbles or plastic chips, kids were enthralled.[32]

Still, Ideal remained the leader in the doll business. In 1920, as the country embraced the Roaring Twenties, Ideal launched Flossie Flirt, a flapper in a slinky dress whose eyes could move from side to side as well as up and down, allowing her to appear coquettish. Indeed, she was marketed with "roguish rolling eyes." She was hardly a baby doll, except in the conventional adult meaning of the phrase. Flossie Flirt was a hybrid in that sense, a baby doll who was also a "baby doll." As the former, she appealed to little girls, but also to their postpubescent independence. One might think of her as Barbie's great-aunt.

On the generic side, innovations were the key to new sales. Ideal sought to launch several new dolls each season, seeking to maximize novelty to drive sales. Each new doll had an innovation, making it the "must have" of the season.

In 1914 at Ideal, Morris Michtom and his team devised a simple mechanism that made the doll close its eyes in simulated sleep when it was laid on its back. Another simulated the sound of crying. A crying doll had originally been developed in the 1890s by Thomas Edison, who had placed a small record player in each doll's body. His dolls could say "Mary Had a Little Lamb" and "Baa Baa Black Sheep" and, most popularly, "Now I Lay Me Down to Sleep." But apparently the sound was muffled, and the dolls failed to take off. The line was scrapped in 1896. Edison removed the phonographs and destroyed them, allowing the now-silent dolls to be sold off at a pittance.[33]

Ideal's version of a crying doll came nearly a quarter century later. Snoozie Smiles, introduced in 1923, had a dual face—a crying face and a smiling face—and she had a small voice box that "cried." She was, apparently, "the doll that made Queen Mary cry." This doll also provided a particular pleasure for Morris and revealed his impish sense of humor. Morris would occasionally ride the subway with a voice box from the doll in his pocket. When he turned the voice box over, it would "cry," Morris would take quiet delight in watching puzzled people look around for the crying baby.

Creating an Industry

The creation of any industry poses a series of logistical problems, and the toy industry was no different. Where would the materials come from? Where would the toys be assembled? How would the products be moved from the factory to retail stores to the waiting hands of children? How would the industry be regulated so as to promote competition and yet ensure that everyone played fairly? How would American manufacture be promoted against international competition? How would the industry as a whole be promoted, now that *Playthings* magazine (founded in 1903) was serving as the industry's trade journal?

How? By organizing.

The Toy Association was founded in 1916 in New York City, and a year later some toy manufacturers engineered the purchase of a building at 200 Fifth Avenue, across from the Flatiron Building. Several companies moved their corporate headquarters there (though their factories often remained in Queens and Brooklyn). The International Toy Center remained the global hub of the toy industry; the building's more than six hundred individual tenants accounted for 95 percent of all toy transactions every year, making the toy industry, until the early twenty-first century, the country's most concentrated and geographically centralized industry.

The association's mission was "to promote American-made products, encourage year-round sale of toys, and protect the interests of the burgeoning U.S. toy industry." All three elements seemed important. During World War I the association called for embargoes and boycotts of German goods. A. C. Gilbert, creator of the Erector Set, was its prime mover, because he wanted to make sure that the word *toy* was not synonymous with *Made in Germany*, according to Christopher Byrne, who wrote the association's official history.[34]

But once the war ended, international competition would again threaten American industry. Tariffs were clumsy and unreliable, so the Toy Manufacturers of America (now called the Toy Association) was formed to promote American products. (After the war, tariffs imposed by Germany and Japan forced the American hand.) American toys got a seal of approval from the association, a patriotic stamp that was useful in promoting the toys to retailers. For its "Buy American" campaign, advertisements depicted Uncle Sam with a boy and a girl on each knee, holding a model horse or doll; the ads ran in popular magazines such as *The Saturday Evening Post.*

Since about four-fifths of all toy sales took place in the few weeks before Christmas, expanding the toy-buying season to a year-round market required a unified response. The association vowed to work with dealers and retailers to promote gift-giving holidays throughout the year, such as "Christmas in July." The campaign failed to gain widespread traction.

Toy manufacturers worried, collectively, that Progressive-era reforms would handcuff them when it came to labor relations and government regulations. The Toy Manufacturers of America founding document supported the Stevens Bill of 1914, which was supposed to prevent larger manufacturers from driving smaller competitors out of business by undercutting prices. The bill would have allowed manufacturers to set retail prices, which, opponents said, would restrict competition, but it failed.[35] In 1916, the Keating-Owen Child Labor Act dramatically restricted child labor, limiting work for children aged fourteen to sixteen to eight hours a day, six days a week. Here the organization pressed all members to comply.

Marketing usually consisted of a team of salesmen who traveled to retail stores that might be interested in buying the toys. Since so much of the industry depended on Christmas sales, the peak sales time was immediately after the holiday, early in the year, when the orders for the next year's Christmas toys would be taken. The retailers were then flush with post-holiday cash, and the toy manufacturers faced constant pressure to come up with the next year's model a year in advance.

It was expensive to maintain separate sales forces and difficult to come up with new ideas all the time. And if you were a toy inventor out in the middle of the country, you'd have to find a way to travel to every toy manufacturer to pitch your invention. Why not, the Toy Manufacturers reasoned, bring everyone to New York at once, where buyers could see the new offerings and inventors could pitch their wares to the companies? A modest toy fair had been established in 1903, with Lionel Trains as the featured company. The Toy Manufacturers took over the fair and set its dates as mid-February, to showcase the new holiday toys and ensure that holiday orders could be fulfilled.

To develop a promotional strategy, the Toy Manufacturers took inspiration from a seemingly unlikely source: the California Associated Raisin Company. Instead of promoting a specific raisin company, the association would promote the entire industry: Every individual company would contribute and would benefit from the industry's increased visibility. (Later the Raisin Board's own dancing raisins were themselves turned into a toy.)

* * *

Probably no institution was more symbiotically connected to the expanding toy industry than the department store. Here, gathered under one roof, toy manufacturers had the opportunity to showcase their wares all year long. Entire sections could be created for newborns, birthdays, and other gift-giving occasions.

Many of the nation's great department stores had been founded and were run by German Jewish immigrants who had arrived in the mid-nineteenth century. The assimilated German Jews' willingness to showcase the work of often Yiddish Jewish toymakers may have been a major way they helped their newly arrived "cousins" to gain a foothold in America. Here makers and sellers were completely aligned.

Just how many department stores shared this history? In New York, the scene was dominated by Macy's, founded in 1858 by Rowland Hursey Macy, a New England Quaker; it was bought in 1896 by Isidor and Nathan Straus, who turned it into a behemoth that also created Abraham & Straus in 1893. Gimbels, founded by the German immigrant Adam Gimbel and his sons, was so successful that it went public in 1922 and bought Saks Fifth Avenue and Kaufmann & Baer in Pittsburgh. Bloomingdale's was founded in 1861 by German Jewish immigrant Benjamin Bloomingdale. B. Altman was founded by Bernard Altman, first-generation son of a German Jew who opened his flagship store on Fifth Avenue in 1906. Bergdorf Goodman was founded in 1901 by Herman Bergdorf, a Jewish immigrant from Alsace, and first-generation Jewish merchant Edwin Goodman; they opened their first flagship store on Sixth Avenue where Rockefeller Center stands today.

Outside New York, Filene's was founded by William Filene, a German Jewish immigrant in 1884; his sons, Edward and Abraham Lincoln Filene, commissioned Daniel Burnham to build their flagship store in downtown Boston in 1912. Neiman Marcus was founded in Dallas by Herbert Marcus, a first-generation Jew from Kentucky, with his sister Carrie Marcus Neiman and her husband, Abraham Lincoln Neiman, who was raised in a Jewish orphanage in Cleveland. (It is notable how many Jewish arrivistes named their children after iconic Americans—two of those listed here were named after Abraham Lincoln, not to mention Benjamin Franklin Michtom.)

Finally, there were several regional powerhouses. In Atlanta, Rich's was founded by Mauritius Reich, a Hungarian Jewish immigrant in 1867, who Anglicized his name to Morris Rich. In Pittsburgh, Kaufmann was founded by the German immigrant brothers Morris, Jacob, and Isaac Kaufmann in 1871; they built their flagship store in 1913. And in Columbus, Ohio, Lazarus was founded by the German immigrant Simon Lazarus in 1870 and was expanded by his grandson Fred Lazarus, Jr.

In 1929 Fred Lazarus, Jr., helped put together the conglomerate Federated Department Stores with three other founding members: Filene's, Abraham & Straus, and Bloomingdale's. (When Federated acquired Macy's in 1994, the company adopted the Macy's name.)

Even the stores that weren't founded by Jews were either run by them (as Julius Rosenwald transformed Sears, Roebuck into a retailing powerhouse) or bought by them (as George Hecht, founder of *Parents' Magazine*, eventually bought FAO Schwarz, and Federated bought Macy's). This connection between department stores and toymakers, which began in the early twentieth century, would define both worlds for the rest of the century and beyond. From the Gimbel brothers to Sonny Gindi (an Iraqi Jew who founded Century 21 with his brothers in Brooklyn in 1961), and from high-end Bernard Altman and Bergdorf Goodman to low-end E.J. Korvette and Filene's Basement, these sprawling department stores gave toymakers a window onto the world.

Here was a near-perfect assimilationist fantasy, the hermetically sealed, impenetrable claim to revered membership in the American social world. Yiddish Jews created the toys and dolls and manufactured them, and an enormous sales force hawked them to the buyers at department stores owned by German Jews—all to ensure that the Christmas season would be at least as happy for Jews as it was for gentiles.

Novelties and Amusements

Ideal's original name was the Ideal Novelty and Toy Company. Novelties—little gag items that shock, disgust, and amuse, often exactly in their ability to shock and disgust—were also the products of an immigrant Jewish imagination. More specifically, they were products of an immigrant Jewish *male* imagination—puerile, juvenile, gross, and funny, particularly in that same somewhat aggressive way of Jewish comedians, from the age of vaudeville to the present.

Sam Oumano, a Turkish Jewish immigrant, began his career selling picture postcards and Indian moccasins out of a pushcart. In 1910 he and his brothers Dave and Eli founded the Franco-American Novelty Company and opened a store on Lower Broadway in New York. They were the poorer cousins of the more lucrative and respectable toy and doll industry founders, but their prurient and often scatological humor produced many of the century's most famous fads, such as the Snake in a Can, Poo Poo Raspberry Cushion, and Doggie Doo (fake dog poop)—staples on the adolescent gross-out circuit for over a century.[36]

As have Whoops! (fake vomit), nudie sunglasses, and Tricky Dogs (magnetic Scottish terriers, one black and one white)—all the brainchild of Irving Fishlove.[37] Irving was the son of Chaim Fishlove, a bookseller in Ukraine who came to Chicago in 1914. Originally Hyman (his Americanized name) sold toy soldiers door to door, but his impish sense of humor kept getting in the way. Irving was no different but was far more scatological. When he started working for a company that produced dollhouses, he created their tiny toilets. This gave him an idea, and in 1922 he created a series of gag boxes labeled "Smallest Receiving Set," perhaps to make people believe it was a miniature radio. Opening the box revealed a miniature toilet, again, a tiny toilet.[38]

Most of Irving's gag boxes were both scatological and sexist, playing with grammar and double meanings just to get the recipient to say "Eeeuw!" (This facility with language—puns, teasing double meanings—is a fascinating assimilationist phenomenon for people who were raised, at least in part, speaking Yiddish.) For example, another box said "Roses are Red, Violets are Blue," and when you opened it up, you found two pairs of miniature women's lingerie, one red (Rose's) and one light blue (Violet's). Another promised "Flats Fixed," and the unassuming recipient would open it, expecting a car tire patch kit, and instead found falsies.

One particular escapade found Irving scoping out the men's room at Wrigley Field. He created a series of fake urinals that looked real enough and were glued to the wall, but they contained no plumbing. He hid in a toilet stall nearby and watched as everyone "missed." He wasn't caught, but apparently the gag was successful enough that he marketed it.[39]

Some dolls turned out to be novelties, capturing a fad and then fading into obscurity. The Billiken doll was created in 1909 by a St. Louis schoolteacher, Florence Pretz, who claimed to have envisioned it in a dream. A fantastical figure, the Billiken was a fat baby-like creature, with an impish monkey-like face, pointy ears, and a tuft of hair sprouting from an otherwise bald head. Not at all cuddly, Billikens were promoted as good luck charms, as much for the giver as for the receiver (a clever marketing strategy, that one!). After a few years, they faded into obscurity. (For contemporary examples, think of Yoda as a doll or those ubiquitous troll dolls of the early 1960s.)

Perhaps the most famous novelty of all was the Groucho glasses. First marketed in the 1930s, the ensemble consisted of oversize black glasses fitted with a plastic nose, shaggy eyebrows, and mustache. The disguise turned anyone, essentially, into an instant Jew. The look coincided with Groucho Marx's persona—sarcastic, contemptuous of city slickers and country bumpkins alike. The wearer instantly became the outsider, the one who stood in judgment, the international Jew.

One of my friends calls Jews' affection for Chinese food "safe *trayf*"—forbidden but safe, because Chinese cooks never mix milk and meat, because they never cook with milk, so kosher laws are not broken. Groucho glasses were a kind of sartorial safe *trayf*, a cultural appropriation that was also culturally sanctioned.

Groucho glasses.

Almost-Real Amusements

Among the Yiddish Jews were artists who had carved the most ornate arks, with vivid lions guarding the Torahs, in countless synagogues across the European continent, especially in Poland. They arrived penniless in New York with only stonecutters' hands and perhaps got working-class jobs as masons.

So what else did they create? Only the staple of every white urban child's pleasure, the centerpiece of every amusement park—the carousel. Those elaborately detailed horses and lions and other animals were carved, in large part, by Yiddish Jewish wood-carvers. Some were immigrants, some were children of immigrants. The carousel was a staple of Coney Island, the seaside Brooklyn neighborhood that was developed in the late nineteenth century as an amusement park. Then pretty much every other urban outdoor amusement park got one. The era between 1890 and 1925 was "the greatest era of American Jewish carving," according to the artist Murray Zimiles, who curated an exhibit in 2007 at the American Folk Art Museum dedicated to the creators of carousels.[40]

The demand for carousel animals was so great that a local businessman, William Mangels, a German immigrant, opened a studio at Coney Island and hired skilled craftsmen like Solomon Stein, Charles Carmel, Marcus Charles Illions, and Harry Goldstein who together were so influential that they are credited with the "Coney Island style" of carousel animals. Elaborate, bejeweled, expressive, and brilliantly executed, their animals became the elite of the industry. (It was Charles Carmel who created the animals for the carousel in Prospect Park, which opened in 1912 and would have certainly been visited by Ben Michtom as a child—as well as by my father when he was a child, and then by me, and later, by my own son. Four generations of little Jewish boys riding on lions.)

Illions, who came to New York from Russia as a teenager in 1888, is today recognized as the greatest of all these Jewish carvers. As Zimiles shows, his carousel horses are characterized by "their energy, classical proportions, exquisitely carved ornate trappings, and precise anatomical detail." Illions even signed his work.

* * *

By the 1930s, the United States had more than one hundred toy manufacturers—about fifty doll companies alone. Ten doll manufacturers accounted for more than three-quarters of all sales. Shirley Temple, Dy-Dee, and the Dionnes (dolls of the Dionne quintuplets) accounted for three-fifths of all sales.

None of these toy manufacturers, doll makers, novelty inventors, and carousel carvers consciously embraced that new definition of childhood. Had you asked them, they would have told you that all they did was see an opportunity, a niche, and seize it. They tried, failed, tried again, and eventually succeeded far beyond their wildest dreams.

But these poor and often terribly unhappy young men also possessed more than simple business acumen, more than just pluck and the luck to be at the right place at the right time. They took childish pleasure in the joy they brought to millions of children. These were serious men who retained the joy of an "inner child" who had never been given free rein when they themselves were children.

Let's face it: It took a lot of chutzpah for these young entrepreneurs to think they could make a living making toys. Making people happy is a serious business, true, but making *children* happy requires having the ability to think like a child. It requires resisting that biblical admonition from 1 Corinthians that growing up means one must "put away childish things." They refused to put childish things away. It's probably more fun to keep them in your pocket to startle riders on the subway anyway.

5

STRUGGLING AGAINST DEPRESSION

* * *

The Great Depression presented a serious challenge—and not just for the toy industry. Money was in short supply, and a sense of despair gripped the nation. Unemployment spiked, reaching 25 percent in 1933, compared to 3.2 percent just three years earlier, and family farms and fortunes were lost. Parents sacrificed to feed and clothe their families.[1] Toy companies were hard hit and scaled back production.

Morris saw an opportunity for Ideal. After all, the one industry that seemed to prosper during the Depression was Hollywood. When the going got extremely tough, America went to the movies. And America fell in love with a little girl named Shirley Temple, who sang and danced her way into Americans hearts. One of those hearts, apparently, was Morris's, who, as family stories have it, saw one of her first films, *Little Miss Marker* (1934), six times before declaring in a toy trade magazine, "This nation needs a beautiful doll to cure this Depression."

It wasn't easy to create and market a Shirley Temple doll. Ideal secured the rights to it only after promising Shirley's mother that the doll's eyes would be neither blue nor brown, as in every other doll on the market, but rather hazel, like Shirley's own. Ideal's designers cast twenty-eight molds of Shirley's face until they finally got it right.

Then they took the prototype head on the road—which meant that Morris and his executives walked through the streets and playgrounds of Brooklyn and listened as the children squealed, "That's Shirley!"

The launch of the Shirley Temple doll revolutionized the toy industry. After every picture was released, Ideal released a new doll dressed in the costume Temple wore in the film. Lines formed immediately for the lifelike replicas that came in five different sizes—18, 20, 22, 25, and 27 inches (ranging in price from five to twelve dollars). It was, according to Ideal, "the most popular celebrity doll in history." Shirley Temple embodied America as the nation wanted to see itself: spunky, sassy, resilient, adorable--and always willing to teach adults how to behave. The doll fashioned in her likeness was a unifier of families; it "brought together adults and children in a collective fantasy of the adoring and the adored, a celebration of playful parenting and a childhood full of play."[2]

The success of the Shirley Temple doll was unprecedented, matched only by Barbie half a century later. Ideal immediately produced other celebrity dolls based not on product tie-ins but real-life actresses—Deanna Durbin, Fanny Brice's Baby Snooks, and Snow White. Even Charlie McCarthy, the "dummy" in Edgar Bergen's ventriloquist act, had a doll. None came close to Shirley in terms of popularity, but each found its place in the market. Tie-in dolls based on cartoon characters, including Popeye, Superman, and Pinocchio, didn't do as well.

Baby dolls remained Ideal's bread and butter—as long as the firm kept innovating. Earlier in 1934, a woman called on Morris and explained that she had a daring idea—a doll that would drink liquid poured into its mouth; the liquid would pass through the doll and end up in a realistic-looking diaper that would be provided (thus providing a continuing post-purchase revenue stream). Changing the diapers would be the fun part.

Arranbee had passed on the idea. Rose Rothstein, William's wife, was said to have exclaimed, "Mothers would never let their children play with water!"[3] But the idea intrigued Morris. He prodded his engineers and designers to figure out how to do it. It was a nightmare. In the first prototypes, the liquids stayed inside the doll too long, turning rancid. The engineers finally came up with a straight tube from mouth to diaper. It produced rather immediate results, but at least it had no problematic aftereffects. And so Betsy Wetsy was born. Named after Abe Katz's daughter, she was sold in a box with a few diapers and a tiny bottle.

Actually, Betsy Wetsy did a lot of things involving liquids. According to the company's advertisements, she "has sniffles," "blows her nose," "weeps" real tears, "drinks" and "wets" and even "goes to sleep." How much more like a real baby could she possibly be?

Betsy Wetsy was an instant success. When the first shipment arrived in Los Angeles, delivered by a privately contracted service, an escort of motorcycles met the dolls at the airport. Their sirens

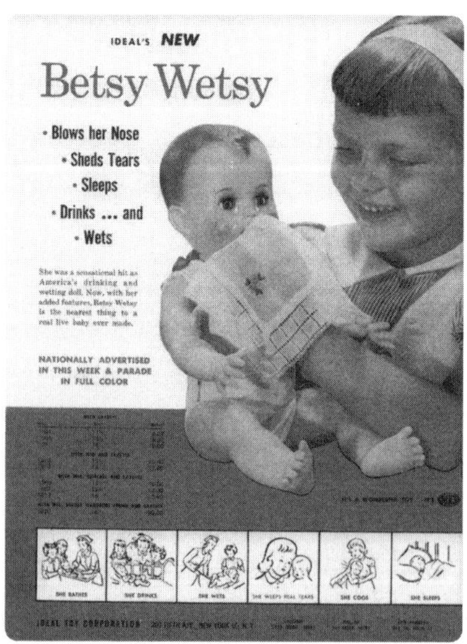

Ad for Betsy Wetsy, 1937. Ideal Toy Corporation. (Photo courtesy of Paula Michtom.)

wailed all the way to the department store that had an exclusive sale deal with Ideal. Within a year, the doll had generated more than $6 million in sales. Betsy Wetsy would remain in production for more than fifty years.

Comic Strip Characters

Creating dolls from celebrities was genius. But where could Ideal turn next? Before the First World War, Morris had successfully mined the world of comic strips, particularly with the Yellow Kid; now many other Jewish toy entrepreneurs were seeking inspiration and models in the funny papers. That they looked there was, as they might have said in Yiddish, *beshert*—destined, foreordained, kismet. Comic strips and comic books were another corner of American culture that was being subtly shaped by Jewish creators. They framed a world of Old Testament themes, of avenging superheroes, where righteousness invariably triumphed over evil, and of gentle satire, where Jewish artists, finding their voice as outsiders on the inside, poked slightly critical, affectionate fun at other Americans. If comics had their roots in "subversive joy and nonsense," as Art Spiegelman later wrote, then immigrant Jewish humor was going to make its presence felt.[4]

Cartoons had appeared in American newspapers and periodicals as early as Benjamin Franklin's 1754 "Join, or Die," an image of a snake chopped into segments: it was a political effort to engage the colonies in unified opposition to George III. In the nineteenth century, Thomas Nast's caricatures had been a staple of *Harper's Weekly*. But it wasn't until *Hogan's Alley*, featuring the Yellow Kid, that a regular character-based comic strip was launched. As we saw in Chapter 4, publication of the Yellow Kid strip became a battlefield in the ongoing turf wars between the Hearst- and Pulitzer-owned newspaper empires. In their funny pages, Pulitzer's *New York World* and Hearst's *New York Evening Journal* went head to head.

Mickey Dugan, aka the Yellow Kid, was not Jewish; nor was his creator, Richard Outcault. But the Yellow Kid was the first in a parade of comic strip characters to inspire dolls and figurines. One reason was that the Yellow Kid comic strip was beloved by both children and adults. For many children—throughout the twentieth century—the comics page was a primary vehicle by which they learned to read. For adults, the comics page might have been a respite, a momentary escape from a dreary working life. Comic strips were a medium for the entire family and often provided opportunities for family bonding. Parents could share the comics page with their children as a linguistic challenge, a cognitive exercise to see if they "got it."

So after the success of the Yellow Kid doll, toy and doll makers went hunting for possible subjects in comic strips. By 1910, America had over twenty thousand newspapers—dailies, weeklies, monthlies and quarterlies—offering plenty of possible fodder.[5]

Frederick Burr Opper's *Happy Hooligan*, which made its debut in 1900 in Hearst's *New York Journal*, was popular, but since Happy was a grown-up, he didn't have enough child-crazy charm to make a doll out of him. Hooligan, a sort of "hapless hobo," wore a tin can as a hat and got involved in zany hijinks until the police invariably arrived, nightsticks swinging, to cart him off to jail. While he was the precursor to other lovable losers like Charlie Chaplin and Bart Simpson, he also seemed to channel ethnic stereotypes about the Irish that made toymakers wary. (And his more pessimistic brother, Gloomy Gus, was even less amenable to becoming a toy tie-in.)

Opper was the first comic strip artist to make the speech balloon a comic strip staple. Born in Ohio to Austrian Jewish immigrants, by 1900 he had made a name for himself with illustrations in magazines like *Puck* (published by two Jewish immigrants, the Austrian-born Joseph Keppler and the German-born Adolph Schwarzmann). Together, Opper and Keppler created a well-known illustration of Uncle Sam parting the Red Sea as "The Modern Moses." Here ethnically identifiable Jewish immigrants stream through the parted waters, the waves labeled "Oppression" and "Intolerance." So ethnically stereotypic were the depictions of the Jewish immigrants—bearded men, obese women, and obstreperous children, all with hooked noses and kinky hair—that the illustration was roundly denounced as a German Jewish calumny against them.[6]

Frederick Burr Opper and Joseph Keppler, "The Modern Moses" in *Puck*, November 30, 1881. (Courtesy of Cornell University—PJ Mode Collection of Persuasive Cartography)

Similarly, Eugene "Zim" Zimmerman, a Jewish immigrant from Switzerland, never got over his early poverty and restlessness; he channeled it into bitingly stereotypic ethnic and racial caricatures in his years working for *Puck* and later *Judge* magazine. His drawings were barely acceptable at the time and are somewhat cringeworthy today.

From the stand-alone caricatures and drawings like these, ethnic stereotypes trickled into the early comic strips. *Abie the Agent* was perhaps the first comic strip to feature an obviously and deliberately Jewish character; it was drawn by Harry Hershfield, born to Jewish immigrant parents in 1885 in Cedar Rapids, Iowa. Hershfield was a columnist for the *New York Journal* and a well-known man about town, dubbed "the Jewish Will Rogers." His comic protagonist Abie, full name Abraham Kabible, was a car salesman, and from the time the strip was launched in 1914, it traded on every ethnic stereotype you can imagine (of plenty of other groups as well as Jews). Yet Abie was pretty mainstream—"a clean-cut, well-dressed specimen of Jewish humor in contrast to the big-nosed banker"—and Hershfield actually softened those traits to enable Abie to assimilate into American society. Still, Abie was not "doll-genic"; he was a comic for grown-ups and barely made a dent in the worldview of children.[7]

Several other comic strips used Yiddish humor and drew on ethnic stereotypes, yet managed to burrow their way into mainstream American consciousness. Gene Ahern's *Our Boarding House* appeared in 1921, followed by *Room and Board* in 1936, when he switched newspapers, and finally *The Squirrel Cage*, also in 1936. Ahern, born in Chicago in 1895 to Jewish immigrant parents, drew his first caricatures on the brown wrapping paper in the butcher shop where he worked. One character, a bearded schlemiel called the Little Hitchhiker, used to mutter "Nov shmoz ka pop?" as he waited for a ride. That Yiddish-sounding nonsense phrase became, almost instantly, a common everyday phase that people would ask each other, like "How's it going?" in meaning, but more like "Wassup" in terms of affable familiarity and innocent cultural appropriation.

So did the phrase "Banana Oil," a strangely nonsequitur-ish putdown that Milt Gross had his characters exclaim at those who postured and puffed pretentiously, in his strip of the same name and later in his collection *Gross Exaggerations*. Gross was born in the Bronx in 1895 to Russian Jewish immigrants. He peppered his cartoons with Yiddish expressions and, most famously, with fractured English expressions rendered in a Yiddish accent. His best-selling book *Nize Baby* (1926) launched a comic strip replete with those fractured malapropisms, mostly uttered by Jewish mothers conversing across tenement alleyways. *Dunt Esk!* (1927) featured the Feitlebaums and the Yifnifs encountering puzzling American behaviors and offering to tell the "nize baby" the story of, for example, "from Jack witt de binn stuck."[8]

Gross's zaniest character was launched in the comic strip *Count Screwloose from Tooloose* in 1929. The Count, "a half-pint, sausage nosed, cross-eyed resident of Nuttycrest Sanitarium" or later Balmycrest Booby-Hatch, often wore a sombrero and had an excitable puppy named Iggy, who wore a Napolean hat. Every week the Count concocted a scheme to escape the loony bin, only to realize

Panel from "Count Screwloose of Tooloose" comic by Milt Gross, circa 1932.

that the world outside was truly quite insane, which would lead him to immediately retreat to his safe haven. His constant refrain upon returning, "Iggy keep an eye on me!" became one of the most memorable catchphrases of the 1930s.[9]

But not even Iggy, the little dog, could lend itself to the doll makers; these were grown-up comic strips, designed to bring joy to Jews, both assimilated and unassimilated, and gentiles alike.

And just try to make a doll out of a Rube Goldberg cartoon! Goldberg was born in 1883 to relatively affluent Jewish parents in San Francisco (his father was the city's police and fire commissioner at different times) and studied engineering at University of California at Berkeley, from which he graduated in 1904. Before the Depression, he had created a couple of comic strips, *Mike and Ike* and *Boob McNutt*. But his comic strip *Inventions of Professor Lucifer Gorgonzola Butts*, launched in 1929, made him so famous that his contraptions now bear Goldberg's name.[10]

Each Rube Goldberg machine was a devastatingly complicated machine designed to accomplish the simplest of tasks, like slicing a piece of bread or using a napkin after taking a spoonful of soup. (Goldberg actually patented many of his designs.) He was always "finding a way to get from point A to point B by traveling through all

Rube Goldberg's design for the "Self-Operating Napkin" (1914).

the other letters of the alphabet," quipped the artist and cartoonist Art Spiegelman.[11]

Fortunately, a couple of well-known comic strip and movie characters did lend themselves to appropriation by doll- and toymakers. One of them was a girl. Besides the stereotypic Jewish mothers and shiksa goddesses, several female characters embodied other stereotypically Jewish traits. Like, for example, Betty Boop, drawn and created by Max Fleischer in 1930.

Fleischer, who had arrived in Brooklyn from Krakow at age four, started his career as a cartoonist at *The Brooklyn Daily Eagle.* A caricature of the Jazz Age flapper, Betty Boop was strong, independent, sexy, and more than slightly impudent. She was sassy and opinionated and knew how to use her wiles and her wits to get ahead. While her comic strip lasted only a few months, her animated cartoons made her one of the two most famous female cartoon stars of the 1930s (alongside Minnie Mouse). The Betty Boop doll, wooden-jointed and standing up, was initially licensed to the Cameo Doll Factory in 1931. Betty became ubiquitous among dolls, with several manufacturers vying for her later favor. Fleischer became known for his animated cartoons of Betty Boop and other characters.

One of those others was Popeye. Popeye the Sailor, the cartoon character, was created by Elzie Segar, born in 1894 to a Jewish handyman and house painter in Chester, Illinois, a small city near the

Mississippi River. Initially intending to work with his father, Elzie (or L.C., the initials he chose to replace his first name) instead took a correspondence course to become a cartoonist.[12] After moving to Chicago, he was encouraged by Richard Outcault (creator of Yellow Kid) to draw for the *Chicago Herald*. There he drew *Barry the Boob*, a strip about an incompetent soldier—this in 1917, just as the country was entering the First World War. Two years later, now decamped to New York and working for the *New York Journal*, he created a new strip, *Thimble Theatre*, with a cast of characters including Olive Oyl, Castor Oyl, and Harold Hamgravy. Popeye joined the cast of *Thimble Theatre* in 1929 and was an immediate hit.

Was Popeye Jewish? Well, you can decide. His superhuman strength came from eating spinach, which was "the centerpiece of traditional Sephardic cooking" according to Benjamin Ivry.[13] Not to mention that his strength came from eating his vegetables in the first place! Other characters, too, had Jewish traits. Wimpy, who replaced Harold Hamgravy, was a classic schnorrer (a ne'er-do-well moocher), and the minor character George Geezil was an older bearded man whose fractured immigrant English led him to perpetually ask "Did you asking me?" In 2018 Hy Eisman, the longtime artist for the ongoing *Popeye* comic strip, told a journalist that he'd deleted Geezil because he was too stereotypic a Jewish immigrant.[14]

Other artists assumed that Popeye was Jewish as well. Albert Bloch's 1941 canvas *March of the Clowns*, painted in Kansas on the eve of America's entry into World War II, depicts a parade of clowns in which the lead clown holds a pike with a swastika at its top, as an effigy of Hitler swings from it. It's all watched by an audience including Popeye, Olive Oyl, Wimpy, Krazy Kat, Moon Mullins, and the Katzenjammer Kids.

The cartoon character Popeye may have seemed Jewish, but the actual living sailor on whom Popeye was based was in fact Jewish. Frank "Rocky" Fiegel, a Polish Jewish immigrant, was, during Segar's childhood, a bouncer at Wiebusch's Tavern in Chester, where he entertained patrons with tales of his seafaring years as a merchant marine. A well-known brawler, Fiegel had massive forearms,

Popeye the Sailorman and Frank "Rocky" Fiegel. (Popeye © King Features Syndicate, Inc. World Rights Reserved)

a deformed eye, and a ubiquitous pipe in his mouth. (Olive Oyl was modeled after Dora Paskel, the owner of a grocery store in Chester.) Segar maintained a relationship with Fiegel until he died and supported him with some of the royalties from the comic strip.

And what, after all, was Appalachia but a poor mountainous area filled with little hamlets of strange folk traditions and meager living—a region of shtetls with a southern accent, an American Pale of Settlement? At least that was what Al Capp created with his family of rural hillbillies from Dogpatch, the Yokums. Pappy Yokum was Tevye with a drawl and fewer teeth.

Alfred Gerald Caplin was born in New Haven in 1909 to a very poor family of Latvian Jewish immigrants. His father, Otto, was an unsuccessful salesman, and his mother, Tillie, daughter of the Grand Rabbi of New York City, had her hands full trying to make ends meet for her husband and four children. "We were poorer than any family today," Capp said. "We had no welfare, no food stamps, none of the sort of things that today, every wretched family has." But at least here in America, his family realized, "it was no crime to be a Jew."

At age nine, Alfred lost his left leg in a trolley accident. "I came out of the hospital determined that this must make no difference," he later wrote. "I strapped on a wooden leg and took my place in the neighborhood." His debility—or rather, his determination to overcome his debility—made him a real scrapper. Capp became, and remained for the rest of his life, a "loud, brash, aggressive East Coast Jew with an almost desperate need for attention." He hung out in Hollywood with movie stars, engaged in notorious feuds and sex scandals, and careened from liberal Democrat New Dealer to right-wing confidant of President Nixon.[15]

Capp launched the comic strip *Li'l Abner* in 1934, in the *New York Daily Mirror*, imagining a world that Jews never entered, could never enter—the rural South. (Capp claimed to have hitchhiked through Tennessee and Kentucky as a teenager, but that is likely a fable.)[16] But Jews didn't have to enter it—they had come from it!

Capp poked good-natured fun at these rubes—the family name, Yokum, was a portmanteau of yokel and hokum—from a place of cosmopolitan sophistication, New York City. (Mammy and Pappy were said to have been modeled on his own parents.) Abner himself was lazy, stupid, and patriotic, with the purest of hearts and the emptiest of brains. He rarely worked, but when he did, his job was as a "crescent cutter" for the Little Wonder Privy Company—yes, he cut the crescents into the doors of outhouses, at the very moment when most Americans had finally installed indoor plumbing. When he lost that job to an actual dummy, he became a professional mattress tester: "He'd get up at 6 A.M., rush to the Little Wonder Mattress Company, flop down on one until noon, eat a hurried lunch, and then go back to sleep until six. It was a hard buck."[17]

Perpetually nineteen years old, Abner was perpetually pursued by Daisy Mae Scragg, a stereotypic shiksa goddess, a buxom blonde whose vain pursuits extended even to that special day when it was required that girls chase after boys for boyfriends and husbands. Sadie Hawkins Day was named for the homeliest girl in Dogpatch. It's hard to imagine a worse-concealed Jewish boy's fantasy. It somehow captured a much wider demographic, so wide, in fact, that when Abner and Daisy Mae finally did marry, the wedding was featured on the cover of *Life* magazine.

To the unknowing reader, *Li'l Abner* was the perfect feat of assimilation; no one would ever have guessed that the pen that drew those panels was a first-generation immigrant Jew. Indeed, in a further step toward Americanization, Capp actually introduced Jews into the strip from time to time: They were almost universally greedy misers with huge noses seeking to swindle the Yokums and other naïve Dogpatch residents. (He routinely mocked their country of origin, Lower Slobbovia, as well.)

Capp's strip certainly caught on; at its peak, *Li'l Abner* was syndicated in more than nine hundred American newspapers and one hundred foreign ones in twenty-eight countries, reaching upward of 90 million readers a week. It ran from 1934 to 1977. John Steinbeck called Capp "very possibly the best writer in the world today," and John Updike called Li'l Abner "an American Candide."[18] There was something charmingly affecting about this clan of some of the obviously dumbest people in America. (Abner himself was said to have the lowest IQ in America.) Like Forrest Gump, everyone in the clan was childlike in their naïveté, innocence, and undiluted patriotism, enabling readers of the strip to feel simultaneously superior and charmed.

Initially, Capp licensed the images of Abner and his relatives for a windup toy band, paper cutout dolls, and a variety of novelties. Dolls and puppets came later, in the 1940s and '50s, after the massive success of the Shmoo, a character launched in the strip in 1948. The Shmoo was a small white teardrop of a fictional figurine, somewhat phallic, that could satisfy every human need and would sacrifice itself when a human needed food. (Consider the Shmoo a mini-golem, protecting not through strength but through sacrifice.) *The Life and Times of the Shmoo*, published in 1948, was a runaway bestseller, selling close to 800,000 copies.

The Shmoo was a natural for the toy industry, and within a year of its inception, seventy-five different manufacturers had issued more than one hundred Shmoo-related products. Nesting dolls, models, dolls, and every conceivable character imitation followed.

The Kigmy, which Capp created the next year, wasn't initially nearly as lucky, perhaps because this pathetic bearded creature (a cross between an African American and a Yiddish Jew who liked to be kicked) was so transparently racist and anti-Semitic in conception

Some of the toys, dolls, and other items based on the Shmoo. (Photo courtesy of Denis Kitchen)

The original drawing of the Kigmy by Al Capp. (Photo courtesy of Denis Kitchen)

that few would touch it. Capp revised it, and after the Kigmy lost its beard and ethnic trappings, it became another novelty success, from lapel pins that proclaimed I KICKED A KIGMY to inflatable creatures to be kicked with glee.

As a comic artist, Capp had once been an assistant to Ham Fisher, creator of the even more popular strip *Joe Palooka* that reached more than 100 million readers a week. Hammond Edward Fisher, born in Wilkes-Barre, Pennsylvania, in 1900, was the son a Jewish scrapyard dealer. In Joe Palooka, he created a good-hearted yet simple-minded blond scrapper with a heart of gold who had, by accident, become heavyweight champion of the world. Palooka was a goyish Everyman, who would inspire Ideal Toy executives to launch the Joe Palooka "Bop Bag," a weighted inflatable doll that you could hit as much as you wanted to, and he would still come back upright. Morris Michtom negotiated the deal personally and made sure that if Joe ever got married or had a baby in the comic strip, Ideal would have exclusive licensing rights to the characters. (Indeed, Morris actually encouraged Fisher to give Joe a wedding and a baby, as he was searching for new toys and dolls.)

Joe Palooka was a comic book version of an American icon, an American ideal. According to the comic strip chronicler R. C. Harvey, Palooka was "an American ideal of manhood. Or of knighthood, for that is what he is: a kindly, gracious knight, righter of wrongs, defender of truth, beauty, justice and the American way."[19]

Well, we all know to whom such a sobriquet might equally apply, don't we?

The People of the (Comic) Book

Superman was Jewish. Don't believe me? Just ask Sammy Klayman, the protagonist in Michael Chabon's marvelous 2000 novel, *The Amazing Adventures of Kavalier and Clay.* "Superman, you don't think he's Jewish?" asks Sammy. "Coming over from the old country, changing his name like that. Clark Kent, only a Jew would pick a name like that for himself."[20]

The world of comic strips, the entire world of superheroes, was a virtual Jewish ghetto—a ghetto created in large part because a slew of young Jewish artists had been frozen out of the higher sorts of artistic endeavors, architecture and advertising. Necessity born of anti-Semitism, talent, and no small amount of moxie—er, chutzpah—combined to usher in what is now considered the "golden age" of comics.[21]

In *Superman Is Jewish?: How Comic Book Superheroes Came to*

Serve Truth, Justice, and the Jewish-American Way (2012), the philosopher Harry Brod explores this *shidduch*—Yiddish for "match"—between Jews and comics. Brod adds gender to the mix, arguing that Jewish men, particularly, "expressed a fight against anti-Semitism through their fantasy comic book creations."[22]

Superman may be the best-known character in the history of American fiction. Created by high school friends Jerry Siegel and Joe Shuster in Cleveland, Ohio, in 1934, Superman was the classic double, the outsider as insider, the insider as outsider. His story begins when a refugee baby, Kal-El (think Moses), is sent from his home planet by his loving parents to an alien land (America). Why? Because his people were about to become extinct. His name, Kal-El, means "All that God is" in Hebrew. It is the tale of the first-generation immigrant, leaving the threatened tenuous life in the old country, sent to find his way in a new country. "It wasn't Krypton that Superman really came from," wrote Jules Feiffer, "it was the planet Minsk." Kal-El was conveyed by a form of *Kindertransport*, taking the vulnerable to a safe place when their home is about to be destroyed.[23]

It's an old story, an old *Jewish* story, "the particularly Jewish theme of the misunderstood outcast, the rootless wanderer."[24] It's Moses floating down the river in a basket, since all the firstborn sons of the Hebrew slaves are to be killed. Or perhaps it's Jesus, his parents wandering Jewish immigrants, unable to find a room at the inn and sleeping in a barn to help their child escape. Or perhaps it's this Jesus story: "a wise and mighty father in the heavens sends his only son to Earth, where he performs miraculous feats for the benefit of mankind." Or perhaps the Jesus story is a mirror: a father sends his only son to Earth to save him, and the son ends up not quite saved himself but saving the entire world.[25]

Siegel and Shuster grew up in Glenville, a "dingy" suburb of Cleveland, both of them sons of shtetl immigrants. The boys dreamed constantly of escape, just as their parents had earlier fled the pogroms. Siegel's father was murdered during a robbery at the clothing store he owned, and young Jerry grew up with the twin fears of imminent danger and the looming terrors in Europe.

The fictive Clark Kent, in their imaginations, grew up in the most American world they could imagine, even more mainstream than some rural Appalachian Dogpatch—the generic midwestern farm. Clark, the fictive son of Jonathan and Martha Kent, is, as Harry Brod writes, "a timid, socially inept, physically weak, clumsy, sexually ineffectual quasi-intellectual who wore glasses and apparently owned only one blue suit." The Italian philosopher Umberto Eco agrees, noting that as Clark Kent appears "fearful, timid, not overly intelligent, awkward, near-sighted, and submissive to his matriarchal colleague, Lois Lane, who, in turn, despises him since she is madly in love with Superman." In other words, writes Brod, Clark is "the classic Jewish nebbish."[26]

But Clark has a secret, a secret that resides in the heart of every unheroic wannabe. Deep down, he is hypermasculine, a hero, the most real man on Earth. "Jewish men had only to tear off their clothes and glasses," writes Jeff Salamon, "to reveal the surging superman underneath, physique fully revealed by those skintight blue leotards and flaunted by that billowing cape." In that sense, Superman is the Jewish Talmudic scholar with the thick glasses who transforms himself into the Übermensch, the hypermasculine, embodying the turn-of-the-century Zionist leader Max Nordau's new muscular Jew. "Clark Kent is the anti-Semitic stereotype Nordau was trying to replace—bespectacled, a coward, and in love with but unable to arouse the interest of Lois Lane, the *shiksa* of his dreams," Salamon continues. He's a one-man New Deal, always intervening on the side of the helpless and oppressed.[27]

Deep down in every bully, beneath the butched-up bravado, lurks the tremulous heart of a coward; their bluster is an effort to mask their fears, ruffling "in a manly pose," as the poet W. B. Yeats put it, "for all their timid heart."[28] Superman's creators reversed the pattern, creating a "revenge of the nerds" fantasy; after all, Jews are the original nerds, high school "brainiacs" whose minds are so much more highly developed than their scrawny, skinny, ninety-seven-pound weakling bodies. As Siegel said:

> As a high school student, I thought that someday I might become a newspaper reporter and I had crushes on several attractive girls who either didn't know I existed or didn't care I existed. It occurred to me: What if I was real terrific? What if I had something special going for me, like jumping over buildings or throwing cars around or something like that? Then maybe they would notice me.[29]

So, he explained, "I'm lying in bed counting sheep when all of a sudden it hits me. I conceive a character like Samson, Hercules, and all the strong men I heard tell of rolled into one."[30]

Superman turns the lives of Jewish nerds upside down: He sees mortal men the way mortal men see Jews—as ineffectual wimps. The

Jerry Siegel and Joe Shuster looking at a mockup of the comic of Superman.

anti-Semitic stereotypes of Jewish men as "feminized physical and intellectual weaklings, greedy, conniving," is actually the world of the goyim. Jews are hypermasculine *Übermenschen,* more powerful than a locomotive. Clark Kent is "the revenge of the Jewish nerd for the world's anti-Semitism."

It's hardly a coincidence that Superman appeared when he did—that is, just when Jews needed him most. In a 1975 press release, Jerry Siegel explained that he and Shuster had European Jewry on their minds when they created the character:

> What led me to creating Superman in the early thirties?
>
> Listening to President Roosevelt's "fireside chats" . . . being unemployed and worried during the depression and knowing hopelessness and fear. Hearing and reading of the oppression and slaughter of helpless, oppressed Jews in Nazi Germany . . . seeing movies depicting the horrors of privation suffered by the downtrodden . . . I had the great urge to help . . . help the downtrodden masses, somehow.
>
> How could I help them when I could barely help myself? Superman was the answer.[31]

While some Americans might have missed Superman's Jewish identity, Nazis saw him for what he was. An article in the Nazi newspaper *Das Schwarze Korps* (The Black Corps) in April 1940 attacked Superman's creator as "an intellectually and physically circumcised chap who has his headquarters in New York, [who] is the inventor of a colorful figure with an impressive appearance, a powerful body, and a red swim suit." (How they knew he was circumcised is anyone's guess.) Later Nazis complained that Superman was corrupting America's youth: "Instead of using the chance to encourage really useful virtues, he sows hate, suspicion, evil, laziness and criminality in their young hearts."[32]

Siegel and Shuster constantly looked for ways to confront the Nazi challenge. In 1940 *Look* magazine commissioned the pair to do a two-page comic answer to "How Superman Would Win the War."

Superman vs. Hitler, *Look* magazine, February 27, 1940.

In the final panels, Superman grabs both Hitler and Stalin by their shirt collars and flies off. "Where are you taking us?" asks Hitler. "Next stop—Geneva, Switzerland"—that is, the League of Nations.[33] That was before the United States even entered the war. Later, in a 1943 issue of *Action Comics*, Superman takes them on directly. I don't have to tell you who won.

Superman spoke to Jews, and he spoke *for* Jews. They were winners, not history's most benighted losers. What made Superman Jewish, aside from the fact that he was created by Jews? For one thing, he's the Messiah, "the patron saint of Jews everywhere." It is at the heart of the Jewish story that the Messiah has not yet come to save God's chosen people. As long as there is war, hatred, persecution, and genocide, Jews must wait for the Messiah to deliver them. "The fantasy of godlike beings who could solve our problems was a cry of hope as well as of despair," writes the comic book historian Danny Fingeroth. "Jews think that a superhero is maybe going to change the world for the better," says Irwin Hasen, the artist of *Green Lantern* and creator of *Dondi*. "He's coming from another planet! He's coming down to help us!"[34]

But Superman isn't just any Messiah. He is a distinctly American Messiah, created by American Jews. That is, he came from somewhere else. Superman, like pretty much everyone else in the country, is an immigrant, and his story is, in that sense, the American story.

He is an alien, an outsider. He is Lady Liberty's soulmate and partner: She lifts her lamp by the Golden Door to welcome the alien, and he embodies those aliens and vows to protect them. Superman, Henry Louis Gates, Jr., writes, is "the hero from Ellis Island, personified as an undocumented alien who had been naturalized by the ultimate American couple."[35]

Superman is the immigrant, possessed of secret powers, blending in, establishing an identity as an average American. It's an assimilationist story—perhaps "the ultimate assimilationist fantasy." "We were aliens," writes Jules Feiffer. "We didn't choose to be mild-mannered, bespectacled and self-effacing. We chose to be bigger, stronger, blue-eyed and sought after by blond cheerleaders. Their cheerleaders. We chose to be them."[36]

In some ways, like all assimilationist stories, it's not a radical story but a conservative one, a story of the desire to fit in, to blend in, to be unnoticed. To be left alone. All Clark wants is to live like a mild-mannered reporter in Metropolis, but the injustices of the world keep calling him out of his camouflage. In a 1972 essay about Superman, Umberto Eco wrote that Superman has "an obsession with preserving the status quo."[37]

That conservative desire to fit in, to not upset the American applecart: This is the Jew's ultimate wish. To be accepted as no different from anyone else. To fit in, to not stand out. Unlike other religions, Jews don't proselytize. Alone among the monotheistic faiths, they have no need to convert you. They just want to be left alone. When you stand out, you are isolated, frightened, and vulnerable to attack. When you fit in, no one sees you. You are the outside-insider, secretly an outsider, but no one knows your secret.

Finally, and perhaps most important, the superhero is misunderstood. The people of Metropolis, or Gotham, or Anytown USA, are constantly turning on the superhero, wondering if he is really their savior, doubting his motives. "No matter how hard he tried to be accepted, to excel, to please and help others," writes Danny Fingeroth, "still he is misunderstood and condemned" and often rejects the very heroics of a Batman or Spider-Man.[38]

"There is no question in my mind that Jerry saw Superman as a kind of projection of his own self-image or his own fantasies about himself," noted the comic book artist Bob Oksner, a contemporary of Siegel and Shuster. "Jerry was Jewish, like I am—like a lot of people in comics in those days—and the rest were Italian. Superman was the story of an unfairly denigrated person who knows that he had the ability to prevail in the end, whoever that person may be."[39]

Though he may have been Jewish himself and was created by Jews, Superman belonged to all of us. He channeled the longings of more than one small immigrant minority. He connected with boys, mostly, and specifically with American boys. His story is the fantasy of power, strength, and muscularity in the service of justice. It is the American story: The immigrant rises to great heights.

Mostly it is the story of the American boy. Just as adolescent boys know that to be a man is to be powerful, they also know they feel powerless. Other boys, their teachers, their parents, the world at large—everyone seems to have power over them. Imagine, just for one moment, that you are the powerful one, that you can do anything you want—and it isn't chores, or homework, or even entering the drab work world of your parents. Further, what adolescent boy doesn't know the feelings of being misunderstood, of being blamed for things that aren't his fault? Superman spoke directly to those boys whose families were struggling to survive the Depression, to maintain their place, or find a place, in American society. By its nineteenth issue, *Action Comics* was selling about half a million copies a month, more than four times more than any other comic. By 1940, *Superman* alone was selling about 1.25 million copies per month.

Superman created an opening. Other superheroes arrived quickly. The golden age of comics began in 1938, specifically in April 1938 (with a cover date of June), when Superman debuted in *Action Comics* number one, a comic series by National Allied Publications, which was owned by Harry Donenfeld. That golden age lasted until the mid-1950s, when Senate hearings on juvenile delinquency implicated comic books. To ward off a government crackdown—it was the McCarthy era, after all—the publishers created a self-regulating organization, the Comics Magazine Association of America, and implemented the Comics Code Authority to regulate the content of comic books.

The writers, artists, and creators of the golden age of comics reads like the roster of the Shtetl Slow Pitch Softball League:

HARRY LAMPERT (born in 1916 in New York to immigrant parents) began working for Max Fleischer, inking *Betty Boop*. He created the Flash in 1940.

SAM GLANZMAN (born in 1924 in Baltimore) worked initially for comic book consolidators and created Hercules, Amazing-Man, and Fly Man.

LOU FINE (born in 1914 in Brooklyn, son of a Russian immigrant house painter) was crippled as a child by polio but became a "meticulous draftsman" who was a ghost artist on *The Spirit*.

JACK COLE (born in 1914) created Plastic Man.

MARTIN NODELL (born in Philadelphia to poor Jewish immigrant parents) collaborated with Bill Finger to create Green Lantern. (Finger, the co-creator of Batman, was born in 1914 to Jewish immigrant parents in Denver.)

MORT WEISINGER (son of Austrian Jewish immigrant parents, born in 1915 Manhattan and raised in the Bronx) created Green Arrow, Aquaman, and the original Vigilante before he became the editor of DC Comics.

CARL BURGOS (born Max Finkelstein in 1916 in New York City to Jewish immigrant parents) started his career as a comic book packager until he branched out and created The Human Torch.

HARRY SHORTEN and **IRV NOVICK** (both sons of Jewish immigrants) created the Shield in 1940, specifically to encourage wartime patriotism and stir up anti-Nazi sentiment.

One more name deserves mention, if only because that story is simultaneously typical and utterly unusual. Lily Renée Phillips was a poor immigrant Jew from Vienna (born in 1921) who escaped the Nazis and was shuttled to Britain as part of the *Kindertransport* in 1939, leaving her parents behind in Austria. When her new British family treated her more like a servant than a child, she struck out on her own, eventually rejoining her original family who were now refugees on the Upper West Side of New York.

Initially, she sought work as an artist. Like other artistic immigrant and first-generation Jews, she was rebuffed at every turn, so when her mother showed her an ad for a comic book artist, she applied for the job at Fiction House. After a two-week trial, she stayed, first as an assistant, revising other artists' work, erasing pencil marks, and painting in color backgrounds. The work was thankless, made all the more unpleasant by her leering coworkers, who would pencil in lewd comments just to watch her erase them. But she stuck with it and eventually got her own strip called *The Werewolf Hunter*, about a nerdy professor who travels the world to expose animal-human monsters. "It was sort of the dog," she recalled in an interview. "It was the one that no one wanted." But she made it her own. "It was a great embarrassment for an artist to lower his/her standard in such a manner," noted one historian. "It was as if a ballerina was doing stripping on the side."

Soon she was also drawing Señorita Rio, a stylish, swashbuckling, buxom American spy in a frilly, revealing white blouse. Señorita Rio is the secret identity of a Hollywood movie star, who enlists as a Nazi hunter after her husband is killed in the attack on Pearl Harbor. This was her "revenge," she acknowledged. "Señorita Rio doesn't fly like that other guy in the comic book," she says in a graphic biography published in 2011, "but she's powerful too."[40]

A year after Superman flew across the pages of AC Comics, DC

Comics introduced Batman. Batman was not Jewish. In fact, he was as far from Jewish as possible. An upper-class WASP, scion to a great industrial fortune, Bruce Wayne is the epitome of blue-blooded aristocratic entitlement. He lives in a large mansion in a wealthy suburb of Gotham, probably restricted. He also has no superpowers, just a lot of money to buy the latest amazing equipment and use it for good, to protect Gotham from a vast array of criminals.

Batman may have been the ultimate goy, the upper-class brahmin, but he was created by first-generation Jews. Bob Kane (born Robert Kahn, son of eastern European immigrants, in 1915) had initially come up with a flying hero named Bird-Man, but he and Bill Finger (born Milton Finger in Denver in 1914) and seventeen-year old journalism student Jerry Robinson, created a little rich boy who loses the one thing that money can't buy: his parents. A character didn't have to be created by Jews to be Jewish; nor did having Jewish creators necessarily make a character Jewish. In Batman's case, it seems to have been a deliberate strategy to create a superhero who was as far removed as possible from the tenements of the Lower East Side. Bob Kane was so ashamed of his Jewish identity that he went to elaborate lengths to conceal it: He didn't even mention it in his autobiography.[41]

Batman may not be Jewish, but his nemesis, the Joker, may have been. Robinson came up with this evil clown sitting in a journalism class at Columbia, according to Arie Kaplan, author of *From Krakow to Krypton: Jews and Comic Books* (2008). The Joker's great love, Harley Quinn, often uses Yiddish slang expressions. (Robinson also created Robin, based partly on his experience as the younger sidekick to Kane and Finger.)[42]

In case Superman needed some help defeating the Nazis before the United States entered the war, Joe Simon and Jack Kirby created Captain America in early 1941. Simon was born in 1913 as Hymie Simon in Leeds, England, to a poor family of tailors and housemaids. Jack Kirby was born Jacob Kurtzberg in 1917, on Essex Street on the Lower East Side, to Austrian immigrant parents. His father worked in the garment industry. Kirby may have been the most Jewish of all the comic book creators; his characters were constantly fighting the Holocaust and anti-Semitism.

Captain America starts his career as Steve Rogers, "a poor scrawny kid who wanted to join the United States Army to fight Hitler" but is rejected as 4F, unfit because of his frail physical condition. So he volunteers to take part in some radical experiments by Professor Reinstein (Albert Einstein anyone?), who is hoping to create a "Super Soldier." Rogers emerges transformed, human perfection. Then a Nazi saboteur kills Professor Reinstein, and Captain America kills the Nazi in response. The professor never wrote down the formula, so Rogers is a one-of-a-kind perfect man.

He arrives on the American scene just in time. "The underfed ghetto kid [was] transformed into a roof-rattling power by seizing American opportunities, the weary old-country survivor [was] reborn as the new fighting Jew through the crucible of American freedom and violence," writes Gerard Jones. "And through this immigrant passion Simon and Kirby captured an entire national awakening: America the provincial stirring itself to become a world power."[43] It was, says Simon, "our only way of lashing out back at the Nazi menace."

> Here was the arch villain of all time. Adolf Hitler and his Gestapo bully-boys were real. There had never been a truly believable villain in comics. But Adolf was live, hated by more than half the world. What a natural foil he was, with his comical moustache, the ridiculous cowlick, his swaggering goose-stepping minions eager to jump out of a plane if their mad little leader ordered it. . . . I could smell a winner. All that was left to do was to devise a long underwear hero to stand up to him.[44]

One thing seems certain: By creating these hypermasculine superheroes, a whole bunch of scrawny, bullied, young Jewish artists asserted their masculinity. Comic books were indeed the revenge of the nerds—with yarmulkes! Their assertions of manhood were simultaneously assimilationist efforts to land squarely in the center

Captain America lets Hitler know who's boss (1942).

of American manhood. Unmasked, they are nebbishy; but when they put on their masks, they are at once unrecognizable as Jews and unique in their superhuman strength and virtue. They simultaneously define and defy the Jewish experience in America.

So it may come as a bit of a surprise that while these first-generation Jewish boys were asserting their manhood through comic book heroism, a scion of the WASP elite ended up creating perhaps the greatest female superhero. (It may not be as surprising, though, considering how male-dominated was the world of the comic books, and how sexist were so many of its practitioners.) Comic book pioneer Max Gaines, concerned with the educational quality of his line of comic books, asked the well-known psychologist William Moulton Marston, a Boston brahmin and Harvard-educated writer, to act as a consultant. Marston proposed Wonder Woman. He wrote the text of the comic under the pen name Charles Moulton. Here's how he explained his creation:

> It seemed to me, from a psychological angle, that the comics' worst offense was their blood-curdling masculinity. . . . It's sissified, according to exclusively masculine rules, to be tender, loving, affectionate, and alluring. . . . Not even girls want to be girls so long as our

> feminine archetype lacks force, strength, power. . . . The obvious remedy is to create a feminine character with all the strength of a Superman plus all the allure of a good and beautiful woman. This is what I recommended to the comics publishers.[45]

From Packagers to Publishers

Why shouldn't the comic book industry be so completely dominated by Jewish artists, writers, and creators? After all, Jews invented the medium, the genre, in the first place.[46]

The first comic book was created by Max Gaines, a curmudgeonly unemployed salesman who was struggling through the Depression, living at home. Born Max Ginzburg in 1894 in Manhattan to a poor Jewish immigrant family, he had, like Al Capp, injured his leg in a childhood accident, the pain from which made him sour and prone to outbursts of rage. Having failed at a succession of jobs, Gaines got a job as a salesman at the Eastern Color Printing Company through the help of a friend, Harry Wildenberg. The company printed Sunday newspaper comic strips. Gaines thought the strips might be useful for promotional campaigns if they were bundled together and published separately from the newspaper.

In 1933 he bundled together a bunch of comic strips into an eight-page pamphlet, which he labeled *Funnies on Parade*. The company offered them to customers of Proctor & Gamble, if they sent in a coupon. It worked even better than anticipated. By the end of the year, Eastern Color Printing had produced several more comic magazines for companies to use in promotions.

Gaines sensed he had a winner, so the next year he produced a stand-alone comic book to be sold at newsstands for a nickel. Thirty-two pages long, *Famous Funnies* sold 35,000 copies. The comic book was born. The next year *Famous Funnies* was sixty-four pages long (since the printing was done in eight-page signatures) and sold for a dime. The company sold nearly all of the 200,000 they printed.

These first comic books were polyglot operations, bringing

together a variety of comics written by different artists. A group of entrepreneurs organized a comic book studio to attract artists to develop their characters, and then a "packager" would sell entire catalogs to the burgeoning comic book publishers. In 1935, for example, Harry "A" Chesler (born in 1897 as Aaron Czesler to Jewish parents who had immigrated from Vilna), established a studio in Manhattan to supply publishers with comic book content. Jack Cole (Plastic Man), Jack Binder (Daredevil), Otto Binder (Supergirl), and Mort Meskin all drew for Chesler in the early days.

Many of the early packagers were themselves artists and writers, and the atmosphere was heady and intense. Profits depended on quantity, and there was a frenzied atmosphere of creativity on the one hand, and a "garment industry-style sweatshop mentality" on the other. At times, these studios churned out comics via an assembly line.[47]

In 1938 Sheldon Mayer (born in 1917 in Harlem to Jewish parents), an artist and editor at National Allied Publications (which eventually became DC Comics) was looking through the "slush pile"—those unsolicited offerings that had found no backers among the editorial team. They were doomed for the trash heap. He noticed some storyboards mocking up a potential comic book character. He picked it up, loved it instantly, and pitched it constantly until the publishers relented. The character graced the cover of *Action Comics* number one, though the publishers put his actual story in the back of the comic book. That is how Superman got published.

Superman was so successful that in 1939 Max Gaines joined up with two other boychiks from the neighborhood, Harry Donenfeld and Jack Liebowitz, to found a company devoted entirely to comic book creation, production, and distribution. All-American Comics was modeled on DC Comics. Suddenly the field was sprouting like weeds: Pep Comics, Archie Comics, Timely Comics, and many more.

The supply of talent seemed endless, partly because young artists were desperate for work and partly because traditional avenues were closed to them due to anti-Semitism. "Comic books," writes David Hajdu, "even more so than newspaper strips before them, attracted a high quotient of creative people who thought of more established modes of publishing as foreclosed to them: immigrants and children of immigrants, women, Jews, Italians, Negroes, Latinos, Asians, and myriad social outcasts." As Jerry Robinson, early Batman artist and creator of the Joker, remembers, there was "a pool of talent in New York from the first- and second-generation immigrants to draw upon. A lot of them were printers in Europe. When comics came along, they saw it as a new form of publishing. . . . Jews couldn't get into other fields. There were quotas in colleges." "We couldn't get into newspaper strips or advertising," recalls Al Jaffee. "Ad agencies wouldn't hire a Jew."[48]

Since "daily newspapers refused to accept illustrations or comic books made by Jews," what choice did they have? Comics were at the bottom of the heap, a "junk field," a "crap medium," said Will Eisner, who would become one of the titans of the comic book industry. That low status opened it up as a haven for those who found more acceptable doors closed to them. It was "just the curious sort of marginality that a range of Jewish entrepreneurs . . . found inviting," writes the historian Paul Buhle. The very fact that the comic book business was held in such low esteem served as a gigantic welcome sign to these wannabe artists and writers. Comic books were "generally thought of as another nutrient-free but essentially harmless confection of kids," writes the historian David Hajdu. The business "was brand new," recalled Eisner. "It was the bottom of the social ladder, and it was wide open to anybody. Consequently, the Jewish boys who were trying to get into the field of illustration found it very easy to come aboard."[49]

The work was plentiful, and the pace frenzied. Joe Kubert, a mainstay of the silver age of comics in the 1950s, recalls that in his earliest years in the industry, the "Antisemitism was just there." But "we were too busy to be too concerned, we were all aware of being Jewish, and even the non-Jews fit into our social circles. We were just working."[50]

This was more or less the route taken by Will Eisner, who began as a comic book creator and became one of the industry's leading publishers, editors, and general impresarios. He was born in 1917 to

Austria-Hungarian Jewish immigrants in the "Pelham Bay shtetl of the Bronx," as he later put it. Young Will's father, who had been an artist in Europe, found it difficult to get work in his new home. His English skills were poor, and anti-Semitism was rife, but he found occasional work painting backdrops for vaudeville and Yiddish theater productions.

Will was determined not to end up like his father. In 1936 a high school friend, Robert Kahn (who, as Bob Kane, would create Batman), suggested that Will bring some of his drawings to Samuel Iger, who was packaging comic books in a shirt factory in the garment district. (Iger, who called himself Jerry, was born in 1903 to Austrian Jewish immigrant parents.) Within a year, Eisner and Iger were operating their own studio and turning out comic books.

A few years later Eisner created his own comic book character, the Spirit. But the Spirit was different from virtually every other character being drawn by all these first-generation artistic wannabes. The main character was Denny Colt, a masked crimefighter, yet the people in the comic "lived in tenements near elevated tracks, gathered on their stoops, and rode the subway to work. They had strong features and wore heavy clothes," writes Hajdu. Jules Feiffer, one of Eisner's assistants, recalled that he assumed that the Spirit was Jewish, despite his Irish-sounding name. Eisner agreed, at least in retrospect. "I suppose he was Jewish, insofar as the fact that he was the product of my experience, and I put a little of myself in him," he told Hajdu. "I never felt like I really fit in anywhere. I certainly didn't feel like I belonged in the superhero field, where everyone was basically trying to do the same thing. I believed in doing my work my way." In essence, "the Spirit was the fantasy image of every outsider, a force of superior cool, strolling through a landscape of woeful normalcy."[51]

First-generation Jews created, wrote, and drew other comics besides those devoted to superheroes. Harvey Comics, for one, used the same medium to go after a decidedly younger set. The company was founded in 1941 by Alfred Harvey (born in Brooklyn in 1913 as Alfred Harvey Wiernikoff to Russian Jewish immigrant parents), who was joined by his brothers, Robert and Leon. Harvey Comics

Collective Portrait of Jewish
Comic Book creators by Dave Sim.

created such characters as Baby Huey and Little Audrey, then simply licensed other characters like Joe Palooka and created comic books around them.

No one could fault Albert Kanter, a New York–based book salesman who specialized in medical appointment books for doctors, for trying to navigate the chasm between comic books and literature. Some comic book critics had argued that reading comic books would distract young readers from digging in to the great literary classics. The son of Russian Jewish immigrants who initially lived in New Hampshire before settling in New York in 1904, Kanter thought the dichotomy too severe: If the children wouldn't go to the classics, he'd bring the classics to them—in comic book form.

In 1941 he founded the *Classics Illustrated* series, which reimagined great literary works as exciting adventure stories, beginning with the *Three Musketeers*, *Ivanhoe*, and *The Count of Monte Cristo*. These comics carried no advertising, which endeared them to school districts across the country. In the 1950s, even as anxious parents and commentators fueled a moral panic about the pernicious effects of comic books, leading to massive countrywide comic book burnings, Kanter's "classics" sold over 100 million copies, many to the more than 25,000 school districts that used them to encourage a reading—any reading—of the classics.[52]

Facts as Fiction

Michael Chabon's Pulitzer Prize–winning novel, *The Amazing Adventures of Kavalier and Clay*, uses facts about fiction as the basis for fiction. The novel brilliantly chronicles the history of comic book heroes and their first-generation creators. Sammy Klayman is working in the office as a clerk when his cousin, Josef Kavalier, arrives from Prague as a refugee in 1939. We, contemporary readers, know what is coming to the Jewish community of Prague, even if these two young men don't. Josef escaped. The friendship and artistic creativity of these cousins compiles stories of the creative cabal of the early world of superhero comics. As Sam puts it:

> Every little skinny guy like me in New York who believes there's life on Alpha Centauri and got the shit kicked out of him in school and can smell a dollar is out there right this minute trying to jump onto it, walking around with a pencil in his shirt pocket, saying "He's like a falcon, no, he's like a tornado, no he's like a goddamned wiener dog," Okay?[53]

The cousins fantasize, draw, dream, and create their character, their contribution to this fantasy world, rhapsodizing romantically about the character and his superhuman abilities:

> "To all those who toil in the bonds of slavery and, uh, the shackles of oppression, he offers the hope of liberation and the promise of freedom!" His delivery grew more assured now. "Armed with superb physical and mental training, a crack team of assistants and ancient wisdom, he roams the globe, performing amazing feats and coming to the aid of those who languish in tyranny's chains! He is"—he paused and threw Joe a helpless, gleeful glance, on the point of vanishing into his own story now—"the Escapist!"[54]

Their superhero was modeled on the Jewish escape artist Harry Houdini. It seemed as if any Jew who managed to get out Europe alive was an escape artist.

Houdini represented yet another element in the tapestry of first-generation Jews who created fantastical worlds that delighted children—and plenty of adults. Born Erik Weisz in Budapest in 1874, his rabbi father packed up the family and moved them to Wisconsin two years later. Harry Houdini was yet another self-made, and self-created, immigrant Jewish American. As the world's most famous escape artist, his escapades enthralled children of all ages. But he wasn't the only first-generation Jew who chose this path; indeed, the list is pretty long and might leave us speculating about some sort of affinity between diasporic Jews and the keen interest in how to escape. Houdini's contemporary "The Great Leon" (born Leon Harry Levy in 1876) performed a "Fire and Water" act in which an assistant was wrapped in paper and set on fire, only to reappear in a tank of water across the stage. Others included sleight-of-hand master Nate Leipzig (born Nathan Leipziger in 1873 in Sweden and moved to Detroit at age ten); and Max Malini (born Max Katz Breit in 1873 in Poland and brought to the United States at age three). Malini's teacher, "Professor" Frank Seiden (born Efraim Zeyden in 1860 in Galicia and came to New York as a teenager) was a fire-eater and a Yiddish recording artist. In the next generation, Al Flosso (born Albert Levinson in 1895 in Brooklyn), owner of the country's most famous magic shop, perfected the "Miser's Dream" illusion of seeming to conjure coins and dropping them loudly into a metal bucket. In their next generation, Ricky Jay (born Richard Jay Potash in 1946 in Brooklyn) became a movie star based on his amazing sleight-of-hand tricks, and David Copperfield (born David Seth Kotkin in 1956 in Metuchen, New Jersey) is perhaps the most famous illusionist in the world today.[55] All but these last two were either childhood immigrants or first-generation American born. That's quite a legacy to inherit.

Comics Come Alive

Comic books are static, even as individual frames suggest action and movement. For some struggling Jewish artists, that wasn't enough. They wanted to see the movement—and for you to see it, too.

No one wanted this more than the Fleischer brothers, Max, Dave, and Lou. (Well, no one perhaps except Walt Disney, whose first animated cartoon was created in 1928.) The Fleischer family came from Krakow to Brooklyn in 1887; Max was four and his younger brothers followed soon after. Their father had been a successful tailor, but by the time Max was a teenager, they were quite poor and lived in Brownsville, a poor Jewish neighborhood in Brooklyn.

During the First World War, Max produced training films for the army. Afterward, relying on that technology, he experimented with short films using a rotoscope, which required drawing hundreds of individually crafted cels, which were then photographed in sequence. Later he developed a rotograph, which allowed for more rapid sequencing using stock-colored frames as backgrounds and filling in only the foreground.

With his younger brother Dave, Max began to create films using cartoon characters that tied in with comic books and comic strips. (Their youngest brother Lou often composed the music.) Some of their earliest and most successful animations were of Ko-Ko the Clown, Betty Boop, Popeye, and Felix the Cat. While Betty Boop hadn't really caught on as a comic strip, she was a smash hit as a cartoon character, a "full-fledged mini–Mae West," writes Adam Gopnik,[56] and she made Max a rich man.

Among their most memorable technological advances was the little animated ball that bounced over song lyrics as Ko-Ko the Clown was singing. This demanded synchronized sound and visuals. Their first use of the bouncing ball, in 1926, preceded by two years Disney's animated film *Steamboat Willie*, which introduced Mickey Mouse to the world.[57]

Disney's feelings about Jews have been debated for decades, but Max and Dave Fleischer were unabashedly Jewish, occasionally peppering their animated cartoons with Hebrew letters and even Jewish themes. While Disney's animated creatures were "sweet and sentimental, and were depicted in rural and suburban settings," the Fleischers' settings were urban and ethnic, their characters less barnyard friends than "street strays."[58]

The Fleischers and their studios were havens for artists such as Seymour Kneitel and Benny Wolf, who drew Betty Boop, and even for voice-over artists: Betty Boop's voice was provided by Mae Questel, a Bronx girl who was the daughter of Orthodox Jewish immigrants. She was also the voice of Olive Oyl in the Popeye animated cartoons.[59]

A Not-So-Super Ending to the Golden Age of Comics

Unlike the more celebrated comic book creators–turned–entrepreneurs, most of the comic book artists and writers never rose to fame and fortune—even if they did rise to fame, their fortunes were virtually nonexistent. Many lived and died in relative poverty and obscurity. Desperate for work, artistically creative but naïve in the cutthroat word of business, they were easy targets for unscrupulous businessmen who ran the packaging shops and publishing houses. They were, in the words of Arie Kaplan, "underpaid wage slaves with no rights or royalties: the characters they created were owned and trademarked by the comic book publishers."

Even the creators of Superman, Siegel and Shuster, were paid $130 by Harry Donenfeld for the first installment, and they got virtually no royalties for the hundreds of spin-offs and subsequent comic strips, movies, television shows, and the like.

A most poignant coda to the saga occurred in 1978, forty years after Superman first appeared, on the eve of the release of the first *Superman* movie. During an audience question segment of a TV talk show promotion for the film, an elderly man stood up and said in a soft voice, "My name is Jerry Siegel. I co-created the character Superman on which they're making this movie, and I work at a supermarket bagging groceries."

The audience gasped, and so did Jerry Robinson, who was watching the show at home. Robinson, a creator of Batman, was by 1978 the head of the National Cartoonists Society. He launched a campaign to force Warner Bros. (which now owned DC Comics) to compensate Siegel and Shuster "for having created one of the most widely recognized characters on earth." After much negotiation, Siegel and Shuster each received a stipend of $20,000 a year, beginning in 1978, which was later raised to $30,000, and they finally got some credit for their creative work.[60]

* * *

It wasn't just in the urban metropolises and Gothams that Jews struggled to assimilate. Perhaps the most "American" comic book series of all, *Archie*, was launched in December 1941, on the eve of Pearl Harbor, by first-generation Jews John Goldwater (born Max Leonard Goldwasser) and Victor Bloom. All-American Archie is the middle-class Everyman, pursued by the darkly sensual and aristocratic Veronica Lodge and by the bobby-soxed, blond-ponytailed Betty Cooper. Playing off characters embodying other masculine stereotypes like the court jester Jughead, the entitled rich boy Reggie Mantle, the myopic genius Dilton Doiley, and the brainless jock Moose, Archie proved that the regular guy would triumph in the end. As contemporary Archie Comics CEO Jon Goldwater (the son of Archie's creator) put it recently, "Riverdale is a safe, welcoming place that does not judge anyone. It's an idealized version of America that will hopefully become reality someday."[61]

Whether set on the beaches of Normandy or in the halls of Riverdale High, these Jewish comic strip and comic book artists and writers provided Depression-era fantasy escape and wartime distraction for America's youth. By 1945 the comic book was the most popular form of entertainment in America, selling somewhere between 120 million and 150 million copies that year.[62] It was calculated that 95 percent of boys and 91 percent of girls between the ages of six and eleven were regular comic book readers, reading an average of twelve comics a month. Their consumption generated a small fortune for the companies (if not for the artists) and for the toy companies that created the tie-in toys. By 1952, more than twenty publishers were producing nearly 650 comic titles per month, employing over one thousand artists, writers, editors, and letterers (who filled in the texts in the quote balloons), among others. Comics, writes David Hajdu, were "capital in the social economy of childhood."[63]

Jews may have been known for centuries as the people of the book. But as America entered the postwar era, it became clear they were also, as many have noted, the people of the comic book. Who'd have thought that a bunch of poor boys from the Lower East Side, Brooklyn, and the Bronx could so utterly captivate the youth of America?

6

THE WAR AND ITS AFTERMATH

* * *

Even before Americans went to war against Nazis in Europe, comic books helped them go to war against Nazis and their sympathizers at home. Through the late 1930s, as Hitler annexed Austria and took over the Sudetenland, a rising tide of concern for the fate of Europe's Jews was met by an equally strong isolationist and anti-Semitic sentiment to stay out of the war and to not let any of "them" into the United States. Charles Lindbergh's America First movement and Father Charles Coughlin's bombastic anti-Semitic radio addresses stoked those passions, especially after the massive Nazi rally at Madison Square Garden in New York City on February 20, 1939.

Organized by the German-American Bund, some twenty thousand people attended this "Pro-American rally" (while at least an equal number protested outside). In front of a massive background portrait of George Washington, flanked by four American flags and two swastika-laden streamers, Fritz Kuhn, the German-born head of the Bund, inveighed against the Jew-controlled media and referred to FDR as President "Rosenfeld" and Governor Thomas Dewey as

"Thomas Jewey." Banners draped along the tiered seats proclaimed SMASH JEWISH DOMINATION OF CHRISTIAN AMERICANS and WAKE UP AMERICA! SMASH JEWISH COMMUNISM![1]

One response? A comic book.

Under George Hecht's leadership, *Parents' Magazine* had branched out dramatically, creating a media empire devoted to parenting and children's lives. Prime among its offshoots were a series of comic books, like *Polly Pigtails, Real Heroes, Jack Armstrong, Calling All Girls,* and *Sports Stars.* By far its most successful and longest-running publication was *True Comics*, which debuted in 1941 and would continue until 1965. The company tried to make ideas accessible, entertaining, and even fun.

In 1943 Hecht was approached by Richard Rothschild, a former advertising executive at J. Walter Thompson and president of the American Jewish Committee (AJC). Joined by Kenneth Gould, the editor at Scholastic Magazines, the two men asked Hecht to turn a special issue of *True Comics* into a comic book version of Gould's short 1942 book *They Got the Blame: The Story of Scapegoats in History.*[2] Gould looked at a series of scapegoats throughout history, including early Christians, Salem witches, and early nineteenth-century Catholics. Then he lit on the Nazi persecution of the Jews and the Nazi effort to "divide and conquer" America from within.

In 1943 Hecht agreed to publish it, and *True Comics* produced the comic book version. The first print run was 500,000. Scholastic's imprimatur helped the group bypass the potential suspicion of teachers toward comic books, and 17,000 copies were sent to social science teachers in high schools across the country. They loved it. Seventy thousand more copies went out to high schools. Theologians were worried that the clergy would be horrified at the sight of comics, but the National Conference of Christians and Jews ordered 200,000. Unions ordered a special issue for workers: another 900,000 went out. When those ran out, the CIO ordered another 500,000. And the army ordered 150,000 just for the air force hospitals. All told, *True Comics* printed more than 4.2 million copies. Later the *True Comics* version was submitted to NBC radio's Blue Network, which broadcast it on December 18, going out to one hundred radio stations from coast to coast.[3]

An Ideal Time for Toys?

The coming of the war coincided with a transition at Ideal, though its centrality in the doll business remained unchanged and indeed would grow under the next generation of Michtoms.

Rose Michtom had died on August 27, 1937, at seventy-one. Morris followed less than a year later, on July 21, 1938. Both were buried in Montefiore Cemetery, in Queens. Obituaries in both the English and the Yiddish press extolled Morris's virtues, even if they disagreed over what those virtues were. The English papers' obituaries hailed him as a great businessman, an entrepreneur whose inventions and creativity brought joy to millions of children, but they failed to mention anything about his Zionism and philanthropic work for Jewish causes. The Yiddish press, by contrast, extolled his *Yiddishkeit* virtues, calling him one of Brooklyn's most respected Jewish leaders and benefactors, but it made no mention of his business activities.

Morris and Rose hadn't been observant Jews, but they had attended synagogue for the High Holidays, and they tried to follow most other Jewish holiday traditions. They hadn't kept kosher, but Rose loved to cook traditional Jewish foods, including, apparently, a gefilte fish that was renowned within the family. Mark (Ben and his wife Hadassah's son) recalled watching his grandmother making gefilte fish, chopping it and tasting it (raw!), stuffing it back into the skin, and sewing it into a fish shape.

This I remember from my own childhood. The family recipe, followed assiduously by my grandmother, may have differed from Rose's in the particulars, but I have a vivid memory of a large carp swimming in the bathtub in the family's Brooklyn apartment.

Alice Michtom, Morris and Rose's great-granddaughter, recalled a story that her father often told her about Morris. One night Rose set a plate of meat down in front of Morris. He asked, "What is it?" She responded, "Never mind, just eat it." He tasted it and asked again,

"What is it?" Again, she responded, "Never mind, just eat it." After finishing, Morris asked, "Okay, what was it?" When Rose told him it was pork, Morris went to the bathroom, stuck his finger down his throat, and threw up.[4]

While they'd never been particularly religious, Morris and Rose did become passionate Zionists after taking a trip to the Mandate of Palestine in the early 1930s. Even then, before the beginning of the genocide in Nazi Germany, the Michtoms came to believe in the need for a homeland for the Jews in the ancient land of their forebears. Following that trip, Morris joined the board of the Jewish National Fund, which sought to buy and reclaim land in Palestine.

Despite his earlier labor struggles, he remained an "ardent socialist," according to his son, Ben; the anarchism and militant socialism of his youth tempered into a more democratic version later in life. He'd founded the Arbeiter Ring (Workmen's Circle) and remained a lifelong friend to and patron of Abraham Cahan, the editor of *The Jewish Daily Forward*. He voted for Theodore Roosevelt in 1912—how could he not?—and thereafter for Norman Thomas in 1928 and for FDR in 1932 and 1936.

Within the family, Morris was hailed as the patriarch, the family lion, loving and generous, "open hearted and open-handed." He was, as Ben put it in a letter to Alice Michtom in 1970, "a born orator, persuasive speaker, honest and courageous, and a firm idealist who hoped to leave a better world than he found."[5]

So when he died, Morris left large shoes to fill—and fill them was exactly what Ben did.

You could say that Ben and Ideal were born together. Both child and company began their lives in the back room of the candy store on Tompkins Avenue—Ben in 1901, and Ideal a mere six years later. Benjamin Franklin Michtom had been named after one of Morris's heroes; he saw Ben Franklin as a man of probity and prudence, for whom a penny saved was a penny earned. In keeping with his namesake, Ben was brilliant, driven, and penurious—the consummate organization man, a natural salesman and marketer. It was Ben who propelled Ideal to become the world's leading toy manufacturer.

Even as a child, he was precocious. In 1913, at twelve, already smart, assertive, and fearless, he was one of several public school students invited to City Hall to respond to a speech by the mayor. The mayor was considering a proposal to build more playgrounds in Brooklyn. Eight students, representing the Brooklyn neighborhoods where the playgrounds were to be built—Brownsville, Ocean Hill, New Lots, Twenty-Fourth Ward, Crown Heights, East New York, and Italian Colony—were chosen to respond. Representing Brownsville, Ben's brief speech was the only one quoted on the front pages of the *Brooklyn Standard Union* and *The Brooklyn Times* in their June 18, 1913, editions. Standing barely three feet tall, the *Times* noted, Ben "let loose a flood of eloquence worthy of a college professor." The rapid growth of the district necessitated more playgrounds, he argued, because, simply, "there is no place for the children to play except in the congested streets where their lives are always in danger."[6]

Ben graduated from Boys High in Brooklyn at fifteen and headed off to the Wharton School of Business, which was then a college at the University of Pennsylvania, where he was the youngest student on campus. (This may sound unusual to contemporary readers, but the New York City school system was ill-equipped to deal with very smart children, so it simply skipped them ahead. My mother, for example, graduated from high school at fifteen and college at eighteen.) His business school thesis was about the financial problems of the toy industry.

Ben struggled financially in college. It wasn't that Ben didn't have the money; it was more that he felt he couldn't access it. His father believed his son needed some financial toughening up.

It was typical of Morris to put his son in such a position, typical for him to torture Ben with that combination of generosity and stinginess. As Ben boarded the train for Philadelphia, Morris gave him a checkbook on the family account, but he didn't tell him how much money was actually in the account. "Remember," Morris told his son, "this is the family account so every time you use it you are taking from others in the family." Ben was always terrified of overdrawing the account and lived abstemiously in college—a lesson he took into adulthood.

After graduation and a year of "seasoning" on Wall Street, Ben went to work at Ideal. Just as he hadn't made Ben's collegiate career easy, Morris didn't immediately bring Ben into the top of the Ideal hierarchy. He expected him to get to know the business inside and out, especially if he was one day to take over. So Ben was sent on the road as a salesman, carrying suitcases full of dolls, to learn how to sell, how to represent the line. He traveled up and down the East Cast at first, and later around the country, playing with the dolls with both children and adults, learning to hear their concerns, and learning, basically, how to think like a child and sell to a grown-up. He loved the work and actually stayed on the road for more than a decade.

In the early 1930s the company moved out of its Brooklyn loft into a factory in Long Island City and, just under a decade later, in 1943, into a large factory on Jamaica Avenue in Hollis, Queens. By then, Ben was happily ensconced as an executive. The company had actually thrived during the Depression, buoyed largely by the Shirley Temple dolls and other innovative products. "The last thing a family will economize on is the happiness of its children," one family member explained to me, a remark that illustrates that Yiddish ideal of childhood.[7]

After Morris's death, Ben, along with Joseph Michtom (Ben's older brother who had previously been a dentist), their cousin Abe Katz, and their brother-in-law David Rosenstein took control of Ideal. Katz attended to the materials side of things, constantly looking for innovative materials and coping with wartime shortages and needs. Joseph and David devoted themselves to production issues—labor, design, and marketing—while Ben handled the front office and was the company's public face.

Before Morris's death, the quintet had met every Sunday at Morris's and Rose's home at 180 Winthrop Street. Abe, Dave, Ben, Joseph, and Morris would sit on the porch, screaming and shouting for hours about the business they loved and the company they ran. (Ironically, given Ben's childhood proclamation for city playgrounds, that the house was later torn down to make way for the Winthrop Playground.)

When he came to head the company his father had started, Ben knew something essential about the toy business: It was run by grown-ups, and its products were bought by grown-ups, but its prime audience was children. And children had a keener bullshit detector than their parents, Ben believed. "Heaven help the toymaker who thinks he can get away with crude and inaccurate models of grown-up jet planes or automobiles or anything else," he said to an interviewer. Once, he recounted, a buyer from a department store came to see Ben in his office. The buyer had brought along his eight year-old son. Ben, delighted, offered the boy one of the company's newest toys, a plastic model of the P-40 fighter plane.

The boy took one look at it, then turned up his nose, scoffing, "Plane like that couldn't even get off the ground. You got the dihedral angle of the wings all wrong."

Ben was aghast. (He had to look up the word *dihedral.*) But it turned out the boy was right. Ben promptly scrapped the entire output and replaced it with a corrected version.

As the company's public face, Ben was always dapper, wearing a double-breasted suit and tie. But he was also notoriously cheap. As a first-generation son of poor—or at least formerly poor—immigrants, he remained frugal, even after he became wealthy: He presented a successful image, but always remained aware of how easily everything could be lost. He never bought himself a briefcase; instead, he arrived at work every morning with his papers and his lunch in a paper shopping bag. Once, in the mid-1940s, a salesman came to the office to talk to him. He noticed a framed photograph on the wall, showing Ben seated with Shirley Temple in the 1930s. The salesman noticed that Ben was wearing the same suit.

As cheap as he was, he was also thoughtful and generous to the family, including the wider family of company executives—especially since many of them were related, at least by marriage. Every year he gave the children of the top executives a subscription to the Book-of-the-Month Club, and when Herb Sand (vice-president for sales and marketing) bought a house on Long Island, Ben had a set of seven dogwood trees planted there to welcome him and his family. All the wives of the executives were good friends, and the families socialized on weekends. Ideal was a family company, and if you were inside the family, you would be taken care of.

If you were an outsider, however, Ben was Scrooge. His definition of family did not include the descendants of Harris, Morris's brother—and my great-grandfather. Morris's children never even knew he had a brother! No Book-of-the-Month Club for my sister and me. No dogwoods. No big box of the newest toys every holiday season. And certainly no inheritance.

Once Ben and Hadassah were out to a fancy restaurant with their son Mark and his wife, Paula. As they left the table and went to retrieve their coats from the cloakroom, Paula reached into her purse and took out a dollar. (This would have been seen as generous, but not lavish, in the early 1960s.) Ben took her hand, gently, and moved it away. He dropped a quarter into the tip jar.[8]

One thing Ben and Hadassah never skimped on, though, was trips to Europe. They always went by boat, in the luxury cabins, and took tons of photographs. They sent "newsletters" back to the family—including all the executives and their families as well. It was their version of the family Christmas letter.

At work, Ben was indefatigable. His colleagues called him "Mr. Poinggg" because when he got an idea, "it was as if a gong had been struck!" One former employee recounted that in 1948, the company had decided to make the Baby Coos doll a bit bigger. Everyone agreed to make her a bit larger, and then, *poingg*—the light bulb went off, and Ben decided to make the first life-size doll. At twenty-seven inches high and weighing about six pounds, she sold for twenty-five dollars—a huge risk in the first years after World War II, when doll prices were falling. But the life-size dolls were a huge success.

Baby Coos succeeded not just because of the noises she made—she cried, sobbed, and cooed—but also because of the new material Ideal used for her arms and legs. In 1940 Abe Katz happened on a new substance in an Ohio balloon factory. Latex looked and felt far more real than any material anyone had ever used, and it proved malleable. Abe recognized the possibilities immediately and sought to make a compound that would be a near-perfect likeness to human skin. He called it Magic Skin, and that doll line, headlined by Baby Coos, was an instant hit. It couldn't have come at a more opportune time, because the year the company began using latex materials, the Japanese cut off America's rubber supply.

Dolls were Ben's passion. "It may sound corny," one of his associates told a journalist, "but Ben loves those dolls like they were his own children. Which they are, in a way, because he usually helps dream them up." While other toymakers expanded into other arenas—games, toy guns, sports—Ben understood something essential about the minds of children and the ways dolls might engage them. Another colleague said that Ben "sees everything with a child's eye view of its possibilities as a plaything."[9]

It was simple, really. Ben believed that what children wanted in a doll was the opportunity to pretend to be adults. "When I was a kid," Ben told a journalist in 1949, "I liked toys because they helped me make believe. And what I wanted to make believe was that I was grown up. Most children are like that."[10]

A doctor? A nurse? A mommy? A soldier? A policeman? A fireman? Toy cars, toy guns, models of airplanes and architectural projects—children wanted to play grown-up, and dolls enabled them to do that safely, without any of the problems of bill paying, home owning, or childcare. "What you have to give them isn't realism but a doll to which they can do something for themselves," he told a journalist.[11] This central insight governed Ideal's toy development philosophy. Ben embodied that childlike desire to be grown-up even as he maintained an entrepreneurial zeal for innovation and competitive advantage. It was a profitable synthesis.

Like his father, Ben was not particularly concerned about knockoffs and copycats. (Remember, Morris didn't even patent the design for the teddy bear.) As long as the company continued to roll out exciting new dolls, he knew the market would always be there. And he was determined that Ideal would produce not only the most numerous new dolls but also, as he saw it, the best ones. He trusted his audience—the kids themselves. “We can depend on the kids for protection,” he told a journalist. “If it isn’t Sparkle Plenty or Baby Coos or whatever the season’s hit happens to be, they let their parents know about it. It’s the same with doll clothes. You’d think we could use cheap stuff. But if it isn’t the finest material and the finest sewing, they won’t take it.”[12]

If Ben’s passion was dolls, his genius was constantly thinking up new variations. Under his watch, dolls were given voices ranging from soft murmuring coos to wails of anguish; they drank from spoons and bottles; they wet their diapers. But Ben always sought more. “A child has five senses to which a doll can appeal. So far, all we’ve been able to do is make a doll that looks good, sounds good and feels good. We’re just wasting the other two senses.” For a long time, he sought to develop a doll with a “sort of built-in baby-powder odor.”

During the war, the company converted about half its factory production to making military equipment for the navy. Next to the production lines for dolls for little girls were production lines for parts for gas masks, cases for fuses, and other equipment. The company introduced military toys as well, like a plastic jeep. Its plastic toy telephone sold more than 7 million units (retail sales about $15 million). This was thought to be a record for a single toy—until Sparkle Plenty topped it.

The Postwar Toy Era

The war produced several technological advances that found uses in the burgeoning children’s market. For example, Silly Putty was the product of both ingenuity and crisis. The Japanese invasion of rubber-producing countries led to a calamitous rubber shortage for the war effort; rubber was rationed for domestic production, and Americans were urged to recycle rubber products. James Wright, a chemist at General Electric, is credited with the idea of mixing boric acid with silicone oil to create a rubber-like product. The resulting putty bounced, stretched more than rubber, and had a high melting temperature, but it turned out to be useless to replace rubber. A few years after the war, a toy store owner came across the putty and marketed it as Silly Putty, a toy that became a staple of children's lives in the early 1950s. (One property was that when spread out and pressed onto a page of newsprint—like, say a comic book—it could pick up the ink.)

Military contracting and new and innovative products enabled Ideal to weather the war years, and the company entered the postwar era stronger and more profitable. More than that, Jews weren't afraid of global trade; after all, it had been a mainstay of Jewish life for centuries. Cosmopolitanism has marketing advantages over provincialism, and American Jews didn't hold much of a grudge against the defeated and rebuilding Japanese. Some American toy companies, like Ideal, were the first ones to resume trading with Japan, and in so doing, they gained competitive advantages that others could only envy.

Baby Coos was Ideal's first big postwar hit. She was filled with foam so that she would coo by means of a clarinet reed, and her hollowed-out head served as a sounding board when she was squeezed below the neck. She was the doll sensation of 1948. Ever the booster, Ben told *The New Yorker* that he felt "just like that Greek fellow—what was his name? Ah, yes—Zaharoff, the one who used to sell munitions to both sides in a war. Here I am in Macy's with Baby Coos, who is going to be our doll of the year. And I'm also in Gimbels with Sparkle Plenty, who was our doll of last year and is still doing fine."[13]

Making Baby Coos life-size was an innovation that struck gold immediately. Orders poured in, and the doll immediately sold thirty thousand units. Some retail stores sought to boost sales by sending a doll "on approval" to every one of their customers with ongoing charge accounts. It was a sales innovation that, in the 1950s, was a huge market booster, used not only for dolls but for lab equipment and for postage stamps for stamp collectors, among other products. "What a terrible thing for these promotion men to be doing," Ben declared at a sales meeting, shaking his head ironically, knowingly. "Once you let a girl hold the doll, how are you ever going to be able to take it away?"[14]

Or boys, I suppose. Some of the dolls got boys' clothes too, which went against the idea that only little girls liked to play with dolls. Ben believed that boys would play with girl dolls that were dressed in boys' clothes but not with "boy dolls."

Since comic strips had served the company so well in the past, Ben tried to parlay some changes in comic strip characters to possibilities for dolls. In 1949 Joe Palooka, the heavyweight boxing champion comic strip character created nearly two decades earlier and syndicated in more than nine hundred newspapers nationwide, finally married his childhood sweetheart, the cheese heiress Ann Howe. The day of the ceremony (in the comic strips) Michtom called Ham Fisher, Palooka's creator. (Morris Michtom and Fisher had worked together on the Joe Palooka Bop Bag and other novelties.)

"Ham, the first child has got to be a girl," Ben told him. "Make her something unusual, something terrific. You owe it to the kids, Ham. They'll love it and she'll make a wonderful doll, maybe the best ever." Fisher wouldn't commit, but Ben was described as looking forward to the event "with the combined excitement of an expectant godfather and a gold prospector on the track of a mother lode."[15]

Ben's efforts to snag the rights to newborn babies as inspirations for dolls extended from the world of comics to real life. When Mrs. John Agar was expecting her first child, Ben let her know that he wished for a baby girl and asked if she would be amenable to a doll of mother and daughter. Mrs. Agar, you see, was Shirley Temple's married name, and as she anticipated her firstborn baby in 1948, Ben was hot on the trail. But alas, John Agar—and his well-known wife—did not approve of the idea.

In the late 1940s, a buyer called Ben with a suggestion. "How about a doll with hair that could be permanented?" The idea captivated him. Long golden tresses that could be combed, shampooed, waved—combining girls' desires to be mothers and also to enjoy going to the hairdresser or even becoming one themselves! "What's one of the most important things a mother does for her little girl?" Ben says. "Why, combing her hair and washing it and setting it, of course. And naturally the little girl wants to do those things for her doll too."

Getting the materials right provided quite a challenge. None of the materials previously used for doll wigs seemed to work. The hair would need to be able to be washed and then set. But the glue would dissolve; the hair could disintegrate. Ideal materials scientists tried several new fibers, but none of them seemed effective. Abe Katz, the materials man, suggested nylon.

Ben contacted DuPont labs and asked if it was possible. DuPont chemists were skeptical but finally agreed to try to come up with something. "That guy is the greatest salesman alive," the DuPont rep said. "By the time he got through with us, the boss was ready to put our whole laboratory on his problem." Ben was excessively modest. "All I did was point out how happy little girls will be if they could have dolls with wavable nylon hair."

And so the DuPont chemists went to work on the problem: how to create a nylon strand that would hold the curl but not for too long, so the children would be able to set the hair over and over. This task alone took months. The problem was that the nylon they created would produce too much static electricity when a comb was passed through it. Another few months passed, and the chemists came up with a superthin wax coating for each strand that could prevent the static electricity.

How would the wig be attached to a doll's head? Ordinary glues wouldn't work because they would dissolve in warm water. Ideal worked with several chemical companies that produced glues to create another binder for the doll's head, to which each strand of the hair to be individually attached.

The Toni doll, launched in 1949, used more nylon than was used in seven pairs of nylon stockings. By September 1949, there were 200,000 orders.

That's when Ben went to work. He used one of his many cruise trips to Europe to engage a dozen Parisian couturiers to design trend-setting fashions for Toni—creating, in effect, a product within a product. "I've just made arrangements with a dozen couturiers to make outfits, one each, for Toni dolls," he told the *International Herald Tribune* in 1951. "Then a dozen dolls, each in a haute couture outfit, will tour the United States, appearing in shop windows all over the country."

"Not since Madame Pompadour decreed tresses has there been such a furor in fashion," read Ideal's ad for the new doll. "Twelve Toni dolls went to Paris, and had dresses designed just for them by the world's leading designers."[16]

That same year, 1951, Ben managed a tie-in to another popular comic strip that had earlier produced a massive hit: Sparkle Plenty. Chester Gould, the artist who drew the enormously popular *Dick Tracy* comic strip, was the artist. Two characters, Gravel Gertie, a disreputable harridan, and B.O. Plenty, a ne'er-do-well, had been married for a year, and Gertie announced she was expecting a baby. Many of Tracy's 26 million readers eagerly anticipated the arrival, but few suspected she would be a cute little girl, blessed with miraculously long and beautiful yellow hair. And her hair could even be shampooed!

Bill McDuffee, a buyer for Gimbels—Ideal always had a great relationship with Gimbels—came to Ben with the cartoon and the idea: a tie-in doll that would be exclusive to Gimbels. Ben jumped at the idea. Ben licensed the character, and that July a new version of Sparkle Plenty rolled into production.

All these doll innovations shared one trait: they had curly hair. Was it deliberate, as curls were seen as stylish, and as women with straight hair often got perms to curl their hair? Or was it a subconscious connection of curly hair with Jewishness? Were all these dolls secretly Jewish girls, loved and cherished by non-Jewish girls all over the country?

The People of the (Children's) Book

On June 14, 1940, Paris awoke to the sound of someone speaking French with a thick German accent informing the city that an eight p.m. curfew was being imposed. German troops had entered Paris, marching in from the northeast, having swept through Belgium, south and west past Lille. That afternoon those same German troops marched down the Champs-Élysées, an indelible event that seemed to signal the collapse of Western civilization as we knew it.

The night before, Hans Augusto Reyersbach searched all over the city for a pair of bicycles so that he and his wife Margarete could get out of the city—and eventually the country. Hans and Margarete (née Waldstein) were Jews, originally from Hamburg, who had moved to Paris after a sojourn in Brazil to further develop their careers writing and illustrating stories for children. They sensed what was coming and could only imagine their fates. They were frantic to escape.

Every bicycle store was empty, as other Parisians had obviously had the same idea. Finally Hans bought a bunch of spare parts, wheels and handlebars, and fashioned two makeshift bikes. He and Margarete took what they could fit into their backpacks, including the preliminary drawings for a children's book character named Fifi, an impish monkey. They rode southwest out of the city, as the German troops moved in from the northeast. After a few days of riding, walking, and hopping a train, they arrived in Bayonne and crossed into Spain, bought train tickets to Lisbon, sailed to Brazil, and eventually landed in New York, where they had a contact in the publishing world.

They brought their mockup of that book about Fifi the impish monkey to their contact. She demurred—the name Fifi sounded too French, too fey, and not nearly impish enough for the monkey. They needed to rename the monkey, she said—and while they were at it, they might as well rename themselves as well. Hans and Margarete thought Reyersbach sounded too German, as the war was expanding, and Germans were becoming suspect. Perhaps it sounded a little too Jewish too. Hans Augusto Reyersbach became H. A. Rey, Margarete became Margret, and Fifi was renamed Curious George.

If Curious George is nothing else, he is a master of escapes! This imp of a chimp always seems to get himself into hilarious jams, only to end up rescuing others in the process of escaping. George unwittingly grabbed too many helium balloons and started to fly away, or he escaped some menace by riding atop a bus, then getting a job as a dishwasher (using four "hands") and a window washer, escaping yet again down a fire escape, and landing a starring role in a movie. All in one book! His madcap adventures, with his nemesis always in pursuit, invariably resolved happily.

The book was an instant hit, and at the beginning of U.S. involvement in the war, it established the Reyersbachs as mainstays of the children's book world.[17] The publication of *Curious George* heralded the explosion of children's books in the postwar era.

It feels like books for children have existed since, well, children existed. But it was only during the early twentieth century that books specifically for children became a cottage industry. In fact, children's books were a rather "late growth" in the literary field, according to C. M. Hewins, writing in *The Atlantic* in 1888.[18] Not until 1919 did a major book publisher organize a juvenile book division. The Newbery Medal was first awarded to the nation's best children's book in 1922. And *Horn Book,* a bimonthly review of children's literature, was founded two years later.

Other countries produced children's books, drawing from the same sorts of sources. In Belgium, Tintin and his mischievous dog Milou debuted in 1929. Many children's book authors lived under those same darkening skies that sent the Reys pedaling for their (and George's) lives. Felix Salten (born Siegmund Salzmann in Pest in 1869), the grandson of an Orthodox rabbi, grew up in Vienna and watched with growing anxiety as Hitler rose to power. His children's book, *Bambi: A Life in the Woods*, was published in German in 1923 as an allegory about the vulnerability of Jews to the anti-Semitism seething around him. (The English edition was published in 1928, translated by none other than Whittaker Chambers, who would later make a name for himself hounding some other Jewish leftists named Rosenberg.)

Still, in the era before the war, comic books reigned supreme. In 1940 the typical American child purchased an estimated 7.5 comic books a month—about ten times the number of children's books. "Comic books were like currency," observed the well-known children's book author Virginia Lee Burton (author of *Mike and His Steam Shovel*) in a 1941 issue of *Horn Book*. "They could be traded for toys.

They were collected like treasures. There must be a reason for it." So she read a few of them. "I soon found out that these books . . . satisfied a natural craving for excitement . . . action . . . drama; gave the children a hero to worship and as escape to thrilling adventure that is wanted by any normal child."[19]

From the beginning, as with toys, American children's books tended to be stereotypically gendered: the boy found adventure outside society while the girl found domestic bliss inside it. This was equally true of the growing world of children's magazines like *Young Knight*, *Chums*, *Grit*, *Boys' Life*, *Pioneer for Boys* for boys, and *St. Nicholas* and *Children's Playmate*, which were more gender-neutral.

Thus, boys would run away, or be orphaned, or get kidnapped, or float down the river on a raft, where their adventurous confrontation with the wild and untamed would enable them to ground their identity as men. Girls would play house, dance and dress up, hold elaborate tea parties, and wonder about marriage.

A girl's adventure tale would involve a cute and lovable creature that could be domesticated, such as *The Cat Who Went to Heaven*, *Mr. Popper's Penguins*, and *Charlotte's Web*. Stories of pioneering women (like Laura Ingalls Wilder's, *Little House on the Prairie* and *The Long Winter*) praised women's ability to create a domestic life in the wilderness. By contrast, the biographies of pioneering heroes for little boys, such as Daniel Boone, Theodore Roosevelt, and Davy Crockett, celebrated their abilities to escape domestic tranquility for the heroic life.*

---

* In the late twentieth century, many of the most successful stories for children have featured ensemble casts, with multicultural girls and boys. And many of them featured average children finding out they are special. Think of Harry Potter, Katniss Everdeen, and Percy Jackson. Harry Potter, for one, is the consummate outsider, a pint-sized Clark Kent—bespectacled, bullied, awkward around girls, and entirely unaware of his powers, of his true identity. These protagonists often have little adult help, so they are alone in the world, orphans (like Harry Potter), children of absentee parents or, worse, cruel and

In the immediate postwar years, first-generation Jews played a pivotal role in the American children's literature. While many of the era's iconic children's books, like *Babar*, *Madeline*, and *Ferdinand the Bull* were created by gentiles, even some of them had Jewish backstories. Ludwig Bemelmans, who created *Madeline*, was even said to have been anti-Semitic, though he worked with Jews on his books. Bemelmans's agent, sometimes described as his "ghost artist," was Ervine Metzl, the Chicago-born (1899) son of Jewish immigrants from Bohemia. Metzl was an American graphic artist and illustrator best known for his posters, including several still-famous posters he designed for the Chicago Transit Authority in the early 1920s, and for postage stamp designs, including commemoratives for the first World Refugee Year, the Lincoln Sesquicentennial, and the 1960 Winter Olympics.[20]

Some, like the Reys and Uri Shulevitz (the Polish-born author of *How I Learned Geography* and the graphic novel *Chance: Escape from the Holocaust*), were fleeing Nazi persecution. Some were fleeing persecution from an even earlier era. Esphyr Slobodkina was born in 1908 in Siberia, where her father was the manager of an oil company. When the Russian Revolution made their lives as Jews untenable, the family moved to Manchuria, where her father got a job with Standard Oil Company and her mother worked as a dressmaker. At nineteen, having completed high school, Esphyr made her way to New York City to join her brother and enrolled at the National Academy of Design. Margaret Wise Brown (author of the celebrated *Goodnight Moon* and *Runaway Bunny*) liked her style and asked her to illustrate her next book, *The Little Fireman*. That freed Esphyr

---

abusive parents. The kids are on their own, just like those first-generation children of immigrants, whose parents might have been stuck in the old ways, and who had no grown-ups to guide them into the new world. The search for a reliable adult, a mentor—heck, just an adult who can be trusted!—is a common theme in many children's books.

to develop her own book, *Caps for Sale* (1940), the tale of an urban peddler and a troupe of impish monkeys. It made her career, and she went on to publish about twenty more children's books.

Arnold Munk, who was born in Hungary in 1888 and moved with his family to Chicago at age three, founded the publisher Platt & Munk, of which he was president. Munk acquired the rights to a famous American story, originally delivered as a sermon in 1906 by Reverend Charles Wing entitled "The Little Engine That Thought It Could." Writing under the pen name Watty Piper, he published it as *The Little Engine That Could*, a tale of perseverance against the odds, that has rung true for every wave of immigrants ever since.

Many other children's book authors and illustrators were born in the United States to immigrant parents. Leonard Weisgard (born in New Haven in 1916) also collaborated with Margaret Wise Brown on *The Noisy Book*, and they won the Caldecott in 1947 for *The Little Island.* Eleanor Estes (Eleanor Ruth Rosenfeld) was born in 1906 in West Haven, Connecticut. Her dressmaker mother was the family provider, and many of Eleanor's stories depicted the pleasures of small-town Connecticut in the first decades of the century. Her *Ginger Pye* won the Newbery Medal in 1951.

Charlotte Zolotow (born Charlotte Gertrude Shapiro in 1915) was a writer and editor at Harper & Row, where she wrote seventy picture books for children. Louis Slobodkin (born in Albany, New York, in 1903) operated an elevator as his day job and developed a way to periodically get it "stuck" between floors so he could read philosophy on the job. He collaborated with James Thurber on *Many Moons.* Eugene Zion (born in New York City in 1913) was close friends with the Reys and created *The Dirty Dog* in part as a companion to Curious George.

Kay Thompson was as assimilationist as they come. Uninterested in merely fitting in among the burgeoning middle-classes, she made a play for the hautest of the haute bourgeoisie. Born Catherine Louise Fink in St. Louis in 1909, she was the daughter of an Austrian Jewish immigrant who made his living as a pawnbroker and a jeweler. From early childhood, she loved music and began a career as a radio singer and choral director. She moved to Hollywood as a musical arranger and then vocal coach to such stars as Judy Garland, Frank Sinatra, and Lena Horne. After a brief stint as a nightclub singer, she moved into the Plaza Hotel, where she lived until her death in 1998.

The children's book she created in 1955 chronicles the antics of a precocious six-year-old girl. Eloise, like Thompson, lives at the Plaza Hotel, on the "tippy-top floor," with her nanny, her turtle, and her dog. Thompson claimed that Eloise was her imaginary childhood friend. She heard her voice so vividly that in the animated films, she insisted on always performing the voice part of Eloise. Her emphatically WASPy accent was evident when Eloise had to take her "bawth." Not a trace of the Old World "baaaath" in that.[21]

If these children's book authors wondered whether to hide their Jewishness, they also struggled, often simultaneously, with whether they could reveal their political leanings, and if so, how much.

For example, Emma Gelders Sterne was among the first white children's book authors to try to take on the subject of racial inequality. She was born in 1894 in Birmingham, Alabama, to a German Jewish family. Her father ran a restaurant. In 1913, during her first year of college at Smith, she heard a speech by W.E.B. Du Bois about racism in America. She was shocked, stunned, and determined to do something about it. That speech, she recalled later, changed her life.

Sterne was involved in the suffrage movement, various leftist causes, and civil rights. She eventually wrote a children's biography of Du Bois, as well as children's biographies of the Mexican leader Benito Juárez and the great civil rights educator Mary McLeod Bethune. She wrote about slavery and about the *Amistad* rebellion, determined to bring these stories to children, to give them a more complete picture of their own history.

No book of hers was more influential than *Incident in Yorkville* (1943). Based on a true story, Sterne depicted the conflicted world of Nazi sympathizers in a well-known German neighborhood in New York City. (Yorkville runs between 79th and 96th Streets on the Upper East Side of Manhattan, east of Third Avenue; today it is quite a bit tonier than in the 1930s, when it was the home of the

German-American Bund, the group that organized the Nazi rally at Madison Square Garden in 1939.)

An actual historical event provided Sterne with the opportunity for a very different kind of children's book. In 1942 the FBI arrested a group of Nazi saboteurs who had landed in Long Island by U-boat with the intention of blowing up key factories, railroads, and the hydroelectric plants at Niagara Falls. What was called Operation Pastorius failed, and the entire team was captured.

Against this backdrop, Sterne describes the interactions of several families living in Yorkville. Two children, Erich (age fourteen) and Carola (age six), are already well indoctrinated into Nazism; Erich is a proud member of the Hitler Youth. The family lives in apartment 2B, directly below the Hersheys, patriotic Americans, whose son is also fourteen and goes to the same school as Erich, and a Polish boy named Stanislaus Prazmian. Stan "disgusts" Erich, who regards him as "inferior." The Hersheys are happy, warm, and loving; the Kulners (Erich and Carola's family) are cold, angry, distant, and unfeeling.

After the exposure of Operation Pastorius, it was Erich, then, who experiences a crisis of conscience. If the Nazis were infallible, how could they have been caught? And why were they sabotaging America in the first place?

While the story brought to light an important real-life incident, it also revealed some of the political allegiances of the author and of many other writers and artists. The association between Jewish writers, artists, filmmakers, and actors and the Left has been long established, and the blacklists of the 1950s prevented many from earning a living in their chosen field. The business of playmaking, it turned out, provided a safe haven and a place to find work.

7

SAFE HAVENS

* * *

The end of the war augured well for America's Jews. Nazism had been defeated in Europe, and at home, anti-Semitism seemed to be on the wane. The State of Israel was officially recognized in 1948. Overt discrimination, especially in housing, higher education, and employment, was increasingly challenged in court. Symbolically, 1945 witnessed not only the end of the war but also a milestone of Jewish cultural acceptance in America. That year Bess Myerson, a Jewish girl from the Bronx, was named Miss America.

Yet anti-Semitism remained a powerful force in American life. Jews did not experience the sort of overt racism or nativism that was directed at Blacks or Latinos or, especially after the war, Asians and Asian Americans. Anti-Semitism, rather, was more insidious, as the journalist Carey McWilliams argued, because it was generated by elites—the urban and suburban Protestants who collectively ran the American economy and government—against a group of well-educated, middle-class, upwardly mobile children of immigrants who were seeking not simply to enter the system but to rise to whatever heights their talents and motivation would take them. In short, Jews tested the promise of American upward mobility in ways that left many at the top feeling truly threatened. This anti-Semitism saw "Jews as rivals who seek to displace members of the old elite, while remaining at least somewhat resistant to assimilation."[1]

Gone, perhaps, was the overt discrimination of NO JEWS ALLOWED and newspaper advertisements for "restricted" resorts and hotels. Instead, "gentlemen's agreements" required few overt statements—only a knowing nod or handshake. Thus did Laura Z. Hobson's 1947 novel, *Gentleman's Agreement*, shock the general public, first as serialized in *Cosmopolitan* and later as a best-selling novel. When it was made into a movie, it won the Academy Award for Best Picture. The fictional story was inspired by Hobson's outrage after John E. Rankin, a long-term racist Democratic congressman from Mississippi, called the journalist Walter Winchell "the little kike," on the floor of the U.S. House of Representatives, where it was met not with censure but with applause. Just how deep and pervasive was anti-Semitism? Hobson wondered.

Hobson herself had grown up in a Jewish socialist household. The daughter of Russian Jewish immigrants—her father was a cofounder and the first editor of *The Jewish Daily Forward*—she'd risen in the publishing world and made a name for herself as a writer of short fiction. In the novel, Phil Green, a non-Jewish magazine writer, poses as a Jew, only to discover, to his surprise, just how pervasive this insidiously invisible anti-Semitism was.*

---

* In a remarkable example of life imitating art, or perhaps the other way around, the film's producer, Daryl F. Zanuck, decided to make the film after being refused membership in the Los Angeles Country Club—its board erroneously thought he was Jewish. Some Jewish film producers, including Samuel Goldwyn, urged Zanuck not to make the film, fearing it might stir up anti-Semitic feelings. After Cary Grant turned down the role, Gregory Peck was cast, despite his agent's pleas not to take the role, fearing it would hurt his career. John Garfield, who was Jewish [born Jacob Julius Garfinkle], begged

The next year Carey McWilliams documented the history of anti-Semitism in America in his landmark 1948 book, *A Mask for Privilege*, one more step in making such discrimination visible and therefore problematic. McWilliams decried the persistence of quotas limiting Jews from entering the professions (like law, medicine, and architecture), academia, and industry. He quoted a Harvard chemistry professor, Albert Sprague Coolidge, who testified before a committee of the Massachusetts legislature investigating anti-Semitism in college admissions, that "we know perfectly well that names ending in 'berg' or 'stein' have to be skipped by the board of selection of students for scholarships in chemistry" because of the "gentlemen's agreement" between the university and the chemical companies donating the scholarships.[2]

Ironically, the very success of Jewish mobility was the foundation for these undercurrents of anti-Semitism. Consider the contrast with racism against African Americans. That racism relied on a self-fulfilling prophecy that the continuing poverty of African Americans, the consequence of racism, was actually its cause. The absence of "Negro Einsteins" stemmed not from lack of opportunity, the racist argument went, but because, quite simply, there were no "Negro Einsteins."

This racist Mobius strip broke down when applied to Jews. After all, Einstein himself was Jewish. And through higher education, Jews were rising rapidly out of the working class and into the middle class—and even beyond. At the beginning of the twentieth century, 60 percent of the American Jewish workforce was concentrated in the blue-collar manufacturing sector. But following the war, these numbers changed dramatically. Between 1948 and 1953, surveys of American Jews in fourteen different communities revealed that only

---

for a role in the film because the story felt so familiar to him. In 1952, hounded by House Un-American Activities Committee, Garfield died of a heart attack at age thirty-nine.

4 percent of them still earned their livelihood through manual labor. Jews were streaming into the professions, especially law, medicine, dentistry, and education. Many non-Jews worried that Jews would "take over" by sheer competence. The speed of Jews' upward mobility made a lot of WASP elites in white-shoe law firms and investment banks very nervous.

In fact, to anti-Semites like Henry Ford, it was Jews' successful Americanization that was most threatening.[3] It was one thing to assert that Jews were outsiders—*international* and *cosmopolitan* were just different words for *outsider* and *not one of us*. After all, hadn't Haman, one of the original biblical anti-Semites, described Jews as "a people scattered abroad and dispersed among the people in all the provinces of thy kingdom?" (Esther 3:8).

But to assert that Jews were plain old Americans—this really got under the skin of older elites. This sentiment was described and analyzed in a landmark book by the Harvard psychologist Gordon Allport. In *The Nature of Prejudice* (1954), Allport allowed that Jews had been history's most convenient scapegoat and that wherever Jews went, they were the "out-group." Allport used this psychological dynamic to explain both racism and anti-Semitism, but he observed a specific self-fulfilling prophecy that underlay anti-Semitism. In the book's opening pages, he reports the following conversation with an anti-Semite:

MR. X: The trouble with the Jews is that they only take care of their own group.

MR. Y: But the record of the Community Chest campaign shows that they give more generously, in proportion to their numbers, to the general charities of the community than do non-Jews.

MR. X: That shows they are always trying to buy favor and intrude into Christian affairs. They think of nothing but money; that is why there are so many Jewish bankers.

MR. Y: But a recent study shows that the percentage of Jews in the banking business is negligible, far smaller than the percentage of non-Jews.

MR. X: That's just it; they don't go in for respectable business; they are only in the movie business or run night clubs.[4]

This singular dynamic of postwar anti-Semitism gave rise to a series of questions among Jewish psychologists and parenting experts about its effects on Jewish American children. As the Rosenbergs were denounced as Communist spies, while other Jews were condemned as infiltrators into New York City public schools—how would Jewish children grow up with a positive identity as both Jews and Americans?

Several psychologists were vitally concerned that growing up Jewish in an anti-Semitic culture was itself a type of "trauma," exacerbated because the discrimination was so subtle and covert. Experiencing anti-Semitism that was pervasive yet universally denied would drive anyone crazy, argued Nathan Ackerman and Marie Jahoda.[5]

The celebrated social psychologist Kurt Lewin was especially concerned with helping Jewish parents promote a healthy self-concept among Jewish children. Drawing on his traditional orthodox Jewish upbringing in Posen (in what is now Poland) and his ideas about what came to be called "sensitivity training," Lewin espoused a positive child-rearing philosophy, believing that a very joyous encounter with Jewishness could shield Jewish children from feelings of inferiority and self-hatred. His essay, "Bringing Up the Jewish Child," first published in 1940 in a small journal, *The Menorah Journal*, was eventually included as a chapter in his posthumous collection, *Resolving Social Conflict* in 1948, was quite influential, underscoring exactly the preciousness of the child and the importance of nurturing the natural precocity and curiosity that defined Yiddish Jews' view of childhood.[6]

In terms of politics, Yiddish Jews were, as a group, significantly to the left. Having brought their anti-tsarist politics—Bolshevik, Menshevik, and Trotskyist, not to mention anarchist and Shachtmanite—into the Lower East Side tenements, they became a major force within the labor movement, particularly in the garment industry and in education, where Jews were the chief organizers of the Teachers Union (which was Local 5 of the American Federation of Teachers).[7] In the 1930s, Jews had been among the most stalwart supporters of Roosevelt's New Deal or, in the words of some critics, the "Jew Deal." It was often said that Jews believed in three things: *die velt* (this world), *yene velt* (the world to come), and *Roosevelt*. To the Michtoms, for example, Roosevelt was such a hero that "he might as well have been Jewish," as my grandfather once said.[8] Many members of the Abraham Lincoln Brigade, who went to fight to defend the Spanish Republic in 1936, had been Jewish; indeed, many of the global International Brigades were heavily populated by Jews. (Yiddish was among the dominant languages in the foxholes.) Many more young Jewish men, like my own father, enlisted to "go kill Nazis" during the war.

Especially after the war, anti-Semitism and anti-Communism collided, converged, and connected. Communism, the new enemy, threatened American society from both without and within. The Cold War transformed the Soviet Union, America's former ally against Germany, into its chief rival for global dominance, signaled by its Stalinist purges, its dropping of the iron curtain over liberated Eastern European countries, and its suppression of the Hungarian Revolution of 1956. The USSR's support for nationalist political movements in Latin America, Asia, and Africa cemented the interwar rivalry over the Third World, while the "race for space" signaled that the competition went beyond even global boundaries.

Jews were convenient targets of postwar anti-Communist zeal. So many Communists were Jews, and so many Jews were, if not party members, at least somewhere on the Left. Leftists and Jews may have been diverse, but their circles overlapped more than those of any other matrix of religion and politics, except perhaps the Quakers. The syllogism was simple, if false: Jews were Communists, Communists were Jews.

I experienced this conflation of politics and religion—along with sexuality—in 1965, when, as a fourteen-year-old, I attended my first march against the war in Vietnam. It was a small march, early in the war, and we marchers were matched by an equal number of hecklers scattered along the sidewalks. If I remember correctly, I carried a sign that said U.S. OUT OF VIETNAM or something equally innocuous. "Go back to Russia!" shouted one of the hecklers. Being only fourteen, precocious and foolish, I thought the right strategy was to engage. "Protest is American!" I shouted back. "It's the essence of democracy." I thought that would settle the matter. "Fuck you, you Commie, Jew, faggot!" was his reply.

Today, at an advanced age, it would be easy for me to say "Sorry, pal, only one out of three!" but I confess, at the time I was shaken by the heckler's easy conflation of politics, religion, and sexuality. This was, in effect, the legacy I inherited from the 1950s, the notion that each of the three identities—Jew, Leftist, homosexual—was somehow alien, other, and certainly not attributable to a "real man."

In the early 1950s, even as formal barriers to Jewish assimilation were gradually lowered, political fears made clear that Jews were "outside insiders." They'd been admitted, but they were still alien. And they were also "inside outsiders"—they'd gotten closer to the center of wealth and power of any other marginalized group. That made their position unstable, precarious, and vulnerable.

It was one way to understand the dilemma of American Jewry: The harder they worked to gain full acceptance into the mainstream of American society, the more they were reminded that they didn't really belong. Yet whenever Jews identified with other marginalized groups, out of their own marginalization, they seemed to be reminded they had already made it and were not really "others" either. Inside the mainstream they were seen as outsiders; outside the mainstream, they were seen as insiders.

The association between Jews and the Left illustrates this dual identity, which the trial and execution of the Rosenbergs—and the intrigues among the other Jewish collaborators and conspirators—seemed only to confirm. This link was reaffirmed in an extraordinary CIA memo from January 1953 (two months before their execution), uncovered by the historian Blanche Wiesen Cook, in which the Rosenbergs were offered the commutation of their sentences if the couple would agree to "appeal to Jews in all countries to get out of the communist movement and seek to destroy it." The "advantages" of this scheme, the memo continued, could "scarcely be overstated from a psychological warfare standpoint."[9]

That didn't materialize. The combination of their deaths, the news of Stalin's crimes, and the brutal repression of Hungary's rebellion in 1956, coupled with the repressive campaigns against the Left at home, drove thousands of Jews into safer suburban burrows, where they believed they could hide. In the frenzied witch hunt of the McCarthy era, though, you might try to hide, but you couldn't necessarily escape your past, however fabricated that past might have been and no matter what damage your persecution would do to the ideals of free speech and constitutional rights.

McCarthyism was especially hard on Jews. The House Un-American Activities Committee (HUAC) and the Senate hearings chaired by Wisconsin senator Joseph McCarthy specifically targeted them. Carey McWilliams wrote that McCarthyism "oozed anti-Semitic innuendos, even though McCarthy himself had Jewish myrmidons, Roy Cohn the most notorious." While some assimilated Jews may have believed they no longer had to hide their Jewishness, just their politics, it was clear to others that "Cold War anti-Communism was inseparable from Cold War anti-Semitism."[10]

Take, for example, the smarmy delight taken by Representative John Rankin—the Mississippi congressman who had called Walter Winchell "that little kike" on the House floor—as he revealed the "real names" of various Hollywood figures—not Communists, but merely liberals—who had signed a petition criticizing HUAC's encroachment on the First Amendment:

> One of the names is June Havoc. We found out from the motion-picture almanac that her real name is June Hovick. Another one was Danny Kaye, and we found out that his real name was David Daniel Kaminsky. Another one here is John Beal, whose real name is J. Alexander Bliedung. Another one is Cy Bartlett, whose real name is

> Sacha Baraniev. Another one is Eddie Cantor, whose real name is Edward Iskowitz. There is one who calls himself Edward Robinson. His real name is Emmanuel Goldenberg. There is another one here who calls himself Melvyn Douglas, whose real name is Melvyn Hesselberg.[11]

It became something of a parlor game: Uncover the Jew! George Burns? Nathan Birnbaum. Lauren Bacall? Betty Perske. Kirk Douglas? Issur Danielovitch Demsky. Tony Curtis? Bernard Schwartz. Woody Allen? Allen Konigsberg. The list feels endless.

McCarthyism's very public persecution of Hollywood leftists and others led thousands to leave the party. Some drifted rightward, while others remained in the non-Communist Left. Many found a new home in the emerging civil rights movement, recognizing racial inequality as somehow akin to anti-Semitism. (Unsurprisingly, many of Nelson Mandela's white comrades in the African National Congress were Jewish, such as Joe Slovo, as was Martin Luther King, Jr.'s, closest white adviser, Stanley Levison.)

But changing one's politics didn't help—the damage had been done. Jews disappeared as creators—as writers, directors, producers—and also as characters. Beginning in 1954, not one prime-time show on network television featured a leading character who was clearly identified as Jewish.[12]

The Hollywood blacklists and the Army-McCarthy hearings had received most of the headlines, offering up the juiciest Hollywood stars for ceremonial degradation. But McCarthyism, the general political campaign to root out Communists from every profession, had a far greater impact elsewhere, especially in education, from public schools to colleges and universities. To say that McCarthyism had a "chilling effect" on free speech and the expression of political dissent would be an understatement. Many educators were summarily frozen out of the world they had earlier known.

Worst hit, perhaps, were public school teachers in New York City, where the general search for a Communist under every bed—and in front of every blackboard—reached a crescendo.

Teaching had become a popular profession for first- and second-generation Jews, the children and grandchildren of the Yiddish-speaking immigrants. Teaching was a major rung on the ladder of upward mobility. Increasingly educated and therefore no longer limited to work in the trades, Jews moved into white-collar professions such as teaching and writing, and many became involved in unionizing these industries, just as they had the garment industry.

The Teachers Union was especially progressive in the era before teaching was routinely unionized.[13] In 1949 the state of New York passed the Feinberg Law, which permitted the investigation of any public school teacher, and the dismissal of anyone who engaged in "treasonable or seditious acts or utterances" or joined any organization that advocated the overthrow of the government by "force, violence or any unlawful means." The Feinberg Law became the Cold War model of a loyalty oath.

New York wasn't atypical; many other states were either adopting or considering such laws, especially as the Truman administration was eager to prove it was tough on Communism. The New York State Board of Regents created a list of organizations it considered subversive, then deemed membership in any of them prima facie evidence of subversion and as justification for the firing of any public school employee.

Between 1949 and 1958, more than eleven hundred teachers were investigated, and according to *The New York Times*, 378 were dismissed or terminated their services, some by resignation.[14] Jews were frequent targets within these fields. According to the American Social History Project, "some 90 percent of the teachers "blacklisted" from working in the public schools in this period due to their alleged subversive activities were Jewish."[15]

Just as Senator McCarthy had Roy Cohn, a Jewish henchman whose presence served to deflect the charge of anti-Semitism, so did New York City superintendent of schools William Jansen have Saul Moskoff, an attorney in the city's law office. Moskoff frequently used Jewishness to frame his interrogations. During one interrogation, for example, the science teacher Maurice Kurzman took Moskoff to

The first eight teachers fired by the New York City Board of Education. From *left*: Alice Citron, Abraham Feingold, David Friedman, Celia Zitron, Abraham Lederman, Mark Friedlander, Isadore Rubin, Louis Jaffe. (Tamiment Library & Robert F. Wagner Labor Archives, NYU Special Collections, New York University)

task for essentially doing the work of anti-Semitism. Kurzman called the entire process "an attempt to impose thought control upon our school system," and noted that among Jews especially, procuring and informing were considered "the vilest, the very basest . . . the most depraved, the most anti-Jewish conduct in the book."

"You had better study the Talmud," Moskoff replied.

"I have studied the Talmud," said Kurzman. "You are following the same pattern which is becoming so popular now wherein the enemies of the people use willing and compliant Jews to do their hatchet work for them."[16]

A Refuge from the Blacklist

Where could they go, these teachers and educators and writers who were hounded out of their jobs by the anti-Communist hysteria that was sweeping the nation? Many found refuge in the world of children. Some teachers who had lost their jobs for political reasons realized they could reach children in a different way—by writing children's books. Celebrated children's book authors who had been blacklisted included Franklin Folsom, Langston Hughes, Dorothy Sterling, Louis Hartman, Priscilla Hiss (the wife of Alger Hiss, who became an editor at Golden Books), and Meridel Le Soeur. In general, many children's book authors in the 1950s were sympathetic with or even identified with the Left.

Children's books were a "freer market" than adult books, and they were a safer space, as children's book authors suffered "far less" than Hollywood screenwriters, novelists, and playwrights. Some children's book authors just hid out, hoping to make a living while riding out the waves of repression. Others found their calling.[17]

Perhaps no one story captures this trajectory better than that of Irving Adler. Born in 1913 to immigrant parents on the Lower East Side, Adler was an early math prodigy, entering high school at eleven and starting at City College at fourteen. At eighteen, he began a thirty-year career teaching math and science in the New York City public schools—a career cut short by his moment in the political spotlight.

Adler was a lifelong leftist; he had joined the Communist Party in 1935. In 1951, as chair of the math department at Straubenmuller Textile High School in New York City, he was subpoenaed to testify before the Senate subcommittee investigating Communist influence in the nation's schools. He refused to answer the committee's questions, citing his Fifth Amendment rights. He was immediately fired, along with more than 378 other teachers in New York City alone, all subject to the state's Feinberg Law.

Adler became the lead plaintiff (the list was composed alphabetically) as several of the fired teachers sued the Board of Education. The case moved rapidly through the courts until it landed at the U.S. Supreme Court. In *Adler v. Board of Education*, the Court ruled 6–3 that there was nothing unconstitutional in the Feinberg Law; that teachers had no "right" to their jobs; and that because they worked "in a sensitive area" where they shaped young minds, the interrogation of their political beliefs was not out of bounds.

Justice William O. Douglas wrote a ringing dissent, joined by Hugo Black and Felix Frankfurter, chastising the court for engaging in "guilt by association." The ruling, they warned, would turn America's schools into a "spying project" and cast "a pall" over the nation's classrooms. The case riveted the world of education, terrifying two generations of public school teachers, including professors at public universities. In 1967 it would finally be reversed in a case brought by a fired SUNY Buffalo professor. In that opinion, Justice William Brennan borrowed that same phrase, "guilt by association." Dozens of teachers who had been fired would be reinstated, and Adler would begin to receive his New York City employee pension in 1977.

Meanwhile, deprived of his livelihood in public education, Adler pursued higher education and received a Ph.D. in mathematics from Columbia in 1961. Unable to find a university teaching job, he turned to writing children's books and became perhaps the nation's best-known writer of science and math books for children. Like the gifted teacher he had been, these books explained scientific discoveries and phenomena in language that children found not only accessible but also entertaining. As he wrote in the opening pages of his first book, *The Secret of Light* (1952), "Part of this story sounds like a fairy tale. But the wonders it describes are all true. This does not make the story any less exciting, for there is no adventure more thrilling than discovering the real wonders of the world we live in."

Some of his books explained the importance of a single phenomenon, like *Fire in Your Life* (1955), *Time in Your Life* (1955), and *Electricity in Your Life* (1965). Others were titled simply *Air* (1962), *Storms* (1963), or *Oceans* (1962). One of his best-known books was the oversize coffee-table book *The Giant Golden Book of Mathematics: Exploring the World of Numbers and Space* (1960), a work that was, perhaps, my favorite tenth-birthday present.[18]

Likewise, Sarah Riedman was fired from the biology department at Brooklyn College after she refused to answer the questions from the Senate Internal Security Committee (SISS). She too started writing science books for children, and by 1983 she had authored or coauthored more than forty of them, occasionally reminding her readers, in the course of recounting the careers of groundbreaking scientists, that "questioning and nonconformity [are] attitudes of mind worth cultivating." But as the historian Marjorie Heins reminds us, Riedman's academic career was over: she never gained university-level employment and remained a freelance scientific writer, then became director of medical literature for a drug and medical supply company.[19]

For others, the world of children's books was a refuge where the vulnerable might find a place. In the 1950s Ruth Krauss, along with her husband, Crockett Johnson, became the "it couple" of children's literature. Krauss was born in Baltimore in 1901 to a relatively prosperous Jewish family. Her grandparents had been among the first wave of German Jewish immigrants in the mid-nineteenth century, and by the time Ruth was born, her community was well established. Although she was sickly as a child (and bedridden for several months), she was artistically precocious. By the early 1930s, she was living in New York, a Parsons graduate, looking for a job.

Following a tumultuous and brief first marriage, Krauss signed up as a research assistant with Columbia University anthropologist Ruth Benedict and trooped off on an expedition to study the Blackfoot nation in Montana. Now fully immersed in the cultural life of the liberal, and largely Jewish, Left in New York, she met the young artist Crockett Johnson at a party. Born David Leisk, Johnson was a cartoonist for and other publications and was at the time working on a comic strip character named Barnaby. They married in 1943.

Krauss hit it big, first in 1945, with *The Carrot Seed*, a sweet book about a little boy who believes his carrot will eventually sprout, even though everyone else says it won't. Johnson waited another decade before his signature book, *Harold and the Purple Crayon*, became a bestseller. In between, they spent a lot of time fending off investigations as suspected Communists. As Ruth was working on a new children's book, she met a twenty-three-year-old artist who was making a living designing window displays at FAO Schwarz. His name was Maurice Sendak, and together they produced *A Hole Is to Dig* in 1952.

It took off. *The New York Times Book Review*'s Ellen Lewis Buell thought it "a unique book" that would "set children thinking"; she found Sendak's drawings "bouncing with action and good humor." The *Horn Book* praised *A Hole Is to Dig* as "original in approach and content" and thought its illustrations "perfect." The *San Francisco Chronicle* called it "that rare and wonderful [children's book] that is genuinely original and imaginative."[20]

That book launched Sendak's career, largely because Krauss had refused to follow the industry protocol to pay Sendak for the illustrations on a piecemeal basis. Instead, she insisted that the art was as important as the story, and so Maurice shared the royalties. This, in turn, meant he finally had enough money to quit his job and become a full-time illustrator. By the end of the 1950s, he had illustrated seven more of Krauss's books.

Johnson and Krauss became Sendak's surrogate parents. Although he was still living at home with his actual parents, Sendak spent every weekend with Ruth and Crockett at their home in suburban Connecticut, where he was finally able to explore both his Jewishness and his homosexuality.

Like Sendak, another children's book author, Sydney Taylor, had always felt marginal. Born Sarah Brenner in New York City in 1904 to Jewish immigrant parents, Taylor never fully felt that she fit in, that she was fully included in the story. She was embedded in the Left, and her social life revolved around the Young People's Socialist League, the youth arm of the Socialist Party. She was somewhat gender nonconforming—while she married and had children, she felt uncomfortable and almost fraudulent within the confines of traditional femininity, and she discarded her birth name for Sydney.

Though she was surrounded by Jewish writers and progressive intellectuals, there seemed to be no children's books about identifiably Jewish characters. It felt as if the unspoken strategy of assimilation for Jewish writers required hiding their ethnicity.[21]

Taylor's daughter changed all that. One day she asked, "Mommy, why is it that every time I read a book about children, it is always a Christian child? Why isn't there a book about a Jewish child?"[22]

Taylor's response was to write *All-of-a-Kind Family*, published in 1951, the first book from a mainstream publisher to feature Jewish children and reach a sizable mainstream general audience. It went on to become a five-book series, chronicling the adventures of five Jewish sisters (and eventually their one brother), daughters of a Lower East Side junk shop owner and his extremely clever and resourceful homemaker wife. It was sort of a Jewish version of *Little Women*, based closely on Taylor's own childhood. The girls' names were the names of Sydney's real sisters: Ella, Henny, Gertrude, Charlotte, and Sarah (Sydney's birth name).

All-of-a-Kind Family represented a new assimilationist strategy for children's book writers. Instead of hiding their ethnicity behind a bland, generic small-town-America backdrop, the series embraced the children's ethnicity as distinctly American. The books are about "*being* Jewish," writes Taylor's biographer, June Cummins, but "they are also about *becoming* American."[23]

It was a claim for assimilation through recognizing difference rather than hiding it, an ironic move for leftist Jews who were trying to hide out from anti-Communist witch-hunters and would-be moralizing censors. In 1952, just a year after Taylor launched her *All-of-a-Kind Family* series, the novelist Howard Fast also published a children's book. Born in 1914 in Brooklyn to religious Jewish immigrant parents (his mother was from Britain and his father was from Ukraine), by the 1930s, Fast was already a well-known figure in leftist literary circles.

In 1950, when a congressional committee was investigating Communist contributors to a home for orphans of Spanish Civil War veterans, Fast refused to name names, for which he was imprisoned. Blacklisted, he was unable to find work. Mainstream publishers avoided him. His 1951 eyewitness account of the riots that had erupted in Peekskill, New York, when the acclaimed singer and actor Paul Robeson was scheduled to perform concerts sponsored by leftist and civil rights groups, was widely distributed by the Civil Rights Congress. In response to his imprisonment, Fast could not find a commercial publisher for his most famous novel, so he self-published *Spartacus*, the heroic tale of a gladiator who leads a slave revolt in ancient Rome, in 1951, in part as a response to his imprisonment. (The 1960 film, produced by and starring Kirk Douglas and directed by Stanley Kubrick, was written by Dalton Trumbo, another blacklisted Hollywood writer.)

In 1952, needing money, Fast wrote a children's book, *Tony and the Wonderful Door*. It tells the story of one Tony MacTavish Levy—from an ethnic hodgepodge of Italian, Irish, and Jewish background and a working-class family. Tony can't be pigeonholed into a singular identity; he's more even than the sum of all three identities. As Fast puts it, his "real national origin" was "Brooklyn." One didn't find the "real" America in the small towns of the hinterland: Brooklyn was "the source."

Syd Hoff, too, had been a professional artist and a dedicated leftist. Born in 1912 in the Bronx to a ladies' garment salesman father and housewife mother, he had published cartoons in *The Daily Worker* and the *New Masses* under the name A. Redfield (get it?). Hoff made his living writing and illustrating more than sixty volumes of the *I Can Read* series for HarperCollins. And over the years he drew more than five hundred cartoons for *The New Yorker*. He, too, found solace in the world of children's books, the best known of which was *Danny and the Dinosaur* (1958), a fetching tale of a young boy's play date with a dinosaur—it sold more than 10 million copies. In another book, *Sammy the Seal* (1959), a seal escapes from the zoo, only to find himself in an elementary school where, after some fun adventures with the kids, he soon discovers that, like Dorothy, although the grass might seem greener, there's no place like home.

Anti-Semitism may have played a role in the trajectory of another beloved children's book author—and he wasn't even Jewish! As an undergrad at Dartmouth, young Ted Geisel was rejected from pledging by several fraternities because they believed him to be Jewish, based on his name and his prominent nose. So Geisel, the non-frat goy, retreated to the campus humor magazine, where he found a home. The children's literature historian Philip Nel credits this experience of misplaced anti-Semitism as an inspiration for the future Dr. Seuss to write such anti-prejudice fables as *The Sneetches* and *Horton Hears a Who!*[24]

To appropriate the old Levy's Rye Bread commercial, "you don't have to have been Jewish" to write children's books, but it sure gave a lot of Jews who needed protection a safe place to land.

The Great Comics Panic

Comic books had consistently provided another such safe haven for many aspiring writers and artists. It was, as the great comic book impresario Will Eisner put it, the "lowest rung" on the publishing ladder. Al Jaffee, who drew cartoons and comics for *Mad* magazine and other venues well into his nineties, told the author Arie Kaplan that he hadn't "want[ed]" to go into the comics industry: "The pay was lousy, you weren't treated very well, you were exploited, you didn't even own your own work." But he couldn't get a job anywhere else. Born Abraham Jaffee in Savannah, he was an easy target for bullies—not because they thought he was Jewish, but because the name "Abraham" reminded the locals of Abraham Lincoln, who was not exactly beloved in the post-Reconstruction South. (Jaffee was born in 1921.) "There was a tremendous amount of anti-Semitic bigotry," he recalled to Kaplan. Newspapers, advertising agencies, and slick magazines all "had an unwritten policy that no Jews need apply." Every time he did apply at an ad agency, they'd ask about his name, and after he told them, they'd ask if he was Jewish. Then they'd tell him the agency had already reached its quota of Jews.[25]

Earlier artists and writers had produced comic books because the traditional fields of art and advertising were closed to them, but by the early 1950s, it had become another way to remain out of the political fray. In the postwar years, the comic book industry exploded. In 1947 one out of every three periodicals sold in America was a comic book. Monthly sales ballooned from 18 million to 60 million. On military post exchanges, comic books outsold *Life, Reader's Digest,* and *The Saturday Evening Post* by ten to one. By 1952, more than twenty publishers were producing more than 650 different titles per month. Indeed, "the comic book was the most popular form of entertainment in America," writes David Hajdu, "reaching more people than movies, television, radio, or magazines for adults."[26]

But such popularity also produced its detractors. We may today remember the 1950s as a time of placid normality, of genial conformity, but dissatisfaction was already rumbling. Beneath the manicured lawns of suburbia lay the gnawing ennui among men "in the grey flannel suit" who took the 7:42 from Greenwich or Scarsdale or Great Neck every morning. Sociologists wrote of the loss of identity in "mass society," while warning that the sudden rise in juvenile delinquency was an outgrowth of the affluence that left people feeling empty.

Social science in the 1950s was preoccupied with "deviance," almost as if things had gotten so good, life so satisfying, that it was hard to understand how anyone would want to break the rules that made us so comfortable. Albert Cohen's *Delinquent Boys: The Culture of the Gang* (1955) linked delinquency to "masculine protest," by which "engaging in 'bad' behavior acquires the function of denying his femininity and therefore asserting his masculinity." Being bad was good—if your manhood was in question.[27]

And being good was "bad." Cohen's book appeared the same year as the films *Blackboard Jungle* (directed by Richard Brooks, born Reuben Sax to Russian Jewish immigrants in 1912) and *Rebel Without a Cause.* Written by first-generation Jews Stewart Stern and Irving Shulman, produced by David Weisbart, and edited by William Ziegler, *Rebel* launched James Dean's career playing a middle-class suburban teenager, contemptuous of his "good" but weak and ineffectual father, desperate for a male role model. In that film's pivotal scene, Jim Stark (Dean) confronts his father Frank (Jim Backus) in the kitchen, while Frank is wearing an apron, doing the dishes. Obviously, he would be of little help to a young rebel seeking to find his way to manhood.

What could be causing this malaise, this descent into degeneracy? According to the New York psychiatrist Fredric Wertham, the answer was clear: comic books! Wertham's mission was to discredit comic books as a scourge that was eroding American society from within, nearly single-handedly destroying literacy, luring children to violence and delinquency, and even promoting homosexuality.[28]

On this mission, he had plenty of company. Sterling North, the snobbish literary editor of *The Chicago Daily News*, called comics "a poisonous mushroom growth," the "cultural slaughter of the innocents." *The Catholic World* sneered that comics represented the "frivolous offspring of yellow journalism." In a 1948 radio broadcast, the drama critic John Mason Brown called comic books "the marijuana of the nursery, the bane of the bassinet, the horror of the house; the curse of the kids; and a threat to the future." That same year the National Institute of Municipal Law Officers expressed its concern that comics "tend to incite juvenile delinquency."[29]

To be sure, comic books had their defenders. Some argued that they promoted literacy: the number of different words used was greater than the vocabulary of the average fifth-grader, noted Sidonie Gruenberg, director of the Child Study Association of America (whom we met in Chapter 3). Kids were reading, noted Catherine Mackenzie in *The New York Times*, and they were buying the comics with money they saved up themselves. Instead of comics being a poor substitute for "real" books, it turned out that kids who read comics were actually more likely to read real books. Child psychologists pointed out that the stories themselves were valuable; they were the "folklore of our times," wrote the psychologists Lauretta Bender and Reginald Lourie, "serving at the same time as a means of helping [young people] solve the individual and sociological problems appropriate to their own lives."[30]

For his part, Wertham seemed the very model of professional probity. The chief of the mental hygiene clinic at Queens General Hospital, he was of German Jewish origin (his given name was Frederich Ignatz Wertheimer) and was a regular contributor and book reviewer at *The New Republic*. In the beginning of his career, he had treated Black patients in Baltimore when other doctors had refused to do so. But now he had a new empirical finding: Many of the men he was treating at the hospital, and many of the boys who were arrested as juvenile delinquents, shared a common characteristic—they read comic books. In this respect, Wertham fell easily into the trap that has ensnared so many psychiatrists seeking to explain deviance: His sample was almost entirely drawn from psychiatric patients. In this case, the patients blamed comic books for their emotional problems. From this evidence, Wertham declared that comic books were a "leading cause of juvenile delinquency."[31]

It was a masterpiece of bad sampling. Instead of looking at comic book readers to see if the percentage of delinquents among them was higher than in a sample of non-comic-book readers, Wertham reasoned backward and used a sample of delinquents to find that many read comic books.

Initially, Wertham trained his attention on "crime comics," eliding his critique of delinquency with the generally misanthropic forebodings found in noir crime fiction. But he soon expanded his critique to include superhero comics. He even went so far as to claim that comic books were "fascist," which was pretty ironic, given that the entire comic book universe seemed to be composed of Jewish writers and artists, creating characters who were fighting for America against the fascists.

In March 1948 Wertham organized a symposium on comic books, sponsored by the Society for the Advancement of Psychotherapy, at the New York Academy of Medicine. All the speakers condemned comic books, grabbing the trendiest ideas in psychotherapy—they were unhealthy escape mechanisms, or they arrested development, encouraged primal instincts over civilization, and taught children that violence was the best way to solve social problems.[32]

That same year Wertham presented his ideas about the link between comic books and delinquency to the annual conference of the American Prison Association. He listed seven ways that comic books could affect children:

1. Comic books may suggest criminal or sexually abnormal ideas.
2. They create a mental preparedness or readiness for temptation.

3. They suggest the forms that a delinquent impulse may take and supply details of the latest techniques for its execution.
4. They may tip the scales in the behavior of an otherwise normal child and act as the precipitating factor of delinquency or emotional disorder.
5. They supply the rationalization for a contemplated act that is often more important than the impulse itself.
6. They set off a chain of undesirable and harmful thinking.
7. They create for the child an atmosphere of deceit, trickery, and cruelty.[33]

In 1954 Wertham's book *Seduction of the Innocent* shot to the top of the bestseller list, peddling a moral panic about comic books that led to public denunciations, comic book burnings, and a fear that the peaceful affluence of American's suburbs and small towns were somehow vulnerable to infiltration by morally and sexually pernicious ideas. That such a moral panic was driven, in such large part, by the most cosmopolitan of elites is but one of the many ironies that characterized the great comic book wars of 1954.

Seduction of the Innocent provided exactly the ammunition that Tennessee senator Estes Kefauver needed to launch a series of hearings about juvenile delinquency. Having run unsuccessfully in 1952 as the vice-presidential nominee on Adlai Stevenson's Democratic presidential ticket, and with presidential aspirations of his own, Kefauver initiated a series of hearings in the Senate Subcommittee on Juvenile Delinquency. Hoping to achieve celebrity but not the notoriety of the McCarthy hearings, Kefauver shone a spotlight on juvenile delinquency as a national problem. He surveyed the elements of youth culture to try to ascertain its cause. Like "Professor" Harold Hill's fictional crediting of billiard parlors as the source of teen malaise in the hit musical *The Music Man*, Kefauver sought to blame youth culture itself and the adults who manipulated those young minds.

Wertham provided just the sort of pseudo-scientific veneer he needed to make his case.

Just as McCarthy had his Roy Cohn, and as William Jansen and the Communist-hunting teachers' investigators had their Saul Moskoff, Kefauver had Fredric Wertham—another Jewish "other" who would obviously have some greater familiarity with the darker forces that were oozing below the surface of civil society.

For his part, Wertham also linked comic books to homosexuality, not necessarily as a cause but as a vehicle for the "normalization" of deviance and the promotion of mental illness. Wonder Woman, he claimed, was clearly lesbian, "a cruel 'phallic' woman" who is "a frightening figure for boys" and "an undesirable ideal for girls, being the exact opposite of what girls are supposed to want to be." With Robin, Batman was "psychologically homosexual," and their relationship represented "a wish dream of two homosexuals living together" in a "subtle atmosphere of homoerotism."[34]

In the early 1950s, psychiatrists were suggesting that homosexuality was the result of overdominant mothers and absent fathers, who rendered the young boy unable to complete the oedipal task of repudiating the mother and identifying with the father. Similarly, they theorized that delinquency was also caused by the presence of overdominant mothers and the absence of strong masculine role models with whom young boys could identify. Instead, boys fantasized about the powerful masculinity of the superhero.

Unlike Roy Cohn, Wertham was a political liberal: The attack on the corrupting influence of comic books was joined on both the political Right and the Left. On the Right were the forces of decency seeking to curtail sexual freedom, promiscuity, and the general disregard for morality that the amoral noir crime comic celebrated. On the Left were those who felt that comic books siphoned off the rebellious energies of youth, channeling what might otherwise be mobilized toward political progressivism into cheap satisfactions. In tones that anticipated the Frankfurt School's critique of jazz, Albert Kahn's *Game of Death* (1953) railed against the corrupting power of comic books:

> The overwhelming majority of comic books are macabre compendiums of mayhem and murder, perverted sex and sadism, weird and ghastly adventures, crime, brutality and bloodcurdling horror. Crudely drawn in garish colors, cheaply printed in magazine form on pulp paper and sold for ten cents apiece, these publications pour an unending torrent of filth and bestiality into the minds of American children. They depict human beings as fiendish degenerates, glamorize the lynch-justice heroics of muscle-bound "supermen," exalt the use of force and violence, and make of agonized death a casual, everyday affair.[35]

Echoing this view was Gershon Legman, a marginal character who wrote obsessively, penning hundreds of essays and pamphlets, and always seemed to show up at psychoanalytic conferences. (Later in his life, Legman would be known as a compiler and editor of erotica.) But when it came to comic books, he was as lurid as he was certain about the harmful effects of reading them:

> The effect, if not the intention, has been to raise up an entire generation of adolescents—twenty million of them—who have felt, thousands upon thousands of times, all the sensations and emotions of committing murder, except pulling the trigger. And toy guns, advertised in the back pages of the comics—cap-shooters, bb rifles . . . paralysis pistols, crank'em up tommy guns, six-inch cannon crackers, and rayguns emitting a spark a foot and a half long—have supplied that.[36]

All these critics were first-generation Jews, aware that Jews had been widely accused of degeneracy and the corruption of youth. As Jews, their project was assimilationist, to carry the banner of decency against the poorer, striving Jewish alien arrivistes. They could cement their status as "accepted" if they could portray the other as alien.

But these adults—experts, therapists, scholars all—had only the most superficial and literal interpretation of comics, and only the most mechanistic understanding of their impact on young people: Pavlovian. Monkey see, monkey do. Entirely without nuance, or any agency on the part of the viewer. The kid sees the violence in the comic book and immediately fantasizes about committing it.

But most children reading a comic book about X-ray vision and or leaping over tall buildings don't immediately think it's a good idea to cut school, start smoking, and buy a switchblade, let alone to try leaping over buildings. Just as most worshippers at synagogues and churches don't read the stories of Joshua and then march around their workplaces hoping the walls will fall down so they can slaughter all their workmates, or gang-rape a man's mistress instead of the man himself (Judges 19:25), or boil one's child for others to nibble (2 Kings 6:28–29), or use a primitive circumcision as punishment (Exodus 4:24–25). Most kids would have resonated more with the comedian Jerry Lewis's utterly sarcastic putdown of the entire comic book moral panic. (Lewis was born Joseph Levitch in Newark in 1926 to a Jewish family.) When asked about reading crime and horror comics, Lewis exclaimed, "That's how I got to be a moron."[37]

In his lively and fascinating book about the Kefauver hearings, David Hajdu argues that the hearings were "neither a subset of the Red Scare nor a direct parallel to it." McCarthyism was "a movement out of the heartland to purge the country of modes of thinking associated with the Northeastern intelligentsia and the New Deal," he writes, while the sentiment against comics was the "near opposite, despite the urban New York origin of its target; it was a kind of anti-elitism, a campaign by protectors of rarefied ideals of literacy, sophistication, and virtue to rein in the practitioners of a wild, homegrown form of vernacular expression."[38]

What linked these otherwise disparate efforts was their anti-Semitism. Both were driven by a sense of threat from forces within—dark, menacing, wild; moreover, in both cases those who called for stopping this pernicious challenge cast themselves as the preservers of American morality. The link is that both threats were propelled by

Jews—the perpetual "other," whether as cosmopolitan elites rejecting the heartland's anti-Communist values, or as "degenerate" corrupters of youth outside elite high culture. Either way, Jews were not "real Americans"; their values were imported, alien, corrupt. The Red Scare and the anti-comic-book hysteria were born of the same anti-Semitic family; they were perhaps cousins if not siblings.

An editorial in *The Hartford Courant* referred to comics as "the filthy stream that flows from the gold plated sewers of New York"—a barely concealed dog whistle synonym for "Jewish businesses." After the humor comic *Panic* ran a spoof of the holiday poem "A Visit from St. Nicholas," the attorney general of Massachusetts called for banning the publication, declaring that it was "desecrating Christmas"—as though it were part of an early "war on Christmas." New York police seized and quarantined the issues of *Panic*. The publisher went to court and won their release. As the historian James Gilbert notes:

> For many Americans, mass culture in this equation solved the mystery of delinquency. It was an outside force guided from media centers in New York and Hollywood. It affected all classes of children. It penetrated the home. And it appeared to promote values contrary to those of many parents. It seemed, in other words, to be the catalyst that provoked generational conflict.[39]

Suburban families who worried about all those rebels without a cause had finally found the cause.

The Kefauver hearings were brutal for the comic book industry. A parade of experts testified about the ill effects of comic books on children. Representing the comic books industry was William Gaines, son of Max Gaines, the legendary founder and publisher of EC Comics. Max had been one of the major midwives of the American comic book. At All-American Comics, he had brought such characters as Wonder Woman and Green Lantern to the world. At EC Comics, his son Bill assembled an amazing team of irreverent guys like Al Feldstein, Harvey Kurtzman, and Wally Wood. They had a taste for the macabre, for the darkness of crime noir, and as far as they were concerned, the gorier the better. EC Comics produced such series as *Tales from the Crypt*, *Crime Suspense Stories*, and *Weird Science*.

Cocky and self-assured but also woefully unprepared to testify before the Kefauver committee, Bill Gaines replied nonchalantly to questions that he barely seemed to take seriously.*When Herbert Hannoch, chief counsel to the committee, asked Gaines "You think it does them a lot of good to read these things?" Gaines replied, "I don't think it does them a bit of good. But I don't think it does them a bit of harm either."[40] "It was so unfair," said the *Mad* cartoonist Drew Friedman. "They portrayed him as some slovenly Jewish pornographer."[41] The link between Jewishness and degeneracy was well established in the minds of those who embraced those anti-Semitic tropes.

Today Gaines's testimony is considered to have been a disaster for the industry, but it also rehearsed early-twentieth-century debates about the nature of childhood itself. In his testimony, Gaines faulted Wertham's view that children were "innocent" as fraudulent, unless by "innocent" he meant that they were impressionable sponges incapable of understanding the difference between reality and fantasy, between blood and ketchup.

Gaines made the more progressive case that comic books didn't substitute for literature but instead were a pathway toward it, and a respite from children's often-humdrum lives. "It has weaned hundreds of thousands of children from pictures to the printed word," he testified. "It has stirred their imagination, given them an outlet for their problems and frustrations, but most important, given them millions of hours of entertainment."[42]

Gaines then made the "free speech" case, quoting federal judge John Woolsey who lifted the ban on James Joyce's *Ulysses*: "It is only with the normal person that the law is concerned." Gaines continued:

---

* Arie Kaplan suggests that Gaines's less-than-stellar performance was also due to the cold medicine he was taking.

> May I repeat, he said, "It is only with the normal person that the law is concerned." Our American children are for the most part normal children. They are bright children, but those who want to prohibit comic magazines seem to see dirty, sneaky, perverted monsters who use the comics as a blueprint for action.
>
> What are we afraid of? Are we afraid of our own children? Do we forget that they are citizens, too, and entitled to select what to read or do? We think our children are so evil, simple minded, that it takes a story of murder to set them to murder, a story of robbery to set them to robbery?[43]

In retrospect, it appears parents *were* afraid of their own children. The damage was devastating. The summer of the Kefauver hearing alone, fifteen comic book publishers went out of business. The number of different comic book titles fell from 630 to 250 between 1952 and 1956; sales of individual titles were slashed in half. The golden age of comic books was over.

Those publishers who survived realized that self-reform would be preferable to being shut down. Several banded together to form the Comics Magazine Association of America. They'd self-police, they promised, establishing a common Comics Code to which all comics would have to adhere in order to receive the Comics Code Seal of Approval. The code restricted visual content, images, and even the words that comics could use. Here is what comic book publishers had to promise:

> Comics shall never be presented in such a way as to create sympathy for the criminal, to promote distrust of the forces of law and justice.
>
> In every instance good shall triumph over evil and the criminal punished for his misdeeds.
>
> No comic magazine shall use the word horror or terror in its title.

> Respect for parents, the moral code, and for honorable behavior shall be fostered.
>
> Passion or romantic interest shall never be treated in such a way as to stimulate the baser elements.[44]

The results were entirely predictable. Many of the older comic book heroes suddenly became very tame. As the comic book historian and artist Arie Kaplan puts it:

> Superheroes were now bland incarnations of their former selves. Batman, once a shadowy figure of the night, was recast as a high-camp boy scout battling rainbow colored monsters. Superman, once the nemesis of corrupt politicians and foreign dictators, now embarked on such silly misadventures as keeping himself whole after being split in two (Superman Red and Superman Blue). And Wonder Woman, once a model of female empowerment, now required an escort—her boyfriend Colonel Steve Trevor.[45]

The new heroes of DC Comics—Superman, Batman, Wonder Woman, and the Flash—"were square-jawed, staid, and tended to be dull," as Cass Sunstein puts it.[46]

Yet they were still wildly popular. DC Comics sold about 6.2 million copies per month in 1956, eclipsed only by Dell Comics, which, under the editorial eye of Helen Honig Meyer, published *Little Lulu*, *Tom and Jerry*, and a slew of Disney-themed comic books. Meyer, a first-generation Brooklyn Jew (born in 1907), is credited with bringing Dell into the modern publishing era by championing comic books and that relatively new innovation, the paperback.[47]

While many yielded to the new constraints, or even used them to launch new and profitable ventures, others found new outlets for old themes. Veterans of the comic book industry were joined by a number of new artists and writers in what became known as the silver age of comics. And like its metallic forebear, the silver age was a magnet for Jewish writers and artists who drew on their Jewish background to create the superheroes that animated America's childhoods.

The list of artists and writers is long, but the list of characters they created is even longer and far more memorable. The silver age of comics was perhaps the medium's most creative era, and its writers and artists the most brilliant, as they had to navigate between what kids would like and what the Comics Code would allow. The decision, says Stan Lee, the founder of Marvel Comics and the creator of Spider-Man, Fantastic Four, Hulk, Thor, and Black Panther—among many others—was to "humanize" the superheroes' public identities and to make their feats specialized and even more extraordinary. Marvel heroes were "irreverent, witty, insecure and playful."[48] Several of them were physically handicapped, like the blind lawyer Matt Murdock who became Daredevil, or the physically handicapped doctor Don Blake who became Thor. Anyone could be a superhero. This new generation of superheroes were as much the result of an accident as of genetic inheritance.

Take Spider-Man. Few characters were more human than Peter Parker—and few were more "Jewish." While Superman may have been Jewish by fantasy association (and by the cultural background of his creators), Peter Parker embodies the full range of Jewish experience in the postwar era.

Parker is nothing if not the Charlie Brown of superheroes, always well-meaning and always messing things up. The comic book historian and creator Danny Fingeroth pegs Parker not as the schlemiel, the waiter who spills soup on the customer, but as the schlimazel, the customer who has the soup spilled on him. Spider-Man "was one long cry by a misunderstood adolescent to be accepted as the well-intentioned person he was, echoing the quest of the immigrant Jews to be so accepted," which is, ultimately "Jewish" in nature—"the idea that, no matter how hard he tries to be accepted, to please and help others, still he is misunderstood and condemned."[49]

Spider-Man may have been indirectly inspired by Jewish

folklore. The first spider in Jewish history saves the life of King David. As the story goes (it's in 1 Samuel), King Saul's soldiers are chasing David, intent on killing him. (Although Saul is David's father-in-law, he is demonstrably jealous of David's popularity.) David hides in a cave as his pursuers approach. He is terrified. But just then a small spider appears at the mouth of the cave and spins a huge web in a matter of moments. The soldiers arrived at the cave mouth and are certain that David couldn't possibly be hiding in it since the web was untouched.

Even if this link between Peter Parker and King David is a bit of a stretch, Spider-Man may still be the most "Jewish" superhero of all. He doesn't act when he could, when he knows he should, and his failure leads to the tragic death of his beloved uncle Charlie. A "web of Jewishness" surrounds Spidey: He "fits the Jewish stereotype of the nerdy pathetic guy with glasses who's invisible to the beautiful girl next door, who, in turn, wastes her time with less deserving athletic thugs and rich boys" writes Alan Oirich. He is nebbishy, more akin to characters played by Woody Allen, and when as Spider-Man he wins in battle and in love, he takes genuine pleasure in his triumphs, almost an impish pleasure—something Superman never allowed himself.[50]

Other superheroes have somewhat different motivations. Superman is motivated by morality; he yearns to see righteousness prevail. Batman is motivated by vengeance; Bruce Wayne's parents were murdered, and he will use all his wealth to avenge them (and clean up the city in the process). He suffers from survivor's guilt—which was certainly not unknown among American Jews of the 1940s and '50s. By contrast, Spider-Man is motivated by a very specific post-Holocaust American Jewish guilt. "It is guilt about having not done enough to save one's people," writes Harry Brod, "about having passively stood by in the face of the crime and having let it happen."[51]

Spider-Man was one of a slew of superheroes created by Stan Lee and Jack Kirby at Marvel Comics. Both born in New York City, Stanley Martin Lieber (1922) and Jacob Kurtzberg (1917) were sons of poor Jewish immigrants. Together they created a world of fantasy for millions of American children, an empire of superheroes, each possessing at least one superhuman quality. From Spider-Man to Iron Man to X-Men, each one's special power could save the world from certain destruction. In fact, an old saying among comic book artists had it that if someone's last name had the word *man* at the end, they're either a Jew or a superhero.

Lee was a "relentless self-promoter," often described as the "Jewish Walt Disney" for his ability to create so many fantasy characters that would take up residence in young people's minds. His father was a fabric cutter in the garment industry, poor and observant. The comic book industry was similar in that way—one was paid piecework, and the industry was driven only by volume. The more you produced, the more you got paid. So Lee produced, prodigiously.

Lee famously disavowed religious piety and identification, but virtually all his superheroes seem to have a Jewish backstory. His heroes can be seen "as characters formed by the anxieties of first-generation American Jews who had fought in World War II, witnessed the Holocaust, and reflected—consciously or otherwise—on the moral obligations and complications of life after Auschwitz," writes Lee biographer Liel Leibovitz. "What we have here, intended or not, is a book about racism, bigotry, and prejudice," recalled Chris Claremont, who worked on X-Men for more than sixteen years; he was a British-born Jew whose family moved to Long Island when he was three. "It's a book about outsiders, about people who are beyond the pale so to speak . . . a story about downtrodden, repressed people fighting to change their situation. . . . The Jewish situation [of the Holocaust] is the most obvious genocidal example in the human experience."[52]

According to Leibovitz, many of Lee and Kirby's characters and themes have distinct and deliberate Jewish origins. Mr. Fantastic is a "nuclear age Hasid," he says, while Iron Man embodies "a stern reminder, drawn from the core of Jewish theology, that redemption comes only when human beings get together and pursue common goals." Iceman, introduced in 1963, was born Robert Louis Drake in Floral Park, Long Island, to an Irish father and a Jewish mother. He discovers his superpower when a bully tries to steal his girlfriend, and he puts up his hand to stop him. The bully is encased in a block of Ice. (Drake was one of the original X-Men and later came out as gay.) Izzy Cohen also appears in 1963 as part of *Sgt. Fury and His Howling Commandos*.[53]

Not just superheroes but also villains have Jewish connections. Many of the greatest comic book villains are so stereotyped that they *seem* Jewish—short, bald, with prominent noses; physically weak but possessed with a superior intellect, so brilliant and cunning that they can manipulate others to do their dirty work. Their backstory is almost always the same: Savagely bullied as boys, they bide their time, hone their intellectual skills, and take their revenge. They are puppeteers of their vast criminal empires, but they rarely get into the fray directly.

Take, for example, the first great comic book villain, Lex Luthor, who appeared as Superman's nemesis in 1940. Bald, middle-aged, and physically outmatched, Luthor's genius is "to slip away from justice without getting his hands dirty." Luthor combines "the cutthroat mentality of Gordon Gecko, the intelligence of Stephen Hawking, and the ingenuity of Nikola Tesla," writes Jason Serafino. "This brain-over-brawn equation makes Luthor the perfect foil for the most powerful being on the planet."[54] There is no direct evidence that Luthor was Jewish, but there is considerable speculation. When the Jewish actor Jesse Eisenberg was cast as the young Luthor in 2016's *Batman v Superman: The Dawn of Justice*, he commented that he wanted to humanize Luthor, "play a character who had recognizable pathologies," "not [as] a stock movie villain."[55]

Wilson Fisk, aka Kingpin (introduced as an enemy of Spider-Man in 1967) has no special powers. Born poor, relentlessly picked on as a boy, he rose through the ranks of the underworld on guile, cunning, and smarts. Winslow Schott, aka Toyman, actually uses toys to commit the crimes he thinks up. The Joker and Harley Quinn are both rumored to be Jewish.[56]

Even the Penguin may have been Jewish. On the one hand, like Batman, Oswald Chesterfield Cobblepot could not be more WASPy. His birth into a wealthy family does not shield him from being constantly bullied and tormented because of his freakish appearance—paunchy stomach, short stature, extremely prominent nose. And his overbearing mother, hardly the model of WASP decorum, is more a harping "Jewish mother" of stereotype. She insists he always carry an umbrella because she is convinced he will die of pneumonia were he to be caught in an unexpected storm. As an op-ed in *The New York Times* put it in a critique of the 1992 film *Batman Returns*, Penguin "is a Jew, down to his hooked nose, pale face, and lust for herring."[57]

Incidentally, Lex Luthor and the Penguin usually take up two of the top five slots in lists of the greatest comic book villains of all time. But the number-one archvillain is usually considered Magneto, also introduced by Lee and Kirby in 1963. His backstory is quite explicit: Max Eisenhardt was a Jewish child in Germany during the 1930s and escaped from several concentration camps, including Auschwitz. Like "a cross between Malcolm X and Osama bin Laden," Magneto is a mutant, the archenemy of Professor X (Charles Xavier, the Jewish genius who created the X-Men). "This is a man who lived through the Holocaust and vowed to never let himself or his people become subjected to hate and violence again," writes Jason Serafino. "To achieve this, Magneto strikes at the heart of humanity and uses his limitless powers to destroy us, so that the mutants can conquer."[58]

Jewish heroes, Jewish villains—and Stan Lee surrounded himself with other first-generation Jews whose prodigious output defined the new era of comic books. Joe Simon, co-creator of Captain America, born in 1913 as Hymie Simon, to a poor tailor who had immigrated to America from Britain, was the first editor of Timely Comics (which later became Marvel). So numerous were these writers and artists that by naming only Mort Meskin, Irv Novick, Harry Shorten, Morris Coyne, and Louis Silberkleit, we're barely scratching the surface.

Joe Kubert was born in 1926 to a poor butcher in a Polish shtetl—his family moved to Brooklyn when he was two months old. (A good thing, too: The shtetl was obliterated in World War II.) At age ten, Kubert took the subway from Brooklyn to Manhattan by himself, walked into a comic book studio, showed some drawings, and was instantly hired as an artist.

Golems in Gotham

The fantasy of the golem shadows several original comic book superheroes. The golem was a superhuman creature of clay and stone who emerged in sixteenth-century Prague, at the behest of Rabbi Loew, and would protect the Jewish community in eastern Europe. One comic superhero is unmistakably a golem come to life: the Thing, created by Lee and Kirby as one of the original Fantastic Four. He's quite explicitly Jewish. As Benjamin Jacob Grimm, he grew up in the tough Lower East Side; when he was eight, his older brother was killed in a street gang fight. Grimm becomes an astronaut and an air force test pilot. He is exposed to massive amounts of radiation, and with three friends he hijacks a rocket that mutates them all into superheroes. Grimm becomes a rock-hard monster "with a heart of gold," as the Marvel promotional material claims.

His religion was rarely mentioned during his career in the comic (he was introduced in 1961), but in the early 2000s he returns to his old neighborhood on the Lower East Side, is bar mitzvahed after thirteen years as the Thing, and becomes the first superhero who is explicitly religious. In a *Fantastic Four* comic book in 2002, he tries vainly to remember the Jewish prayer "Shma Yisroel," in order to say it over an elderly pawnbroker who has been injured during a fight. The pawnbroker asks the Thing why he's never said he is Jewish in all those years—is he ashamed to be Jewish? "Nah, that ain't it," Grimm replies. "I don't talk it up is all. Figure there's enough trouble in this world without people thinkin' Jews are all monsters like me."[59]

More important, this particular superhero was modeled after the golem: "He was a being made of clay . . . but he wasn't a monster. He was a protector." Several other comic book heroes are patterned after the golem—large, animate, humanoid "protectors" of Jews. The Hulk has some of those qualities; indeed, a 1970 issue of *The Incredible Hulk* is entitled "Among Us Walks the Golem."* As Harry Brod puts it, these golem-like figures:

> are liberators, watchfully waiting in the shadows until they emerge in the darkest hour to enable the oppressed to escape the shackles of tyranny. They are the fantasy creations of the little guys, the kids who got beat up in the neighborhood, and they fight not just for them but for their people, who are also unable to protect themselves against overpowering forces.[60]

Ben Grimm is the consummate New York Jew, right down to his secular upbringing until his adult "awakening." More than that, he is also one of the many "Jewish" comic book heroes whose fates are

---

* Later characters also reveal Jewishness. Optimus Prime is the most powerful Transformer and leader of the Autobots. Yes, his spaceship is called "the ark," but it's more than that. In an episode of *Family Guy*, Max Weinstein takes the Griffins to Sabbath services at Temple Beth Thupporting Actor. Optimus arrives in vehicle form and transforms into an observant Jew in yarmulke and tallis, declaring "I am Optimus Prime," the way God announces himself to Moses through the burning bush. The current series of *Transformers* movies, directed by Michael Bay, who was raised Jewish and was Leonard Nimoy's cousin, chronicle a shape-shifting band of golems searching for a home after their world has been destroyed. Pariahs on earth, they must hide in plain sight in order to do good in the world and defeat the Decepticons. These robots assume the form of cars, trucks, tanks, airplanes—whatever will help them blend in, Zelig-like, "morphing between machine and robot with chameleon-like ease." They embody Jewish mimesis, mimicry in the service of assimilation and acceptance. See Nathan Abrams, "Why the Transformers Movies Are Really Stories of Jewish Resilience and Adaptability," *Jewish Forward*, June 20, 2017.

Jack Kirby, the Thing (of the Fantastic Four) drawn as Jewish.

The Thing at Shul, drawn by Jack Kirby
for a family holiday card, 1976.*

entwined somehow with Columbia University. Peter Parker was bitten by a spider on a high school field trip to an entomology lab at Columbia (sometimes referred to as Empire State University). And Jerry Robinson is said to have thought up Batman's sidekick, Robin, while sitting in a journalism class at Columbia.

Many comic book creators got their start at DeWitt Clinton High School in the Bronx—Stan Lee (class of 1939), Will Eisner (1936), Bill Finger (1933), and Bob Kane (1933), to mention four of the most prominent—and many of their superhero creations got *their* start on Morningside Heights. Indeed, if DeWitt Clinton was Comic Book High, Columbia may have been Comic Book U. Reed Richards (Mr. Fantastic) got one of his many degrees at Columbia, after serving in the army with his freshman roommate, Ben Grimm, the Lower East Side football star from Stuyvesant High School. Richards lived

---

* Apparently, Kirby did not intend this image for the actual comic book but drew it for a friend.

in a boardinghouse run by the aunt of Sue Storm (Invisible Woman), who had also attracted the attentions of the Quiet Man, also a Columbia student. Matt Murdock (Daredevil) and Franklin Nelson (Foggy Nelson) were roommates at Columbia Law School. Another Columbia student, Elektra Natchios, dropped out after her father was killed, only to recast herself as Elektra, the assassin. Vance Astrovik (Justice) was a Columbia student who accidentally killed his abusive gay father, but fortunately after he was released from prison, Columbia readmitted him and accepted all his course credits!

Several Columbia faculty members play a role in the superhero comic book universe. Lee Wing (Asian studies) is the father of Colleen Wing, of the Daughters of the Dragon; James Power (physics) is the father of the Power Pack; and Professor Meredith McCall's first boyfriend was Tony Stark, the future Iron Man. The 1940s comic book villain Simon Meke reinvents himself in the 1960s as Dr. Sanderson, a physics professor.

In the 2004 film *Spider-Man 2*, Columbia sits squarely on both sides of the equation. Peter Parker is a scholarship student at the school, where one of his professors is Curt Connors, who later becomes the Lizard, Spidey's archenemy, at least in the comic book version.[61] And in *Spider-Man: No Way Home* (2022), Peter still seems to be a student there while Dr. Strange wears a Columbia sweatshirt.[62]

Why was Columbia University the Superhero Ivy? Perhaps because it was the New York Ivy and, even more, the Jewish Ivy. At a time when Harvard and Yale were instituting quotas limiting the number of Jews they admitted, Columbia drew most of its students from the New York City public schools (though it tried to steer many of them toward City College or Seth Low Junior College, the latter, built to siphon the "surplus" of Jewish—including Isaac Asimov—away from upper Manhattan and back to Brooklyn). And at a time when New England schools were turning their back on the flood of Jewish intellectuals feeling the terrors of the Third Reich, Columbia welcomed them, as did the New School for Social Research, which transplanted the Frankfurt School to Lower Manhattan. An old Harvard fraternity ditty went something like this:

Oh Harvard's run by millionaires
And Yale is run by booze
Cornell is run by farmers' sons
Columbia's run by Jews.[63]

Unlike Harvard, Yale, and Princeton, Columbia had no country club atmosphere, a breeding ground that sons of America's hereditary aristocracy would attend before assuming their place at the top of the social hierarchy. It had no finals clubs, no eating clubs, no secret societies—no "schools within a school" that enabled the old elites to maintain their status in the face of "alien" newcomers. And it issued no Gentleman's C's. Instead, Columbia was the strivers' university, a school not of genteel entitlement but of social mobility. It was perhaps *the* Ivy League school for social mobility. When poor Lower East Side–based Jewish artists who created and drew comic book heroes looked uptown from the Lower East Side to Morningside Heights, Columbia was perhaps the farthest they could dream of going, the world apart, just out of their reach, but not, in their fantasies, out of the reach of the characters they created.

The Madness of *Mad*

Mad magazine also provided refuge. After Bill Gaines testified disastrously at the Senate HUAC hearings, industry self-censorship became the solution to the public outcry against delinquency. Gaines and others at EC Comics decided the only option was to make fun of everything. *Mad* made fun of anyone who had the temerity to be in the public eye.

Along with the editor Harvey Kurtzman and the "usual gang of idiots," Gaines produced a relentlessly satirical magazine. Pretty much every one of those "idiots" was a first-generation Jew. Kurtzman, born in Brooklyn in 1924, was a natural cartoonist. As a boy, he created characters named Ikey and Likey, and he drew cartoons on the sidewalks near his house using some "shards of plaster from hunks of walls in abandoned lots."[64]

Al Jaffee (born Abraham Jaffee in 1921 to immigrant parents from Lithuania) was one of the magazine's stalwart cartoonists—for sixty-five years! One of his creations was a spoof on comic book superheroes called Inferior Man. "The core of Jaffee's work," according to Will Forbis, is "the idea that to be alive is to be constantly beleaguered by annoying idiots, poorly designed products and the unapologetic ferocity of fate. Competence and intelligence are not rewarded in life but punished."[65]

The magazine itself had a Jewish flavor. Its mascot, the dorky, gap-toothed Alfred E. Neuman, was the Everyman-as-Nebbish. Neuman wasn't specifically Jewish (his last name was not Newman), but his tagline, "What Me Worry?" always had a bit of Yiddish in its inflection. The magazine was peppered with Yiddishisms like *feh*, *oy*, and *fershugginer*.

At its heyday, *Mad* was enormously popular. In 1960, with a paid circulation of 1.4 million a month, it was read by 43 percent of American high school students and 58 percent of college students. In the early 1960s, as its circulation surpassed 2 million, it was also widely imitated (who remembers *Cracked*?). As Gloria Steinem (who worked for a time as Kurtzman's assistant) put it, "There was a spirit of satire and irreverence in *Mad* that was very important and it was the only place you could find it in the 1950s."[66] Loaded with juvenile, sophomoric quips and general adolescent male inanity, the magazine was just this side of gross-out fart jokes. "Oppressed people resort to humor," said Jaffee, "They can't afford to get angry."[67] Without *Mad* there would never have been a Beavis or a Butthead, a Stan Marsh or a Kyle Broflovski or even a Bart Simpson.

* * *

Hounded by censors, persecuted by zealots, the targets of panics both political and "moral," these misfits and malcontents found the world of children to be more welcoming, and they brought their creative imaginations with them into the shaping of American children's lives.

There were, of course, costs to their refuge, a certain stripping of the political and perverse edges that propelled their humor and energized their teaching. As Harry Brod put it:

> The Jewish sons of immigrants who created the first wave of superheroes had succeeded all too well in their attempts to embody the immigrant's American dream in their pages. They'd become assimilated. They'd left the working-class urban streets behind for new homes in the middle-class suburbs. And their characters seemed to have made the same transition. They lost that urban ethnic edge that gave them their vitality and became bland WASPs, trading in their outsider status for badges of respectability.[68]

As a result, comic book characters got less and less interesting, but in compensation the special effects got wilder, crazier, and more violent. What drives the superhero today is less his backstory, less his internal motivation, than the maniacal menace of his adversaries and the special effects he has at his command. And as they moved from the shtetl to the ghetto, from the Lower East Side to the Bronx and Brooklyn, and then after the war, from the outer boroughs to northern New Jersey, Long Island, and Westchester, Jewish leftism may have softened somewhat into a comfortable liberalism, but such is the "price" of successful assimilation.

PART III

The Baby Boom

8

THE BABY BOOM

* * *

The post–World War II baby boom was more than a simple demographic bulge in the number of births between the end of the war and the mid-1960s. Yes, it's true that more than 76 million Americans were born between 1946 and 1964, about 4 million each year. But the baby boom also signaled a change in consciousness, a cultural shift whose magnitude is still being felt. Sometimes the entire culture seemed to have shifted its axis around those 76 million children.

The end of the war ushered in the great suburban diaspora, fueled in part by the GI Bill (and the expansion of federal funds for schools and roads), which transformed the landscape of childhood. The suburbs lured parents from cities into single-family homes, far larger than the urban apartments they'd grown up in. These larger homes had dens, family rooms, and even individual rooms for children—allowing far more room for toys—and families had more money with which to buy them.

This was true at least for middle-class white families, the ones who could afford to move out of the cities and take advantage of those spurs to suburban expansion. But in the prevailing ideology of the postwar era, life was to be about family: family time in family rooms, consuming family-sized products. There's no question that the baby boom era got its name because it was all about the children. If the twentieth century was going to be the century of the child, as Ellen Key had predicted, the midpoint was its apotheosis. The 1950s was the decade of the child.

Everything suddenly seemed geared to children. A child could watch children's television, play with more toys than anyone could count, spend the afternoon—or several days!—at a children's amusement park, and eat candy by the mouthful. No wonder the American assumption at midcentury was, as David Michaelis writes, that "children were happy, and childhood was a golden time."[1]

But making sure that those children were perpetually happy, that the golden surface was never scratched or blemished—well, that in itself was a full-time job. An early postwar Playskool toy catalog included a short essay, "What Toys Shall I Buy for My Child?" by the University of Chicago child development expert Ethel Kawin, who reminded parents, "It is not enough that toys are educational—they must be correctly educational so that they teach the right things at the *right time* in the *right way*!"[2]

So much for the secure serenity that was supposed to accompany the move to the suburbs. So much was on the line! Affluence bred the exact opposite of contentment: Behind those manicured lawns seethed an unquenchable anxiety.

Within that fraught cauldron of parental anxiety, childhood itself became an industry, a big business, marketing toys and games and dolls for kids and advice books for parents. Soon amusement parks like Disneyland in Anaheim, California (begun in 1955)—and on the East Coast, the short-lived Freedomland (1960–64), in the Bronx—spread the terrain of leisure outward, creating new spaces where children could play, and new opportunities for entrepreneurs to give them something with which to play.

Into that space rushed another cohort of first-generation Jewish entrepreneurs. In 1948 in South Pasadena, Arthur "Spud" Melin and Richard Knerr, two aimless USC grads, started a toy company

Art (Spud) Melin and Rich Knerr in 1958 publicity photo for Hula Hoops. (Photo courtesy of Wham-O)

called Wham-O in Knerr's garage, where they pioneered Frisbees, Hacky Sacks, and Superball—all from southern California's burgeoning plastics industry. When an Australian friend visiting them in 1957 mentioned that in his country, children twirled bamboo hoops around their waists in gym class, Knerr and Melin created one of the biggest fads of the twentieth century, Hula-Hoops, which sold nearly half a million within the first four months of release.*

A Doll Bonanza

By 1948, the toy industry was worth $300 million, and Ideal had 10 percent of the entire U.S. market. At its factory in Hollis, Queens, the company employed 3,500 men and women. The company made and sold more than 200 kinds of dolls, 250 different stuffed animals, and

* Gay Talese mistakenly attributed the success of the Frisbee to some Ivy Leaguers at Princeton and Dartmouth, without noticing that they had already come to dominate the beaches of southern California. Gay Talese, "Frisbees, Yo-Yos, Goo-Goos, Etc.," *New York Times*, August 11, 1957.

more than one thousand rubber and plastic toys—model planes, cars, miniature telephones, washing machines, and doll furniture. Every single working day its workers turned out 10,000 dolls and 4,000 stuffed animals, along with 50,000 plastic, 10,000 latex and 6,000 wooden toys. By 1949, Ideal was making more than 2 million dolls a year—they alone generated a retail value of $12 million.

Dolls were—and remained—the centerpiece of Ideal's toy line. In the decade that followed the end of the Second World War, under Ben's leadership, the company produced many notable successes and a few spectacular flops. The larger version of Baby Coos inspired the introduction of other large dolls in the 1950s, like Patti Playpal (thirty-five inches) and Saucy Walker (twenty-three inches). Thumbelina, also introduced in the 1950s, had limbs that moved when a key was inserted into her back and turned like a windup clock.

Ben was experimenting with small recorders to allow dolls to do more than coo or cry. In 1959 Ideal released Chatty Cathy. She talked! In fact, she said eleven different things. A string attached to her back was connected to a tiny record in her abdomen. The string wound a metal coil that activated random statements. "Let's play school." "I hurt myself." "Please take me with you." And "I love you." (Cathy's voice was recorded by June Foray, a well-known voice actor who was best known as the voice of Rocket J. Squirrel from *The Adventures of Rocky and Bullwinkle and Friends.* And yes, she too was a first-generation Jew, born in 1917 to a Lithuanian mother and a Russian father.) Chatty Cathy was the most desired toy of the 1960 Christmas season, ahead of Ken (number two) and Barbie's Dream House (number three). A talking Barbie wasn't far behind.

In 1953 the company produced the first Smokey Bear toy, based on an illustration in *The Saturday Evening Post.* Ideal's line expanded into games like Mouse Trap, their first (based on cartoons by Rube Goldberg), and Kerplunk! By 1970, games accounted for about one-third of all of Ideal's sales.

The expansion of the plastics industry created a revolution in materials that transformed the toy industry, making toys far cheaper to produce. One significant complication to this expansion was

Japan. After the war, Japanese manufacturing exploded, threatening U.S. domestic manufacturing, as the label MADE IN JAPAN appeared on myriad products. In 1957 several major toymakers wanted to impose high protective tariffs that would drive up the cost of Japanese toys and provide a boost to domestic companies. Ideal bucked the trend. It supported lower tariffs and began producing in Asia, soon opening factories in Taiwan, Singapore, and Korea, as well as in Haiti and the Dominican Republic.

In 1957 Ben seized on what he thought would be a brilliant idea. As Christmas approached, he noticed children eagerly anticipating the latest toy, then walking with their families past Christmas manger tableaux in front of every church in America and worshiping baby Jesus. Why not put them together? Why not a Baby Jesus doll? *Poinggg!*

It's not as if dolls based on religious characters were all that unusual. In the 1940s, Diana Forman had created Children of the Bible as "dolls with a purpose" to elevate children's play by creating "happy experiences and memories which are associated with the Bible." The daughter and granddaughter of rabbis, Forman envisioned the dolls as a way to anchor Jewish children, especially, in their faith. Entirely self-taught, she clothed each of these foot-tall dolls in "authentic" garb—Rebekah, Sarah, and even Mary. Each doll came with a vial of sand from the Holy Land, some ornaments, and a scroll with a narrative of their story. "People spend a lot of money on buying Teddy Bears, Golliwogs, and Donald Ducks," Forman said, "but they never think of buying a doll that can do more than just amuse children for a short period."[3]

Ben was completely sold on the idea of a Baby Jesus doll, and so he and his wife, Hadassah, sailed to Rome. In an audience with the pope, Pius XII gave them his express permission for the doll. (The Holy See was to receive a royalty.) The company rolled out a huge advertising campaign, ready for the 1958 Christmas season.

Anyone could have seen this kind of thing coming. Since 1900 Christmas had been increasingly commercialized—driven in part by Jewish toy manufacturers and Jewish-owned department stores like

Left picture: Ben and Hadassah Michtom meet with Pope Pius XII, 1958. From *left*: Hadassah Michtom, Ben Michtom, Vatican translator, Pope Pius XII. (Photo courtesy of Paula Michtom) *Right picture*: The Baby Jesus doll by Ideal, 1958. (Photo courtesy of Paula Michtom)

Macy's and Gimbels. These stores invented the Christmas "season," heralded by the appearance of Santa Claus at the end of every Macy's Thanksgiving Day Parade since the event's founding in 1924. Christmas was becoming quite profitable, leading to conservative calls to "Keep Christ in Christmas," which might just as well have said "And Keep the Jews Out" in parentheses.

Alas, the Jesus baby turned out to be too great a reach over the line separating piety and profits, even for an utterly commercialized holiday. "What a bomb," Paula Michtom, Mark's widow, remembered. "Being Jewish, [the family] didn't understand that no one was going to buy the toy. No one was going to have their children playing with the Christ child." How Ben had managed to sweet-talk the pope into endorsing it is still a mystery, perhaps explainable only by the royalty to be paid to the Vatican.

The Postwar Toy Boom

New toy companies proliferated. Creative Playthings, founded by Frank and Theresa Caplan in 1945, capitalized on suburban sprawl by creating huge play sets, with well-crafted structures for gross motor play and huge hollow blocks for construction sets.

Many of the era's most successful toymakers started out in other fields, then realized that toys would make their original business far more profitable. Take Max Klein, owner of a paint company in Detroit, and his partner Dan Robbins. When Robbins started working for Klein, he was looking to develop a children's art project. He recalled that many of the old masters, especially Leonardo da Vinci, would hand out numbered patterns to their apprentices, who filled in the backgrounds of his paintings. "Why not do the same for anyone who wants to paint but does not have the talent to draw or mix colors?" he thought. "All I have to do is create a numbered outline and provide the corresponding numbered colors." Klein was initially unimpressed, but gradually he warmed to the idea. Craft Master was born, and Paint by Numbers was its hugely successful product.

Robbins's first numbered canvases were abstract, like cubist paintings by Picasso or Braque. Adult hobbyists scoffed at the kits, unable to see the art in these abstract shapes. So Craft Master hired the artist Adam Grant, a Holocaust survivor, to create more generic canvases. Its edition of *The Last Supper* remains the company's best-selling kit, while those of the Matterhorn, and of fishermen, and of beautiful lakes and hillsides were solid sellers with both children and adults, easily surpassing the sales at Palmer Paint. They even created a kit for Alfred E. Neuman, poster boy for *Mad* magazine. "Every man a Rembrandt!" was the slogan. Today there is even a Paint by Number Museum.[4]

Kenner Products, founded by the Steiner brothers—Albert, Philip, and Joseph—in Cincinnati in 1947, had its origin in the soap business. To increase their sales, the brothers added a small novelty gun that created soap bubbles to their packaging. The Bubbl/Matic Gun was such a hit the brothers changed course, dropped the soap, and started making the toys. Their great fortune came with Play-Doh in 1956 and the Easy-Bake Oven (which used a small light bulb to generate enough heat to "bake" things) in 1963. Play-Doh had begun its life as a compound for cleaning coal residue and soot from wallpaper. But the transition from coal heat to oil and natural gas left the compound with little commercial value. The company initially took it to an educational convention to suggest it as a modeling compound.

Founded by Maurice Greenberg in 1932, Coleco began as a leather business, supplying shoe repair outfits. Maurice's sons, Leonard and Arnold, expanded the company into toys, as well as aboveground swimming pools. In 1954 Leathercraft selected Coleco's leather moccasin kit as the prestige toy of the year, and the company went full time into the toy business. Along with several others, Coleco would go on to become a leader in the video game and console business. (Its last great toy, before being gobbled up by Hasbro, was Cabbage Patch Kids.)

Likewise, Remco (short for "remote control") was founded in the 1940s by the Newark, New Jersey, cousins Isaac Heller and Saul Robbins. They started out selling walkie-talkies that were so successful that they moved their headquarters from Newark to Cape May Street in Harrison, locating their factory on land now occupied by Red Bull Arena. Remco also created the Coney Island Penny Machine, which combined a crane-operated miniature arcade toy with a piggy bank. And if Hasbro was making a fortune with its doctor and nurse kits, Remco came up with its Medicine Chest, endorsed by the TV actor Pinky Lee (born Pincus Leff in St. Paul in 1907), which included a packet of Kleenex, a toothbrush and toothpaste, and a few other "medical" essentials.

Kohner Bros. began as a wood-turning business in a little town on the German-Czech border. Moritz Kohner had used birch and beech wood to create curtain rods and sword decorations. His sons, Paul and Frank, kept the business going until Hitler rose to power, and then they brought the business to Brooklyn. They made toys from different sized wooden beads and eventually bought the patent for a little puppet that stood three to four inches high, was made entirely of wood, and was jointed at the waist, knees, elbows, and ankles. The puppet was mounted on a base, and when you pushed up on the base, the puppet collapsed in a heap. Release the button, and it snapped back into place. Push Button Puppets were a massive hit with kids, but because they were so small, they were also found on many corporate executives' desks.[5]

Cardinal Industries, founded by Les Berger in Brooklyn's Williamsburg neighborhood in 1945, made dozens of games and puzzles, including dominoes. Rosebud Art Company, founded in 1923 by Isidor Rosen, originally made coloring books for children, then added games and puzzles, but in the postwar era, his sons Irving and Sydney took control, renamed the company Rose Art, and added art and school supplies. Next to Crayola, it was the nation's largest supplier of crayons, arts and crafts materials, and school supplies.

Henry Orenstein was a relative latecomer to the toy business, but he landed with a bang. Born in a small Jewish village in Poland in 1923, he and his two brothers survived several concentration camps, then were able to emigrate to New York in 1947. Henry founded Topper Toys right after the war.

Like Louis Marx, Orenstein's first hit doll was the product of chance and connivance; like Marx, his strategy was basically to undersell his competitors. At first, he sold cheap dolls on grocery store shelves. In 1958 he saw a beautiful bridal doll in a store window, selling for $29.95 (about $250 today). Outrageous! So he had his designers come up with a taller (thirty-inch) doll with an ornate dress and layers of ruffles, which he sold for $9.99. She was Betty the Beautiful Bride. "That's how I made my first million," he told a journalist. The next year Betty was joined by bridesmaids.[6] More millions followed.

Topper soon came out with more cheap knockoffs, sending the company into the stratosphere. By then Suzy Homemaker appliances were competing with the Easy-Bake Oven. But the company encountered controversy with its Johnny Seven O.M.A., which was seven guns in one. It was a big seller, but it pushed a lot of parents—and parenting experts—to consider how these toy guns might be linked to the explosion of gun violence. By the end of the 1950s, Topper was the country's fourth-largest toy company.[7]

Orenstein, like many others, saw the potential of harnessing celebrity power to his low-priced toys. In 1964, he hired Louis Armstrong to sing a little ditty about Suzie Cute for a television commercial. And six years later he sponsored race car driver Al Unser's winning car in the Indianapolis 500, which catapulted the sales of Topper's Johnny Lightning toys (a lower-priced competitor to Mattel's Hot Wheels).

After leaving Topper (the company tried, and failed, to go public in 1971 and declared bankruptcy in 1973), Orenstein became an independent toy developer. His biggest hit came in a partnership with Hasbro. In 1982, in a back room at the Toy Fair, he found a castaway toy car that turned into an airplane and thought to himself, "This is it!" He took it to Hasbro, and Alan Hassenfeld loved it. Transformers debuted in 1984.

It wasn't until the early 1950s that Hasbro made its transition to a full-on toy company. You'll recall that the company was founded by three Jewish immigrant brothers—Herman, Hillel, and Henry Hassenfeld (hence the Hasbro name)—in Pawtucket, Rhode Island, in 1923. The brothers started with nothing except each other and a driving work ethic. They began, as did so many, in the *schmatta* business—in their case, a small business in scrap textiles. They used some of the scraps to create textile boxes, then started filling the boxes with school supplies—erasers, pencils, and rulers. That caught on, so they soon began to manufacture the pencils and other items. Henry's son, Merrill, thought the scrap-covered boxes might have other uses. They put in some fake pill boxes and plastic stethoscopes and marketed them to children. Presto! Doctor and nurse bags!

Then in 1951 George Lerner, a Brooklyn-born son of Romanian Jewish parents, came to the Hassenfeld brothers with an idea for a toy. He had become familiar with the exploding possibilities of plastics during World War II and came up with something new and original. He and his partner Julius Ellman created small arms and legs and eyes and eyebrows and a nose and mouth, then designed them with small spikes that could be stuck into potatoes, resulting in funny faces and preposterous poses. This first iteration of Mr. Potato Head failed utterly because parents thought it was wasteful of food,

The original Mr. Potato Head (*right*) and his plastic brother (*left*). (Photo courtesy of Tim Walsh of The Playmakers)

especially after World War II rationing. "Clean your plate!" I can still hear my grandparents cry. "People are starving in Europe."

So Lerner and Ellman created a plastic mold with holes for the designer parts. Mr. Potato Head was the first toy to be advertised on television—at a time when there were not even 10 million TV sets in the whole country. Mr. Potato Head sold over a million units in its first year alone. The second version, with the plastic torso, became a runaway hit and remained an iconic toy for a very long time.

Mr. Potato Head vaulted Hasbro into the top echelons of toy companies. Alan Hassenfeld, grandson of the company's founders, called the industry a magical world where "you never have to grow up."[8]

Just as Ideal and most of the other toy companies had their "women creators behind the scenes," so too did Hasbro, which today owns Parker Brothers. The conventional story of the board game Monopoly is that it was created by Charles Darrow, who brought the game to Parker Brothers in 1935 (after Milton Bradley turned it down) and so created one of the world's most recognizable modern board games. But actually Darrow got the idea originally from a

Publicity photo of Alan Hassenfeld, and some Hasbro toys.

woman, Elizabeth (Lizzie) Magie, who patented a game based on the economic theories of Henry George that national progress was more likely to be the result of individual entrepreneurship than of inherited wealth. George argued for a single tax system. So even as the players' goal was to gain a "monopoly" over particular sets of properties, the game also offered a critique of monopolists. In fact, Magie called it a "practical demonstration of the present system of land grabbing with all its usual outcomes and consequences." She saw it as a way to teach people how capitalism actually works.[9]

As intended, Magie's game was a hit with leftist intellectuals. She herself became famous in 1906, when she put herself up for sale as a "young woman American slave" to raise awareness about the thankless drudgery of housework and women's exclusion from many occupations. Her stunt quickly went viral—well, as viral as it might have gone today if she offered herself for sale on eBay. Eventually the game reached Atlantic City, New Jersey, where Darrow encountered it and changed the street names, tinkered with the rules, and made the successful acquisition of a monopoly a goal rather than a "problem." In effect, Darrow turned the game on its head—and made the very fortune that its creator had decried.

Independent Toy Inventors

Toy companies had internal product development departments where artists and engineers concocted new ideas for toys. But they also relied on a steady stream of independent inventors who created their own toys and pitched them to the companies at the annual Toy Fair in New York City.

In cluttered basements, suburban garages, and backyard sheds, hundreds of ambitious young creative types tried to create the next Nerf ball, Pet Rock, or Mr. Potato Head. Many were too poor to go to college for industrial design or engineering, so they took regular jobs and tinkered on the weekends and evenings, or they enlisted in the military and learned the engineering needed to operate submarines or radar equipment.

Perhaps the king of the independent toy creators was Marvin Glass. Born Marvin Goldberg in Chicago in 1915 (he changed his name in his early twenties because of anti-Semitism), Glass sold his toy ideas to virtually every toy company. A short, slight middle-class boy, he had had a terribly unhappy childhood; his father was a salesman and was away most of the time, while his mother was severely depressed and likely schizophrenic. If he misbehaved, she would tie him to a chair and prevent him from eating, drinking, or going to the bathroom. Once when he was six years old, she tried to throw him out of a third-story window. She was committed to a mental hospital when Marvin was eight, and he went to live with an aunt and uncle.

Growing up in a poor neighborhood, Marvin retreated into his imagination, creating toys and dolls from whatever materials he could find. Early on he learned that the best way to avoid being bullied was to make toys for the neighborhood gangs. After graduating from the University of Chicago in 1935, he started a small studio on Chicago's south side to make toys. He pretty much single-handedly "invented the business of independent toy design," recalled Jeffrey Breslow, who came to work in the Glass studio in 1967.[10]

Initially, he created toys based on their sound—a radical approach for such a visual industry. He created a frying pan that sizzled, a time bomb that ticked a countdown to a cap "explosion," and even a robot that would release missiles and rockets when it "heard" a command. In 1959 he created the Ric-O-Shay toy pistol that made the sound of a ricochet. His team worked on it for months, watching episodes of *Gunsmoke* over and over to get the sound right. He sold it to the Hubley Manufacturing Company but had a change of heart four years later, after the assassination of President John F., Kennedy, whom Glass revered. "A toy gun is made to pretend that one is killing," he told the *Chicago Tribune* in 1968.

> A manufacturer has the responsibility not only to profits, but also to the mental health and character of children. Realistic guns, advertised realistically, convey the idea that violence is a legitimate persuader. The toy gun may be the ingredient that sets in motion another potential assassin.[11]

Glass later became a fierce opponent of all war toys.

A cigarette-smoking, overcaffeinated workaholic, who "slumps through the world with the pained expression of a depressed dachshund," Glass ran what must have been the most imaginative toy-invention studio ever created. And he was the shrewdest of businessmen. Not only did he create toys for virtually every American toy company, but he was also the first to demand royalties based on sales rather than flat fee for the design, the industry standard. (He was also a perfectly tailored man-about-town, who palled around with fellow Chicagoan Hugh Hefner at the Playboy mansion.)

For Glass, the point of a toy was to unleash the child's imagination, to generate a sense of "fantasy and wonderment." "A toy," he said, "must have a certain amount of fantasy that reawakens an echo in a child, but at the same time, it must be the umbilical cord through which he perceives the world of reality.

> A toy is really three-dimensional mythology. Mythology is wish fulfillment using the real world to create that

> fulfillment. If you just copy the real world, it's no good. It won't work. It'll be just another piece of completely forgettable plastic or metal. But to be a truly successful designer of toys today, you have to be able to straddle the world of the practical as well as the world of the possible. You have to have a sense of fantasy, but you have to coordinate it with the practical world.[12]

Among Glass's best clients was Ideal, as he and Lionel Weintraub, Ideal's president, made an odd couple alliance and friendship. Among their biggest hits together was Mr. Machine in 1960. Mr. Machine was a man-as-machine, "modern man tyrannized by his mechanical creations, turned into a mechanical man himself," Glass said. *Time* magazine called Glass "the Frankenstein who set Mr. Machine clunking and whirring through a million living rooms." Glass created the toy for Ideal. (Lionel Weintraub liked Mr. Machine so much that he kept it on his desk and used it as his mascot.) And the man who first came up with the model plans was Glass's employee Leo Kripak, a fifty-year-old Russian Jewish immigrant, and former slave laborer in a Nazi prison camp.

You'd think that a studio that produced more than five hundred toys and games—including Mr. Machine, Mouse Trap, Rock 'Em Sock 'Em Robots, and Lite-Brite, and that employed such toy creators as Eddy Goldfarb, Jeffrey Breslow (Bucket of Fun, Ants in the Pants, Upset, Snap Bowling, and Twiddler), Allison Katzman (Blythe dolls), and Rouben Terzian (Big Monster Toys)—would be constantly hosting children of all ages to try out the toy prototypes. You'd be wrong.

Actually, Glass did not like children at all. (His five marriages were all childless.) He adamantly opposed testing toys and games on kids. Once a new client who came in for a presentation asked Glass if he ever tested prototypes with kids. He looked the client straight in the eye and said, "I haven't seen a kid in twenty years." In part, he was afraid the children would talk about the prototypes with their friends, thus revealing company secrets, even to other seven-year-olds.

He wouldn't even let his employees take toys home to let their own children play with them.[13]

But if Glass didn't want to be around children, he surrounded himself with grown-ups who were as playful and creative as children. Perhaps no one better embodied this childlike impishness than Eddy Goldfarb, a poor first-generation Jew from Chicago, born Adolph Goldfarb in 1921 to immigrant parents from Romania and Poland. He dropped his first name for obvious reasons and went by his middle name, Eddy, for the rest of his life. A child of the Depression, he lost his father at a young age; his father, stressed and beaten down by poverty and anxiety, died of a heart attack at forty-four. Eddy and his two siblings went to work to support the family, selling newspapers on street corners, hustling odd jobs, doing anything. All the while, he was inventing technical contraptions and drawing them on whatever materials he could find.

When the war broke out, Goldfarb enlisted in the navy and did technical work on a submarine. With lots of free time, he began creating all sorts of mechanical gizmos and began to think about how to parlay this knack for invention into something resembling a career. "I thought toys were the easiest industry to get into if you were mechanically inclined like me, and had no actual training. It was definitely the bottom of the ladder of engineering prestige," he told me. He left the navy with a satchel full of drawings for toys.[14]

After Goldfarb got back home to Chicago, he found his way to Marvin Glass's workshop. Glass had recently had a terrible failure with tiny stained glass ornaments for Christmas trees that hardly sold at all. He'd misunderstood Christmas, the way that Ben Michtom's Baby Jesus doll at Ideal had been an utter failure. "Christmas isn't really a religious observance anymore," Glass said. "It's a time for fun and this wasn't fun." Just then, in walked Goldfarb with a little cardboard box standing on two cardboard "legs." When the box was pressed down, a mechanism inside caused a marble to fall out. Eureka. Goldfarb's cardboard box became a chicken, which, when pressed down on its legs, laid an egg (still a marble). Busy Biddy Chicken, which Ideal introduced in 1949, sold more than 14 million units.

Eddy Goldfarb in 2023 with Yakity-Yak chattering teeth. (Photo courtesy of Lyn Goldfarb Productions Inc., www.eddysworld.net)

Their next toy, also created in 1949, was a stratospheric hit. Goldfarb asked his dentist for one of the plaster molds used to create dentures. He molded plastic teeth, added a mechanical wind-up device, and Yakity Yak Talking Teeth was born. He brought it to Glass, and they developed it together, then took it to Irving Fishlove, who organized the production. It still sells well today.

In 1952 Goldfarb decided to work independently, and he and his family decamped to California. Glass, furious, felt abandoned; he withheld Goldfarb's royalties for the first toys they had created together. Goldfarb designed model airplanes and cars for Revell, the plastics company founded by Lewis Glaser in the 1940s to create models of ships and planes. Over the years, he created over eight hundred toys and games and continued to invent new ones into his late nineties.

Goldfarb's first encounter with Ideal went less than ideally. In the early 1950s, money was tight, and he heard about an upcoming show in Chicago where toymakers would display the hobby kits that they were developing to tap into the suburban boom. In those days the hobby world was exploding: Everyone—especially men who had returned from the war to become domesticated suburban dads—was encouraged to develop hobbies, engrossing pastimes that would tether them to their families and homes. Millions of suburban basements and garages were being converted to workshops.

Goldfarb had a few inventions he thought might work. He and his wife saved up for him to take a bus to Chicago, but when he arrived, he couldn't get into the show. He was only an inventor, not a buyer, and the show was closed to anyone who wasn't already in the trade. "I was completely dejected," Goldfarb told me. "I had saved all this money in order to get here, and now I couldn't get in." He walked around the building and came upon a door that was slightly ajar. It led to the area behind the exhibition booths. He sneaked in and made his way in the darkness, behind the curtains of the various booths.

That is, until he tripped over a power cord and fell into one of the curtains. The exhibition booth came crashing down around him. It was Ideal's booth. Ashamed and mortified, he tried to walk away nonchalantly, but someone from Ideal caught up with him and asked him what he was doing there. "I told him I was an inventor and I had a few things I wanted to show to some of the companies there. 'Okay,' he said, 'show me.' And they liked them!" So the sales people arranged for Goldfarb to meet Lionel Weintraub, the company president, when he came to the show. "We got along great," Goldfarb remembers. "I must have sold forty-eight or fifty items to Ideal over the years."

Over those years, in fact, Goldfarb worked with nearly all the major toymakers, once accidentally burning the desk of Mattel cofounder Elliot Handler, while showing him an idea that became Vac-U-Form. Vac-U-Form was a toy that let a child become the toymaker: You could melt a sheet of plastic to mold little cars, boats, or log cabins. Like many of Goldfarb's creations, Vac-U-Form objects have since become a highly prized collectors' item.

The world of the independent toy designer is precarious, as one lives from invention to invention. "It's definitely a 'What have you done for me lately?' business," says Elliot Rudell, who conceived such games as Weebles (wobbly figures for preschoolers) and Splash Out (a game that employs an exploding water balloon). "You're on your own out there."

"We have a saying among inventors that R&D in the independent toy-creating world doesn't mean Research and Development. It really means Royalty and Decadence. Or Rejection and Depression," he says. "Being an independent creator gives you time to chase dreams. The downside is that if you don't perform, you don't eat."[15] It's literally feast or famine.

The inventor's creative carrot, however, is the possible high of producing a monster-selling toy. Reuben Klamer, an Ohio-born toy inventor, was the son of Romanian Jewish immigrants. He went to work for Ideal after graduating from Ohio State and created a few toys for them that were modestly successful. But then in 1959, after a failed pitch for another toy, Milton Bradley approached him and suggested he try to develop a new game to celebrate the centennial of the Milton Bradley company. He came up with the Game of Life, which became a staple of many a suburban home, right next to Monopoly, Clue, and other "all-age" games.[16]

Finally, there was George Hansburg. Born in Ukraine in 1887 to German Jewish parents, he emigrated alone to the United States at eighteen, put himself through night school, learned English, and took classes at the Arts Students League. George was one of those independent creative types who was constantly inventing new products. But he just happened to marry into the Michtom family. (He married my grandfather's sister, Frances, and thus was my great-uncle.) He waited for years for a call that never came—the call from Ben to bring him into the toy business at Ideal.

George invented what he called a "bathinette," which was a bathtub for children, basically a basinet molded in plastic that could be inserted into a bathtub, a transition between the sink and the full tub. And he also created Babee Tenda, basically a small fortress: The baby was inserted into the center and was surrounded by a chest-high play surface on three sides. The baby could sit or walk but couldn't hurt itself.

But George Hansburg is best known neither for the bathinette nor for the Babee Tenda but for a child's toy: the pogo stick, which he created in 1917. So the pogo stick is Jewish?

An old Burmese tale tells of a man whose daughter is about to be married during monsoon season. The father creates a set of stilts made of bamboo so his daughter will be able to walk over the puddles in her bridal dress. Unlike actual stilts, though, the feet can move up and down on the steps. Hansburg, who at the time was dabbling in furniture making, was hired by Gimbels to create something like those stilts that moved while walking. The wood was imported from Germany, but it arrived water damaged and warped. So Hansburg created an all-metal, spring-enclosed version and began producing them at a small factory on the family's large manor house property in Ellenville, New York.

Hansburg loved showing off his pogo sticks and would give them to children in Central Park or on busy New York streets to promote them. He also taught all the dancers at the New York Hippodrome and the Ziegfeld Follies how to pogo. The Follies incorporated them into a show in the 1920s.

And who else but a Jew would be responsible for video games in the early 1960s? First-generation Jews had been major players in the development of the pinball machine since the 1930s, when they were first introduced. (They'd begun in Britain in the 1870s, based on a French game called Bagatelle.) Bally was founded in 1932 by Raymond Moloney, but David Gottlieb had already begun producing Bingo and Baffle Ball, countertop mechanical games, in 1931, and within a year he was joined by Stern Pinball, founded by Sam Stern. These three companies remain the largest pinball machine companies today.

But about those video games. Ralph Baer, a German Jew, fled Germany at sixteen in 1938, just before the Kristallnacht attacks, because his family saw what was coming, especially after Ralph was expelled from his gymnasium and forced to attend an all-Jewish school. A self-taught electrical engineer, Baer worked on surgical equipment, circuit boards, and some military projects for Sanders Associates in Nashua, New Hampshire. In 1966 he was well aware that there were television sets in a substantial number of American homes—over 40 million of them, in fact—but they were one-way machines. "Maybe," he said, "we can figure out a way to interact with these things."

In 1966 he created a television-based target-shooting game, using a light gun; he also created a two-person sports video game. By 1969 he had fashioned a video game console that could play multiple games, and he'd developed the cartridges on which the games could be loaded. The Odyssey was born, acquired by Magnavox—it would later be licensed to Atari to develop Pong. He also created Simon, which also sold millions of units.

The Toy Nexus

The first-generation Jews who created the toys that so fully defined American childhood also developed downstream relationships—the sales forces, marketers, distribution platforms, and retail outlets that sold the toys. It wouldn't be too far-fetched to say that the toy industry in America was a Jewish industry because it married these two first-generation qualities: the childish curiosity and playfulness that had been denied these men and women as children, and the entrepreneurial spirit of seeing, and seizing, the main chance. The downstream collaborations were also a significant point of contact between the German Jews, who had established many of the department stores, and the Yiddish-speaking Jews who were establishing the toy companies.

Hundreds of young Jewish boys entered the toy industry through the selling side, not the making side. A wide regional nexus of toy distributors relied on hundreds of salesmen.[17] Among the biggest, with the largest national reach, was Shepher, which began in 1931 and morphed from being a mammoth distributor into a reseller, buying unsold inventory from Toys "R" Us and other stores and reselling to closeout stores like Dollar Stores. Pincus Monchik, a Yiddish-speaking immigrant from Poland, found himself living in squalor on the Lower East Side with eight children to care for. In 1945, four of his six boys—Sidney, Bert, Irving, and Bill—returned from the war wondering what to do with themselves. They settled in the East New York section of Brooklyn, on Shepherd Avenue. By accident, opportunity, or a little bit of both, they ended up selling toys, then distributing them. They tried to incorporate as Shepherd, after their street address, but the name was already taken, so they lopped off the *d* and became Shepher. "All the big distribution companies were groups of Jewish brothers," Richie Monchik, whose grandfather was one of the four founders, told me. It's remained a family business.[18]

Bernard, Nathan, and Stanley Greenman were a group of Jewish brothers in Long Island, whose teams of salesmen fanned out across the Northeast. Farther afield from the International Toy Center, Melvin Lachman founded Lachman-Rose just after the war in San Antonio and distributed all across the Southwest. Jacob Blatt started out as a buyer for a toy distributor in Pittsburgh and moved to Los Angeles in the early 1950s, capitalizing on the great western migration. These and dozens of other outfits were virtually all owned and staffed by Jewish men, many the sons and grandsons of those first salesmen. They formed the nexus that linked the toy companies to the children who gleefully opened their presents at Christmas. The Grinch may have tried to steal Christmas, according to Dr. Seuss, but it was Jews who sold Christmas back to the Christians. Who do you think originated the "Spirit of Christmas" parade in Memphis but department store owner Jacob Goldsmith? And where else but at Rich's department store would hundreds of thousands of Atlantans assemble every year for the annual lighting of the Christmas tree?[19]

Regional chains were other powerhouses. Boston-based Zayre, founded by Morris and Max Feldberg in the mid-1950s, was a discount retail chain operating throughout the Northeast. Neisner's, founded in Rochester in 1911 by brothers Abraham and Joseph Neisner, outgrew its origins as a five-and-dime store to operate nearly two hundred stores nationwide. Likewise Kuhn's, founded in 1913 in Tennessee as a five-and-dime, grew, under Lee Kuhn's leadership, to more than fifty stores across the South, then transformed itself into a big-box store, Big-K, in the early 1960s (before selling out to Walmart in 1981). And Bradlees, the New England discount retail giant, was founded by Ted Frankel and other local Jews; they named it after Bradley Airport in Hartford, which was where they had initially held their meetings and concealed their ethnic origin in WASPy New England.[20]

Several of the discount retail chains grew in size and scale as America suburbanized. Bigger-box stores anchored the new shopping malls across the country, and their toy departments grew to accommodate their increasingly outdoorsy clientele. But then Charles Lazarus entered the picture, and the toy world was forever transformed.

Lazarus was born in 1923 in Washington, D.C., to Jewish parents who owned a bicycle repair shop. After service in World War II, he went to work in a children's furniture store, eventually taking it over. He opened his first toys-only store in Rockville, Maryland, in 1957. He called it Toys "R" Us. Lazarus transformed the toy-selling business from a seasonal affair—close to 70 percent of all toy sales in the 1930s and '40s took place during the Christmas season—to a year-round affair, with shelves constantly stocked. Toys "R" Us was a veritable toy supermarket, containing every toy from every manufacturer under one roof. For the next forty years, it was the country's largest toy retailer, surpassed only by Walmart in 1998, the year Lazarus stepped down as CEO. (In an ironic coda, Toys "R" Us bought FAO Schwarz in 2009 and was responsible for closing the flagship store on Fifth Avenue and 59th Street in Manhattan.)

Lazarus wasn't the only one. Two other giant retailers, taken together, commanded the lion's share of the toy market. K-B Toys was founded as a wholesale candy store by the Kaufman brothers (hence the K-B), Harry and Joseph, in Pittsfield, Massachusetts, in 1922. Immediately after the war, they acquired a wholesale toy store from a client who owed them money. The company transitioned from wholesale to retail and moved into shopping malls all across the Midwest and Northeast. At its zenith, K-B Toys had more than 170 stores.

Child World was even bigger. Begun in 1962 by Sid Schneider and Joseph Arnesano, also in Massachusetts, Child World had over 180 stores, and the owners often placed them in malls close to Toys "R" Us stores, seeking to compete directly. (In this respect, they took a page from Ray Kroc's playbook, as he had a habit of placing his McDonald's franchises across the street from local competitors.)

After Child World acquired The Children's Place, they became for a time, the second-largest U.S. toy retailer. (It was in a Child World store that Tom Cruise worked as a clerk in Martin Scorsese's film *The Color of Money*.)

All these stores eventually succumbed to industry consolidation, the retreat of shopping malls in the face of online shopping, and management missteps. But during the baby boom and for some time beyond, the nexus of Jewish-owned manufacturers, distributors, wholesalers, salesmen, and retailers didn't simply "dominate" the toy industry in America. They defined it.

Novel Ways to Sell Novelties

But why create toys, made for children, only to market them to grown-ups, advertise them to grown-ups, in grown-up magazines, and send out legions of salesmen and women to sell them to other adults who owned and operated department stores? Why not advertise directly to children themselves, and let kids become the toys' sales force?

In an earlier era, a clever candy store owner might strategically place a box of some new knickknack or novelty at the cash register, where a child with a few cents left over could spend it. But as the 1950s prosperity created the suburban middle class, kids suddenly had more pocket money and an eagerness to spend it. It was difficult, as we've seen, for children to escape the pull of comic books in the 1950s and '60s, so that seemed a logical place for marketers to start. And as any child raised on Superman comic books can tell you, the back cover was almost always taken by ads for Charles Atlas's bodybuilding kit, promising to turn scrawny little boys into brawny he-men through a regimen of barbells, weights, and spring-action muscle building apparatus.

Increasingly, a comic books' inside covers, and a growing number of their back pages, were taken up with ads for novelties that were designed to delight comics readers. Just as advertisements dominated magazines for adults, they increasingly provided a solid revenue stream for comic book publishers.

Milton Levine, for one, took full advantage of the moment. Born in 1916 in Pittsburgh to Jewish immigrant parents, he was working in the plastics industry when he teamed up with a company to create supercheap flat toy soldiers. You may have seen his ads in comic books that read "100 Toy Soldiers for $1.00!" He also created the "shrunken heads" that were a fad in the early 1960s.

Levine's big breakthrough came one Fourth of July at a picnic where found himself fascinated watching ants in an anthill. "We should make an antarium," he told a friend. He worked on it for a while and eventually created the Ant Farm, with his brother-in-law, E. J. Cossman. They formed their own toy company, Uncle Milton Toys, to produce them.

It was complicated. When you bought the Ant Farm, you received a plastic case with a farm scene on the surface and visible tunnels for ants. The ants didn't come with the case. You got a coupon that you sent back and then received the ants in the mail. It was a toy that kept on giving. Since it was illegal to transport queen ants, you had to order new ants every few months.

Why stop at ants? Harold Nathan Braunhut was born in Memphis to a Jewish family who moved to New York City when he was five. He became a prolific inventor and a brilliant, if unscrupulous, marketer of novelties and toys, including X-Ray Specs, Crazy Crabs, and Invisible Goldfish. His biggest hit, though, was Sea Monkeys. They weren't monkeys at all; they were brine shrimp, tiny crustaceans that came with their own aquarium, food, a water purifier, and a packet of "Instant Live Eggs." When released into the tank, they would magically "come alive" in a matter of minutes, and you'd have tiny creatures that looked like a cross between miniature capuchin monkeys and sea horses, about the size of the ants in Uncle Milt's Ant Farm.

Braunhut's life was nothing like those of the other first-generation Jewish toymakers and inventors. While many remained reliable Roosevelt liberal Democrats, others drifted rightward to the Republican Party as their fortunes grew. The cartoonist Al Capp, for example, went from a quasi-socialist to a Nixon Republican, vehemently opposed to welfare and civil rights. (He denounced his own campus followers as Students Wildly Indignant about Nearly Everything, or SWINE.) But regardless of their domestic political alignment, they all remained fervent Zionists, supporting the new state of Israel and funding Jewish charities at home.

Not Braunhut. As he aged, in the 1980s, he dropped his middle name and added "von" to make it sound more Germanic. Increasingly drawn to the extreme Right, he bought firearms for a faction of the Ku Klux Klan and regularly attended Aryan Nations meetings. Under the name Harold von Braun (perhaps to connect him to the German atomic physicist, Wernher), he founded and ran an organization called the National Anti-Zionist Institute. (You can figure out the acronym.)[21]

One novelty appealed to both children and adults—or as the manufacturer might have said, to children of all ages. How many corporate desks and children's bedrooms had a Magic 8 Ball sitting there, an oracle of vague predictions and constant amusement? It was created by Albert Carter, the son of a Cincinnati clairvoyant, who brought what he called the "Syco-Seer" to two first-generation Jews to develop and market. First he turned to Lucien Cohen, a local psychology professor, who devised the twenty possible answers the ball could provide—ten positive, five negative, and five neutral. These he thought would answer the largest range of yes-or-no questions. In the prototype ball, the answer cube sat in a viscous liquid—one toy historian says Carter originally used molasses. Carter then showed it to Max Levinson, a local store owner, who saw the marketing possibilities and turned to his brother-in-law, Abe Bookman (born Abe Buchman to Russian Jewish immigrant parents).

Alabe Crafts (a portmanteau of Albert and Abe) began production of a crystal ball, but it didn't sell particularly well. But Brunswick Billiards Company saw in it a possible novelty they could use to promote their pool tables, which were becoming a big sales item for those suburban playrooms. Bookman engineered a complete redesign to the black eight-ball, and the Magic 8 Ball soon became a crossover hit with both children and grown-ups.[22]

Toys and the Tube

At five p.m. on October 3, 1955, the world of childhood changed again—and with it, the world of children's desires. That was when *The Mickey Mouse Club* debuted on ABC.

Television and the suburbs grew up together, mutually reinforcing the new postwar family. Television brought families together and also separated them into segments. There were shows for kids, shows for grown-ups, and shows for entire families. By the late 1950s, television played an increasingly important role in the creation of childhood and spurred debates on its effects on the kids themselves.

Some parents, and parenting experts, fretted that the new medium was making children more docile and passive, while others worried that it stimulated aggressive thoughts and that seeing violent images on television would make children more violent. Some believed that television could spur creativity and curiosity; others worried that children would become dull and dumb and take school less seriously. Still others worried about its possible ill-effects on health, especially eyesight. This concern is commonly expressed for media innovations, including comic books, video games, and later, iPhones.

Since precious little empirical research had been conducted on the effects of television, these debates rehearsed earlier discussions about the effects of comic books, and even radio, on consumers. In the mid-1950s the British researcher Hilde Himmelweit and her colleagues conducted the first large-scale empirical study of the effects of television on children. (At the time, Britain had only two television networks, the state-run BBC and ITV, which had been formed in 1954 to permit commercial television.) In a study of 4,500 children in four cities, Himmelweit and her colleagues found little evidence on either side: Children did not simply absorb television like uncritical sponges; nor did the medium lead them to prefer a truncated version of life or to lose initiative. Far from leading to a "jaded palate," television actually expanded children's curiosity.[23] Television did, however, have one major effect. While it didn't reduce or dilute children's interests, it tended to displace other hobbies. (There are only so many hours in a day.)

Television replaced radio as the centerpiece of the living room. There, during prime time, families would gather together to watch westerns, sitcoms, and game shows. Since television was initially a group medium, TV programming was designed to please the whole family, sitting together around their one television set. As families increasingly re-centered their family hours around television set, the bonds between children and the industries that catered to them were duly and durably cemented.

For toy companies, television was the perfect medium to reach children directly, resulting in a productive symbiosis between programs and advertisements. Television created a new class of potential consumers: children.[24] Often the relationship between the shows and the products being advertised was truly seamless. Just as, in adult television, game show and variety show emcees would slip into the role of pitchmen for products of companies sponsoring the shows, so too would kid show hosts pitch products during commercial breaks. If not live, then in a filmed spot, these same hosts, speaking in the same camp counselor voices children knew from the shows, would hawk breakfast cereals, milk additives, and toys and games. This bond between the medium of television and companies that ministered to the needs and desires of children enabled TV to become the most important constitutive element in the new American childhood.

In Hollywood film studios, many heads were either Jewish immigrants or first-generation American Jews; so too in New York television studios. The first TV networks were nearly entirely Jewish-owned: CBS (William Paley), NBC (David Sarnoff), and ABC (Leonard Goldenson). But most of the time they stayed in the background, content to have "real" Americans in front of the camera, representing "real" America to "real" Americans. "The trouble-free, all-white, Christian world of fifties television was largely the product of immigrants," as the culture critic Susan Bordo puts it, "who created that world from their own fantasies of what it meant to be American, their fears of repelling Christian viewers, and/or their ambivalence about reinforcing Jewish stereotypes."[25] In the mid-1950s, those stereotypes were seeping into American homes through that magical box.

Just as the studios were largely owned by first-generation Jews, many backstage and producer roles were played by first-generation Jews as well. Mark Goodson and Bill Todman, two Jewish New Yorkers, produced a long run of successful prime-time game shows, including *I've Got a Secret*, *The Price Is Right*, *Password*, *Beat the Clock*, *To Tell the Truth*, *Family Feud*, and many others.

A few times it didn't go so well. In 1957 a payola scandal swept across the American TV landscape, prefiguring the payola scandal that would engulf radio stations two years later. Goodson and Todman had created such a formidable lineup that any effort to break through was going to have to be daring—or illegal. Enter producers Dan Enright and Jack Barry. A couple of Long Island boys, Enright (né Ehrenreich) and Barry (né Barasch), would produce the shows, and Barry would front them as emcee. Among their contributions were *Tic-Tac-Dough* and *Concentration*. But their infamy came from *Twenty-One*, a short-lived (1956–58) quiz show that pitted two contestants against each other answering questions weighted between one and eleven points. The first contestant to reach twenty-one points would be the winner. The problem was that the questions were too hard, and the contestants got too many wrong. Besides, audiences had a tough time figuring out which contestant to cheer for.

The show's sponsor, Geritol, purveyor of a dietary iron supplement, was increasingly dismayed. To placate them, after a few episodes Enright and Barry seized upon a solution. They picked a nerdy Jewish guy from the Bronx, Herb Stempel, to be a contestant, then fed him the answers in advance. For six straight weeks, Stempel was a star, returning to play every night against a different competitor. Then Enright and Barry made a brilliant move, born of Jewish self-hatred: They found a worthy adversary for Stempel in Charles Van Doren, the son of the illustrious Columbia professor Mark Van Doren. The aristocratic scion would be pitted against the Jewish arriviste. America could cheer for the WASP traditionalist over the craven ethnic climber. The Jew could be allowed in the door, but he couldn't be allowed to win every single time. Armed with the answers and some advance coaching, Van Doren prevailed and was crowned the new champion. It provided a morality tale about assimilation, about growing too comfortable, about feeling so much like you belong that you actually begin to feel entitled. Stempel eventually went public and exposed the fraud, which resulted in the mid-decade quiz show scandal that rocked the television world. For Stempel, it provided a small amount of revenge. *You can't give him the answers*, he seemed to be saying. *You can only give them to me!*

Mickey

If suburbanization, affluence, and plastics created a revolution in the production of toys, the invention of television further changed toy marketing forever. It is hard to overestimate the effects of television on the toy industry. For the first time, on a massive scale, toymakers could market directly to children. Previously, toymakers would take out ads in national circulation magazines, especially magazines that appealed to mothers. The sales job was somewhat reversed: The toymakers had to sell, say, a doll to parents through a magazine, then the parents had to "sell" the doll to their children. Only comic books allowed direct sales pitches to kids. Tie-in dolls were especially convenient for that direct marketing strategy. But no matter how popular comic books were, television added more: instant visual and auditory demonstration of the joy that a toy could bring, real live testimonials from other kids, eager endorsements from contented parents, and most of all, the ability to see a child actually playing with a toy. Shows like *Howdy Doody* permitted a nonstop barrage of direct marketing to children.

The Mickey Mouse Club, which began in 1955, perfectly illustrates this dynamic relationship between content and advertising. Broadcast on weekday afternoons after school let out, the show permitted children to come home to their own entertainments. On that very first show, Louis Marx and Company advertised its toys, and Mattel joined the chorus with its Mouse Guitar. Sales were brisk.

Later, Hasbro promoted Mr. Potato Head. (Ideal lagged behind, latecomers to TV advertising.) This decision to advertise to children fifty-two weeks a year, as the business economists Sydney Ladensohn Stern and Ted Schoenhaus write, "so revolutionized the industry that it is not an exaggeration to divide the history of the American toy business into two eras, before and after television."[26]

In fact, the relationship between the shows and the products being advertised was often truly seamless. On *The Mickey Mouse Club*, Jimmie, the adult head Mousketeer, wrote a little jingle for Ipana toothpaste that he sang while the product's mascot, Bucky Beaver, brushed his oversize teeth. The toothpaste more than tripled its sales.

The Children's Hour

Saturday morning was kids' time. Reverend Martin Luther King, Jr., once said that "the most segregated hour of Christian America is eleven o'clock on Sunday morning," but Saturday mornings from eight a.m. to eleven a.m. were surely the most age-segregated hours of a family's day, as kids watched *Fury*, *The Adventures of Rin-Tin-Tin*, *Andy's Gang*, and *Sky King*—a welcome relief from the restricted weekday "family" programming that benefited both parents and children.

I recall that on Saturday mornings, before my parents were awake, my sister and I had a ritual that lasted a couple of years. She would come into my room and climb into my bed, and we'd watch television together. (I would have been nine or ten, and she six or seven.) I'd get some of those individual-size boxes of Sugar Pops or Frosted Flakes from the kitchen, and we'd eat them right out of the box as we watched kids' TV shows for hours. Those were glorious mornings together, and the shows and the ads for toys and games constructed our fantasies as well as our more mundane wishes for birthday and holiday presents.

Children's television shows on Saturday mornings rehearsed the frontstage-gentile and backstage-Jew dynamic that held sway in prime time and during family TV time. The front men were almost always "real" Americans, but the guys in the back rooms, writing, producing, and editing, were often what you might call TV Jews: Men like Jack Chertok, who took over producing *Our Gang* from Hal Roach, then went on to produce *The Lone Ranger.* And Herbert Leonard, who produced both *Circus Boy* and *The Adventures of Rin-Tin-Tin.* And Sidney Salkow, who created *Fury.* And Howard Friedlander, who wrote the scripts for *Captain Kangaroo*, which ran for twenty-nine years.

Jay Ward (born Joseph Ward Cohen in 1920 in Berkeley, California) created *Crusader Rabbit*, *The Adventures of Rocky and Bullwinkle and Friends*, and *George of the Jungle*, among others. (He also created a character named Oski Bear, which became the cheerful mascot of University of California athletics.) These clever cartoons appealed to children but also contained sly messages to older viewers. Short interludes like "Dudley Do-Right of the Mounties" and "Fractured Fairy Tales" (send-ups of classic stories) could amuse both parents and children, while the main show's villains—a ne'er-do-well Soviet spy couple Boris Badenov and Natasha Fatale—constantly encouraged kids to the most outrageous antics.

One of the greatest behind-the-scenes creators was the voice of many of the most iconic cartoon characters: Mel Blanc. Born Melvin Jerome Blank in 1908 in Portland, Oregon, Blanc as a child was surrounded by different languages and dialects, most notably his family's Yiddish, "Brooklynese" from his Brooklyn-born father, and Japanese, which he heard in the market. As a boy, he watched silent cartoons and made up voices for the characters.

In Blanc's menagerie of animal characters, everybody was a goofball or a wise guy. Through their voices, Blanc channeled the tough streets of Brooklyn into Daffy Duck and Bugs Bunny. "So, I thought 'what are the toughest voices I know?' " he reminisced. "They've got to be Brooklyn or the Bronx, so I put the two of 'em taggeda, Doc." When the film producer Leon Schlesinger asked him to develop the voice of Porky Pig, Blanc asked, "You want me to be the voice of a pig? That's some job for a nice Jewish boy."[27] Schlesinger was Blanc's patron, promoter, and producer. Born to a poor Jewish family in

Philadelphia in 1884, Schlesinger was the producing muscle behind, first, Leon Schlesinger Productions, which eventually became Warner Bros. cartoons, producing both *Looney Tunes* and *Merrie Melodies.*

Every type of show that adults enjoyed had a miniature version for children. Variety shows like *Ed Sullivan* and *Jack Benny* had parallels with *The Mickey Mouse Club* and *Andy's Gang.* Prime time game show like *What's My Line?* and *The Price Is Right* had children's spinoffs, like *Wonderama*, hosted by Sonny Fox from 1959 to 1967. A friendly, avuncular, and animated host, Fox was from an Orthodox Jewish family in Brooklyn.

Fox wasn't the only Jewish host of TV shows for kids. Some shows blurred the line between school and home by being set in a studio done up as a classroom. As "Miss Frances," Frances Horwich hosted *Ding Dong School. Romper Room* was created by Bert and Nancy Claster in Baltimore in 1953. When the original host dropped out, Nancy filled in and stayed. Her regular segment of "Do Bees" and "Don't Bees" became a staple of child culture. Perhaps her most radical moment was to get a polio shot on live television, to allay children's (and their parents') fears of the vaccine.

The puppeteer and ventriloquist Phyllis Naomi Hurwitz also entertained children with puppets like Lamb Chop using the stage name Shari Lewis. Born in 1933 in New York City, Lewis was the daughter of immigrants from Vilnius; her father was a professor at Yeshiva University who had been named New York City's "official magician" by Mayor La Guardia. He taught Lewis magic and encouraged her to become a performer.

Several young Jewish performers found being a clown on children's television a far easier way to make a living than trying to be a full-fledged comedian, like so many others from the neighborhood. Lawrence Weiss changed his name to Larry Harmon—but he was far better known as Bozo the Clown. Milton Supman entertained two generations of kids—the first sincerely and the second generation ironically—as Soupy Sales. Pinky Lee, as mentioned earlier, was born in 1907 as Pincus Leff in St. Paul, Minnesota, and had, as his trademark, a too-small plaid bowler hat, a too-big bow tie, and high-energy antics. His show began in 1954 and was sponsored by Tootsie Roll. Lee and Sales were both somewhat less "wholesome" than other characters in children's programming, with frequent kiddie violence: Lee wore a flower that squirted seltzer at his foes, and Sales often got a pie in the face. They often conspiratorially winked to the kids, as when Sales instructed them to take the "green pieces of paper" from their parents' wallets and send them to him. No wonder their shows were embraced ironically by suburban teenagers as much as they were by their target audience.[28]

Many of these children's variety shows had regular segments that were broadcast in each show. Few of the performers were as successful as the Three Stooges, who took the Marx Brothers' physical antics and nudge-nudge double-entendre comedy, stripped it of all intellectual pretension, and produced nearly two hundred individual slapstick knucklehead episodes. While their parents were watching the likes of Jack Benny, George Burns, Milton Berle, Sid Caesar, Woody Allen, Mel Brooks, Rodney Dangerfield, and countless others on grown-up variety shows like *Ed Sullivan*, the kids were watching three boychiks from Bensonhurst—the Horwitz brothers—Moses, Samuel, and Jerome, joined by their neighbor and friend Louis Feinberg—playing Moe, Larry, and Shemp or, later, Moe, Larry, and Curly. These sons of an Orthodox garment cutter and a housewife who dabbled in real estate were "grade school mischief makers fascinated by silent movies," according to the historian Paul Buhle. With their physical comedy, they were among the few, and best, original vaudeville troupes to make the transition to movies and television.[29]

For my sister Sandi and me, if watching the shows wasn't enough, we could even appear on them. One of my father's patients (he was a chiropractor) had a connection to *Wonderama*, hosted by Sonny Fox, and on one Saturday in 1962 Sandi and I were in the audience. In an impromptu interview, Sandi was asked what advice she got from our mother that morning. "Don't talk like a Dead End Kid," she replied. "And don't fight with *him*!" she added, pointing at me. As for me, well, I won the spelling bee, the finale of the morning show, the big kahuna of *Wonderama*—which was, I think, the proudest moment of my twelve-year-old life. (I won a complete home workout set—barbells, wrist and chest crushers, and ankle weights—which I never used but couldn't bear to throw away.)

Earlier in my kid-television career, I'd had one of those moments that could only happen on live TV, a moment that taping shows would eventually eliminate, much to the relief of the sponsors and censors. Because of another of my father's connections, this one to a producer on *Howdy Doody*, I was chosen to participate in a commercial during one of the breaks. It was for Bosco, a chocolate syrup that was added to milk, no doubt to encourage kids to drink more milk. Buffalo Bob, the show's emcee and host, mixed Bosco into the milk and handed it to me. As the cameras were rolling, he ask if I liked it, anticipating that I would say something along the lines of "Yum, it's delicious." Instead, I took a big gulp and blurted out, "My mommy always gives me Ovaltine!" (Bosco's chief competitor). Fortunately, I didn't know enough to be mortified. Buffalo Bob couldn't go to a commercial since I *was* the commercial, so they did the next best thing—they pivoted to a filmed segment.

The King of Saturday Morning

One toy inventor created so many action figures and dolls that he became known as the "King of Saturday Morning." Developing toys for all the major toy companies, Bernard Loomis may have been the most successful toy creator in history. Advertisements for toys he developed dominated the airwaves of children's television in the 1950s and '60s. Indeed, he stitched marketing, advertising, and creation into a seamless cloak.

The "King of Saturday Morning" did not exactly have a regal childhood. In fact, Bernard Loomis, born in the Bronx in 1923, hardly had any childhood at all. His father was a Russian immigrant who eked out a meager existence in the garment industry. When that didn't work out, he became an agent for the Yiddish theater, mostly burlesque, then became an agent for many Jewish comedians.[30]

Bernie was so poor, in fact, that he later said he had had no toys as a child—yet another first-generation Jewish boy whose own privation led him to entrepreneurial stardom. What he did have was imagination. A precocious child, a voracious reader with an animated mind, he constructed a vast railroad empire using only the pictures in a Lionel train catalog. As an avid Yankees fan, he used a regular deck of playing cards to create an entire imaginary American League baseball season, noting every card as a ball, strike, pop fly, single, and so on, and filling notebooks with the statistics of these "games."

In a sense, Loomis's career encapsulates the experience of so many of the creative first-generation Jews. His family's financial instability gave him a feeling that he needed to be connected to a big company, protected by its size and power, rather than go off on his own. He was an "intrepreneur," creating and inventing, but always within a large company. Thus, as the eternal inside-outsider, or outside-insider, he worked for every major toy company but didn't start one of his own; he was eager to succeed and be accepted as an insider, only to be reminded, from time to time, that he really didn't fit in. When he worked for Mattel, he moved his family to Palos Verdes, an affluent suburb, but was barred from membership in the local country club because he was Jewish. Later, as CEO of Kenner, he moved the family to Cincinnati, where he was barred from joining the local *Jewish* country club because they considered him a "lower-class" Jew.

Is this not the perpetual plight of the outside-insider/inside-outsider? Too Jewish, not Jewish enough. Not quite one of us, not quite one of them. The Jew is the Goldilocks of history: too hot, too cold; too big, too small; never just right.

But he was "just right" within the several companies he worked for. Each one of them became the largest toy company in the world while he worked there. His story began in 1961, when a chance meeting with Ruth and Elliot Handler, co-founders and CEO[s] of Mattel at the Toy Fair in New York, led him to join their company just as it was about to take off. In 1969 he created a line of toy cars called Hot Wheels. To market them, he thought, instead of buying advertising time on children's television shows, why not give them a show of their own? So the TV show *Hot Wheels* was born, a virtual thirty-minute

Toy-Machers! CEOs of major toy companies at banquet dinner at Toy Fair, 1961. Starting at the bottom center and working counterclockwise: Ruth and Elliot Handler (Mattel), Sylvia and Merrill Hassenfeld (Hasbro), Fred Ertl (ERTL toys, not Jewish), Bernie and Lillian Loomis (Kenner) and Lionel and Bette Weintraub (Ideal), Philip Behrman and Bertha Alexander Behrman (Madame Alexander).

commercial for one product. (The show was short-lived: the FCC found that it blurred the line between programming and advertising, and networks that carried it had to list it as "advertising." It would be years before the infomercial was created as a legitimately scheduled program.)

Loomis also pitched to Mattel the idea of action figures based on characters in TV shows and movies, like *The Six Million Dollar Man* and *Jurassic Park*. His great gift seemed to be his understanding of how to marry television to character-driven toys. He left Mattel and began working at Kenner, when he noticed a short article in a newspaper in 1976 about a forthcoming sci-fi movie. He knew nothing about the director, George Lucas, but he liked the title: *Star Wars*. For next to nothing, he bought the "intergalactic" licensing rights to make games and toys based on the movie. "I contend that George Lucas is one of the world's great toy designers," he told a journalist.[31]

Just as the film *Star Wars* exceeded everyone's wildest imagination, so did the demand for *Star Wars* action figures. As Christmas 1977 approached, Kenner realized it couldn't possibly meet the demand for the toys by Christmas. In other words, it was screwed.

Not so fast, Bernie said. What was the typical Christmas morning scene? Everyone opened their presents, left the boxes by the side, and played with them for a month or two. "So what if we sell them an empty box with a certificate to redeem for the toy in February, when the excitement of Christmas would be over, and the kids had something new and exciting to play with?" Bernie asked. "Are you mad?" said one of the marketing execs. "You want to sell people an empty box and a promise?" "Exactly."

And they did. *Star Wars* action figures debuted that Christmas with a small box containing a bunch of "Early Bird Certificate" stickers. You'd send the company your certificate, and a few months later it would send you the toy. It worked, much to everyone's surprise. That is, it worked far beyond anyone's wildest fantasies. The company sold about 40 million action figures that first year.[32] Over the years, the toys tallied more than $1 billion in sales. (At the same time, Loomis turned down a chance to license action figures based on Steven Spielberg's *Close Encounters of the Third Kind* because he thought the characters were not, as he put it, "toyetic.")

Loomis's last stop on his illustrious career was at American Greetings, a greeting card company, seemingly an unlikely landing for a toy developer. (It was founded in 1906 by the Polish immigrant Jacob Sapirstein, who made a living selling cards from a horse-drawn cart.) By the 1970s, second only to Hallmark in size and sales, American Greetings was looking to expand into the licensed toy business. Tom Wilson, who'd been creative director there, was developing a line of products based on a comic strip character named Ziggy. He proposed it Loomis as the basis for a toy.

Loomis thought the comic strip was cute but didn't find Ziggy particularly "toyetic," so he passed on the project. "You got anything else?" he asked Wilson. Wilson showed him some greeting cards that were in development, and one of them caught Bernard's eye. She was called Strawberry Shortcake. "Now *she's* toyetic!" he exclaimed, and they developed a licensing program for one of the most successful lines ever.[33]

As a final gesture to the industry that he embodied for half a century, Loomis decided to do something about gender and toys. His daughter Merry would later recall that he'd always been uncomfortable with the strict gendering—girls with pink dolls and boys with action figures and guns. Now he wanted to see if he could bridge a divide that had been so well implanted in people's minds. At a meeting with the American Greetings development people, he posed a question for a brainstorming session: What was the most successful best nongendered toy in the world? The teddy bear. And what was the foundation of greetings cards? Feelings, sentiments, comfort, and love. Perhaps the emotional expressiveness of the cards and the genderlessness of the teddy bear could be married. Care Bears were born.

The Kidvid Controversy

The marriage of medium and message, of TV shows and the products that were advertising on them, was always fraught. After all, the companies were marketing directly to children, bypassing their parents. Ads made to appeal to children directly, not to their parents, could be a little more adventurous, a little more animated.

Not everyone was happy about this arrangement. And just as the baby boom years had begun with political investigations into the effects of comic books and Communists on impressionable young minds, the official baby boom ended in the 1970s with hearings on the effects of television advertising on those minds. The 1970s kidvid hearings focused not on the content of children's shows but on the nearly twenty thousand advertisements that an average child watched every year—mostly for sugary cereals and other foods that promoted bad dental hygiene. Michael Pertschuk, chairman of the Federal Trade Commission, argued that advertising to children was inherently unfair because children didn't understand the persuasive power of the ads and couldn't distinguish between shows and advertisements. As a result, the FTC argued, television was creating "a generation of fat children with decaying teeth who are intellectually passive, prone to violence, and profoundly materialistic."[34]

When executives at the toy companies and the advertisers were called to testify, Abe Kent, from Ideal, had the last word. Children had more sensitive radar than the reformers thought they did, he said. They were not simply passive sponges, sopping up uncritically whatever the shows offered, desiring every new object, unable to distinguish between a story and a commercial. *But hey,* he testified, *don't believe me.* He had asked his six-year-old daughter, "What is a commercial?" She had replied, "It's when someone tries to sell you something."

This and other testimonies convinced the lawmakers, and the kidvid hearings were a colossal failure, an example of government overreach. But the argument that children are shaped by the culture around them and by the environments in which they find themselves arose straight from conceptions of child development that had been ushered in by child psychologists earlier in the century and had become universally accepted truths.

Another consequence of the saturation of suburbia by television, and television's direct marketing to children, was that toys became increasingly gendered. Toys had always been gendered—just remember Erector Sets and all those dolls. But in the days before television, the marketing of toys had been to adults—on radio, in magazines, and in newspapers. Adults had had some choices about what to buy for their children. Most parents hewed to the traditional separation of genders assiduously. This wasn't a time of gender nonconformity, after all. The binary was asserted and accepted.

But television exaggerated the separation of the sexes, just at the very moment when women were entering the workplace, and dads were coming home from the war and being advised to anchor themselves in their home lives. Just as there were rumblings of critique of the separation of the sexes for grown-ups, the gendering of toys reasserted the naturalness of gender separation for children. Boys played with boys, and girls played with girls, and the two rarely met anywhere close to the middle. Boys' play centered on sports, soldiers, and cars; girls', on dolls, tea parties, and more dolls. Girls would learn to be mothers; boys would learn to be adventurers. TV made sure they got the message—and only that message.

9

THE EXPERTS AND THE STORYTELLERS

* * *

If the baby boom was the era of the child, it was also the era of psychological theories *about* the child—theories designed to map children's development with healthy markers by which parents and teachers could gauge their charges' progress. As we learned more about how children develop, the path to their healthy development suddenly seemed more perilous, more strewn with obstacles large and small.

During the baby boom, writes the cultural critic Nicholas Hammond, the United States was "poised between two opposing ideals of child care—older ideals of behaviorism aimed at instilling obedience, versus neo-Freudian 'permissiveness.' "[1] While behaviorism sought to train a child toward a specific outcome in a somewhat impersonal, authoritarian manner, child-centered neo-Freudianism sought to uncover the young individual's independent sense of self and allow them to actualize as individuals on their own terms, within a culture that idealized the American Dream of self-made prosperity and belonging.

One strategy to cope with this bewildering postwar project of raising healthy children was to return to pre-Progressive ideas about child-rearing through structure and discipline. In the view of the behaviorist John Watson, children were just like other animals and could be trained and socialized by behavioral conditioning: Give them a reward when they do something you want them to do, and punish them when they do things you don't want them to do. If that sounds like Pavlov's dogs, well, that's the point. Earlier in the twentieth century, Watson had advised that mothers "never hug or kiss" their children or even "let them sit in your lap." Advising fathers not to do so probably was unnecessary: "If you must," he advised, "kiss them once on the forehead when they say goodnight. Shake hands with them in the morning."[2]

Many observers—experts and parents alike—regarded this view as both regressive and, frankly, appalling. Imagine treating your children as if they were house pets! Parents needed to know how to raise children when the choices were much more numerous, the paths so much more strewn with potential obstacles, and the consequences of getting it "wrong" so much more consequential.

During the Depression and the two world wars, child-rearing had often been fraught with anxiety and instability. After the war, government assuaged parents' anxieties, or at least managed them, with massive initiatives to stabilize the middle-class white family: the interstate highway system, suburbanization, and a building frenzy of public schools. Ready and eager for the material culture of the new American childhood, parents consumed a proliferation of child-rearing books.

The most famous parenting expert was the Connecticut pediatrician Dr. Benjamin Spock, whose *Baby and Child Care* has sold more than 50 million copies since it was first published in 1946. (It's still the best-selling parenting book of all time.) Dr. Spock soothed parental anxieties with a positive vision of childhood as resilient. His permissive child-rearing methods broke with a century of manuals that had instructed parents to impose discipline and structure on their children and to demand obedience and conformity from these otherwise unruly and ill-tempered creatures. Instead, Dr. Spock's book, revised more than twenty times, advised parents—especially mothers—to enjoy their children, to not keep them on rigid schedules, to delay toilet training, to feed them on demand, and to treat their impulses as valid and legitimate. In so doing, he gave children a lot more freedom, while letting parents breathe a sigh of relief that they were doing an adequate job. "Trust yourself," he counseled. "You know more than you think you do."[3]

This model of child-rearing—provided by parents who were loving, nourishing, nurturing, and physically affectionate, and who gave children the freedom to test boundaries, express their curiosity, and explore their worlds—fit perfectly with the postwar era. Toys, puzzles, and family games all bent to the new model of the nuclear family. It articulated that earlier vision of childhood that those Yiddish-speaking Jews had carried into Castle Garden and Ellis Island.

The vision was not only rooted in that migration, it was now articulated by the children of those immigrants. First-generation Jewish psychologists, parenting experts, and doctors led the parade of Progressive-informed child-rearing, and first-generation Jewish parents cheered the parade as it went by. Indeed, among the most venerated child-rearing books, parenting magazines, and websites today, the majority of their creators are Jewish, including Harvey Karp (*The Happiest Baby on the Block*, 2002), Jennifer Waldburger and Jill Spivak (*The Sleepeasy Solution*, 2007), Adele Faber and Elaine Mazlish (*How to Talk So Kids Will Listen and Listen So Kids Will Talk*, 1980), Daniel Siegel, though not coauthor Tina Payne Bryson (*The Whole-Brain Child*, 2011). Richard Ferber's *Solve Your Child's Sleep Problems* (1985) introduced the concept of "ferberizing" a baby by letting them "cry it out." Heidi Murkoff and Sharon Mazel's *What to Expect When You're Expecting* (2008) has sold over 42 million copies worldwide and is read by 93 percent of all pregnant American women who read a pregnancy book.[4]

Don't get me wrong. I'm not claiming that all the pioneering developmental psychologists of the twentieth century were Jewish. Of course not. Dr. Spock himself came from an old patrician family of Dutch origin (both he and his father went to Phillips Andover and Yale) and he had won a gold medal in rowing at the 1924 Olympics. I'm referring to the influence of Jewish *ideas* on the development of the field in the first place.

Many of the postwar developmental psychologists embraced Jean Piaget's "constructivist" theory, a far more sanguine view of child development than previous notions. Piaget had held that young children learn through experience; they decipher meaning and decode themes by manipulating physical objects. So toys were now considered essential building blocks of self-concept. Teachers, in this framework, are guides and mentors, not disciplinarians. One can easily see the symbiotic relationship with the toymakers.

Erik Erikson was the dean of developmental psychologists. Born Erik Salomonsen to a Jewish mother in 1902, he took the name of his stepfather, Homberger, in 1911. His own identity crisis, his own search for a stable identity, gave a personal side to his psychological theories. Erik created himself, rechristening himself Erikson, literally "Erik son of Erik." Erikson gave birth to himself, or so he claimed in his self-naming. Talk about a self-made man! And not by accident, his theory of development was based on the capacity of boys to become men on their own—without the aid or influence of women.

His was a theory of active engagement, not passive acceptance or rote behavioral training (also known as operant conditioning). Children, adolescents, and adults were all active agents, in his view, able to navigate their own developmental crises and create themselves. Erikson's stages of development are about learning through interaction with the environment. By age two or three, he argued, if children are criticized, overly controlled, or denied the ability to assert themselves, they will feel inadequate, lack self-esteem, and experience shame or doubt. By age three to five, the child should be active and engaged; it is a "time of vigor of action and of behaviors that the parents may see as aggressive."

Central to the entire schema is play, which provides children with opportunities to develop their interpersonal skills. Central to play is the ability to animate the inanimate environment and to interact with other children through the use of toys, whether by anthropomorphizing these toys with human characteristics or by using them to mediate and adjudicate interactions with other children.

Thus an entire generation of developmental psychologists broke with the prevailing orthodoxy that child development was simply a matter of the child, either actively or passively, internalizing the norms and values of society. Some of them focused on children's cognitive development, such as Jerome Bruner (born in 1915 in New York City to Polish Jewish parents), while others investigated moral development, such as Lawrence Kohlberg (born in 1927 in New York suburbs to an affluent German Jewish family) and Carol Gilligan (born in 1936 in New York City as Carol Friedman to first-generation Jewish parents). Dorothy Baruch explored language acquisition in her 1949 her child-rearing manual *New Ways in Discipline*.

Urie Bronfenbrenner (born in Russia in 1917, arriving in the United States at age six) argued for a more ecological theory of the self, shaped through constant interaction with the environment. Bronfenbrenner was the architect of the Head Start program in 1965, on the principle of taking children out of toxic environments so that they can thrive in new ones. We're not biologically programmed, he argued; nor are we blank slates. It's the interaction that matters. We *learn*. This emphasis on active agency, modeling, experimenting, and creating, while not exactly Talmudic, does have a certain resonance with a certain religious tradition.

Finally, Haim Ginott's *Between Parent and Child* (1965) codified the developmental model of childhood. He recommended a parent-child relationship was not one of parental dominance over children but rather one of mutual, reciprocal engagement. Ginott (born Haim Ginzburg in Tel Aviv in 1927) had graduated from Teachers College at Columbia in 1948 and earned a Ph.D. in clinical psychology from Columbia in 1952. As a professor at New York University, he wrote a weekly syndicated newspaper column and served as "resident psychologist" for NBC's *Today* show. His book encouraged parents to attend to every feeling, want, or need expressed by their children. He advised them to personalize rules—"Little sisters are not for hitting"—and to depersonalize problems, as in "I see a messy room." He counseled parents to draw on their own experiences as children, in a process akin to method acting, to arrive at an empathic identification with their children.[5]

For Erikson, Ginott, and the others, the goal of child development was not sublimation and self-control but happiness and self-actualization. What a difference! Marrying Freudian ideas of developmental stages to American pragmatic ideas about self-creation, these first-generation Jewish psychologists created a distinctly American theory of child development.

But was there also something distinctly Jewish about the theory? In the sense of being American, it was a decidedly assimilationist project, one that could have been attached to any ethnicity. But these theories center on how the individual finds a place in the world, navigates interactions with others (whether friendly or hostile), and creates a life of stability, safety, and meaning. Perhaps that is why psychology today is so often understood as a "Jewish" field.

Propelled by this theory of child development, with its sense that children were naturally creative and curious, a new sort of children's literature emerged in Europe and the United States. Perhaps no author more successfully—or more seamlessly—fused the world of child-rearing advice with storytelling than Judy Blume, born in 1938 as Judith Sussman. Her books, most notably, *Are You There God? It's Me, Margaret* (1970), dealt frankly with topics that were difficult, if not impossible, for parents to discuss with their children or teachers with their students. They thereby normalized the topics, reassuring both children and parents that everything was going exactly as it should, and that they had nothing to be afraid of. Blume fused the work of Dr. Alfred Kinsey, who had normalized sex simply by describing (and counting) what people were doing and with whom, with that of Dr. Spock, who had assured parents that kids could survive childhood just fine without their own constant parental dread.

But for both Spock and Kinsey, the representative child was the boy. Blume centered girls and spoke directly to them, helping them redefine puberty from a mystery to a normal life passage. In that sense, Judy Blume is arguably responsible for inspiring more American feminist women than even Betty Friedan.

Taming the Wild Things

In the 1946–47 *Jewish Book Annual*, Fanny Goldstein, a librarian at the Boston Public Library, proclaimed, "The 20th Century may well be termed 'The Children's Century,' for everywhere people are striving to create for their children a more ideal environment and a more secure future." Half a century after Ellen Key proclaimed that century's focus in a book about parenting, Goldstein shifted her attention to children themselves. "Books," she continued, "are essential to proper character building and the happiness and enrichment of a child's life."[6] Goldstein, an immigrant from Russia (at age five), had founded Jewish Book Week in 1925 by displaying Jewish children's books at the Boston Public Library. Her mission, as she put it, was to promote book reading among Jewish children.[7]

She was following a path that many Jewish experts and pundits had previously trod. As early as 1922, Rabbi Stephen Wise had advised parents that they could do nothing better for their children than to "foster a taste for worth-while books."[8] After the war, children's books were plentiful. The baby boom exploded the market, and a new generation of children's book authors rushed in to meet the swelling demand, coming not only from the numerous children themselves but also from the many anxious parents who were eager to make sure their offspring had everything needed for a "successful" childhood.

As the culture changed, the content and tone of children's books shifted too. Some became more multicultural, even as the country looked different than it had before. Even as white suburban parents seemed to require cheerful books to match their manicured lawns, some children's book authors probed a somewhat darker, more unsettling, underbelly to those seemingly perfect suburbs.

Many first-generation Jewish authors, not necessarily pushing the limits, sought simply to delight children. They drew not on their own backgrounds—often as poor, Brooklyn-born children of immigrants—but on their beliefs in children's imaginative flights of fancy. To be sure, first-generation Jews didn't represent the majority of children's book authors, but they were dramatically overrepresented in proportion to their numbers. When the New York Public Library surveyed its children's literature librarians in 2013 for the hundred best children's books of the previous century, nearly one-third were written by Jews, nearly all of them first-generation.[9]

Leo Lionni, a Sephardic Jew, was born in 1910 in Amsterdam and came to the United States as a child; he went on to win four Caldecott Medals for his delightful collage books like *Inch by Inch* (1961), *Swimmy* (1964), *Frederick* (1968), and *Alexander and the Wind-Up Mouse* (1970).

Simms Taback, born in the Bronx in 1932 to a working-class immigrant family, was named after Harry Simms, a Jewish labor leader. Taback went on to cofound the Illustration Guild. He illustrated the Caldecott-winning children's book *Joseph Had a Little Overcoat* (2000) and was a runner-up for *There Was an Old Lady Who Swallowed a Fly* (1998). (He was also the designer of McDonald's Happy Meals box.)

Norton Juster was born in Brooklyn in 1929 to a Romanian father and a Polish mother. After training to be an architect, he was posted to a job at the Brooklyn Navy Yard. Possessed of an impish and clever sense of humor, he used his downtime at the navy yard to create the entirely fictitious "Garibaldi Society." Juster advertised for members, created elaborate logos, and wrote application forms and rejection letters. The society's main mission was, actually, to reject all applicants—that is, he had just wanted to see how many people would apply for membership to a society they knew nothing about and that had no public profile, just because of a desire to be accepted. One day while taking out the trash, he met his neighbor, Jules Feiffer; they became fast friends. His first children's book, *The Phantom Tollbooth* (1961), was a colossal success, with illustrations by Feiffer. *The Dot and the Line* (1963), written and illustrated by Juster, is one of the sweetest romances you'll ever read about a line who falls in love with a dot.

Jane Yolen, born in 1939 to Ukrainian immigrant parents, wrote mostly fantasy fiction for children. Her best-known book was about a young boy named Henry who is sent to Wizard's Hall to learn how to be a wizard. Sound familiar? *Wizard's Hall* appeared in 1991, six years before J. K. Rowling's *Harry Potter and the Philosopher's Stone*. Yolen is generous in her assessment of the coincidence:

> I'm pretty sure she never read my book. We were both using fantasy tropes—the wizard school, the pictures on the wall that move. I happen to have a hero whose name was Henry, not Harry. He also had a red-headed best friend and a girl who was also his best friend—though my girl was black, not white. And there was a wicked wizard who was trying to destroy the school, who was once a teacher at the school. But those are all fantasy tropes. . . . There's even a book that came out way before hers where children go off to a witch school or a wizard school by going on a mysterious train that no one else can see except the kids, at a major British train station—I don't know if it was Victoria Station or King's Cross. These things are out there. . . . This is not new.[10]

Arnold Lobel wrote sweet children's books about companionship as a way to compensate for his own terribly unhappy childhood. Born in 1933 in Los Angeles, he was raised in Schenectady where he was constantly bullied. As an adult, he moved to Brooklyn and in 1955 married Anita Kempler, who had been born in Warsaw, hid for several years from the Nazis, and was captured and sent to a concentration camp. In 1945 she'd been rescued by the Swedish Red Cross. The couple lived across from the Prospect Park Zoo, where Arnold spent his time drawing the animals.

Arnold's books are sentimental stories of dear and close friendships. *Frog and Toad Are Friends* was perhaps his most famous book (it won the Caldecott Medal in 1971), and the sequel, *Frog and Toad Together*, won the Newbery Medal in 1973. (Two other books of his won Caldecotts as well.) Anita, too, became a well-known children's book author—her *Sven's Bride* was named one of the *New York Times* best-illustrated books of 1965. *On Market Street*, a collaboration with Arnold, won the Caldecott.

In 1974 Arnold came out as gay. He later described how his being bullied as a boy had spurred his fantasy life. Marginalized as both Jewish and gay, he drew from both streams for his creative vision and his childlike sensibility.

So did Maurice Sendak, perhaps the most celebrated children's book author of the twentieth century. But unlike Arnold Lobel, Sendak derived a dark, ruminative picture of childhood from his marginality. What marked his work was perhaps his profound belief in children's resilience. He is credited with "wrench[ing] the picture book out of the safe, sanitized world of the nursery and plung[ing] it into the dark, terrifying and hauntingly beautiful recesses of the human psyche," which made him both accessible and emotionally profound—and widely beloved.[11] Rather than painting rosy pictures of childhood, Sendak believed that kids could face their demons, look them squarely in the eye, and come out the other side.

Perhaps that's because he did.

Sendak didn't have the happiest of childhoods. Born Moishe Barnard Sendak in 1928 in Brooklyn, he described his childhood neighborhoods in Bensonhurst and Gravesend as tree-lined Brooklyn ghettos comprising Jews and Sicilians. (As a young child, he mistakenly perceived the Sicilian as a type of Jew who drank wine and laughed more.) His parents, Philip and Sadie, had immigrated alone as teenagers from shtetls near Warsaw, Poland, shortly before the First World War. They both enjoyed reading Yiddish authors who also wrote for children, such as Sholem Aleichem.[12]

Philip Sendak, who worked in the garment district, spun tales out of the fabric of his eastern European childhood, mixed with remnants he had picked up along the way, including some sexualized shards of Torah stories. Maurice recalled him as a great father figure, somewhat Abrahamic, who was always available to reassure him. Philip missed his own parents terribly and wrote his stories to reassure himself as much as his son. Maurice's mother was psychologically unstable—he called her a *vilde khaye*, a wild beast.[13]

The central fact of Sendak's life was his marginality. He fit in nowhere—by class, religion, sexuality, or physicality: "an emotionally sensitive, serious, physically frail, gay son of Yiddish-speaking immigrants," as his friend Tony Kushner described him. He had a "Yiddische kopf, a large, brooding, circumspect, and contemplative mind," with an "enduring sense of displacement, yearning for and not securely possessing a home [and holding a] conviction, passed through hundreds of generations, that true home is elsewhere, promised but not attained, perhaps not even attainable."[14]

It was from this place of hybrid identity that Sendak drew his imaginative identities. He described his own background as

> composed of disparate elements strangely concocted, a childhood colored with the memories—never lived by me—of shtetl life in Europe, vividly conveyed to me by my immigrant parents—a conglomerate fantasy life typical perhaps of many first-generation children in America. It was composed, on the one hand, of feeling as though I lived in the Old Country—the fabulous village world of my parents—and, on the other, of being bombarded with the full intoxicating gush of America in that convulsed decade called the thirties.[15]

Sendak's central characters are odd and defenseless, always feeling out of place. The writer Nat Hentoff noted that they are not "the bright, handsome boys and softly pretty little girls who are so numerous in picture books for children." Instead, they "appear truncated, having oversized heads, short arms, and quite short legs." They are young people superimposed on old bodies, or are old before their time. As Sendak put it:

> During my early teens, I spent a lot of time at the window, sketching the kids at play, and those sketchbooks

> are, in a sense, the foundation of much of my later work. Maybe that's another reason the children in my books are called European-looking. Many of them resemble the kids I knew growing up in Brooklyn. They were Jewish kids, and they may well look like little greenhorns just off the boat. They had—some of them, anyway—a kind of bowed look, as if the burdens of the world were on their shoulders.[16]

This sense of difference is central. Sendak is the insider, always looking out that window, and at the same time, he is the outsider, always looking in at the world of well-adjusted, "normal" kids. He is the consummate alien, just as the child is alien to the world of adults. (The converse is equally true: The adult is an alien to the world of children.) The question isn't whether children will eventually enter the world of adults; they will. The question is how they can create a community of aliens, occupy a space before adulthood, and carve out their own territory.

The child sees the world from the outside, and Sendak's great gift, according to the scholar Golan Moskowitz, was that he "wrote *through* the child more than he wrote *for* the child."[17] As Sendak put it:

Maurice Sendak at the Rosenbach Museum & Library, Philadelphia. (© 1985 by Frank Armstrong)

> Too many parents and too many writers of children's books don't respect the fact that kids know and suffer a great deal. My children show a lot of pleasure, but often they look defenseless, too. Being defenseless is a primary element of childhood. And often, I am trying to draw the way children feel—or, rather, the way I imagine they feel. It's the way I know I felt as a child. And all I have to go on is what I know—not only about my childhood then, but about the child I was as he exists now.[18]

In an early book, *The Happy Rain* (1956), which Sendak illustrated for his brother Jack, children grow up in the fictional village of Troekan, where it is the norm for the skies to pour rain that drenches their clothes and muddies the streets. The villagers love the rain and are traumatized when it suddenly ceases and the sun comes out to shine:

> The people of Troekan were certain that it indeed was the end of the world. They shut their shutters tight. They shook with fear. And they wept, and they wailed, and they wrung their hands. . . . The comforting dark clouds were gone; now there was only the harsh, glaring sun. And the soft, warm mud had become hard, and difficult to walk on. . . . Very wisely, to protect themselves from the terrible sunny weather, most of the villagers carried umbrellas.

Attempting to bring back the rain, the villagers of Troekan follow various misinformed advisers and proceed to fire cannons into the sky while standing upside down and wearing paper bags over their heads—all to no avail. Finally two children save the day by considering the clouds' feelings and sending them a note.[19]

This inside-outsider status is best illustrated in Sendak's most celebrated children's book, *Where the Wild Things Are* (1963). Like many comic book superheroes, its protagonist, Max, is alone, out of place in this world but longing to fit in. He's also furious with his mother, who just sent him to bed without his supper. (His father makes no appearance in the book.)

He's a strange boy, this Max, a "wild, dark, and unapologetic child sensitively attuned to menacing forces beyond their understanding." He sails off to worlds of threat, menace, danger, and wildness, to lands of dreams and nightmares, or of fantasies and terrors. An alien, he arrives in these dangerous lands and assimilates almost without effort, so successfully that not only does he fit in but becomes the leader. Most important and most inspiring, Max faces his demons on his own, without relying on his parents or other outside forces.

No wonder his biographers and critics see the book as projecting Sendak's "alien-ness" as a closeted gay man, a Jew, the consummate outsider, onto children as a group. And yet all Max really wants to do is to return home, to fit in there. In that sense, Golan Moskowitz says the story is "permeated with a Jewish sensibility."[20]

Where Sendak used his different-ness, his particularity as an outsider, to embrace a universal experience of childhood, another children's book author took a very different tack to explore that universality. If Sendak made the different feel normal, Ezra Jack Keats made what should have been normal feel obviously different.

In the 1950s pretty much every character in every single mainstream children's book was white. You didn't notice that whiteness; it just looked "normal." That is, until it wasn't there. Suddenly in a 1960 children's book, an eight-year-old Puerto Rican boy named Juanito has lost his dog and needs to find him. So, in *My Dog Is Lost*, Juanito roams all over Manhattan to find his dog, passing through Chinatown, Little Italy, Harlem, and even Park Avenue, encountering a wide variety of New Yorkers.

My Dog Is Lost was the first offering by the first-generation Jewish writer Ezra Jack Keats. Born to very poor Polish immigrants in Brooklyn in 1916, Keats grew up in an unhappy home. His father was a waiter in a restaurant; his mother, a deeply unhappy housewife who warned Ezra never to get married. (He never did.) His uncle Max, who lived with them, was a "chicken flicker," plucking chicken

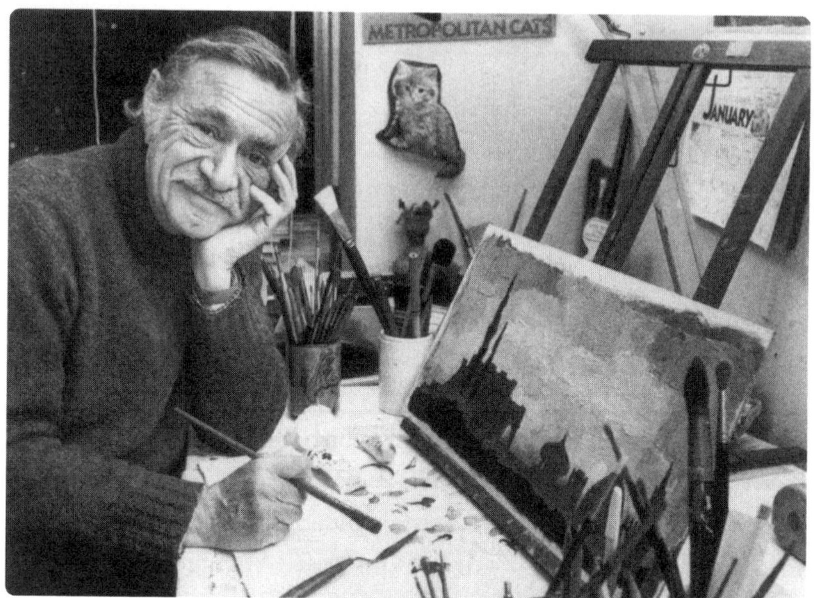

Ezra Jack Keats at his easel, circa 1960. (Reprinted by special permission from the Ezra Jack Keats Foundation)

feathers in a meat-packing plant. Keats remembers his uncle as terribly cruel, gratuitously so. He used to heat pennies on the stove until they were molten hot, then use a spoon to put them on the street, where children would pick them up and burn their fingers.

In his unpublished memoir, Keats recalls being so poor that he had no toys; he used to collect matchsticks to "make castles, log cabins, and train tracks." As young boys, he and his best friend Irving Pope were walking when they first saw the local library. Keats remembers being "stunned." The pair of friends vowed to walk together to the library every day—a promise they kept for years, walking to the library to spend their days reading and talking. The walk took them from their poor neighborhood through more middle-class neighborhoods, with their manicured lawns and yards. Knowing they could never live there, they fantasized, imagining the lives outside the "glass tunnel" that held them inside. Think of an aquarium at a zoo—you walk by tanks where fish swim to your left and right, and also above you, and you are surrounded by their world. Ezra and Irving were encased in a glass tunnel; outside were all the things they could never have.

Keats's major breakthrough came in 1963, just as the civil rights movement was gaining momentum. In *The Snowy Day*, a little boy named Peter wakes up and decides to take a walk in the snow. He makes a snowman, creates snow angels, climbs a mountain of snow, and tries to save a snowball overnight in his pocket. In short, Peter does what absolutely any little child would do on a walk in the snow.

But Peter is Black. *The Snowy Day* was the first mainstream children's book about a boy of color. What made this children's book so revolutionary, though, is that the story is not about his race. It doesn't pivot on his race at all. It's never even mentioned. It's simply taken for granted. He is a boy, a child, and his race has nothing to do with his pleasure in playing in the snow. In a sense, Keats embraced Martin Luther King's dictum that what mattered was not the "color of his skin" but the "content of his character." The book won the Caldecott Medal for 1963.

Keats had revealed something essential about the culture of postwar American childhood that was being celebrated and promoted: Some Americans were absent, both from that pageant and from the reality of childhood that children across the country were experiencing.

10

BEYOND BEN'S "IDEAL" GIRLHOOD: GIRLS AND DOLLS

* * *

One morning just before Christmas 1949, in Belle Glade, Florida, Sara Lee Creech was leaving her local post office when she noticed two Black girls playing outside. "What a lovely sight," she thought to herself. But then she noticed they were playing with white dolls. Just a few days earlier, she had been talking with a Black mother, who complained that the only high-quality dolls were white. "Where are the Negro dolls?" the woman had asked.

The question haunted Creech. Where, indeed, were the Negro dolls? A "red headed sixth generation white southerner," she was a well-respected florist in Belle Glade, where she had earlier founded a preschool for the children of migrant workers. She'd long been involved in women's organizations and in the fledgling civil rights movement. In the late 1940s, she was the first president of the Florida Federation of Business and Professional Women's Clubs and had helped found the Inter-Racial Council in Belle Glade. Her good friend Zora Neale Hurston wrote to Carl Sandburg that Creech was "perhaps the foremost individual of the area for better race relations"—a "white phenomenon."[1]

Unable to let go of the image of Black girls playing with white dolls, Creech decided to create a Black doll, one that would "represent the beauty and diversity of black children." "A black child playing with a white doll would not assist these young girls in developing a healthy self-image," she said. "Therefore, it was important that all children, both black and white, be able to see a quality black doll."[2]

A Brief History of the "Negro" Doll

Sara Lee Creech wasn't the first person to contemplate creating a Black doll. For centuries, slaves had pulled together scraps of cloth and pieces of scrap wood to create dolls for their children, just as poor people the world over have used their creative wits to offer their children pleasure.

Before the early twentieth century, mass-produced "Negro dolls" were mostly gross caricatures of African Americans, mostly, as Walter B. Abbott put it in 1918, "mammies or picaninnies." That was just fine with many consumers, since many of those Black dolls were purchased for white girls "who desire these dark playmates to be used as servants in their doll establishments, as maids, coachmen, butlers, and the like," according to a 1909 article in *Playthings*.[3]

Even those dolls designed for Black children, dolls that weren't stereotypes, still often used white models for the faces and almost never used anything but straight hair. Indeed, "a large number of the negroes themselves spurn the efforts of toy manufacturers to provide the children of the brown and black races with negro dolls." Apparently, Black children "do not seem to want them, and they go to the other extreme and choose dolls representing white children, white children which are notably the fairest haired, brightest cheeked, bluest eyed and altogether the most brilliant blonds obtainable."[4]

This was precisely the problem Sara Lee Creech wanted to fix. The truth was, white-owned doll companies just didn't know what to do about Black dolls. Were they "Black *dolls*" (that is, dolls that just happened to be Black) or were they "*Black* dolls" (dolls whose real purpose was their Blackness and that therefore served a political purpose). To choose the second would inevitably raise the issue of the whiteness of other dolls, for if these dolls were defined by their Blackness, didn't that logically define the other dolls by their whiteness? In other words, if Black dolls were truly Black, then white dolls were no longer just "dolls."

As a result, white-owned doll companies produced a series of Black dolls that rehearsed Black stereotypes, thereby reassuring white doll owners that theirs was the generic doll. In the process, white-owned doll companies produced a series of failures. There was Snowball in 1913 and Patsy in 1930, both made by Effanbee. E.I. Horsman made the Baby Bumps doll. The Amosandra doll, which fused the well-known characters Amos and Andy, went on sale on Valentine's Day 1947. According to *Ebony*, despite a "crippling" snowstorm, the doll sold four hundred units in the first two days—mostly to white patrons. A Jackie Robinson doll was produced in 1950.[5]

Some of these dolls drew on well-known derogatory stereotypes. During the Depression, the Works Project Administration of Milwaukee commissioned a Little Black Sambo doll. Sambo was the main character of an 1899 story set in India about a well-dressed little South Asian boy who distracts some hungry tigers with his clothes to escape being devoured. Such a story might have been "amusing undoubtedly to the white child," wrote Langston Hughes, but it was "like an unkind word to one who has known too many hurts to enjoy the additional pain of being laughed at."[6]

Topsy, a character in *Uncle Tom's Cabin*, and Kid Chocolate (modeled after a Cuban-born featherweight boxing champion) also became dolls. An Aunt Jemima doll—a rag doll dressed in a maid's uniform with a red handkerchief wrapped around her head—was so popular that her image was used to promote breakfast syrup. Ideal entered the Black doll market with the non-ironically named Black Snow White in 1938, and Sears did the same with Noma's Mammy with Charge, which included a Black "mammy" doll with hyper-red

Topsy-Turvy doll, unidentified maker, ca. 1850–80. (Collection of the New York Historical Society)

lipstick and a red dress and scarf, pushing a pink baby carriage with a little white baby in it.[7]

One of the more intriguing dolls of the period was Topsy-Turvy, half white and half Black. She had two heads, one white, the other Black. Her dresses could be pulled over one head to allow the child to play with the other, either white or Black—or the child could play with both at the same time.

No one really knows how children played with these dolls. One doll collector believes they were mostly played with by Black children who desired to play with a white doll—like the white babies their mothers might have cared for as nannies. Perhaps they were created initially by slave women as a way to prepare their daughters to be both mothers and maids, and to learn the differences in how to care for other people's children and their own. Playfully ambiguous and potentially subversive, Topsy-Turvy was one more "means of expressing the complexities of race relations."[8] Topsy-Turvy allowed for clandestine play with the "other"—though it's not so clear which way it went.

Black doll makers often tried the opposite tack, to create dolls for uplift rather than for stereotypes. Early in the twentieth century, Leo Moss, a Black doll maker from Macon, Georgia, sought to market Black dolls to Black children but found few takers. The problem was neither supply nor demand—there were companies ready to create the dolls, and certainly a growing potential market ready to buy them. It was that the connection between supply and demand was missing: marketing and advertising. Potential buyers had no way to know that such a product existed.

Realistic African American dolls had existed before World War I, but they were imported by and sold almost exclusively in Black churches. Dr. R. H. Boyd, one of the founders of the National Baptist Congress, traveled to Germany to attempt to convince toymakers to produce a nonstereotyped Black doll. No one was interested, and so it was left to his son, Henry Allen Boyd, to remedy the problem.

Henry Allen Boyd led the National Baptist Congress after his father died, but he was more than just a religious leader. He cofounded the Citizens Bank, providing low-interest loans to Black businesses. He headed the National Baptist Publishing Board, perhaps the most important religious publisher serving Black churches—it provided hymnals, religious texts, Bibles, and other educational materials to more than twenty thousand churches and Sunday schools. Boyd also was the editor of *The Union Review* and *The Nashville Globe*, newspapers that served the Black community. And he manufactured toys and dolls.

In 1911 Boyd founded the National Negro Doll Company, with a mission to use dolls to uplift the race. His extensive networks enabled it to become the first reasonably successful producer of Black dolls. He harnessed the growing African American media to advertise, placing ads for the dolls in *The Nashville Globe*. "These Toys," the advertisement promised, "are not made of that disgraceful and humiliating type that we have been accustomed to seeing. They represent the intelligent and refined Negro of today, rather than that type of toy that is usually given to the children, and as a rule used as a scarecrow." These dolls were meant to "teach the people that they may teach their children how to look upon their people."[9]

"Refined" was hardly the word used for rural or even urban poor folk, whether Black or white. Boyd designed his dolls for the Black middle class that W.E.B. Du Bois promised was emerging. Indeed, Boyd's company was a regular advertiser in *The Crisis,* the magazine founded by Du Bois in 1911.

Later that decade, others entered the Black doll market. In 1919 Marcus Garvey's United Negro Improvement Association supported a host of Black enterprises including a chain of grocery stores, restaurants, laundries, tailor shops, a publishing house—and a doll factory.[10]

Walter B. Abbott created the Sun Tan Doll in 1921. His cousin had founded *The Chicago Defender*, and Walter was dispatched to Harlem to manage the New York office. Moonlighting on the side, he decided to try to create positive Black dolls. The key, he believed, was the color of the doll's skin. He worked long nights to develop "sun tan paint" to use to color the originally white dolls. In 1921, he incorporated the

Advertisement for the National Negro Doll Company in *The Crisis*, 1911.

Nutshell Variety Sales Company to market the paint. All the companies that produced white dolls rejected the paint proposal. Undeterred, he found a white doll company that was failing, bought a 50 percent stake in it, and started manufacturing Sun Tan Dolls himself. Which, naturally, he advertised in *The Chicago Defender*.[11]

The Clarks' Research

After the Second World War, the timing was once again right to promote a Black doll. In 1947 the Terri Lee Doll Company introduced a nonstereotypic Patti-Jo doll, based on the comic strip character drawn by the Black cartoonist Jackie Armes.[12] The marketing problems proved insurmountable, however, and the doll faded quickly.

By now, however, the nascent civil rights movement had achieved some notable successes, like the formal integration of the military by President Truman's executive order. Campaigns for voting rights and against segregated schools, neighborhoods, and other public accommodations were under way. The Supreme Court had proclaimed in 1896 that segregation was "separate but equal," but it had proved, in fact, to be dramatically unequal.

The large-scale, institutional inequality of segregation lacked a human quality, a sense of the disparate impact of inequality on people's lives. One could look at aggregate statistics that demonstrated racial inequalities, but such numbers didn't lead to an understanding of how inequality felt, how those at the bottom experienced it. And that's where new ideas about developmental psychology entered the story.

As we have seen, developmental psychologists had been studying how children develop their identities and come to thrive as adults. But what about groups that did not thrive, for whom prejudicial attitudes and discrimination led to negative self-images and a sense of inferiority? In the late 1930s, the psychologists Kenneth and Mamie Clark ran a series of psychological experiments designed to assess the impact of segregation on Black children's self-concept. Their methodology involved dolls.

Developmental psychologists had realized by now that childhood play with dolls is crucial to identity formation—a finding that had been transformed into a steady stream of advertisements for Ideal dolls and their competitors. But the Clarks' study startled both the research community and policymakers. They presented two groups of Black children, ranging in age from three to seven, with a set of four dolls, identical except for their color. (Of the 253 children in their study, 134 attended segregated nursery schools in Arkansas, and 119 attended an integrated nursery school in Springfield, Massachusetts.) They observed the children's preferences, how long they played with which dolls, and then asked a series of questions about them. A majority of the children preferred the white or lighter-skinned dolls and ascribed more positive attributes to them. This finding held in both the segregated southern school and the northern integrated school.

In short, the Clarks reasoned, by the time the children reached nursery school, they had internalized society's stereotypes about them. In one particularly memorable episode, while Kenneth was conducting the experiment in rural Arkansas, he asked a child which doll was most like him. The boy smiled and pointed to the dark brown doll. "That's a nigger," he said. "I'm a nigger." Clark found this episode "as disturbing, or more disturbing, than the children in Massachusetts who would refuse to answer the question or who would cry and run out of the room."[13]

The Clarks concluded that "prejudice, discrimination and segregation" has created a feeling of inferiority among Black children, and that they suffered from significantly lower self-esteem than white children. They experienced a form of "self-rejection."[14] The effects were particularly pronounced among children who attended segregated schools in the South. That finding eventually provided an important empirical foundation for the NAACP's arguments in *Brown v. Board of Education* in 1954. (Kenneth Clark provided expert testimony in that case.)

What could remedy the "self-rejection" these children experienced? A mass-produced and nationally distributed Black doll. All that was required was a champion (or two)—and a toy company willing to design and produce it.

Sara Lee Creech was stunned when she read about the Clarks' research. What, she asked herself, could she do to help this process happen? She decided right then and there to try to create a truly non-stereotypic Black doll. She enlisted a friend, Maxeda von Hesse, a New York City socialite, to help her.

The first dilemma they faced was color. White dolls were "easy"; they could be produced generically, with a single pigment capturing the entire race. All white children, in that sense, looked alike. But the enormous range of skin color among African Americans proved a serious design challenge. Creech and von Hesse took nearly five hundred photographs of African American children in Belle Glade, to observe the different shades of their skin color.

When the acclaimed writer Zora Neale Hurston moved to Belle Glade in 1950, the second piece of the puzzle fell into place. The three women became fast friends, and Creech spent virtually every evening socializing at Zora's home. When she showed Zora the photographs, Zora became effusive. "Please allow me to say how pleased I am that you let me see pictures of the Negro dolls that you plan to put on the market," Hurston wrote to Creech.

> The thing that pleased me most . . . was that you, a White girl, should have seen into our hearts so clearly, and sought to meet our longing for understanding of us as we really are, and not as some would have us. That you have not insulted us by a grotesque caricature of Negro children, but conceived something of real Negro beauty. Those dolls are adorable. . . . They will surely meet a long-felt need among us. It [is] a magnificently constructive thing you are doing for the whole of America as well as for Negro children.[15]

Creech also sent the photographs to Sheila Burlingame, a St. Louis sculptor. Burlingame had encountered the problem before; she had sculpted *Negro Boy Praying* that stood in front of the St. Louis Urban League. Burlingame created four molds for prototype heads that might work for the dolls.

The three women enlisted the aid of an old family friend of von Hesse: Eleanor Roosevelt. Late in 1949 the three women traveled to New York, where they met with the former first lady. Together they proved a powerful quartet. That next summer, at Eleanor's cottage at Val-Kill, they determined to put their plan for a Black doll in motion. "I was so interested to see the Negro dolls you are proposing to manufacture," Eleanor wrote to Creech. "I like them particularly because they can be made and sold on an equal basis with white dolls. There is nothing to be ashamed of. They are attractive and reproduced well with careful study of the race. I think they are a lesson in equality for little children and we will find that many a child will cherish a charming black doll as easily as it would a charming white doll."

Before they approached potential industrial collaborators from the toy industry, however, they wanted to demonstrate the dolls' marketability. Roosevelt, with Hurston's help, compiled a virtual "who's who" of Black intelligentsia who might endorse the product and support it through a marketing campaign. Hurston provided letters of introduction to university presidents and prominent Black leaders. She arranged for influential members of the Black community—including Mordecai Johnson, president of Howard University; Benjamin Mays, president of Morehouse College; Rufus Clement, president of Atlanta University; Jackie Robinson; Ralph Bunche (who had, that year, become the first Black recipient of the Nobel Peace Prize), and others. All agreed that the best solution would be for a toy company to bring out all four dolls simultaneously, each with a different hairstyle and skin color.

The reaction was uniformly positive. "I feel that a good bit of good will and human understanding can be promoted if you can get the right type of dolls manufactured, which would portray the Negro child in the proper light," Mays wrote to Creech on November 9, 1950. "I think it is the things that we learn unconsciously that will determine the extent of our prejudice towards others and the extent of our human understanding."[16]

Even with the backing of such prominent people, no toy manufacturer would touch the idea. Then Creech came up with a plan to work from back to front. Instead of creating the doll and then seeking retail outlets like large department stories, she thought of engaging the retail stores first, thus "proving" that if the doll were to be manufactured, it would have strong sales outlets. Mays wrote to Sears, Roebuck, setting up a meeting for Creech with its southern merchandise manager—a man named Harley Kimmel (no relation)—and it was through Kimmel that Sears got in touch with Ideal. Kimmel enlisted General Robert Wood, chief executive officer at Sears to broker the deal.

Wood had always enjoyed a mutually profitable relationship with Ideal, so he went to them first. Ideal's company president David Rosenstein championed the doll; in college, Rosenstein had worked in the settlement houses in New York City, and his heart remained partly in social work. But neither Ben Michtom nor Abe Katz, Michtom's cousin and chairman of the board, was so enthusiastic. They thought Rosenstein was "letting his social conscience cloud his business sense," so they put the project on the back burner: The doll was a possibility but not a certainty. Rosenstein discussed it with a public relations consultant, Charlotte Klein, who persuaded Ben Michtom that "the Negro doll would make news for the company."[17] Now the doll had both a possible retail outlet and an enthusiastic toy company executive. Ben and Abe's resistance was finally worn down, but they needed the doll to make a big splash.

Creech and von Hesse met again with Eleanor Roosevelt on October 15, 1951, and the former first lady hatched a plan to attract national attention. She hosted a tea in a New York City hotel suite, inviting major Black and white figures to launch the doll. Mordecai Johnson, Mary McLeod Bethune, Ralph Bunche, and Jackie Robinson were there. "You don't turn down an invitation to Mrs. Roosevelt's tea," Creech says proudly. "The people that attended the tea were interested. They endorsed it. They were people who were firmly dedicated to changing the atmosphere of the country."[18]

From *left*: Walter White, president of the NAACP, David Rosenstein (Ideal), Eleanor Roosevelt, Ralph Bunche, Ben Michtom (Ideal), Abe Katz (Ideal). Ben holds the doll, and Eleanor holds one of the four differently colored prototype heads. (Photo courtesy of Paula Michtom)

So on October 22, 1951, the Saralee doll was "revealed" and covered by major magazines and newspapers. "It's high time there were a quality Negro doll which would give Negro children a new respect for their heritage and would give White children a new respect for the Negro," proclaimed the press release.[19]

Ideal's plan was to roll out the release of four different Saralee dolls, each with a different skin tone and hairstyle. This, they believed, could answer the objections that would be raised about color—concerns that the company had never encountered with its white dolls. When Saralee debuted, the media was initially effusive. This is not "just a white doll painted black, not one of those travesties of the Negro race represented by the caricatured Pickaninnies or colored maids," Gertrude Penrose wrote in the December 1951 issue of *Independent Woman*, a monthly magazine for working women. "She was a real Negro doll." *Better Homes and Gardens* gushed that the Saralee doll was "designed to replace the 'mammy' dolls of the past." *Ebony* called it "one of the most beautiful Negro dolls America has ever produced."[20]

Right off the production line, Ideal sent a crate of them to Creech in Florida. She took a few to Lake Shore Elementary School, the school that her organization, the Inter-Racial Council, had lobbied to build. She wanted to see the children's reaction. "They were just thrilled to death," she later remembered. "They ran their fingers through the dress material and looked up at me and smiled. That meant that, although they couldn't express it in words, they felt the quality of the doll. That convinced me that this was something that needed to be done."[21]

Saralee Negro Doll—the doll's official name—made her debut for the Christmas season in 1951 wearing a yellow organza dress with a yellow bonnet, color-coordinated with her medium brown skin. She sold for $6.95. *Esquire*, *Life*, *Time*, *Newsweek*, and *Ebony* announced

The Ideal promotional photograph for the Saralee doll, 1951. (Photo courtesy of Paula Michtom)

her arrival, and she was advertised in the Sears, Roebuck catalog. It was, to use Hurston's terms, the first "anthropologically correct" Black baby doll to be mass-produced and marketed nationally.[22]

Typical was the flowery editorial in *Ebony* in January 1952:

> This Christmas, a half million little girls of many races found under their Christmas trees some of the most beautiful Negro dolls America has ever produced. A transformation has taken place in toyland and new colored dolls with delicate features, lighter skin, and modish clothes are being introduced in the world of childhood fantasy where always before the Negro doll was presented as a ridiculous, calico-garmented, handkerchief-headed servant.[23]

The "experts" expected a hit. The New York school system made Saralee its official doll and ordered several hundred.[24] Several large New York City department stores like Gimbels and Abraham & Straus ran advertisements featuring the doll. Sears, Roebuck promoted it as well. Jordan Marsh and Marshall Field featured the dolls in their stores. Some large stores, notably Saks Fifth Avenue and Macy's, however, did not carry the doll because they believed that stocking it would bring in more Black customers, who would scare white customers away.[25]

But sales were soft. Although Sears stores in Atlanta and Dallas reordered it, national sales were disappointing. Salesmen didn't have the time to sit with buyers and explain the dolls' social significance. "It had to be important to the person who was selling it to the stores," Creech remarks. A doll that contravened so many industry norms needed time and serious marketing and advertising skills to find its niche in the market. Ideal gave Saralee neither. Its indifference in this instance deprived the nation of a potentially iconic doll.

Clearly, Ideal had no idea how to market to African Americans. Direct marketing to Black girls was, the company thought, impossible: What did they read? What radio shows did they listen to? Was there a "Black" television show? It was only slightly easier to market to the parents: At least there were some identifiable radio and TV shows and magazines that catered to minority audiences. The company had little experience and even less interest in working out how to segment its market. *Jet* had just begun publishing the year before, and the more established *Ebony* had begun in 1945, but most Black women still read mainstream magazines that were read also by white women, and Ideal couldn't imagine advertising there. Nor could the marketing department conceive of an ad that didn't also feature a cute little white girl, to give the Black doll the authenticity of being a "real" doll.

Then the vinyl turned out to be unstable—it would harden and leak color onto the doll's clothes. The dolls needed to be recalled, but Ideal, lukewarm at best, used this problem as an opportunity to pull out. It refused to produce the other three dolls in the set, and it ceased production in 1953. Ultimately, Ideal sabotaged the doll.[26] "When we got into these products," Lionel Weintraub, Ideal's president in the 1970s and son of Abe Katz, recalled, "we were ahead of our time and the results were just about zero." Even today, he continued, "black dolls are ill-defined as a distinct market, and our sales are not at all in proportion to the black population."[27]

Girls and Their Dolls

The Saralee doll broke the mold in one sense: By creating a "negro doll," Ideal had, unintentionally rendered all other dolls "white." But in another sense, she still fit neatly into the paradigm that Ideal had established for decades. Much of Ben Michtom's success had come from following one simple axiom of the toy business: Girls want to play with dolls because they want to play Mommy. Call it simplistic or sexist, but at the time, this axiom was the framing understanding, the paradigm if you will, of the toy business. From the introduction of the Shirley Temple doll in 1936, the Michtoms, both father and son, followed it so assiduously that they continued to produce a series of hits through the 1940s and into the '50s. Dolls encouraged little girls to play Mommy, or to be the hostess at the tea party—precisely the activities they would be expected to perform in the decade after Rosie the Riveter returned to the suburban housewifery she must now embrace (or endure).

Among girls, there were plenty of rumblings of discontent. If suburban housewives were chafing against the "problem that has no name"—which was what Betty Friedan called the predicament of women who had given up their career aspirations to be homemakers—their daughters may also have shown some restlessness with the stereotypic assumptions that choked off their ambitions and channeled them into what they might see as less fulfilling lives.

In a sense, daughters may simply have looked around their suburban neighborhoods and noticed that the boys seemed to be having more fun. Boys got to play sports, play soldier, and go on adventures (even just sleeping in the backyard on warm summer nights). If they got into trouble, they would be excused by a resigned parental shrug of "boys will be boys." Indoors, they could watch sports on TV; they got to make more noise and had to clean fewer dishes. They could be Cub Scouts or Boy Scouts, try archery, tie knots, or play with pocketknives. By contrast, girls could be Brownies or Girl Scouts, sell cookies, and hone their baking and cooking skills.

Toys reproduced the gendering of children's lives. Television ads seemed relentlessly sex-segregated: Boys huddled around model cars or trains, while girls delighted in having their dolls come to tea. A visit to a large toy store often felt like children's lives were neatly divided into his and hers. A wide aisle might divide "his" world (sports equipment, model cars, chemistry sets, toy guns) from "her" world (mostly dolls and their outfits). More than few little girls realized that the world on the other side of the aisle might contain some pleasures yet unknown.

These rumblings of girls' discontent found their way into the corporate offices of the country's major toy companies. But how could they tap into it without abandoning what had been so profitable for so long? How could they embrace change and yet reproduce the status quo?

Maybe they could make a doll that wasn't a baby?

In 1956, Ideal began to develop a more mature, teenage doll. It was designed by the company's favorite doll developer, Bernard Lipfert, who had earlier designed its successful Toni doll. Lipfert came up with a toned-down Marilyn Monroe doll, perhaps, according to his daughter, the first doll with "boobs." "It's not a sexy doll," Ben said, "it's just got the lines of any beautiful, normal, young woman." Ben was a booster, even if a little defensive in anticipating criticism. "There's never been anything like it," he told a reporter. "Always before, dolls have had child-like bodies, but now we're breaking down age-old prejudices against dolls with maturity, and we're doing it with taste and dignity." He insisted "there's nothing wrong with little girls wanting to look like their teen-age sisters."[28]

Initially, the company had toyed with a proposal for an even more buxom and mature Marilyn Monroe doll, but it abandoned that idea. If the doll couldn't enable a girl to fantasize about being a mother, what was the point of a doll in the first place? Melvin Helzer, Ideal's advertising director, explained, "Ideal makes dolls which talk, walk, cry, wet, and blow their noses, but recently we were approached with the idea of making a Marilyn Monroe doll. After a good deal of thought, we decided against it. Nobody could figure out what the doll should do."[29]

Well, nobody at Ideal anyway.

Cue Barbie.

Bild Lilli, Barbie, and the Transformation of Girlhood

Barbie's story is already well known. Library shelves sag with the hundreds of books about her and her impact on American girlhood and even womanhood. Was she a protofeminist heroine? Or was she Little Miss Anti-Feminist, addicting girls to striving for elusive perfection? Perhaps she was both—"an early rebel against the domesticity that dominated the lives of baby-boom mothers," as well as a clever marketing strategy to link self-expression with consumption and accessorizing.[30]

Like the Teddy Bear, Mr. Potato Head, and many other dolls and toys, Barbie began in a Jewish immigrant family. Ruth Moskowicz, known as Ruth Mosko, was the youngest of ten children, born in 1916 to a Jewish family in Colorado. Her father was a poor blacksmith who had emigrated from Poland. Ruth grew up to marry Isadore Elliot Handler, the son of Ukrainian Jews; his grandfather had been a rabbi. His father had found his way to Chicago at sixteen and later to the small but prosperous Jewish community in Denver, where he met Ruth at a high school dance in 1929. They wed and had two children, Barbara and Kenneth. After the war, they drifted to L.A. and initially worked in designs for plastics, especially Lucite and Plexiglas.

In 1945 Elliot and his business partner Harold Matson founded Mattel, the company name being a combination of Harold's last name and Elliot's first name. From the beginning, Ruth Handler was a full and equal collaborator. At first, Mattel produced plastic picture frames and miniature furniture for dollhouses, made from the plastic scraps left over from the manufacture of airplane nose cones. Ruth acted as saleswoman, pitching the frames to local businesses, which snatched them up hungrily.

The team decided the toy industry was an alluring market. so they jumped in. Their first products were pure genius. Reasoning that little boys would want to play the adult roles that their fathers had played just a few months before, they produced toy guns (and toy ukuleles). Forget doctor bags, they thought. Toy guns enabled boys to play soldier and cowboy, the two most palpable fantasies for boys in the 1950s. (The most popular television shows of the 1950s were westerns.) Mattel was an instant success as a toy company.

In the beginning, just as Ideal "got" what girls wanted, to pretend to be mommies, Mattel got what boys wanted, to pretend to be heroes. When I was a child, all my male friends owned a Mattel toy gun. Some had "caps," a red paper strip with tiny amounts of gunpowder that would make a bang loud enough to sound real, but not so loud as to sound dangerous. The toy burp gun fired multiple shots, like a tommy gun. Hundreds of thousands of pretend Elliot Nesses finally caught up with Baby Face Nelson and Al Capone in the backyards of suburbia.

In 1956 (the year Ideal commissioned, then abandoned, the Marilyn doll) Ruth was on a family trip to Switzerland when she came across a German doll called Bild Lilli. A popular doll in postwar Germany, Lilli was based on a character in a German newspaper cartoon. She was lithe and sexy, always dressed in skimpy bras and panties, interacting with fully dressed adults. In one cartoon, a bikini-clad Lilli is confronted by a policeman who tells her that two-piece swimsuits are illegal. "Oh and in your opinion, which part should I take off?" she replies. Lilli was so popular that the newspaper commissioned the toymaker Max Weissbrodt to create a doll that it could use as a promotional item.[31]

Weissbrodt created an "adult" toy as a novelty item based on the cartoon. *Adult* meant she was full-bodied and fully formed, with ample breasts, a slim waist, and full hips. Produced between 1955 and 1964, she was sold mostly to men in bars and tobacco stores. "Bluntly, Lilli dolls were designed for sex-hungry German men who bought her for girlfriends and mistresses in lieu of flowers, or as a suggestive gift," writes Orly Lobel. Promotional brochures used such phrases as "Gentlemen prefer Lilli" and "Whether more or less naked, Lilli is always discreet."[32]

Lilli was diminutive, standing only twelve inches tall, so she could hardly have been a "sex doll" in the way we understand them today. But she was a *sexy* doll, oozing an impish sexuality, a woman who knows what she wants and uses her sexual wiles to get it.

Ruth saw a possibility that the German toymakers had not foreseen. A "real" postpubescent doll would allow prepubescent girls to play something other than Mommy—they could play high school cheerleader, prom queen, and girl about town; later nurse, teacher, and secretary; and later still, astrophysicist, dentist, doctor, and soccer star. People initially scoffed. "Ruth, little girls want baby dolls," one toy buyer told her dismissively. "They want to pretend to be mommies." "No, they don't," she replied. "Little girls want to pretend to

Bild Lilli and Barbie.

be *bigger* girls."[33] For them, dolls needed to look like bigger girls, with shapes and figures, and, well, you know what else. "I believed it was important to a little girl's self-esteem," Handler said, "to play with a doll that has breasts."

Barbie Millicent Roberts appeared in 1959, named after Ruth and Elliot's daughter, Barbara, who was fifteen at the time. Ken, who came two years later, was named after their son—which is a little strange since he was billed as Barbie's boyfriend. A series of novels filled in their backstory, transforming Barbie from a Jewish American princess living in the San Fernando Valley to the WASP daughter of George and Margaret, in Willows, Wisconsin—a backstory closer to Clark Kent's than to those of the Yiddish Jews who created these perfectly "American" characters. Her hair was straight, her nose pointy. (Ken Handler's story is sad: According to one account, he grew up embarrassed and humiliated by having "an anatomically incorrect boy doll named after him with no hint of genitalia." He died of a brain tumor in 1994.)[34]

Barbie was an instant success, beyond Shirley Temple, beyond Patti Playpal, beyond any other doll before or since, perhaps rivaled only by teddy bears. Well, her success was not exactly "instant." Elliot Handler consulted with Ernest Dichter, an Austrian-born

Ruth Handler with Barbies and Kens, 1961.

psychologist who, on immigrating to the United States, had turned himself into a marketing guru. For Barbie, Dichter designed a marketing campaign that persuaded American mothers that a sexy but wholesome teenage doll would neither threaten maternal authority nor hypersexualize their daughters nor turn them away from motherhood. That sealed the deal.

As soon as Barbie appeared, Lilli's owners sued for patent infringement, but Mattel turned the tables and simply bought the exclusive rights to Lilli. The German doll went out of production in 1964. Unlike the British queen, Barbie both reigned *and* ruled supreme among dolls for the next sixty years. (In the early 2000s, she was challenged by Bratz, the creation of another Jewish entrepreneur, Isaac Larian.)

For girls, Barbie is neither their baby nor their mother; she is more like their older sister, a subject of her own admiration and the object of the male gaze, desiring and desired. She is beloved by girls the world over. More than 10 million Barbies are sold every year—that's one roughly every three seconds. Mattel makes nearly as much money on her outfits as they do on the dolls. (The company bills itself, with some legitimacy, as the world's largest producer of women's wear.) The first truly successful African American doll turned out to be Barbie's friend Christie, launched in 1968.

Barbie is more than a toy—she is a trope, a symbol, a screen against which societal fears have long been projected and enlarged. To some, she represents the subordination of girls' ambitions to the "beauty myth," the sexualization of young girls, their near enslavement to fantasies of attractiveness to boys. To others, she represents agency, ambition, and a proto-feminist "be all you can be" ethos. To yet others, she is a she-devil. The ruling family in Kuwait issued a fatwa against her in 1995 and prohibited the buying or selling of Barbies. In 2003 in Saudi Arabia, the Committee for the Propagation of Virtue and Prevention of Vice announced that the "Jewish Barbie" is the symbol of decadence in the "satanic west." At least they got her religion right! One wonders what they make of the Creatable World collection, a set of gender-neutral dolls that Mattel announced in 2019.[35]

The Handlers guided the company for more than thirty years. In 1974 an investigation into Mattel's finances revealed that the company had filed false and misleading financial reports. The two founders were banished from Mattel. The company went on an acquisition spree, gobbling up competitors like Fisher-Price, and it rode on the success of Hot Wheels to count among its products four of the world's top ten. But nothing else ever approached the success of Barbie. Like the teddy bear, Barbie is an icon that captured something essential about America and the aspirations of its children. And like the original Teddy Bear, Barbie was created by a woman.

Notably, in her 1994 autobiography, *Dream Doll*, Ruth discussed some of the ways that, as a woman, she was ignored or dismissed by toy industry magnates, big banks, and others. But she never mentions the fact that she was a Jewish woman. In one sense, that's because the entire industry was so dominated by Jews that she hardly stood out. But like some of her contemporaries, such as Bella Abzug and Betty

Friedan, she was bold, brash, opinionated, and every bit the equal of her husband. She had things to say and expected people to listen to her. Sometimes those stereotypes of Jewish women made an indelible mark on the culture.

For decades, Ideal had been the leader in the doll wars, but it was a latecomer to the grown-up-doll wars. Ideal came to believe that Barbie's success was due less to her sexualized femininity than to her age. "We had noticed how many teen-agers buy stuffed toys to put on their beds or bookcases," said Abe Kent, the company's vice-president. "So we thought we should make a toy designed specifically for this age group." The result was the Klunks, a "family" of five roly-poly walrus-looking "heroes" with silly backstories, launched by the company in 1962. Like the Baby Jesus doll, it was a complete flop, making it impossible to resist saying the entire line was a Klunker.[36]

Coda: Back to Black

As for Black dolls, it wasn't until 1968 that Christie joined Barbie's entourage. The next year Mattel went further, supporting the development of a Black doll that was conceived and produced within the Black community. In that sense, Baby Nancy was the first "Black Power doll." In the aftermath of the Watts riots in 1965, two civil rights workers, Robert Hall and Louis Smith, began a community organizing effort in Los Angeles to promote Black enterprise, educational reform, and community uplift. Operation Bootstrap ran community-based enterprises to provide jobs and remedial education in skills for a better-equipped workforce. Soon the organization was sponsoring a daycare center, a clothing boutique, and even a gas station.[37]

Operation Bootstrap's most commercially successful initiative, however, was Shindana Toys. In 1968 Hall and Smith met with executives from Mattel, which was based in nearby Hawthorne. Mattel offered to back a project for Black dolls: It provided equipment, expertise, and over $500,000 in grants and another $1 million in loans to get it started. The goal was to produce authentically Black dolls, not a "white doll dipped in chocolate," as Smith put it. Shindana's first doll, Baby Nancy, appeared in 1969, followed by Wada and several other successful dolls, all with natural hair and African features. As one Shindana worker proudly explained, Baby Nancy "is not a white doll with black skin. She is not a black doll with Negroid features that is unpleasing to look at. She is an authentically beautiful black doll."[38]

The promise of Saralee Creech, Zora Neale Hurston, and so many others was finally realized. Barbie for the assist.

11

BOYS AND THEIR TOYS

* * *

Girls played with dolls. It didn't matter whether the dolls were babies whom the girls could mother, or larger three-foot tall dolls who could be their friends, or Barbies who could be their older sisters, to be adored and emulated. They played alone or with other girls. Rarely would you see a doll advertisement that showed a parent. Mothers were noticeably absent from ads for girl-themed toys: Who needed mothers when the girls were pretending to *be* mothers? Girls would have tea parties with their dolls and perhaps a friend or two, but they rarely, if ever, set a place for Mom. Girls' play was not cross-generational. It didn't have to be.

Not so for boys. Talking about toys for boys in the postwar baby boom invariably means talking about fathers. Even the most casual glance at the toy catalogs at the Strong Museum of Play in Rochester reveals the consistent presence of fathers in ads for toys geared for boys. Unlike mothers and daughters, fathers and sons were engaged in a complicated, mutually reinforcing pretense: The boys were pretending to be adult men, while the adult men, the fathers, were pretending to be boys. Father-son bonding was both the means and the end. It would save both of them, because they both needed saving.

Saving from what? For the boys, it was pretty straightforward: delinquency and/or homosexuality. That the two could be linked was evident in the palpably eroticized Marlon Brando in *The Wild One* and in the rebellious James Dean in *Rebel Without a Cause.* Young boys must have had difficulty figuring out why these on-screen heroes made their hearts beat a bit faster and their palms sweat a bit more. Identification, attraction, admiration, desire—it's hard for anyone to sort them out.

But figure it out they must. The prevailing culture regarded neither homosexuality nor delinquency as innate or biological. Boys weren't born gay, and delinquents weren't the result of a "bad seed." No, the era's diluted Freudian pop psychology attributed the origins of both to the family. The parenting literature of the 1950s regarded the cause of both problems as "father absence"—too little fathering, too little attention paid by fathers to the lives of their sons. Father absence left a boy "prey" to his mother's overdomination: she could "feminize" him as a mama's boy, rendering him gay, or force him to rebel against her by becoming a delinquent. Either way, both absentee fatherhood and boys' dilemmas were clearly seen, at bottom, as mothers' fault.

Boys left to themselves were in danger of being enticed, seduced into what was considered deviance. While the culture celebrated the boy gang as a realm of freedom, fun, and harmless mischief—think of the *Our Gang* comedies—it also considered boy gangs dangerous, always a step away from morphing into the cruel, even murderous scenario of *Lord of the Flies.* Boy gangs were best when they had strong adult male leaders that kept the boys in check, as in the real-life Boy Scouts or in *Andy's Gang,* a Saturday-morning TV show for kids, led by an adult Andy Devine.

The notion that overdominant mothers and absentee fathers produced "deviant" sons, whether delinquent or gay, had its origin in psychiatrists' studies of their patients. Fredric Wertham's assertion that comic books led to delinquency came entirely from his psychiatric practice interviewing troubled youth (see Chapter 7). It was the same with "deviance." Psychiatrists found that their gay male patients seemed to have a common family configuration: a feckless, ineffective, or absent father and a smothering mother.

Methodologically, such studies almost always suffer from a sampling bias. How much can one generalize from a clinical sample of people in psychiatric treatment? What about gay men who were not seeing a psychiatrist? And what about heterosexual men who *were* seeing a psychiatrist? It turns out that many gay men who were not in psychiatric treatment did not have an overdominant mother and absent father, and while many straight men in treatment did. In fact, one might say that having an overdominant mother and absent father was a good predictor of whether a man would seek out a psychiatrist, but it would tell you next to nothing about his sexual orientation.

Nonetheless, the association stuck. Virtually every parenting book or advice column stressed the central importance of a strong father figure in the life of a boy—an adult male role model who could guide the boy toward healthy, responsible manhood. "The process of transferring from the mother to the father is essential for emotional development, since the girl has to love and respect some man early in life if she is to grow up to marry one, and the boy needs to have some male ideal early in life if he is to wish to grow up to be a high type of man," wrote one sociologist.[1] Studies of delinquency and homosexuality saw these identities as problems with masculinity, with inadequately internalizing the masculinity their fathers had achieved. Father absence was the source of the problem.

If parenting experts regarded father absence as the cause of delinquency or homosexuality, it's ironic, yet predictable, that at the same time they managed to divert the blame away from fathers. Delinquency or homosexuality were, they said, mothers' fault. Fathers were not exactly absent but were victims of overdominant wives who kept their sons tied securely to their apron strings (keeping them "feminized") and who kept fathers away from their sons. Serious social science and pop Freudianism buoyed this notion that in order for a boy to achieve a secure masculinity, he must repudiate his mother and identify with his father. Philip Wylie's *Generation of Vipers* (1942) excoriated mothers for emasculating their henpecked husbands and turning their sons gay, delinquent, or both. Fathers were too weak to stand up to mothers, too absorbed in their careers to spend time at home, and too distracted by the material pleasures of postwar affluence to insert themselves into the lives of their sons. Wylie's book, as well as David Levy's *Maternal Overprotection* (1943) and Edward Strecker's *Their Mothers' Sons* (1946), initiated an assault on "megaloid momworship," as Wylie so artfully put it.[2]

It was an extraordinary sleight of hand, this mother-blaming, and it coincided with general anti-Semitic slanders against Jewish mothers. What Jews often valued, that women were strong and assertive, was transmuted to an image of women who were domineering and dominating. The stereotypical Jewish mother was overbearing and overinvolved, a "smotherer" rather than a "motherer," who poured her own suppressed ambitions onto her "golden boy" son. It's interesting to see how the word for this sort of involved motherhood became a slur. The Yiddish word *balabusta*, which means a perfect homemaker, cook, cleaner, and baker, became *ball buster* just a little too casually.[3]

Involved fathers could save their sons from the emasculating clutches of these overweening mothers. "You have the horror of seeing your son a pantywaist," wrote *Life* magazine, "but he won't get red blood and self-reliance if you leave the whole job of making a he-man of him to his mother."[4] Men were on a mission—to save their sons and in the process themselves. This was key: Home wasn't a retreat—it was a field of battle against delinquency and homosexuality. Men were going to war again!

Life magazine declared 1954 the year of the "domestication of the American man." This was a good thing: Men would return to their homes, save their sons, and find meaning and purpose in their postwar identity. Still, men too faced temptations, like dropping out, becoming a beatnik, or simply failing to integrate into the postwar suburban boom.[5]

So in the process of saving their sons, dads could also save themselves. *Parents' Magazine* ran a column called "Specially for Fathers," though it's not clear how many men read the magazine to which their wives routinely subscribed. An article in *American Home*, "Are You a Dud as a Dad?" suggested that involved fatherhood gave men a chance to prove their masculinity, when their jobs as faceless factory workers or corporate clones rendered them less masculine. "Here is one area of your life," the article said, "which doesn't depend on 'breaks' or ability, on education or money. A man can be a success as a father, a real 'dad,' if he cares enough to try."[6] Suburban dads were encouraged to develop hobbies like woodworking or stamp collecting—and hopefully to include their sons.

Many of the era's toys promoted father-son bonding. Many suburban basements were converted into miniature countrysides with small towns connected by railroad tracks, on which miniature trains supposedly transported goods across the country—all for suburban boys who had never seen a real-life freight train. Lionel Trains made this mutually reinforcing father-son bonding the leitmotif of its annual ad campaign and cemented the place of their train sets as one of the toy industry's few evergreens.

Fathers and sons were also to share activities. Boys would go out

Ad for Lionel trains, late 1950s. (LIONEL L.L.C © Lionel® brand name and logo used with permission)

for Little League baseball, Cub Scouts, or Boy Scouts, and their dads would follow. The 1950s were the era not of the soccer mom but of Umpire Dad, Coach Dad, Scoutmaster Dad. Boys would become men, men would become boys again, and each would rescue the other.

Sporting Boys

Sports were the glue of boyhood.* Sports cemented the boy to history, to an entire family's long-standing love for a particular local or national team. "Baseball is fathers and sons," wrote the poet Donald Hall. The lazy arc of the baseball, languid and pastoral, bound families together and bound communities to tradition. Football, by contrast, Hall wrote, is "brothers beating each other up in the backyard."[7]

But football also binds boys together; the team is a pack, a band of brothers. Since the turn of the twentieth century, when President Theodore Roosevelt trumpeted sports as instilling manly fortitude in emasculated men, sports have been the primary vehicles for competition, aggression, physical efficacy, and male bonding. Both physically exerting and rule-bound, the circumscribed aggression was even considered necessary for a healthy boyhood. Boys learned to play, to play hard, and to play by the rules.

Obligatory sports activity provided an opening for all sorts of equipment. While Jews were dramatically overrepresented in the ranks of toy inventors and creators, they were markedly absent from the world of sports equipment. Spalding, Rawlings, and Wilson provided the baseball gloves and balls, the tennis racquets, the footballs

---

* Such a gender-specific statement could not be written about the twenty-first century, especially as girls playing sports, and girls and women watching sports, has been one of the major cultural changes of the past half-century. In the 1950s fewer than 200,000 high school girls played sports—nationwide. Even by 1972, when Title IX was passed, less than 4 percent of girls played sports. Forty years later, in 2012, nearly 40 percent of girls played sports. Jaeah Lee and Maya Dusenbery, "Charts: The State of Women's Athletics, 40 Years After Title IX," *Mother Jones*, June 22, 2012.

and the helmets—all midwestern companies, with headquarters in Chicago and St. Louis.

What explains this absence? Perhaps because Jews—Hank Greenberg and Sandy Koufax excepted—were not a particularly sporty culture, more cosmopolitan than rural, more comfortable in the library than in the sandlot. Perhaps because Lower East Side tenements provided few spaces large enough to play organized sports, and residents had little free time to play them. Or perhaps because calls to hale and hearty manhood fell on relatively deaf ears among a people for whom the highest calling was to be a man of the book.

Maybe. But in the 1930s many of the nation's best collegiate basketball teams were stocked with Jewish players, as were the ranks of the lighter-weight boxing championships. Benny Leonard reigned as the world lightweight champion from 1917 to 1925 and is ranked among the greatest fighters ever. Barney Ross (born Dov-Ber Rasofsky in 1909 in New York after his father, a Talmudic scholar, escaped a pogrom) won world championships in three weight classes, lightweight, welterweight, and light welterweight. (One can often track the waves of ethnic groups who have immigrated to New York by looking at the boxing champions for the lighter-weight classes. Irish, Jews, Italians, Blacks, Puerto Ricans, Filipinos, Thais—every group had to fight, literally, to get a seat at the table and a chance at the crown.)

The National Collegiate Athletic Association ranks the LIU Brooklyn Blackbirds as the best collegiate men's basketball team of the entire 1930s. The team voted to boycott the 1936 Olympics in Berlin—the first Olympics to actually include basketball.* Three of the starting five on the team were Jewish, including All-Americans Jules Bender and Ben Kramer.[8]

The absence of Jews from the sports equipment industry may also have been a matter of timing. Rawlings was founded in 1887, and Spalding in 1876. Hillerich & Bradsby, makers of the Louisville

* The move prefigured L.A. Dodgers pitcher Sandy Koufax's refusal to pitch in the World Series on October 6, 1965, because the game fell on Yom Kippur.

Slugger baseball bat, was founded in 1855. Wilson was the latecomer, founded in 1913. Certainly shtetl dwellers had little interest in, or time for, sports, and Lower East Side tenements offered opportunities for play only with whatever "equipment" was at hand. But by the time Yiddish Jews arrived in the United States, the sports equipment industry was already well established. There was no niche that they could create, no seam that they could exploit. Nor did the upper echelons of those established companies much like Jews anyway.

But in the 1950s, if playing sports wasn't enough for Jewish boys, then thinking about sports, playing at playing sports, might prove a terrific diversion. *That* was a niche, a seam. Of course, I'm talking about baseball cards.

Topps, a major manufacturer of baseball cards, was originally founded as the American Leaf Tobacco Company by first-generation Jewish entrepreneur Morris Shorin. Morris Chigorinsky, as he was originally named, and his wife, Rebecca, had emigrated from Russia to New York in 1892, settled in Brooklyn, and changed their names. By 1910, Morris was running the tobacco company, but it faced a crisis during the First World War when its supply of Turkish tobacco was suddenly cut off. To avoid bankruptcy, Morris's four sons decided to rename the company Topps and focus on a new product: chewing gum.

Chewing gum had been a successful confection for a long time. Topps began to market it in 1938, and during the Second World War, the company's motto, "Don't Talk Chum, Chew Topps Gum," was widely known. After the war, in 1947, the company launched Bazooka bubble gum, wrapping it in a red, white, and blue wrapper and giving it that military-sounding name. It then got the idea of cross-marketing the bubble gum: It inserted a tiny comic strip about a young hero into every piece. Bazooka Joe was one of the Yellow Kid comic book characters, a wise guy—wearing an eye patch, a cockeyed baseball cap, and rolled-up jeans—with a heart of gold. Here was a perfect amalgam: candy confection, comic book, and novelty all rolled into one. Bazooka bubble gum, with *Bazooka Joe* comics, soared past its competitors

Beginning in 1950, Topps, now based on 36th Street in

Brooklyn, tried to package the gum with small cardboard cards featuring Hopalong Cassidy. They sold reasonably well and remained the company's major product until early in 1951, when Sy Berger (born in 1923 on the Lower East Side to a furrier father and homemaker mother, and by then a twenty-eight-year-old World War II veteran) decided to design a set of cards with images of baseball players that could be packaged with the chewing gum. He and Woody Gelman sat down at the kitchen table of his Brooklyn apartment and designed the cards: they would have a picture of the player, the logo of his team, a facsimile signature on the front of the card, and a bunch of statistics and personal information (birthplace, birthday) on the back. Berger signed exclusive agreements with the players, and for a fee, they autographed up to one thousand cards each. The cards were placed in the packets. "We wanted the cards to sell more gum," Berger recalled.[9] Their basic design is still in use today, and Topps continues to produce cards for baseball, football, basketball, and pretty much every other sport.

Baseball trading cards had been around for a long time. Soon after the Civil War, Peck & Snyder, a sporting goods store in New York, had created cards of baseball teams to promote its wares. By the turn of the century, several tobacco and confectionery companies were bundling trading cards with their products. In the years after the Second World War, one company, Bowman, competed with Topps for baseball card dominance. Berger ingeniously worked the clubhouses of the Dodgers, Yankees, and Giants, bringing the players free bubble gum (and even helping to wean a few from chewing tobacco). He promised that Topps would produce cards in color (Bowman's were originally in black and white) and signed the players to exclusive contracts for $125 and nonexclusive for $75. The first full set appeared in 1952, and in 1956 Topps bought out Bowman and became the undisputed dominant card company.

Sy Berger thought the success of cards based on sports teams (by the 1950s there were basketball and football cards; hockey cards came later) might spill over into other arenas. In 1962, when President John F. Kennedy's popularity was at its height, Topps produced JFK cards—seventy-seven cards with black and white photos of the president, often with his family, on the front, and historical information on the back—putting them in every pack of bubble gum. Alas, the cards disappeared after Kennedy's assassination in 1963. By 1964, they were collectors' items.

But that didn't stop Sy Berger. After the Beatles appeared on Ed Sullivan's show in February 1964, Topps sent Berger to London to negotiate the rights to cards featuring the Fab Four. The Beatles were uninterested; Britain had no tradition of cards for soccer players, and the idea seemed silly to them. Undeterred, Berger expressed his disappointment to Brian Epstein, the Beatles' manager. According to his obituary, Berger said a few choice phrases in Yiddish. Epstein responded, also in Yiddish. They returned to the room and made the deal. Beatles cards began appearing soon afterward.[10]

Even today Berger is considered the "father of the modern baseball card."[11]

Boy Toys

Boys had plenty of toys that were geared to playing either alone or with other boys. Alone, they had dolls—boy dolls—but they went by a different name.

Ideal simply didn't "get" boys in the same way that it understood girls. Year after year, the company rolled out new and improved dolls for girls, and ever more teddy bears, which were gender-neutral and embraced by boys and girls alike. Then one day in 1963, one of the doll developers at Ideal, Larry Reiner, approached the top executives with a new doll idea: a soldier doll. It would not be a small toy soldier, like the legions of plastic or tin soldiers that little boys had played with for years. Nor would it be one of those hundred-soldiers-for-one-dollar sets that were advertised in comic books. Reiner was thinking of a larger figure, more like the dolls that had captivated American girls, that had movable arms and legs, that could strike realistic poses, and move alongside tanks and planes. Ben Michtom and Lionel Weintraub told him he must be crazy. "Boys will never play with dolls," exclaimed Michtom. "Well, in that case," said Reiner, "would you mind if I tried to sell it to another company?" "Be our guest" came the reply, freeing Reiner to take his idea elsewhere.

Had Ideal ever been more stupid? (Well, maybe. Remember that the company had also passed on the Marilyn grown-up doll two years before Barbie showed up. And then there was that Baby Jesus doll.) Reiner's agent, Stan Weston, brought the idea to Don Levine, who was research director for Hasbro. Merrill Hassenfeld recognized the possibility at once. G.I. Joe was born.

Introduced in 1964, Hasbro was careful to call G.I. Joe not a doll but an "action figure." Boys flocked to it. The genius of G.I. Joe mirrored the genius of Barbie. Barbie took a traditional feminine, girly experience—playing with dolls—and made it into a grown-up experience. Barbie is decidedly not a baby to be mothered. She is an equal, a peer, a friend, an older sister. Dolls need not be babies to be coddled—they can be confidantes to share your secrets with. Barbie enters masculine realms, enabling little girls to enjoy the feminine experience of dolls while also imagining themselves as surgeons, astronauts, and athletes (while never being condescending about teachers, cheerleaders, and nurses). Barbie was at once nonfeminist, anti-feminist, and protofeminist. She was anything you wanted her to be, because she was you.

And just as Barbie enables girls to enter masculine realms with no loss of femininity, G.I. Joe enables boys to engage in the utterly feminine pastime of playing with dolls with no loss of masculinity, since G.I. Joe was anything but feminine. He became buff, hypermuscular, and palpably male.

G.I. Joe arrived, it seems, at just the right time. Toy gun sales, after their initial meteoric popularity, had declined after JFK's assassination and would continue to decline as the culture soured on militarism during the Vietnam War. G.I. Joe enabled boys to play with guns without actually playing with guns, and they could stay indoors, where the parents might be better able to keep an eye on them. Given his strength, power, and formidable, posable features, this twelve-inch action figure might actually win, in fantasy, the war that America was

Three G.I. Joes. From *left*: 1982 G.I. Joe "Grunt," 1991 G.I. Joe, and 1997 G.I. Joe "extreme." (Photo courtesy of Harrison G. Pope, Jr., MD)

losing in reality. It will come as no surprise that G.I. Joe was the model on which the cinematic Rambo was based.

Over the years, Barbie's physical dimensions have remained pretty much the same. Were she an actual woman, her measurements would be 39-inch bust, 19.5-inch waist, and 28-inch hips, and she would wear a size three shoe, even when she entered masculine spheres. She has the same body whether she is Brain Surgeon Barbie or Cheerleader Barbie. (In 2016 Mattel released a series of new Barbies, including Curvy Barbie, whose measurements come closer to reality.)

But G.I. Joe's dimensions have changed dramatically. In 1974, were he an actual man, he would have stood at five feet ten inches tall, with a 31-inch waist, a 44-inch chest, and 12-inch biceps. He was strong and muscular, to be sure, but still within the realm of the possible. By the early 2000s, he was still five foot ten, but his waist had shrunk to 28 inches, his chest had expanded to 50 inches, and his biceps were now 27 inches, not that far from the size of his waist. G.I. Joe today is more a circus freak than a role model; he is such a hypermasculine ectomorph that were he real, he would be unable to touch his fingers to his own shoulders because his biceps would get in the way.*

Mattel also struck gold in the market for boys. Reasoning that boys would want to play the roles that their fathers had played not long before in the theaters of World War II and Korea, the company's first post-Barbie toys were toy guns (and toy ukuleles). Toy guns enabled boys to play soldier and cowboy, the two most palpable fantasies for boys in the 1950s. One-tenth of all fictional titles in the 1950s were westerns, and eight of the top ten television shows of the 1950s—a total of thirty prime-time TV shows in all—were "horse operas."[12]

Suburban neighborhoods had plenty of space for boys to play, so sales of the equipment for playing cowboy and soldier soared, soon nearly eclipsing sales of chemistry sets. Dozens of cap-firing six-shooters and faux-Winchesters found their way into the hands of boys at pony rides wearing Davy Crockett coonskin caps. Thousands of seven-year-old "cowboys" tied thousands of younger brothers and sisters to backyard trees as "Indian" captives, only to switch midgame into G.I.'s defeating Nazis or "Japs" who were hiding in the bushes.

Davy Crockett was promoted as a more "wholesome" alternative to the juvenile delinquent and comic book superhero, "a healthy sign by those who have deplored the vogue of the comic-book superman," according to *The New York Times* in 1955. While Disney had created the myth of Davy Crockett, it didn't see the marketing potential, and so they didn't think to copyright the name or the image.

---

* Whether G.I. Joe was a "doll" for boys has been a subject of dispute ever since he was introduced. It seems to have finally been decided in 1989 by the U.S. Court of Appeals, which upheld the designation of the U.S. Custom Service: G.I. Joe is a doll, not, as Hasbro company executives claimed, a "toy soldier." This designation is about more than a name—it's about millions of dollars. Dolls produced abroad are subject to a 12 percent import tariff; toy soldiers are not. Hasbro continues to avoid the word *doll*. Since his introduction in 1964, it has called him an "action figure." "Say It Ain't So, G.I. Joe," *Washington Post*, July 26, 1989.

Morey Swartz, a Baltimore notions manufacturer, jumped right in, creating and distributing millions of coonskin caps, toy guns, faux-deerskin outfits, and replicas of Ol' Betsy, Crockett's musket, before Disney got wise and copyrighted "Disney's Davy Crockett" to cash in. (The Disney company never made that mistake again, as any visitor to a Disney park can attest, as they exit from rides into themed gift shops.)[13]

If the fantasy of Crockett wasn't enough to bring fathers and sons together, the real thing might work better. BB guns, air rifles, and even real guns would do the trick. Like sports equipment, the production of "real" fake guns, as opposed to toy guns, was a world apart from Jewish entrepreneurs. Established rifle companies had developed out of the world of hunting and fishing; now they produced real rifles that shot pellets, BBs, and other nonlethal projectiles. The Daisy air gun (the company was founded in Michigan in 1882) was a first step for boys itching to get a real rifle from Remington or Colt. But because few Jewish fathers were hunters or fishermen, their sons' exposure was likely more of the make-believe variety.

Playing "war" or "Cowboys and Indians" allowed boys to participate in another activity that had, like doll play, been "coded" as feminine: dressing up. Davy Crockett coonskin caps were just the tip of the iceberg, as entire western ensembles—chaps, fringed shirts, kerchiefs, and even the occasional cowboy hat to replace the raccoon fur—were ubiquitous among those tough hombres of Thousand Oaks, Highland Park, and Great Neck. While Ideal made dolls based on TV characters like Hopalong Cassidy, Roy Rogers, and Gene Autry, costume designers outfitted real boys to match.

Insulated from the privations of the Depression and the violence of World War II, boys of the 1950s grew up nurturing heroic fantasies that toymakers were more than ready to serve. And as hundreds of thousands of urban Jews, a generation or two removed from the tenements, decamped for the suburbs, the established toy companies ministered to their every need to stake their claim for hardy masculine boyhood and devoted daddydom. In the Jewish suburbs, for the first time, they weren't "Jewish boys." They were just boys.

Military Models

Father-son bonding provided not only a secure route to manhood for boys but also a route back to a grounded normality for fathers who had been traumatized in war and faced the economic pressures of the modern breadwinning dad. While toy guns enabled boys to play grown-up, the world of models provided a way for fathers and sons to bond while miniaturizing, and thus sanitizing, the fathers' wartime experiences. (No doubt some mothers and daughters enjoyed building model airplanes, but the marketing was directed entirely toward boys, and only boys were pictured on the packaging boxes.)

Southern California, the home of the American plastics industry, was also a major center for military manufacture, home to many shipyards, military bases, and military contracting. We saw in Chapter 10 how the explosion of the plastics industry transformed girls' toys, setting the career path of Elliot Handler, who created plastic picture frames before going on to develop the doll that changed girlhood forever. You may remember an early scene in the film *The Graduate* (1967), where a friend of Benjamin Braddock's father approaches the newly graduated college star and says, "One word." Ben looks at him. "Plastics." That's what southern California was like—about a decade earlier, in the early 1950s. (Every one of the plastic model company relatives I spoke with mentioned that movie scene.)

In 1943, just as my father was preparing to ship out to the Pacific from the gigantic naval base in San Diego, a young Jewish plastics inventor in Venice, California, Lewis H. Glaser, had the idea of making plastic replicas of the fighter planes and battleships that were engaged in the massive war effort.

Glaser was born in Brooklyn in 1917 to a Hasidic tailor father and seamstress mother who had arrived from Krakow only a few years before. After his father abandoned the family, Glaser and his mother decamped for Los Angeles, where Lew excelled in high school, especially in science, but was too poor to attend Caltech. Needing money, he started as a radio repairman, but in the late 1930s he began experimenting with plastics. His small company, Precision Specialties, built plastic miniature replicas of other companies' products, such as plastic compact and lipstick cases for Revlon. Precision's most successful products were novelties like the Pluto flashlight (licensed through Disney) and the Woody Woodpecker Laff-amonica.[14]

An avid fan of the comedian Jack Benny's popular radio program, Glaser thought it might be fun to make a model of the 1913 Maxwell, Benny's oft-mentioned misbegotten car. He tinkered with using plastic to create models of cars, and by 1950, he'd developed a scale that would enable perfect replicas of the Maxwell, the Ford Model T, and others. The toys, marketed under a new name, Revell, were an instant hit. (Rumors that the company name was derived from the Revlon connection aren't true, Glaser's daughter Kim tells me; it was simply the result of a brainstorming session with employees.)[15]

In 1953 Revell produced a replica of the USS *Missouri*, the nearly forty-one-ton battleship that had played a crucial role in ending the Second World War. (The formal Japanese surrender ceremony took place on that ship in Tokyo Bay on September 2, 1945.) It was so successful that Revell instantly became the world's largest manufacturer of plastic model kits of military airplanes and battleships. Glaser was proud of a letter he received from Admiral Robert Carney of the U.S. Department of the Navy. "The Revell ship models I have seen all possess a sailor's concern for nautical detail as well as an engineer's attention to workmanship and design," the admiral wrote. "You are to be congratulated on your Navy line which has made so many millions of Americans more aware of the ships and planes of our fleet."[16]

Revell may even have had a hand in the reconciliation between Germany and the United States after the war. Its model ships and planes were so popular that in 1956 it opened a German subsidiary, first in Bielefeld and later in Bünde. To say that German youth embraced the models would be an understatement. They've sold in the millions there every year, most notably the model of the *Bismarck*, among the largest and most celebrated (and from the U.S. point of view, notorious) German battleships. Revell models were so accurate in their scale that it was rumored that the Kremlin had purchased hundreds of different models to help the Soviets fill in the gaps in

Lewis Glaser with some of his model kits, c. 1955. (Photo courtesy of Kim Glaser Selbert)

their knowledge of U.S. weapons systems. While boys were playing war, real war makers were playing with those same models.

Young boys spent hours gluing the models together, applying decals and other insignia to the planes and boats. Those hours brought fathers and sons together, enabling boys to imagine being men, and their fathers to return home safely—all at a scale of 1 to 87.

Another major model company, Monogram, was founded in Chicago in 1945 by two friends and colleagues working at Comet Kits: Bob Reder, a designer, and Jack Besser, a marketer. Besser was a first-generation Jew who had returned from the war to try to find a job in sales. In Reder's family basement, they conceived of a line of models made of balsa wood that would not only provide the pleasures of model building but, once built, could actually fly. To be honest, the balsa planes didn't fly especially well, but the pleasures of building them far outweighed their technical problems. When Monogram switched to plastic models, it took off, so much so that it became one of the country's top three model companies.

One of Monogram and Revell's chief competitors was Aurora, founded in 1950 in a Brooklyn garage by Joe Giammarino and Abe Shikes. Giammarino was born in Brooklyn in 1916 to Italian immigrant parents; Shikes was Jewish, born in Russia in 1908, and he arrived in Brooklyn in 1918, after the revolution. A World War II veteran, Shikes had fought in the Battle of the Bulge. They were young men on the make, producing plastic molding for other companies. Giammarino was the design-obsessed engineer; Shikes, the organizational whiz and marketing genius. As hobbyists themselves, they were fascinated by the military equipment created during the war. They launched their first models in 1950, a cheap version of the Lockheed F-90 and the Grumman Panther F9F. Perfect accuracy in the model was sacrificed for a cheaper price; their models appealed to younger boys who found their models easy to assemble and seemed less invested in perfectly scaled accuracy.

Aurora competed successfully with Monogram and Revell until 1962, when it accidentally stumbled on a new idea: a Movie Monsters line. When the sales and marketing executives unveiled a model of Frankenstein at the hobby industry's annual convention, they were laughed out of the room. On the convention's last day, though, the executives were invited to bring their families to the convention exhibit hall. There the kids went wild over the Frankenstein monster. They absolutely had to have one! The parents hadn't realized that these 1930s monsters were recycled on Saturday-afternoon TV—the kids knew every single monster that their parents had tried to forget. Dozens more monster models appeared. Aurora alone steamed into the 1960s with a full line of games, models, and other toys—nearly 250 different models. At the end of the 1970s, the bottom would drop out of the model business, after the OPEC oil embargo decimated the U.S. plastics industry for a time.

One thing seemed to be missing from all these plastic models of military planes and ships: their interiors. That would be the contribution of Irving Rosenbloom, a Long Island, Jewish entrepreneur who was also experimenting with injection molding of plastics. (Rosenbloom's parents had emigrated from the Lomza district of Poland in 1896, and he was born Israel Kravietsky in 1903 on the Lower East Side.) Rosenbloom, a born kibitzer, worked as a pitchman selling kitchen gadgets on the Coney Island Boardwalk. At the 1939 World's Fair, he saw an exhibit of the new technique of plastic injection molding. It was one of those eureka moments that successful inventors and entrepreneurs often mention, like Lew Glaser's epiphany while listening to Jack Benny.

Rosenbloom worked for Renwal, a company founded in 1939 by Irving Lawner—Renwal is his name spelled backward. Renwal made waffle irons, manufactured housewares, and had also been responsible for making "proximity fuses" for American bombs during the war. (The fuse is an awful device, using radar to sense when it is close to the target, so it can explode early and send lethal fragments in a wider radius than a normal bomb.) In 1949 Rosenbloom was fiddling with injection plastic molds and came up with the design for a line of well-crafted 1:24 scale furniture for dollhouses. When manufactured, they sold extremely well, especially since suburban homes were large enough for more girls to own dollhouses.

By the early 1950s, just as Revell began producing plastic model cars on the West Coast, Rosenbloom started playing around with military models on the East Coast. In his first efforts, he worked from original army blueprints to create replicas of antiaircraft guns, tanks, and massive artillery weapons. (He called it, appropriately enough, the Blueprint Series.) In 1959 the company created a replica of the USS *North Carolina* that featured rotating turrets, cannons that lifted, and other realistic equipment. This was followed by a realistic model of the USS *Washington* Polaris submarine that added a new feature: The walls of the sub would fold down to reveal the entire miniature interior, fully crafted to scale.[17] These see-through models were more accurate, and much larger, than Revell's submarines, and they proved enormously popular.[18]

Their success inspired Rosenbloom to think outside the box, or rather outside the military. One day on a trip to the American Museum of Natural History in New York, he was mesmerized by the skeletons in the Hall of Human Origins. They were empty of anything but bone, yes, but so suggestive. "Eureka!" he thought. He took some photographs and brought them back to his head of production, Irving Lubow, who contacted a model maker, Marcel Jovine, to see if he could make a model of a human. (Jovine had also worked for

Ideal and had developed several toys for Ben Michtom, including the Blessed Event Lifelike Baby Doll in 1950, notable for its stretchy plastic "lifelike" skin.) Jovine went to work, and the Visible Man appeared that next year. This immediate hit was followed by the Visible Woman, the Visible Cow, the Visible Horse, and the Visible Dog. Ever since, these models have been used in high schools, and in medical and veterinary schools, all over the country as an introduction to the human and animal body.[19]

The early 1950s through early '70s were the heyday of plastic models. In fact, in 1959, plastic model building was the number-one boys' hobby; four out of five boys listed it as their favorite pastime. Ten years earlier it hadn't even been on the list, and twenty years later it had disappeared altogether. In the mid-1970s, the plastic model business waned, in part because of the critique of military glamorization in the era of the Vietnam War. Parents were less thrilled about war; kids were increasingly uncomfortable with the war machine. Companies producing plastic models merged, folded, got absorbed into larger conglomerates, and changed their product lines, so that by the late 1970s, models had become a niche market for detail-obsessed enthusiasts and ex-military men seeking to relive their past glories.

For nearly three decades, boys and their dads cemented more than model planes and tanks; they had cemented the bonds of suburban manhood. Guns and sports—these were the fantasies of American boys during the postwar era. And their needs were ministered to largely by the least "sporting" of American immigrants.

PART IV

Creating Childhood

12

HOW FIRST-GENERATION JEWS CREATED AMERICAN CHILDHOOD

* * *

"So, *nu* already?" as Morris and all the others might have said. "Tell me why. Why did it fall to these Jews to practically "invent" American childhood?

My aim in this book has not been to recount some triumphalist parade of extraordinary Jews, nor to celebrate Jewish creativity and entrepreneurialism, however tempting or gratifying that might be. The parade merely raises the question: Why were these first-generation Jews able to create such a large part the material culture of American childhood? How were they able to do it?

The general answer to such questions always focuses on the men and women themselves, on their experience as the children of immigrants (or as immigrants who arrived very young) and as the first generation raised in the United States. Was there something about their experience, specifically their *Jewish* experience, that led them, and not other immigrant groups, to enter certain fields and create fantasy worlds there? It could have been Irish or Italians or Chinese. But it wasn't. It was those Yiddish Jews.

Just as important, why did America prove such a fertile ground? One reason was America's openness, its invitation to those who were entrepreneurial, adventurous, creative, or curious, to come and give the American Dream a try. It is a Jewish story, yes, but it is also an American story. It's the story of entrepreneurial creativity, of a culture schlepped in cardboard suitcases across a continent and an ocean, of a drive for assimilation, and of finally finding a home, only to bump headlong into a kinder, gentler version of the anti-Semitic exclusion from which they had just escaped.

The sociologist Max Weber wrote about the "elective affinity," the particular relationship, between the Protestant ethic, a theological doctrine of ascetic self-denial, and the "spirit of capitalism," a secular cultural sensibility that requires economic sacrifice to sustain and grow an enterprise. The relationship isn't causal: Protestantism didn't *cause* capitalism. The two systems, one religious and the other economic, mutually reinforced each other's ideas and values, grafting a social psychology of motivation onto a theological cosmology.

Such was the relationship between Jews and America. The Jew, as we've seen, is the "rootless cosmopolitan," and Jewish history is a story of wandering from country to country. *Bodenlosigkeit*—a German word literally meaning "soil-lessness"—is the story of the Jews. To be cosmopolitan, a citizen of the world, is simultaneously to not have a place of one's own.

To the Yiddish Jews, America was going to be that place. (For many European Zionists, that place could also be Israel.) As much as America is a place, it is also an idea, a vast terrain of opportunity, freedom, and the possibility of mobility. In America, through hard work, discipline, and dedication, so the ideology goes, a man could rise as far as his aspirations and talents would take him. In a land of immigrants, Jews felt they might have just as much of a right to be here as anybody else. Perhaps for the first time, Jews found a home.*

* I realize I am leaving out Native Americans from this story of the American ideal. Of course, the "American" story is the story of settler colonialism, of

A growing country had so many niches to be filled. Post–Civil War expansion had pushed the frontier from sea to shining sea; industrial and financial opportunities abounded. Even the closing of the frontier, declared by the historian Frederick Jackson Turner in 1896, didn't end that expansion; now the frontier would continue to push outward, to colonies, and internally, to internally colonized peoples.

It's been that way for a long time. In 1840 Henry Clay declared on the floor of the U.S. Senate that the United States was a "nation of self-made men." That idea of "self-making" is America's contribution to the world's stock images of masculinity. The American man makes his own way, pitted alone against the environment. Self-making is a project that would have been impossible in Europe, where traditions of aristocratic and theological rule placed most people in fixed positions.

On the other hand, those fixed positions gave life the certainty that what had been would continue to be. Born into a position, you would die there. Status was fixed. You needn't strive; there was no point. A chief characteristic of fixity is security.

Self-making, by contrast, is inherently unstable, insecure. If you can rise as high as your aspirations will take you, you can also fall. Who will be there to catch you? What sort of safety net will you have? And perhaps the hardest question of all: Who's to blame if you fail? For generations, the frontier was that safety net. You failed in New York or Philadelphia? You could start over in Chicago or St. Louis. You failed there? Well, you could move on to Denver or Houston. Couldn't make it there? Try Los Angeles.

The emotion most associated with such self-making is, naturally,

---

white westward expansion and the slaughter and displacement of Native peoples. Yes, of course, they were here first. But to immigrants in the eastern cities, regardless of their European origins, the story of Natives and whites had little effect on their daily lives. They contended instead with older elites and other recent arrivals. There was plenty of racism to go around. It's not that Native Americans didn't play a role in this story; it's that the East Coast urban immigrants didn't see their role.

anxiety. "Will I make it? Do I have what it takes? How hard can I work?" Nearly two centuries of commentators have noted that a peculiar anxiety characterizes the American man, a restlessness, a sense of insecurity.[1] The elective affinity between anxiety and upward mobility seems obvious. Anxiety propels us forward, drives us like sharks, to swim or die, eat or die. Any rest stop might be a permanent resting place, a death sentence.

Yiddish Jews were true believers in the American Dream. They believed in it with everything they had. They forsook their obvious Jewishness in order to fit in, to create themselves. Think of Erik Erikson, literally "Erik Son-of Erik," giving birth to himself, and the hundreds of thousands, even millions of immigrants who Anglicized their names so they could fit in, only to find they were still blacklisted, quota-ed out of university admissions, job prospects, and professional training. Think of J. D. Salinger (born Jerome Daniel Salinger to a Lithuanian-born kosher cheese merchant) creating the alienated teenage Everyman who was fed up with all the "phonies."

They expected more from the country they believed in. They expected America to live up to its promise of equal opportunity. So when they didn't get it, they set about creating it for themselves.

How?

Well, for one thing, they stumbled into an area that had not been "settled" earlier by other ethnic groups. Waves of ethnic entrepreneurs have historically secured a foothold in American society by achieving a monopoly or near monopoly in one industry, like Chinese laundries, and Korean groceries, and Irish police and fire departments, and Italian food importers, masons, and organized criminals.

The first-generation Jews didn't exactly survey the landscape and say, "Hey, toys and games, and TV, and music and movies! Now, there are some niches we can take over!" On the contrary, they sought to enter established arenas, like banking and advertising, but were shut out by WASP elites. Possessing skills in the garment industry, many settled there, and retail outlets for clothing soon followed, with the rise of large department stores in the 1920s and '30s. For some excluded groups, it meant crime. "Gentile society excluded Jews and forced them to enter socially tainted businesses," Michael Alexander wrote of the Jewish gangster Arnold Rothstein.[2]

But no matter where they turned, entrepreneurial Jews always bumped up against anti-Semitism. "Accumulating wealth, pursuing power and influence previously accorded to WASP counterparts," writes the historian Paul Buhle, "Jews still experienced those exclusions for several generations, formal and informal, that kept them out of locker rooms of exclusive clubs and the boardrooms of most giant corporations, therefore in the offices of marginal enterprises capable of sudden expansion or equally sudden collapse." Perhaps, Buhle suggests, it was exactly this marginality that fueled the "edge" needed to create, innovate, and invent.[3]

If not exactly exile, then perhaps anti-Semitism pushed Jews to be creative and entrepreneurial. In 1938 the sociologist Robert Merton wrote a classic study of deviance in which he theorized it as an alternative opportunity structure. That concept may allow us to make sense of the concentration of first-generation Jews in certain fields. Merton's original intention was to explain crime and deviance sociologically; that is, to explain not why some *individuals* became criminals (a psychological approach) but why some *groups* did. He argued that society holds out certain ideals, like wealth and status, that pretty much everyone would like to achieve, and it offers acceptable ways for everyone to pursue them, like hard work, discipline, and sacrifice. However, certain social arrangements may prevent some groups from attaining those goals through the accepted means. Racism, sexism, homophobia, anti-Semitism—all these may make it difficult for some groups to achieve what everyone equally wants. Given this mismatch, how do people respond?

Merton saw four possible outcomes, which we can organize into a two-by-two table of means and ends. (1) *Conformity*, when you pursue culturally approved ends through socially approved means. (Think of Ben Franklin, the Protestant work ethic, and typical stories of upward mobility.) (2) *Innovation*, when you accept the ends but are somehow blocked from using the accepted means and have to resort to creativity, wiles, or deviance in order to achieve them. (Think of drug dealers, bootleg alcohol sellers during Prohibition, and Don Corleone explaining that everyone wants justice, but sometimes his people don't get it from legitimate institutions and so have to resort to indirect means.) (3) *Ritualism*, when you don't really care about the culturally approved ends and simply go through the routines of the accepted means. (Think of people who go to work every day with no expectation of ever getting ahead.) And finally (4) *Retreatism*, when you reject both the means and the ends offered by society and drop out, so to speak. (Think of hippies who dropped out of prestigious colleges to live like medieval peasants on rural communes.)

You can see where I'm going with this, right? Some immigrants saw a niche, an opportunity, a space where they might, as an ethnic group, establish a toehold in the new world and stake a claim for their own pursuit of the American Dream. New York is a microcosm of ethnic succession, where different groups found ways to bring others of their background into the business. Every ethnicity started enclaves for its people's cuisine in restaurant ghettos. Jews and Italians provided services that people wanted but that were unavailable through legal channels: drugs, alcohol, prostitutes (all of which were called, before feminists critiqued the term, "victimless crimes"). Arnold Rothstein and Bugsy Siegel, like Lucky Luciano and Al Capone, were all "innovators" who saw in America the chance for mobility, even if the means they used weren't always respectable.*

* I must point out that Merton himself was the living embodiment of his theory. Born Meyer Robert Schkolnick to a Yiddish-speaking family of Russian immigrants, he adopted Merton as a stage name for his magic act because it sounded more American. He kept it all his life, in an apparent reference to the Oxford college he never attended, and later added King to his name. In an academic world characterized by Jewish quotas and overt anti-Semitism, Merton's trajectory captures the very innovation he observed in others. He was himself a first-generation Jew who devised a creative way to get around the obstacles in his path.

Michael Chabon once asked Will Eisner, the great comic book creator who established the graphic novel, why so many of the young men in the comics business in the 1930s and '40s had been Jews. Eisner replied "that the opportunity was just there. That if you were a young Jewish kid who wanted to be an artist, the more respectable forms of commercial art, illustration, advertising art—all those fields were closed to you at the time. But comics would take you." Then Eisner stopped, thought for a moment, and added: "There is something in the Jewish storytelling tradition that's exemplified by the golem, this idea of an imaginary champion that is going to come along and right all wrongs for an oppressed people."[4]

Stan Lee, the creator of so many "marvels," echoed this idea:

> Could it be that there was something in our background, in our culture, that brought us together in the comic book field? When we created stories about idealized superheroes, were we subconsciously trying to identify with characters who were the opposite of the Jewish stereotypes that the propaganda tried to instill in people's minds?[5]

The interconnections among toymaking, comic books and comic strips, children's books, and television allowed for a cross-pollination that enabled the enterprises in each industry to feed off the others. Comic book characters created by Jews were licensed to Jewish toymakers whose manufactured toys were sold in department stores run by Jews. Hollywood stars licensed their images for product tie-ins. As we've seen, Ben Michtom even tried to reverse that causal trajectory and make the original follow the artifact, when he begged Ham Fisher, the creator of Joe Palooka, to make sure that Palooka's wife, Ann, gave birth to a boy.

The biography of each individual obviously had something to do with their success. So many of the men had fathers who had failed, yet instilled in their sons a drive, a need—no, a compulsion—to succeed well beyond themselves. Against what Neal Gabler called a "patrimony of failure," Hollywood moguls were driven to succeed. Upward mobility in America wasn't simply a possibility, a path to the American Dream—it was a necessity. There was no alternative.

As the historian Rich Cohen writes, most of the most notorious 1930s Jewish criminals seem to have had similar family constellations: their immigrant fathers were poor shopkeepers, peddlers, and scroungers. Louis Lepke, Arnold Rothstein, Bugsy Siegel, Abe Reles, Meyer Lansky—all were true believers in the American Dream, much like the fictional Corleones and the real-life Castellano and Gambino crime families. They drove nice cars, lived in leafy suburbs, and dressed in designer suits. They made it.[6] Their sons inherited what the poet Robert Bly once called "the father wound," a deep injury that left a hole in their hearts, a gaping need to achieve, to earn attention and love, to be better than their fathers. My own father once told me that he would not consider himself a success unless I were more successful than he was—and that his own father had told him the same.[7]

But to speak of Jewish men, we must also speak of their mothers. Growing up in poverty, these boys were deprived of maternal coddling, the attention and nurture of full-time motherhood. Their mothers worked, often in the garment industry, or by taking in laundry and sewing, or in factories and sweatshops around the city. The boys often awoke on dark mornings in an empty tenement and got themselves to school, if they bothered to go at all, only to return in the evening to an empty house. They raised themselves in some sense, and they resented it. They resented that some other children had full-time stay-at-home mothers, and they resented that they didn't get what other children got.

These young men took those twin facts—the patrimony of paternal failure and the gaping wound of the nurturing but absent mother—and projected them onto little children, by creating dolls that enabled little girls to "play Mommy" and little boys to be strong and successful, whether as soldiers or doctors, and thereby create the very childhoods that these men wished they had had.

Outside-Insider / Inside-Outsider: The Double Consciousness of the First-Generation Jew

The social dynamics of Jewish innovation are at least as important as the psychology. The philosopher Isaiah Berlin argued that what drove them was not their outsider status but their desire to be an insider. It was "not alienation but an intense desire for acceptance" that "led Jews to study their neighbors with almost obsessive care."[8] As the journalist Richard Cohen so aptly put it, "Jews are foreign correspondents in their own country."[9]

Perhaps the best articulation of these social and cultural dynamics comes from the pioneering sociologist W.E.B. Du Bois, who wrote about the "double consciousness" of the American Negro. As he explains the concept:

> It is a peculiar sensation, this double-consciousness, this sense of always looking at one's self through the eyes of others, of measuring one's soul by the tape of a world that looks on in amused contempt and pity. One ever feels his two-ness—an American, a Negro; two souls, two thoughts, two unreconciled strivings; two warring ideals in one dark body, whose dogged strength alone keeps it from being torn asunder.

The history of the American Negro is the history of this strife—this longing to attain self-conscious manhood, to merge his double self into a better and truer self. In this merging he wishes neither of the older selves to be lost. He would not Africanize America, for America has too much to teach the world and Africa. He would not bleach his Negro blood in a flood of white Americanism, for he knows that Negro blood has a message for the world. He simply wishes to make it possible for a man to be both a Negro and an American, without being cursed and spit upon by his fellows, without having the doors of Opportunity closed roughly in his face.[10]

This double consciousness is both a privilege and a curse; one always sees and experiences oneself not only through one's own eyes but also through the eyes of others. It gives one access to how others think and perceive the world, but also reminds one constantly, relentlessly, of one's own otherness. (Double consciousness, or split vision, helps explain why people of color understand white people better than white people understand people of color; why LGBT people understand heterosexuals better than heterosexuals understand LGBT people; why women understand men better than men understand women; and why Jews understand gentiles better than gentiles understand Jews. In one sense, they'd better; their lives could depend on it.)

First-generation Yiddish Jews were, in their own way, achingly aware of possessing this double consciousness. Their outsider position had many parallels with that of the African Americans Du Bois described, although it was not in the least identical. Black people are always reminded of their outsider-ness, the legacy of centuries of racism and its subtle and not-so-subtle expressions today. The twoness of "African American" identity always indicates this double consciousness.

Historically, this racial othering has been a way other immigrant groups, Jews included, have made their claim for "whiteness." In *How the Irish Became White* (2009), the historian Noel Ignatiev argues that by aligning with racist and nativist political sentiments, in the mid-nineteenth century, Irish immigrants distanced themselves from people of color (they had been called "black" by the English) and thus consciously identified as white.[11]

In *Blackface/White Noise* (1996), political scientist Michael Rogin argues Jewish immigrants undertook a similar assimilationist project. They too sought to gain greater acceptance in society by demonstrating their difference from Blacks, who represented an even lower social category. Jews "become white" through racism, symbolized by blackface, by cultural appropriation as cultural assimilation. By pretending to be Black in blackface minstrelsy, Jews showed audiences that they were not Black at all but were just pretending—as *any* white person could do! In essence, Rogin argues, the Jews became white by "blacking up."[12]

This is a dynamic between different ethnic groups, each one staking its claim to be American by distancing itself from some other group. The particular experience of African Americans often constructs them as everybody else's "other," the single group that every succeeding group references, thus ensuring that African Americans continue to have the distinction, in effect, of being the eternal other.

At least in the United States. In Europe, Jews long held the dubious distinction of being the eternal other, the eternal outsider, although Muslims may hold that position in Europe today. The existence of an "other" helps the center define itself; the "other" is necessary for there to even *be* a center. For how would the center know itself except in opposition to something not there, something excluded?

So then, were Jews white? It depends on whom you ask. The German Jews who assimilated before the great eastern European and Russian diaspora would tell you they were white, but those Yiddish newcomers? Well, perhaps not. In the American South, Jews were "allowed" to be seen as white only to the extent that they embraced Jim Crow and segregation. In 1893 the *Richmond Times* reported on an altercation between a "Polish Jew and a white man"—as if the Polish Jew weren't white; a candidate in that city's municipal elections sought in a campaign speech to single out "Jews and niggers" as political troublemakers. In the North, by contrast, Jews often sided with other marginalized groups rather than stake their whiteness on repudiating them. Perhaps it was political: Jewish leftists sought to make common cause across race and ethnicity to foment a class-based revolution.[13]

The cultural critic J. Hoberman asks: "How can Jews be seen simultaneously as cultural outsiders—a minority seeking integration into the American mainstream—and as the ultimate insiders—a group with decisive 'disproportionate' influence over a nation's cultural sensibilities?"[14] The historians James Barrett and David Roediger call it a racially "inbetween" state, ranking slightly above African Americans on the racial hierarchy but significantly below "whites."[15] "Now everybody knows that a black man is inferior to a white man (except, of course, Jews, Italians, and Slavs)," W.E.B. Du Bois is said to have quipped in 1924.[16]

The anthropologist Karen Brodkin suggests that Jews experienced "a kind of double vision that comes from racial middleness: of an experience of marginality vis-à-vis whiteness, and an experience of whiteness and belonging vis-à-vis blackness." Gradually, Jews benefited from a kind of "conditional whiteness," earned through a series of compromises with racial exclusion.[17]

In his compelling history of "how America's immigrants became white," Roediger tells the story of David Pearlman, who arrived in Georgia in the late nineteenth century. As he set out to make his fortune, he was advised by his cousin to stay away from Black people because it would hurt his prospects. Staking a claim for "whiteness," David's cousin warned him that Black people in America were "like we are in Russia. Do you understand? They are to *goyims* Jews—outcasts, nothing, dirt!" But David replied with a claim for continued marginality: "It is easy for you to forget how to feel and what it is like to be hurt and stepped on when you think of yourself as white today and forget what it was like being a Jew yesterday." The cousin mulled it over before asking rhetorically, "Is it so bad that they should hate someone else for a change?"[18]

Roediger argues that in-between-ness was characteristic of all the immigrant groups who arrived poor and precarious at the turn of the twentieth century. They were apart from the mainstream, yet no longer tethered to their old traditional worlds, seeking to fit in and also, at the same time, to preserve those national ties that had given their families' lives meaning for generations.

True enough. But while the condition of in-between-ness may have been jarringly unfamiliar for Italian, Hungarian, or Irish immigrants, their roots had been earlier planted firmly in a known soil called home. By contrast, in-between-ness was the chronic condition of Jews, who had never had a home, never been able to plant secure roots anywhere. Jews had been in-between in Russia and Poland in many of the same ways they were in-between on the Lower East Side.

The territory wasn't unfamiliar to them; in fact, that cultural uncertainty was very familiar. Culturally, Jews had experienced generations of uncertainty, planting roots in one generation only to have to pick up and move when their neighbors decided they'd had enough of them. The chronic restlessness that defined the American temperament had been the Jewish temperament since the destruction of the Second Temple.

Perhaps, wrote the political economist Thorstein Veblen (at the same time that Du Bois was writing), Jews' in-between-ness contributed to their success in Europe: not because Jews, Veblen thought, had some innate cultural characteristic but rather because the pressures of life in an alien and unfriendly society gave Jews a skeptical animus, a chronic sense of themselves as outsiders. Their marginality set them apart; among their own kind, they were as ordinary as anyone else. To Veblen, "only when the gifted Jew escapes from the cultural environment created and fed by the particular genius of his own people, only when he falls into the alien lines of gentile inquiry and becomes a naturalized, though hyphenate, citizen in the gentile republic of learning," does he come "into his own as a creative leader."[19]

But, Veblen cautioned, that posture could cut both ways: "the skepticism that goes to make him an effectual factor in the increase and diffusion of knowledge among men involves a loss of that peace of mind that is the birthright of the safe and sane quietist."[20] The price of being on the cutting edge was a chronic restlessness. The desire to fit in often insures that one will stand out, in part because one has to try so hard to pretend it's effortless.

In an arresting essay, the historian David Biale echoes Du Bois's notion of a double consciousness to understand the particular position of the Yiddish Jews. Theirs was a quest to assimilate and to remain distinct, to be both utterly Americanized and entirely Jewish. Their marginality, enforced by anti-Semitism, and their insularity kept them "wandering between two worlds," as Matthew Arnold had put it—at home in both, then at times at home in neither.[21] American Jews, Biale writes, were "one of the most quickly and thoroughly acculturated [groups] yet, among European immigrant ethnicities, equally one of the most resistant to complete assimilation," fulfilling, it would appear, the old Jewish Enlightenment slogan, "Be a human being on the street and a Jew at home."[22]

Jews possess a version of the double consciousness that Du Bois described, but it worked in two distinct ways. Jews are both "inside outsiders" and "outside insiders." Other marginalized groups often perceive Jews as having made it, as already "insiders," but those on the inside see them as outsiders. (It's often difficult to convince people of color that Jews suffer discrimination, but also difficult to convince landed elites to admit Jews to their country clubs.)

Upward mobility for New York Jews could be tracked geographically. My grandparents were born in those squalid Lower East Side tenements at the turn of the twentieth century, but they moved, as did all the Michtoms, to Brooklyn, where they raised their families. That is, they moved to the outer boroughs—Brooklyn, the Bronx, Queens. From the outer boroughs, these Jews experienced both their belonging and their otherness. "We were of the city," writes Alfred Kazin, "but somehow not in it."[23]

I was born there, too, in Brooklyn, but we moved to Long Island when the Dodgers left—"Brooklyn is over," my father, a chiropractor to several Dodger pitchers, announced somewhat prematurely. We joined the great suburban migration of the mid-1950s, when, aided by the GI Bill, single tract homes, good schools, and safe neighborhoods lured upwardly mobile families. Moving from the Lower East Side to Brooklyn to Long Island was the pattern not only of my family but of nearly everyone I knew. (If Jews weren't considered white, they certainly participated in white flight.) The historian Samuel Heilman captured my—and virtually all my friends'—experience:

> Grandma and Grandpa stayed behind in the city, in the apartment blocks in the old neighborhood. Indeed, the flow of traffic between the suburbs of Long Island and the old neighborhoods of the Bronx in New York City became a kind of choreography of the residential pattern.[24]

Yes, the Jews had made it—up and out, up, up and away. They were insiders.

But were they?

Cultural impulses often move from margin to center; it is on the edges that new trends emerge, where fashion speaks to the daring. Most fashion originates on the margins, usually with the working class, or with inner-city African American youth, or with LGBT people. Blue jeans, work shirts, flannel shirts, and Timberland boots all originated among the white working class, were appropriated as fashion by LGBT or African American youth, and then were sold back to white middle-class consumers with a new air of authenticity.

So, too, with the material culture of childhood, as misunderstood orphans end up the heroes of young adult adventure stories, and nerdy outsiders end up exhibiting enviable superpowers. And in the toy business? "Everyone in the toy business is looking for the next big thing," says the toy historian Tim Walsh, but coming up with a truly successful toy "takes an outsider. . . . The things that are huge hits, people never see coming."[25]

Assimilation and Its Discontents

For the first generation of American Jews, assimilation was a driving passion, an obsession, a ceaseless craving that was nearly insatiable. The founders of the Hollywood studio system felt a "desperate longing for security," Neal Gabler writes, a "yearning to belong." They craved a safe space, a sanctuary, an asylum. "One would have had to be so fearful of being outside and alone that one would go to any lengths to fabricate America as a sanctuary, safe, and secure, and then promulgate this idealization to other Americans." And so "within the studios and on the screen, the Jews could simply create a new country—an empire of their own, so to speak, one where they would not only be admitted, but would govern as well."[26]

Similarly, the creators of the comics invented nebbishy guys, frightened in an unsafe world, who magically transform into super-Aryan heroes, who can make the world secure. And so too, like the

Hollywood moguls, that first generation of toymakers "had a peculiar sensitivity to the dreams and aspirations of other immigrants and working-class families."[27] In that same vein, one would have had to yearn desperately for a warm and loving childhood to so fantastically create the toys of such a childhood.

They didn't want to take over. They just wanted to be left alone. They wanted to merge, to dilute themselves until they became indistinguishable; to change their names, their noses, their accents; to shed the language, religiosity, customs, and cuisine of their parents and grandparents.

Yet in the process, they sacrificed something, gave up something as vital as, perhaps more vital than, what they received. A 1931 novel, *Rabbi Burns*, by Aben Kandel put the matter succinctly:

> Consider this. A Jew becomes Americanized only in direct proportion to his becoming de-Judaized. But that's a tight-rope performance. Yearning to be Americanized, that is, to be accepted at par by the *goyim*, he begins by renouncing everything Jewish about him. He sheds his accent, shaves his beard, changes his clothes, curtails his names, plays golf and tennis, subdues his fire, and makes his whole religion conform to an elite Protestantism. Then, suddenly, he becomes aware that he has nothing left which is intrinsically himself. He has a crazy quilt make-up of foreign patches which serves as a good temporary covering.[28]

The Jew becomes Americanized—or so he thinks. This is the tragedy of the assimilationist craving: It can never be satisfied. No sooner does the Jew believe he is safe than he is reminded of his Jewishness. He will never be safe. Not completely.

But now he has nothing to protect him, no more the tight-knit, Yiddish-speaking culture of parents and grandparents. "The Jewish sons of immigrants who created the first wave of superheroes had succeeded all too well in their attempts to embody the immigrant's

American dream in their pages," writes Harry Brod. "They'd become assimilated. They'd left the working-class urban streets behind for new homes in the middle-class suburbs."[29]

The costs of assimilation have been written about by countless scholars and novelists. Ironically, the very things that you craved as a way to proclaim your new identity are now leading you to isolation and loneliness. The first- and second-generation Jews resembled other ethnic groups: Embarrassed by their parents' old-world accents, clothes, customs, and parochial old-world morality, they rushed headlong into a modern alien world that reminded them they didn't really belong. Precisely that tension created something much larger, something distinctly American—from which they would still be partially excluded. "As Jews become more American, America becomes more Jewish" is the way cultural critic J. Hoberman put it.[30]

The Second Generation

The second and third generations inherited all the trappings of success in America: They were heirs to the family fortunes built by their first-generation parents or grandparents, built so that they would never have to experience the privation, the discrimination, the fear of the Old World Jew in the New World Order. What happened to these next generations? They were "real" Americans, neither immigrants nor nouveau riche arrivistes. No longer wandering between two worlds, in Matthew Arnold's phrase, they were as assimilated as they could be.

This is the great intergenerational (and gendered) story of American immigration: The poor immigrant works his way up to amass a fortune and stakes his claim for legitimacy in the new world; his son embraces that new world, building the business, so that his own son can take that wealth, power, and legitimacy for granted.

Ben Michtom's son, Mark, born in 1928, bore none of the markings of his immigrant grandparents. Not named after an American hero in order to stake his claim, he was simply Mark, athletic, musically talented, and handsome. (His older brother, Anton, born in

1926, was troubled from the start and walked away from the family to become a rancher in Montana.) Mark prepped at Choate and went, as if preordained, to Yale, then on to Oxford to study music. Back in New York, he started his own jazz combo before his father put his foot down and demanded he join Ideal as senior executive vice-president.

But the truth was that Mark didn't really like toys. The company launched only a few successes during his tenure, most notably Rubik's Cube, but his heart wasn't in it, and when the company went public, he and his wife, Paula, sold his 11 percent of the company and bought a winery in Napa Valley. That was far more fun, so when Ben died in 1980, Mark engineered the sale of Ideal to CBS for $58 million. (At the time, the company had annual sales of about $200 million.) Skiing in the Sierras, eating the nouvelle cuisine of California, making wine—it was a truly idyllic life for a blueblood American heir.[31]

The other second-generation children were equally uninterested in maintaining the family business. The children of Louis Marx, the man who'd been dubbed "America's toy king" in a glowing profile in *Time* magazine in 1955, had no interest at all in the toy business. (One daughter married Daniel Ellsberg and assisted him in the release of the Pentagon Papers; one son was a virulent anti-Communist who denounced his brother-in-law; one became a futurist, and another a venture capitalist.) Saddened by this lack of interest, Marx sold the company to Quaker Oats in 1972 for $54 million, and it was closed for good in 1979.

What about the "real-life" Barbie—Barbara Handler? Well, she followed the same trajectory as the others, though she had a lot more to live down. As the "real-life" Barbie, she had a tough time in school and even on the street, as people ached to make her a celebrity. "Barbara is not Barbie!" she wanted to scream. She even insisted that her mother, Ruth, stop calling her Barbie. She wanted nothing to do with Mattel, the company that had made her rich; she assimilated into a sedate, decidedly un-Jewish upper class. "Today," as Ruth described it, "Barbara has done a complete turnaround on what constitutes an 'ordinary' life. She lives in a beautiful home in a gated community, wears designer clothes, plays a good game of golf, helps organize golf tournaments at our country club, and skis and golfs all over the world." And to top it all off, "her boyfriend of eleven years is an Englishman!" Ah, a real American at last, even with a nod to the fictive "old country."*

One Last Moment of Creation

During a single week in November 1969, it all came together: the outsiders' creativity, entrepreneurialism, and dreams of assimilation, as well as the insiders' assumptions that they were part of the mainstream now. On Thursday, November 6, Congress passed, and President Nixon signed, the Child Protection and Toy Safety Act (15 U.S.C. 1261), a significant piece of legislation aimed at making toys safer, especially from electrical, thermal, and mechanical hazards. The chief driver of the law was the large number of children who were putting small toy parts in their mouths. (Choking was among the leading causes of toy deaths.) For those legislators who wanted to rein in the toy industry, the act was a significant compromise. Jerome Fryer, CEO of Gabriel Industries and president of the Toy Manufacturers of America, testified before the committee, flanked by top executives of virtually every major American toy company, including Ideal, Hasbro, Mattel, Fisher-Price, Kenner, Tonka, and Remco.[32] Forming a unified front, the toy companies managed to push Congress to step back from what they perceived as overregulation. Like the comic book publishers before them, the toy companies proposed self-regulation and promised to put age limits and a warning of any possible choking hazard on their packaging.

Four days later the landscape of childhood changed yet again. On Monday, November 10, 1969, *Sesame Street* premiered on public television stations across the country.

---

* Until his retirement as president and CEO, Alan Hassenfeld, of the Hassenfeld family's third generation, remained, happily, at Hasbro, the family business.

From the opening slightly off-key singing of "sunny days, sweeping the clouds away," *Sesame Street* was different. Broadcast on PBS, the show was commercial free, and so hosts and guests and the stations themselves did not simultaneously hawk products to kids. But even as they sang of "sunny days," their perch was hardly the clean manicured lawns of suburban housing developments. Rather, they sang from the inner city, a gritty neighborhood of dented trash cans and littered streets, laundry hung in airshafts, and hosts who were as "street" as their environs.

The show was populated by a motley multispecies crew of puppets—a grouch who lived in a garbage can, a neurotic huge yellow bird who fit in nowhere, a wisecracking but insecure frog, and much later, a relentlessly cheery red furry mini-monster named Elmo—as well as a truly multicultural cast of humans. *Sesame Street* promoted the same vision as Mr. Rogers; together they put the "neighbor" back in the hood.

Sesame Street evolved from the same ethnic mélange as the earliest toys, comic books, and children's books. It was the brainchild of Joan Ganz Cooney, who was born in Phoenix in 1929, the daughter of a Jewish father and Catholic mother. By the 1960s, she'd produced documentaries for public television and was well traveled in New York's heady intellectual circles. At one party, she talked with Lloyd Morrisett, an executive at the Carnegie Corporation, and he agreed to underwrite an assessment of the feasibility of an educational television show for preschool children.

There was nothing of the kind then on television. The show would be not just for children, but for preschool children specifically. Cooney cast a wide net, interviewing child psychologists and other experts, catching mostly first-generation Jewish experts. To help them develop the show, Cooney and Morrisett tapped Gerald Lesser, a developmental psychologist from Harvard. Born in Queens in 1926 to Jewish immigrant parents, Lesser was already studying the effects of media on child development. With Cooney and Morrisett's support, he convened a series of seminars bringing together some well-known developmental psychologists, many of his Harvard colleagues from the Human Development Program at the School of Education, and several children's book authors, among them Maurice Sendak and Ezra Jack Keats.

The task was to determine if—and how—to gear a television show to children from three to five years old. Was the goal to reproduce Mr. Rogers's neighborhood and provide warmth, comfort, and emotional closeness at the expense of actual learning? Or would the show try to engage the children with preschool "work"? Tensions arose in the seminars between the "professors," who sounded off with psychological jargon about brain development and cognitive capacity, and the "practitioners," the children's book authors, like Sendak, who appeared colossally bored and spent most of the time doodling on a memo pad.

Eventually, everyone agreed that preschool children could process a few bits of information, so they determined to include a word or number each day. Simple emotional pleasantness without any intellectual effort would seem empty, offering all form and no content. So they determined to engage the children emotionally and intellectually, hoping that, as one Harvard child psychology professor, and one of Cooney's advisers, put it, such a show could be used "to teach children how to think, not what to think."[33]

They produced a television show that expressed the ideas about childhood that by then had been brewing for nearly a century. It offered "the first truly multicultural cast on TV, the first show to integrate educational content with full-on entertainment; the first children's program that adults watched in large numbers."[34] *Sesame Street* was the product—no, the fulfillment—of the vision of childhood, articulated by the Yale child psychologist Arnold Gesell two decades earlier, that by nature, the child was a "creative artist of sorts. . . . We may well be amazed at his resourcefulness, his extraordinary capacity for original activity, inventions, and discovery."[35]

That day in November 1969 transformed the landscape of children's television. The shows that followed, from *Zoom* and *Electric Company* to *Free to Be*, reinforced a view of children as fun, curious, and happy—even in the most adverse conditions. It is an irony of sorts that it embodied the vision of those writers and artists and creators on the Lower East Side who, some seven decades earlier, had imagined a world outside the ghetto, the tenements, the dented trash cans, and the hanging laundry.

* * *

First-generation Jews were central to the creation of contemporary childhood. They created the toys, the dolls, the games and puzzles for children, enchanted their imaginations, and inspired their fantasies of superhero powers or glamour or teenage popularity. They created the ideological apparatus to support it: the advice books for anxious parents, the advice columns in newspapers and magazines, and the fields of child and developmental psychology. In their struggle, over the course of the twentieth century, to assimilate, they stood out, transforming the culture they sought to embrace.

As Americans born into poverty, they created the materials for a childhood they had been denied. Their belief in the American Dream was so strong that they believed they could actually call it into existence. As adults, they created the childhoods they wished they had had—seeking to create the perfect version of that childhood, the one that had been denied them by poverty and anti-Semitism. To do so, they drew upon the values they inherited from their ancestors and adapted them to the contradictory environment, both welcoming and hostile, that they found in twentieth-century America. The ideal had become real.

Acknowledgments

This book started as a modest family memoir, a small project to trace the history of this exotic and extraordinary side of my mother's family tree. As often happens with small projects, when you open one door, suddenly dozens of other ones reveal themselves. The project sent me sprawling into a forest that kept getting deeper and thicker the more I researched it. From one successful Jewish toymaker to so many other Jewish toymakers, to the comic strip and comic book artists, children's book authors, and even the developmental psychologists who theorized it all, the landscape kept expanding. But the goal of mapping it all became increasingly elusive. This book is as far as I got—I'm sure others will explore further.

Over the course of this project, I've incurred more debts than I could ever repay. The Michtoms are both my family and the family I never had. My mother, née Barbara Hope Michtom, kindled my fascination with the family story, gave me one of the original life-size Shirley Temple dolls (though I had no idea what to do with it!), and indulgently watched my sister and me jump on pogo sticks for hours. She loved this project from the outset and truly enjoyed reminiscing with me about those early years. I wish she were still alive to read what I eventually came up with, but her spirit animates the work.

Jay Michtom, my great-uncle, is the keeper of the family flame, brilliantly and tirelessly managing the family tree, corresponding with relatives near and far. His research into the transformation of Moshe Charmatz into Morris Michtom got me started. As a descendant of Morris's brother Harris, Jay was largely frozen out of the Morris side of things. For my entrée into that realm, I'm grateful to Paula Michtom, my cousin thrice removed, for her generosity in granting access to all the file cabinets of the family's personal papers and memorabilia. (I'm saving the Michtom cabernet for a toast at the book party.)

Many toymakers, artists, and entrepreneurs—and their children and often their grandchildren—opened both their hearts and their files and generously reminisced about their families. I'm so grateful to Barbara Attie, Melissa and Doug Bernstein, Jeffrey Breslow, Eddy Goldfarb, Lyn Goldfarb, Bill Hanlon, Alan Hassenfeld, Eric Kimmel, Merry Loomis, Billy Monchik, Richie Monchik, Jim and Donna Pressman, Kim Selbert, Laurie Stein, and Robert Wanderman. I learned so much from them all. And I'm grateful to the entire Rosenbloom family—three generations—who regaled me with stories about Renwal and their meticulously crafted model ships and planes.

Many scholars, collectors, and researchers helped me navigate this enormous field, parts of which they had already so expertly tilled. Especially helpful were interviews and correspondence with Michael Alexander, Chris Bensch, Mel Birnkrant, Chris Byrne ("The Toy Guy"), Sherm Cohen, Gary Cross, Rick DesRochers, Hasia Diner, Lawrence Fleischer, Danny Fingeroth, Bryan Ganaway, Debbie Garrett, Rob Goldberg, David Hajdu, Marge Heims, Karen Hesse, David Hornisch, Stephen Jacobs, Arie Kaplan, Melissa Klapper, Seth Lerer, PJ Mode, Deborah Dash Moore, Miriam Mora, Golan Moskowitz, Lynn Moylan, Phil Nel, Mark Newgarden, Bill Paxton, Joe Perry, Deborah Pope, Peter Reitan, Lawrence Rubin, Jan Schein, Mark Schwartz, Roy Schwartz, Daniel Soyer, Mardi and Stan Timm, Kimberly Wallace-Sanders, Tim Walsh, and Bob Wande.

Throughout my work on the book, I depended on the mercies of dozens of libraries and archives. I'm particularly grateful to Timothy Horning (Wharton archives), Erik Johnson (Theodore Roosevelt Center at Dickinson State University), Beth Merkle, Claire Pingel (Weitzman National Museum of American Jewish History), Ellen Hunter Ruffin (University of Southern Mississippi), Chloe Gerson (Brandeis University archives), Christopher Bensch and the staff at the Strong Museum of Play, the staffs at the Columbia University

Library, National Archives, YIVO Institute for Jewish Research, Center for Jewish History, and especially the Park Slope branch of the Brooklyn Public Library, who met my near-daily requests for interlibrary loans with cheerful competence.

My agent, Doug Grad, has been a booster, a friend, and a reliable Mets fan. A writer cannot possibly get luckier than to have John Glusman as an editor. It's one thing to believe in a project and quite another to adopt it so thoroughly and to read it so carefully—it restores one's faith in the entire publishing industry. Thanks also to Wickliffe Hallos for making sure every detail was handled with grace, and to Jane von Mehren for talking about the project over many months.

My friends have always been that support network everyone hopes for. I'm grateful to Martin Duberman, Pam Hatchfield, Michael Kaufman, Mary Morris, Larry O'Connor, and Mitchell Tunick for decades, approaching lifetimes, of friendship and love. Near daily walks in Prospect Park with my neighbor and friend Daniel Levy have been a source of constancy and Jewish humor. Throughout my work on this book, I've missed the forty years of animated conversations about Jewishness I had with Lillian Rubin, Michael Rogin, and especially Harry Brod, who was a source of both deep knowledge and whimsically Talmudic aphorisms. It pains me that they will not get to read it.

Amy and Zachary have been enthusiastic and supportive of this project from the start. With many of my earlier books, I had theories, hypotheses, and went searching for empirical evidence to back them up. Not this time. My ignorance of the fields I was trampling through led me to near-daily discoveries, to twists and turns in a road it that I felt like I was paving as I was driving on it. "You won't believe this!" I'd often shout as I came upstairs from my study to prepare dinner, only to be met by bemused smiles, slight eye rolls, and forbearance from those who truly love me. My message to them is less "I couldn't have done this without you" than "I could only have done this with you." There's a difference.

This is for them—and for my sister, Sandi, with whom I shared the childhood that these people created.

Notes

1: TEDDY'S BEAR

1 Gilbert King, "The History of the Teddy Bear: From Wet and Angry to Soft and Cuddly," *Smithsonian*, December 21, 2012.
2 Louisiana v. Mississippi, 202 U.S. 1 (26 S. Ct. 408), 50 L. Ed., 913, 1906.
3 Melissa Korn, "University of Mississippi Will Remove Name of White Supremacist from Building," *Wall Street Journal*, July 7, 2017.
4 Edmund Morris, *Theodore Rex* (New York: Random House, 2001), 174.
5 Morris, *Theodore Rex*, 174.
6 Morris, *Theodore Rex*, 174.
7 Seth Rogovoy, "The Secret Jewish History of . . . Teddy Roosevelt," *Forward*, February 21, 2022.
8 Peter Tamony, "The Teddy Bear: Continuum in a Security Blanket," *Western Folklore* 33, no. 3 (1974): 232.
9 See, for example, Strobel & Wilken ad in *Playthings* 4 (May 1906): 3; A. S. Ferguson, *Playthings* 4 (May 1906): 69; Kahn & Mossbacher, *Playthings* 4 (May 1906): 70.
10 Tamony, "Teddy Bear," 235, 237.
11 Katie Ryder, "A Piercing View of the Twentieth Century, Through the Eyes of the Teddy Bear," *New Yorker*, September 18, 2016.
12 " 'Teddy Bear' Creator Dead: Seymour Eaton, Author, Was Noted for His Newspaper Promotion Work," *New York Times*, March 14, 1916, 11.
13 Seymour Eaton, *More About Teddy B and Teddy G The Roosevelt Bears* (Philadelphia: Edward Stern & Co., 1907).
14 Dan Foley, *Toys Through the Ages* (Philadelphia: Chilton Books, 1962), 11–12.
15 Card in gift shop of Smithsonian Institution, obtained September 25, 2022.
16 "All for Dear Bruin," *Playthings* 4 (October 1906): 65.
17 "Teddy Bear Is a Menace to Nation," *Telegraph Herald* (Dubuque, IA), July 8, 1907; also parodically discussed in *Playthings* (November 1908): 48. See also Alice George, "The Teddy Bear Was Once Seen as a Dangerous Influence on Young Children," *Smithsonian Magazine*, December 2023.
18 "The Roosevelt Bears," letter to the editor, *New York Times*, June 2, 1996.
19 Sam Roberts, "When You're 100 Years Old, Bear It and Grin," *New York Times*, December 22, 2002.
20 Anna Freud, *The Ego and the Mechanisms of Defence* (1936; reprint London: Routledge, 1966), chap. 6.
21 See, for example, Gerald Alan Fox, *Teddy Bear and Freud: Stroll Through a Century of Talking Therapies* (London: Independently published, 2019). Quote

is from Richard Miniter, "Teddy Bear Therapy Versus the Mental Health Professionals," *American Thinker*, January 16, 2016.

22 Ray Moseley, "How a Spared Cub Became an Ideal Toy," *Chicago Tribune*, December 26, 1977.

2: COMING TO AMERICA

1 John Klier, "What Exactly Was a Shtetl?," in *The Shtetl: Image and Reality*, ed. Gennady Estraikh and Mikhail Krutinov (Oxford: European Humanities Research Centre Studies in Yiddish, 2000), 32.

2 See, for example, Paul Buhle, *From the Lower East Side to Hollywood: Jews in American Popular Culture* (New York: Verso, 2004), 24.

3 "Yelisavetgrad," in *The Jewish Encyclopedia: A Descriptive Record of the History, Religion, Literature, and Customs of the Jewish People from the Earliest Times to the Present Day*, ed. Isidore Singer (New York: Funk & Wagnalls, 1906), 12:592.

4 "Yelisavetgrad," 12:592.

5 David Laskin, *The Family: Three Journeys into the Heart of the Twentieth Century* (New York: Viking, 2013), 20; Jacob Rader Marcus, *United States Jewry, 1776–1985* (Detroit: Wayne State University Press, 1993), 4:14.

6 Michael Alexander, *Jazz Age Jews* (Princeton, NJ: Princeton University Press, 2001), 4.

7 Yaffa Eliach, *There Was Once a World: A 900-Year Chronicle of the Shtetl of Eishyshok* (Boston: Little Brown, 1998), 782.

8 Mark Zborowski and Elizabeth Herzog, *Life Is with People: The Culture of the Shtetl* (New York: Schocken Books, 1952), 61; Yohanan Petrovsky-Shtern, *The Golden Age Shtetl: A New History of Jewish Life in East Europe* (Princeton, NJ: Princeton University Press, 2014), 11.

9 Michael Aronson, *Troubled Waters* (Pittsburgh: University of Pittsburgh Press, 1990); Russo-Jewish Committee, *The Persecution of the Jews in Russia* (London: Spottiswoode, 1882), 13.

10 Russo-Jewish Committee, *The Persecution of the Jews in Russia* (London: Spottiswoode, 1882), 4.

11 Aronson, *Troubled Waters*. See also Daniel Jonah Goldhagen, *Hitler's Willing Executioners: Ordinary Germans and the Holocaust* (New York: Alfred Knopf, 1996).

12 Barbara Cohen, *Gooseberries to Oranges* (New York: Lathrop, Lee & Shepard, 1982).

13 Russo-Jewish Committee, *Persecution of Jews in Russia*, 21. See also Alexander Orbach, "The Development of the Russian Jewish Community, 1881–1903," in *Pogroms: Anti-Jewish Violence in Modern Russian History*, ed. John Klier and Shlomo Lambroza (New York: Cambridge University Press, 1992), 158.

14 Aronson, *Troubled Waters*, 234.

15 Stephen Berk, *Year of Crisis, Year of Hope* (Westport, CT: Greenwood, 1985), 147.

16 Marcus, *United States Jewry*, 4:19.

17 These family history tidbits are from Emily's notes of conversations with Ben Michtom.

18 "RIAA Top 365 Songs of the 20th Century," Recording Industry Association of America, https://open.spotify.com/playlist/4OQaRbhuJJETp6Q0c

mhiay#:~:text=RIAA%20Top%20365%20Songs%20of,The%20Stars%20and%20Stripes%20Forever; National Endowment for the Arts, https://www.arts.gov.

19 Moses Rischin, *The Promised City: New York's Jews, 1870–1914* (Cambridge, MA: Harvard University Press, 1962), 33; Stephan Brumberg, "Going to America, Going to School: The Immigrant-Public School Encounter in Turn-of-the-Century New York City," paper presented at the annual meeting of the American Educational Research Association, New York, 1982.

20 Deborah Dash Moore, *Jewish New York: The Remarkable Story of a City and a People* (New York: NYU Press, 2017), 4; Adam Hochschild, "Obstruction of Injustice," *New Yorker*, November 11, 2019, 30.

21 Jim Pressman and Donna Pressman, interview by the author, May 13, 2023; see also Jim Pressman and Donna Pressman, *A Century of American Toys and Games: The Story of Pressman Toy* (New York: Abbeville Press, 2022).

22 Buhle, *From the Lower East Side*, 19; Danny Fingeroth, *Disguised as Clark Kent: Jews, Comics and the Creation of the Superhero* (New York: Continuum, 2007), 30.

23 Woodrow Wilson, *A History of the American People* (New York: Harper & Brothers, 1902), 5:212–13, quoted in Rick DesRochers, *The New Humor in the Progressive Era: Americanization and the Vaudeville Comedian* (New York: Palgrave Macmillan, 2014), 2.

24 Eric Goldstein, "The Great Wave: Eastern European Jewish Immigration to the United States, 1880–1924," *The Columbia History of Jews and Judaism in America*, ed. Marc Lee Raphael (New York: Columbia University Press, 2008), chap. 3.

25 Alan Silverstein, *Alternatives to Assimilation: The Response of Reform Judaism to American Culture, 1840–1930* (Hanover, NH: University Press of New England, 1994), 149; Wasserman quoted in Roy Schwartz, *Is Superman Circumcised? The Complete Jewish History of the World's Greatest Hero* (New York: McFarland, 2021), 195.

26 Stephen Birmingham, *The Rest of Us: The Rise of America's Eastern European Jews* (New York: Berkley Books, 1985), ix.

27 Moses Rischin, *The Promised City: New York's Jews, 1870–1914* (Cambridge, MA: Harvard University Press, 1962), 238.

28 Carey McWilliams, *A Mask for Privilege: Anti-Semitism in America* (Boston: Little, Brown, 1948), 27.

29 Paula Hyman, *From Dreyfus to Vichy: The Remaking of French Jewry, 1906–1939* (New York: Columbia University Press, 1979.

30 Hasia R. Diner, "German Immigrant Period in the United States," *The Shalvi/Hyman Encyclopedia of Jewish Women*, https://jwa.org.

31 See Naomi Cohen, *Encounter with Emancipation: The German Jew in the United States, 1830–1914* (Philadelphia: Jewish Publication Society, 1984).

32 Stanley Nadel, "Jewish Race and German Soul in Nineteenth Century America," *American Jewish History* 77, no. 1 (1987): 8.

33 Jeremiah Berman, "Jewish Education" (1954), quoted in Brumberg, "Going to America, Going to School," 36.

34 Brumberg, "Going to America, Going to School," 31.

35 Steven Ujifusa, *The Last Ships from Hamburg: Business, Rivalry and the Race to Save Russia's Jews on the Eve of World War* I (New York: HarperCollins, 2023), 52.

36 Hochschild, "Obstruction of Injustice," 30.

37 Eric L. Goldstein, *The Price of Whiteness: Jews, Race, and American Identity* (Princeton: Princeton University Press, 2006).

38 Jacob Riis, *How the Other Half Lives: The Tenements of New York* (New York: Charles Scribner's, 1890), 106.
39 Charles Silberman, *A Certain People: American Jews and Their Lives Today* (New York: Simon & Schuster, 1985), 49; Allon Schoener, *Portal to America: The Lower East Side, 1870–1925* (New York: Holt, Rinehart & Winston, 1967), 57–58.
40 Abraham Cahan, *Yekl: A Tale of the New York Ghetto* (1896; reprint New York: Dover, 1970).
41 See, for example, David Nasaw, *Children of the City: At Work and at Play* (New York: Oxford University Press, 1985).
42 Anzia Yezierska, *Bread Givers* (New York: Doubleday, Page, & Co., 1925), 138, 297.
43 Abraham Cahan, *The Rise of David Levinsky* (1917; reprint New York: Harper & Row, 1960), 29.
44 Cahan, *Rise of David Levinsky*, 380.
45 Cahan, *Rise of David Levinsky*, 39.
46 Moore, *Jewish New York*, 6; Marcus, *United States Jewry*, 4:253.
47 Jillian Gould, "Candy Stores and Egg Creams," in *Jews of Brooklyn*, ed. Ilana Abramovitch and Sean Galvin (Hanover, NH: Brandeis University Press, 2002), 202–5; Nasaw, *Children of the City*, 117.
48 Nasaw, *Children of the City*, 117.
49 Benjamin Reich, "A New Social Center," Year Book of the University Settlement Society of New York, 1899. I am grateful to Megan Scauri of the American Jewish Historical Society for her help in tracking down this document.
50 Irving Howe, *World of Our Fathers: The Journey of the East European Jews to America and the Life They Found and Made* (New York: Harcourt Brace Jovanovich, 1976), 209.
51 Barbara Attie, interview by the author, April 15, 2020.
52 Moore, *Jewish New York*, 138; Hutchins Hapgood, *The Spirit of the Ghetto* (New York: Funk & Wagnalls, 1902), 179; Robert Park, *The Immigrant Press, and Its Control* (New York: Harper & Brothers, 1922), 89.
53 Marcus, *United States Jewry*, 4:268.
54 Anzia Yezierska, *Children of Loneliness* (New York: Funk & Wagnalls, 1923), 122.
55 Matthew Arnold, "Stanzas from the Grande Chartreuse" (1855).
56 Hapgood, *Spirit of the Ghetto*, 35.
57 Thorstein Veblen, "The Intellectual Pre-Eminence of Jews in Modern Europe," *Political Science Quarterly* 34, no. 1 (1919): 33–42; Charles Hirschman, "Immigration and the American Century," *Demography* 42 (2005): 595–620.

3: A NEW IDEAL OF CHILDHOOD

1 Viviana Zelizer, *Pricing the Priceless Child* (New York: Basic Books, 1985).
2 Paula Fass, ed., *The Routledge History of Childhood in the Western World* (New York: Routledge, 2014), 15.
3 Steven Mintz, *Huck's Raft: A History of the American Child* (Cambridge, MA: Harvard University Press, 2006), 76; the unnamed man is quoted in David Macleod, *The Age of the Child* (New York: Twayne, 1998).
4 Philippe Ariès, *Centuries of Childhood: A Social History of Family Life* (New York: Vintage, 1965); Barbara Tuchman, *A Distant Mirror: The Calamitous 14th Century* (New York: Knopf, 1978).

5 Tuchman, *Distant Mirror*, 97.
6 See Barbara Hanawalt, *The Ties That Bound: Peasant Families in Medieval England* (New York: Oxford University Press, 1988); Barbara Hanawalt, *Growing Up in Medieval London: The Experience of Childhood in History* (New York: Oxford University Press, 1993); and Shulamith Shahar, *Childhood in the Middle Ages* (New York: Routledge, 1990).
7 Lothrop Stoddard, *The Story of Youth* (New York: Cosmopolitan Book Corp., 1928), 264.
8 Howard Chudacoff, *Children at Play: An American History* (New York: NYU Press, 2007), 24–25.
9 Richard Baxter, "Christian Economics," in *The Practical Works of Richard Baxter* (Morgan, PA: Soli Deo Gloria Publications, 1996), 1:450, quoted in Gerald Moran and Maris Vinovskis, "The Great Care of Godly Parents: Early Childhood in Puritan New England," *History and Research in Child Development* 50, no. 4/5 (1985): 24–37.
10 See also John Demos, *A Little Commonwealth: Family Life in Plymouth Colony* (New York: Oxford University Press, 1970); "The American Family in Past Time," *American Scholar* 43 (1974): 422–46; Moran and Vinovskis, "Great Care of Godly Parents," 24–37, quotation on 26, though Moran and Vinovskis soften Robinson's ideas and question his representativeness.
11 Hugh Cunningham, *Children and Childhood in Western Society Since 1500* (New York: Longman, 1995), 47.
12 Geoffrey Wilson, "Obstinate Angels: Some Aspects of Child-Rearing and Popular Attitudes Toward Children, 1865–1885" (M.A. thesis, Columbia University, May 1953), 44, 45.
13 Moran and Vinovskis, "Great Care of Godly Parents," 28.
14 Catharine Beecher and Harriet Beecher Stowe, *The American Woman's Home, or Principles of Domestic Science* (Bedford, MA: Applewood, 1869).
15 Wilson, "Obstinate Angels."
16 Mary Cable, *The Little Darlings: A History of Child Rearing in America* (New York: Charles Scribner's Sons, 1975), 19.
17 Wilson, "Obstinate Angels," 82–83.
18 William Sadler and Lena Sadler, *The Mother and Her Child* (Chicago: McClurg, 1916), 316.
19 Sadler and Sadler, *Mother and Child*, 310.
20 B. G. Jefferis and J. L. Nichols, *The Science of Eugenics* (Naperville, IL: J.L. Nichols & Co., 1920), 289, 315. For more of the same, try Oscar Chrisman, *The Historical Child* (Boston: Gorham Press, 1920).
21 John F. W. Ware, *Home Life, What It Is, and What It Needs* (Boston: William Spencer, 1864), 42.
22 Jacob Abbott, *Gentle Measures in the Management and Training of the Young* (New York: Harper & Brothers, 1871), 18.
23 Stoddard, *Story of Youth*, 313; Christine Stansell, "Women, Children, and the Uses of the Streets: Class and Gender Conflict in New York City, 1850–1860," *Feminist Studies* 8, no. 2 (Summer 1982): 309–35.
24 I am grateful to Melissa Klapper for helping me see this notion of childhood innocence as a necessary intermediate step between infant damnation and Progressive ideas about childhood.
25 Marion Kaplan, *Jewish Daily Life in Germany, 1618–1945* (New York: Oxford University Press, 2005).
26 Malcolm Cowley quoted in Julia Mickenberg, *Learning from the Left: Children's*

Literature, the Cold War, and Radical Politics in the United States (New York: Oxford University Press, 2005), 25.

27 Sarah Chinn, *Inventing Modern Adolescence: The Children of Immigrants in Turn-of-the-Century America* (New Brunswick, NJ: Rutgers University Press, 2008), 14.

28 Felix Adler, "Child Labor in the United States and Its Great Attendant Evils," *Annals of the American Academy of Political and Social Science* 25 (May 1905), quoted in Zelizer, *Pricing the Priceless Child*, 70.

29 Francis L. K. Hsu, *Clan, Caste and Club* (New York: Van Nostrand Reinhold, 1963), 194.

30 Gary Cross, *Kids' Stuff: Toys and the Changing World of American Childhood* (Cambridge, MA: Harvard University Press, 1999), 128.

31 Danny Fingeroth, *Disguised as Clark Kent: Jews, Comics and the Creation of the Superhero* (New York: Continuum, 2007), 28; see, for example, Ilan Stavans and Josh Lambert, eds., *How Yiddish Changed America and How America Changed Yiddish* (Brooklyn: Restless Books, 2020).

32 Marcus Eli Ravage, *An American in the Making: The Life Story of an Immigrant* (New York: Harper & Bros., 1917), 60–61.

33 Jenna Weissman Joselit, *The Wonders of America: Reinventing Jewish Culture, 1880–1950* (New York: Hill & Wang, 1996), 55.

34 Mark Zborowski and Elizabeth Herzog. *Life Is with People: The Culture of the Shtetl* (New York: Schocken Books, 1962), 310.

35 Zena Smith Blau, "The Strategy of the Jewish Mother," in *The Jew in American Society*, ed. Marshall Sklare (New York: Behrman House, 1974), 165–87.

36 George Henry Payne, *The Child in Human Progress* (New York: Knickerbocker, 1916), 158–59.

37 Joselit, *Wonders of America*, 56.

38 Campbell Gibson, *American Demographic History Chartbook, 1790-2010*, DemographicChartbook.com, chap. 9.

39 Mickenberg, *Learning from the Left*, 33.

40 Floyd Dell, "Among the Prophets." *Masses*, 6, no. 12 (September 1914) 13; Mickenberg, *Learning from the Left*, 39.

41 Cross, *Kids' Stuff*, 19.

42 Cross, *Kids' Stuff*, 19.

43 Norman Brosterman, *Inventing Kindergarten* (New York: Abrams, 1997).

44 Steven Mintz, *Huck's Raft: A History of the American Child* (Cambridge, MA: Harvard University Press, 2006), 174–75.

45 Margaret Naumburg, "Life in a New School," *World Tomorrow* 5, no. 9 (1922): 265–66.

46 Margaret Naumburg, *The Child and the World: Dialogues in Modern Education* (New York: Harcourt, Brace, 1928), 3, 103, 243.

47 Mintz, *Huck's Raft*, 204. Nonkosher soaps used various animal fats; it wasn't until Israel Rokeach opened the first kosher soap factory in New York, in 1914, that kosher soap was even available.

48 Alicia Gil Lázaro, "A Comparative Overview at the Spanish and Italian Historiography on Return Migration, 1880–1930," *Storia e Future* 31, no. 3 (2013).

49 Mintz, *Huck's Raft*, 204–5.

50 Melissa Klapper, *Small Strangers: The Experiences of Immigrant Children in the United States, 1880–1925* (New York: Ivan R. Dee, 2007), 73–74.

51 Rick DesRochers, *The New Humor in the Progressive Era: Americanization and the Vaudeville Comedian* (New York: Palgrave, 2014), 90.

52 Zelizer, *Pricing the Priceless Child*, 56; Mintz, *Huck's Raft*, 135.
53 Hugh D. Hindman, *Child Labor: An American history* (Armonk, NY: M.E. Sharpe, 2002), 25.
54 Walter I. Trattner, *Crusade for the Children: A History of the National Child Labor Committee and Child Labor Reform in America* (Chicago: Quadrangle Books, 1970).
55 Edwin Markham, Benjamin B. Lindsey and George Creel, *Children in Bondage: A Complete and Careful Presentation of the Anxious Problem of Child Labor—Its Causes, Its Crimes, and Its Cure* (New York: Hearst's International Library, 1914).
56 Bart Dredge, "David Clark's 'Campaign of Enlightenment': Child Labor and the Farmer's States Rights League, 1911–1940," *North Carolina Historical Review* 91, no. 1 (2014): 30–62.
57 Zelizer, *Pricing the Priceless Child*, 56.
58 Mickenberg, *Learning from the Left*, 27.
59 Zelizer, *Pricing the Priceless Child*, 11, 57, 72.
60 Cross, *Kids' Stuff*, 30.
61 Mintz, *Huck's Raft*, 181; Rose Cohen, *Out of the Shadow* (New York: George Doran, 1918).
62 George Dobsevage, "Jews of Prominence in the United States," *The American Jewish Year Book*, vol. 24, *September 23, 1922, to September 10, 1923* (New York: American Jewish Committee, Springer Publishers, 1923), 218.
63 "Rose Berdych, Bluffton, South Carolina," *Mornings on Maple Street*, 2011, https://morningsonmaplestreet.com/2015/01/18/rose-berdych/
64 Markham, Lindsey, and Creel, *Children in Bondage*, 58.
65 Mickenberg, *Learning from the Left*, 28.
66 G. Stanley Hall and E. Caswell Ellis, *A Study of Dolls* (New York: E.L. Kellogg, 1897), 43.
67 Chrisman, *Historical Child*, 412.
68 Kate Douglas Wiggin, "Children's Rights," *Scribner's Magazine* 12 (July–December 1892), 246.
69 Kate Douglas Wiggin, *Children's Rights: A Book of Nursery Logic* (Boston: Houghton, Mifflin, 1898), 57, 56.
70 William Leach, *Land of Desire: Merchants, Power and the Rise of a New American Culture* (New York: Pantheon, 1993), 329–30.
71 Roberta Wallons, "Sidonie Matzner [*sic*] Gruenberg, 1881–1974," *The Shalvi/Hyman Encyclopedia of Jewish Women*, n.d., online edition.
72 N.a., *George Joseph Hecht: A Lifelong Commitment to Children* (New York: Parents' Magazine Press, 1975), 27; Steven Schlossman, "Perils of Popularization: The Founding of Parents' Magazine," *History and Research in Child Development* 50, nos. 4/5 (1985): 71.
73 The story is spelled out in Schlossman, "Perils of Popularization," 76. Though the anti-Semitism is hard to miss today, Schlossman recounts the story as a clash between academic legitimacy and business boosterism.
74 N.a., *George Joseph Hecht*, 7.

4: FURNISHING THE NEW IDEAL CHILDHOOD

1 Victor Hugo, *Les Misérables* (1887), vol. 2, bk. 3, chap. 8.
2 Brian Ganaway, "Engineers or Artists? Toys, Class and Technology in Wilhelmine Germany," *Journal of Social History* 42, no. 2 (Winter 2008): 373.

3 All quoted in David Hamlin, *Work and Play: The Production and Consumption of Toys in Germany, 1870–1914* (Ann Arbor: University of Michigan Press, 2007), 147, 149, 154.
4 Bryan Ganaway, *Toys, Consumption and Middle-Class Childhood in Imperial Germany, 1871–1918* (Oxford: Peter Lang, 2009).
5 "Fifty Years of Progress," *Playthings*, December 1928, 300–1.
6 Stephen Jacobs, "A Brief Jewish History of the Toy and Game Industry: The United States," *Global Toy News*, December 22, 2022.
7 Untitled editorial, *Playthings*, October 1903, 33.
8 W. W. Ferrier, *Origin and Development of the University of California* (Berkeley: University of California Press, 1930); see also Myra Sadker and David Sadker, *Failing at Fairness: How Schools Shortchange Girls* (New York: Simon & Schuster, 1994), 22.
9 See, for example, Jean Frances, "Late 1800's Farm Clothing," *Classroom*, September 29, 2017.
10 "Pink or Blue?" *Infants' Department*, June 1918; "What Color for Your Baby?" *Parents' Magazine*, March 1939. Both are quoted in Jo Paoletti, *Pink and Blue: Telling the Boys from the Girls in America* (Bloomington: Indiana University Press, 2012).
11 Miriam Formanek-Brunell, *Made to Play House: Dolls and the Commercialization of American Girlhood, 1830–1930* (New Haven, CT: Yale University Press, 1993), 14.
12 "Nobat Base Ball" advertised in *Playthings* 1, no. 6 (June 1903): 1.
13 Paula Petrik, "The Self-Made Boy and the Scientific Capitalist: Gender and the Toy Industry, 1880–1920," in *Small Worlds: Children and Adolescents in America, 1850–1950,* ed. Elliott West and Paula Petrik (Lawrence: University Press of Kansas, 1992), 125–43.
14 Harry Rinker, "A Short History of a Classic: Tinkertoys," *Morning Call* (Allentown, PA), November 4, 1990.
15 Ron Hollander, *All Aboard! The Story of Joshua Lionel Cowen and His Lionel Train Company* (New York: Workman, 1981), 12–14.
16 Hollander, *All Aboard!,* 14, 29.
17 Benjamin Spock, "What Toys Mean to Children," *Redbook*, December 1963, 121.
18 "The Little King," *Time*, December 12, 1955, 92. See also "Louis Marx: Toy King," *Fortune*, January 1946, 122–23; J. P. and Peggy McEvoy "Talk with the Toy King," *Reader's Digest*, January 1955, 125–28.
19 The entire saga is recounted in Peter Jensen Brown, "Margarete Steiff, Morris Michtom and Teddy Roosevelt—Hunting Down the Origin of 'Teddy Bear,'" Early Sports and Pop Culture History Blog, November 22, 2017, available at https://esnpc.blogspot.com/2017/11/margarete-steiff-morris-michtom-and.html #google_vignette.
20 "Teddy Bear Makers Struck. Two of the Strikers Arrested for Assaulting Two of the Strike Breakers," *Brooklyn Daily Eagle*, November 12, 1907, quoted in Brown, "Steiff, Michtom and Roosevelt."
21 "Art in Teddy Bear Making. Union Says Strike Breakers Miss the Half Human Expression," *Wichita Beacon* (Kansas), November 27, 1907, 6, quoted in Brown " Steiff, Michtom and Roosevelt."
22 See Brown "Steiff, Michtom and Roosevelt."
23 Jeremy Dauber, *American Comics: A History* (New York: W. W. Norton, 2021), chap. 2.
24 "Doll Making Industry in Brooklyn Which is Making Big Cut into Germany's

Trade." *Brooklyn Daily Eagle*, August 29, 1915, 12, quoted in Brown, "Steiff, Michtom and Roosevelt."

25 "Toy Makers Strike. Ask Wage Raise and Recognition of Union," *Brooklyn Daily Eagle*, June 22, 1916, 4, quoted in Brown. "Steiff, Michtom and Roosevelt."

26 "1,800 Dollmakers Strike," *New York Times*, June 23, 1916, 14, quoted in Brown, "Steiff, Michtom and Roosevelt."

27 Ralph Kovel and Terry Kovel, "Pioneering Patsy Doll Fondly Remembered," *Tampa Bay Times*, August 31, 2005; Gerri Hirshey, *Not Pretty Enough: The Unlikely Triumph of Helen Gurley Brown* (New York: Farrar, Straus & Giroux, 2016), 28–29.

28 Robert Wanderman (son-in-law of William Rothstein), interview by the author, December 15, 2020.

29 Marian Ellias, "Madame Alexander: 'American Dolls for American Children," *Playthings*, July 1, 1984; Marjorie Ingall, "The Woman Behind the Dolls," *Tablet*, May 7, 2013.

30 Ingall, "Woman Behind the Dolls."

31 Jim Pressman and Donna Pressman, interview by the author, April 20, 2023. See also Jim Pressman and Donna Pressman, *A Century of American Toys and Games: The Story of Pressman Toy* (New York: Abbeville Press, 2022); Jim Pressman, "Pressman Toy—A Short History," People of Play, October 12, 2021; and Joan Verdon, "A 100-Year Old Toy Story: How Pressman Toy Shaped the Business of Play," *Forbes*, December 22, 2022.

32 Susan Lederer, "Playing Doctor, Playing Nurse: Perspectives on the Origins of the Toy Doctor and Nurse Kits," *Nursing History Review* 25, no. 1 (2017): 117–30; "Charles Raizen of Toy Company," *New York Times*, May 15, 1967.

33 Patrick Feaster, "A Cultural History of the Edison Talking Doll Record," National Park Service, April 13, 2015, https://www.nps.gov/edis/learn/photos-multimedia/a-cultural-history-of-the-edison-talking-doll-record.htm.

34 Christopher Byrne, interview by the author, October 27, 2020. See also Christopher Byrne, *They Came to Play: 100 Years of the Toy Industry Association* (New York: Toy Industry Association, 2016).

35 Byrne, *They Came to Play*, 17.

36 Lawrence Bush, "Jews in the Toy and Novelty Industry," in *Jews and American Popular Culture*, ed. Paul Buhle (Westport, CT: Praeger Perspectives, 2007), 1:152. The company is still in existence, located and still based in Queens. Robert Oumano, Sam's son, is the father of Carole Crist, former first lady of Florida.

37 My discussion of the Fishloves is based on the superb research of Stan and Mardi Timm. Mardi Timm, interview by the author, January 16, 2024. See also Lisa Hix, "The Inside Scoop on Fake Barf," *Collectors Weekly*, August 23, 2011.

38 Lisa Hix, "How Your Grandpa Got His LOLs," *Collectors Weekly*, August 24, 2012.

39 Mardi Timm to the author, March 28, 29, and 30, 2024.

40 Murray Zimiles, "Gilded Lions and Jeweled Horses: The Synagogue to the Carousel," *Folk Art* 32, no. 3 (Fall 2007): 42–51.

5: STRUGGLING AGAINST DEPRESSION

1 "Great Depression Facts," Franklin D. Roosevelt Presidential Library and Museum.

2 Gary Cross, *Kids' Stuff: Toys and the Changing World of American Childhood* (Cambridge, MA: Harvard University Press, 1999), 117.
3 Robert Waldeman, interview by the author, December 15, 2020.
4 Art Spiegelman, "Foolish Questions," *New York Review of Books*, March 12, 2020.
5 "Breaking the News in 1900," Teaching History, https://teachinghistory.org/history-content/ask-a-historian/22927.
6 "From the Land of the Czars: Escape from the Pogroms" Jewish Virtual Library, American-Israeli Cooperative Enterprise, https://www.jewishvirtuallibrary.org/escape-from-the-pogroms-judaic-treasures.
7 Jeremy Dauber, *American Comics: A History* (New York: W. W. Norton, 2021). See also Jeffrey A. Marx, *Smoothing the Jew: Abie the Agent and Ethnic Caricature in the Progressive Era* (New Brunswick, NJ: Rutgers University Press, 2024), 72–73.
8 See Paul Tumey, *Screwball! The Cartoonists Who Made the Funnies Funny* (San Diego: Library of American Comics, 2019).
9 Spiegelman, "Foolish Questions."
10 See, for example, Jennifer George, *The Art of Rube Goldberg: (A) Inventive (B) Cartoon (C) Genius* (New York: Harry Abrams, 2013); and Peter Marzio, *Rube Goldberg: His Life and Work* (New York: Harper & Row, 1973).
11 Spiegelman, "Foolish Questions."
12 Glen Berd, "I'm Popeye the (Jewish) Sailor Man!," Shul By the Sea, February 4, 2024, https://shulbythesea.co.uk/im-popeye-the-jewish-sailor-man/.
13 Benjamin Ivry, "The Secret Jewish History of Popeye the Sailor Man," *Forward*, May 31, 2019. Ivry provides a long list of Jewish references to Popeye through the rest of the century, from Roy Lichtenstein's painting of Popeye punching Bluto to references in the work of Philip Roth and Michael Chabon, among others. And remember that Jules Feiffer wrote the script for the Hollywood movie of Popeye—and it starred Robin Williams, who called himself an "honorary Jew."
14 Larry Yudelson, "Popeye the Sailor's Man in Glen Rock," *Jewish Standard*, December 28, 2018.
15 Michael Schumacher and Denis Kitchen, *Al Capp: A Life to the Contrary* (New York: Bloomsbury, 2013), 9, 206.
16 Denis Kitchen to the author, December 21, 2020.
17 Schumacher and Kitchen, *Al Capp*, 8.
18 R. C. Harvey, "Hubris and Chutzpah: How Li'l Abner Kayo'd Joe Palooka and Both Their Creators Came to Grief," *Comics Journal*, pts. 4–5, n.d., online at TJC.com.
19 Harvey, "Hubris and Chutzpah."
20 Michael Chabon, *The Amazing Adventures of Kavalier and Clay* (New York: Random House, 2000), 585.
21 The history of Jews and comic books has been told many times but nowhere better than in Harry Brod, *Superman Is Jewish? How Comic Book Superheroes Came to Serve Truth, Justice, and the Jewish American Way* (New York: Free Press, 2012); Danny Fingeroth, *Disguised as Clark Kent: Jews, Comics and the Creation of the Superhero* (New York: Continuum, 2007); Arie Kaplan, *From Krakow to Krypton: Jews and Comic Books* (Lincoln: University of Nebraska Press, 2008); and Gerald Jones, *Men of Tomorrow: Geeks, Gangsters, and the Birth of the Comic Book* (New York: Basic Books, 2004). Except, of course, in fiction, in Chabon, *Adventures of Kavalier and Clay*. You'll notice, of course, that all four nonfiction works are preceded by, and likely inspired by, Chabon's fanciful fictional recreation, which won the Pulitzer Prize in 2000.

22 Brod, *Superman Is Jewish?*, xxvii.

23 Jules Feiffer, "The Minsk Theory of Krypton," *New York Times Magazine*, December 29, 1996.

24 Simcha Weinstein, *Up, Up, and Oy Vey: How Jewish History, Culture and Values Shaped the Comic Book Superhero* (Baltimore: Leviathan Press, 2006), 18.

25 David Hajdu, *The Ten-Cent Plague: The Great Comic-Book Scare and How It Changed America* (New York: Farrar, Straus & Giroux, 2008), 29.

26 Brod, *Superman Is Jewish?*, 7; Umberto Eco and Natalie Chilton, "The Myth of Superman," *Diacritics* 2, no. 1 (Spring 1972): 14–22.

27 Jeff Salamon, "Up, Up, and Oy Vay! The Further Adventures of Supermensch," *Village Voice*, August 4, 1992, 86–88.

28 William Butler Yeats, "Coole Park" (1929).

29 Brod, *Superman Is Jewish?*, 8.

30 Quoted in Otto Friedrich, "Up, Up and AwaaaaY," *Time*, March 14, 1988.

31 Danny Fingeroth, *Disguised as Clark Kent: Jews, Comics and the Creation of the Superhero* (New York: Continuum, 2007), 41.

32 Reid Mitenbuler, *Wild Minds: The Artists and Rivalries That Inspired the Golden Age of Animation* (New York: Atlantic Monthly Press, 2020), 231.

33 Jerry Siegel and Joe Shuster, "How Superman Would End the War," *Look*, February 27, 1940.

34 Fingeroth, *Disguised as Clark Kent*, 17.

35 Henry Louis Gates, Jr., "A Big Brother from Another Planet," *New York Times*, September 12, 1993.

36 Feiffer, "Minsk Theory of Krypton," 15.

37 Eco and Chilton, "Myth of Superman," 14–22.

38 Fingeroth, *Disguised as Clark Kent,* 100.

39 Hajdu, *Ten-Cent Plague*, 30.

40 Neil Genzlinger, "Lily Renée Phillips, Pioneering Comic Book Artist, Dies at 101," *New York Times*, September 19, 2022. See also Trina Robbins, *Lily Renée, Escape Artist: From Holocaust Survivor to Comic Book Pioneer* (New York: Graphic Universe, Lerner Publishing, 2011); Jim Amash, "I'm Not Typical for Doing Comics, You Know!," *Alter Ego* no. 85, November 12, 2012; Bass Schuddeboom, "Lily Renée," *Lambiek Comiclopedia*, n.d.; Adriane Quinlan, "A Real-Life Comic-Book Hero," *Newsweek*, July 30, 2010.

41 Fingeroth, *Disguised as Clark Kent*, 51.

42 Ariel David, "Holy Borscht Belt, Batman! The Jewish Roots of the Joker," *Haaretz*, October 5, 2019.

43 Gerard Jones, *Men of Tomorrow: Geeks, Gangsters, and the Birth of the Comic Book* (New York: Basic Books, 2004).

44 Roy Schwartz, *Is Superman Circumcised? The Complete History of the World's Greatest Hero* (Jefferson, NC: McFarland & Co., 2021), 102.

45 William Moulton Marston, "Why 100,000,000 Americans Read Comics," *American Scholar* 13 (Winter 1943–44): 42–43, quoted in Amy Kiste Nyberg, "Seal of Approval: The Origins and History of the Comics Code" (Ph.D. diss, University of Wisconsin–Madison, 1994), 82–83.

46 Fingeroth, *Disguised as Clark Kent,* 23.

47 Fingeroth, *Disguised as Clark Kent,* 17; Hajdu, *Ten-Cent Plague*, 26.

48 Hajdu, *Ten-Cent Plague*, 25–26; Fingeroth, *Disguised as Clark Kent,* 27; Brod, *Superman Is Jewish?,* 2.

49 Mark Mietkiewicz, "People of the (Comic) Book," *Canadian Jewish News*, February 9, 2017; Fingeroth, *Disguised as Clark Kent,* 28; Paul Buhle, *From the Lower*

East Side to Hollywood: Jews in American Popular Culture (New York: Verso, 2004), 90; Hajdu, *Ten-Cent Plague*, 35; Arie Kaplan, "How Jews Created the Comic Book Industry, Part I: The Golden Age (1933–1955)," *Reform Judaism*, https://reformjudaism.org/reform-jewish-life/arts-culture-travel/how-jews-created-comic-book-industry-part-i-golden-age-1933-1955.

50 Brod, *Superman Is Jewish?,* 2.

51 Hajdu, *Ten-Cent Plague*, 49–50.

52 Paul Buhle, ed., *Jews and American Comics: An Illustrated History of an American Art Form* (New York: New Press, 2008), 58–59.

53 Chabon, *Adventures of Kavalier and Clay*, 94.

54 Chabon, *Adventures of Kavalier and Clay*, 121.

55 See Jerry Z. Muller, "An Entrepreneurial American," *Jewish Review of Books*, Winter 2022; Mike Caveney, *The Great Leon: Vaudeville Headliner* (Pasadena, CA: Magical Publications, 1987).

56 Adam Gopnik, "Hot-Ice-Cream Dreams," *New Yorker*, December 28, 2020, 80.

57 See Richard Fleischer, *Out of the Inkwell: Max Fleischer and the Animation Revolution* (Lexington: University Press of Kentucky, 2005); Reid Mitenbuler, *Wild Minds: The Artists and Rivalries That Inspired the Golden Age of Animation* (New York: Atlantic Monthly Press, 2020).

58 Brod, *Superman Is Jewish?,* 72.

59 Brod, *Superman Is Jewish?,* 74.

60 The story is told well in Kaplan, "How Jews Created Comic Book Industry."

61 Goldwater made that comment in 2012, just as the American Family Association and One Million Moms demanded that Toys 'R' Us remove Riverdale's newest pal, Kevin Keller, a gay veteran. Keller was introduced in 2011 after the *Today* show found that if Archie was going to get married, Betty was preferred by 4 to 1 over Veronica—but Jughead came in third. "Kevin Keller will forever be part of Riverdale," Goldwater continued, "and he will live a happy, long life, free of prejudice, hate and narrow-minded people." John Parkin, "American Family Association Targets Kevin Keller Comics at Toys 'R' Us," *Comic Book Review*, February 29, 2012, available at:American Family Association targets Kevin Keller comics at Toys 'R' Us.

62 Bradford W. Wright, *Comic Book Nation: The Transformation of Youth Culture in America* (Baltimore: Johns Hopkins University Press, 2001).

63 Hajdu, *Ten-Cent Plague*, 5, 37.

6: THE WAR AND ITS AFTERMATH

1 "22,000 Nazis Hold Rally in Garden," *New York Times*, February 21, 1939, 1, 5. Archival footage at Marshall Curry, "A Night at the Garden," *Atlantic*, October 10, 2017. See also "Americans Hold a Nazi Rally in Madison Square Garden," History.com, February 20, 2019. Kuhn, a naturalized citizen, was denaturalized in 1943 and deported to Germany in 1945, just in time to witness the collapse of the Nazi regime.

2 Kenneth M. Gould, *They Got the Blame: The Story of Scapegoats in History* (New York: Association Press, 1942).

3 "They Got the Blame—A New Venture in Education," *Committee Reporter* (New York: American Jewish Committee, March 1944). See also E. C. Phillips, memo, May 9, 1944, AJC Record Group 347.17.10 GEN 10, Box 17, Folder 4, YIVO Archives.

4 Jan Schein, "Morris Michtom: Birth of Teddy's Bear," unpublished manuscript, courtesy of the author.
5 Ben Michtom to Alice Michtom, August 12, 1970, Ben Michtom Papers.
6 "Children Plead for Playground," *Brooklyn Standard Union*, June 18, 1913; "Mayor Favors Many More Playgrounds," *Brooklyn Times*, June 18, 1913.
7 Paula Michtom, interview by the author, May 12, 2019.
8 Paula Michtom interview.
9 Robert Froman, "Ben Loves Little Dolls," *Collier's*, December 17, 1949, 24.
10 Froman, "Ben Loves Dolls," 24.
11 Josef Israels, "Oh, Those Beautiful Dolls!," *Coronet*, December 1948, 111.
12 Israels, "Oh, Those Beautiful Dolls!," 114.
13 "Coloratura," *New Yorker*, July 10, 1948, 12–13.
14 Froman, "Ben Loves Dolls," 77.
15 Froman, "Ben Loves Dolls," 77.
16 Michael Horton, "Mostly About People," *New York Herald Tribune*, January 6, 1951.
17 See, for example, Louis Bordens and Allan Drummond, *The Journey that Saved Curious George* (New York: Houghton Mifflin Harcourt, 2010); Rivka Galchen, "The Unexpected Profundity of Curious George," *New Yorker*, June 3, 2019.
18 C. M. Hewins, "The History of Children's Books," *Atlantic*, January 1888.
19 Virginia Lee Burton, "Symphony in Comics," *Horn Book Magazine* 17, no. 4 (July 1941).
20 Saul Jay Singer, "Ludwig Bemelmans' Madeline and the Jewish Connection to Léon Blum," *Jewish Press*, October 1, 2020.
21 Sam Irvin, *Kay Thompson: From Funny Face to Eloise* (New York: Simon & Schuster, 2010).

7: SAFE HAVENS

1 W. Carey McWilliams, introduction to McWilliams, *A Mask for Privilege: Anti-Semitism in America* (New Brunswick, NJ: Transaction, 1999), xv.
2 McWilliams, *Mask for Privilege,*138.
3 Henry Ford, *The International Jew* (Dearborn: Dearborn Publishing Co., 1920).
4 Gordon Allport, *The Nature of Prejudice* (New York: Anchor Books, 1954), 13–14.
5 Nathan Ackerman and Marie Jahoda, *Anti-Semitism and Emotional Disorder: A Psychoanalytic Interpretation* (New York: Harper & Brothers, 1950).
6 Kurt Lewin, "Self-Hatred Among Jews" and "Bringing Up the Jewish Child," both in *Resolving Social Conflicts: Selected Papers on Group Dynamics*, ed. Gertud Weiss Lewin (New York: Harper & Row, 1948).
7 See, for example, Tony Michels, *A Fire in Their Hearts: Yiddish Socialists in New York* (Cambridge, MA: Harvard University Press, 2005); and Clarence Taylor, *Reds at the Blackboard: Communism, Civil Rights and the New York City Teachers Union* (New York: Columbia University Press, 2011).
8 This adoration for FDR has come under considerable revision, as in Laurence Zuckerman, "FDR's Jewish Problem," *Nation*, August 5, 2013.
9 Blanche Weisen Cook, "The Rosenbergs and the Crimes of a Century," in *Secret Agents: The Rosenberg Case, McCarthyism and Fifties America,* ed. Marjorie Garber and Rebecca Walkowitz (New York: Routledge, 1995), 25.
10 McWilliams, *Mask for Privilege,* xvii; Joseph Litvak, *The Un-Americans: Jews,*

the Blacklist, and Stoolpigeon Culture (Durham, NC: Duke University Press, 2009), 74. See also Marjorie Garber and Rebecca Walkowitz, eds., *Secret Agents: The Rosenberg Case, McCarthyism and Fifties America* (New York: Routledge, 1995).

11 Neil Gabler, *An Empire of their Own: How the Jews Invented Hollywood* (New York: Anchor, 1989), 371–72.

12 David Zurawik, *Jews of Prime Time* (Waltham, MA: Brandeis University Press, 2003).

13 Taylor, *Reds at the Blackboard.*

14 Irving Adler and Ben Zelman, "Aftermath of a Witch Hunt: New York's Subversive Teachers," *Nation*, April 9, 1977, 434–36.

15 Lori Shaller and Judith Rosenbaum, "Jewish Radicalism and the Red Scare: Introductory Essay," Jewish Women's Archive, https://jwa.org/teach/livingthelegacy/jewish-radicalism-and-red-scare-introductory-essay#_ftn2.

16 Marjorie Heins, "Insubordination and 'Conduct Unbecoming': Purging NYC's Communist Teachers at the Start of the Cold War," Center for New York City History, January 12, 2016; available at: https://www.gothamcenter.org/blog/insubordination-and-conduct-unbecoming-purging-nycs-communist-teachers-at-the-start-of-the-cold-war.

17 Leonard Marcus, *Minders of Make Believe: Idealists, Entrepreneurs and the Shaping of American Children's Literature* (New York: Houghton Mifflin, 2008), 154.

18 Martin Weil, "Teacher Wrote Lucid Science Books About Man, Nature and the Universe," *Washington Post*, October 4, 2012.

19 Marjorie Heins, *Priests of Our Democracy: The Supreme Court, Academic Freedom, and the Anti-Communist Purge* (New York: NYU Press, 2013), 231.

20 Philip Nel, *Crockett Johnson and Ruth Krauss: How an Unlikely Couple Found Love, Dodged the FBI, and Transformed Children's Literature* (Oxford: University Press of Mississippi, 2012), 130.

21 June Cummins with Alexandra Dunietz, *From Sarah to Sydney: The Woman Behind All-of-a-Kind Family* (New Haven, CT: Yale University Press, 2021).

22 June Cummins, "Becoming an 'All-of-a-Kind' American: Sydney Taylor and Strategies of Assimilation," *Lion and the Unicorn* 27, no. 3 (September 2003): 325.

23 Cummins, "'All-of-a-Kind' American," 324, italics in original.

24 Phil Nel to the author, September 16, 2020.

25 Arie Kaplan, "From Krakow to Krypton" (video), posted by WLLC Center, April 24, 2017, https://youtu.be/m9jeblhb6lc; Arie Kaplan, *From Krakow to Krypton: Jews and Comic Books* (Lincoln: University of Nebraska Press, 2008), 28.

26 Amy Kiste Nyberg, "Seal of Approval: The Origins and History of the Comics Code" (Ph.D. diss, University of Wisconsin–Madison, 1994), 87; Hajdu quoted in Roy Schwartz, *Is Superman Circumcised? The Complete History of the World's Greatest Hero* (Jefferson, NC: McFarland & Co., 2021).

27 Albert Cohen, *Delinquent Boys: The Culture of the Gang* (Glencoe, IL: Free Press, 1955), 164. See also Joseph Pleck, *The Myth of Masculinity* (Cambridge, MA: MIT Press, 1981), 96–106.

28 Fredric Wertham, *Seduction of the Innocent: The Influence of Comic Books on Today's Youth* (New York: Rinehart, 1954).

29 Jeremy Dauber, *American Comics, A History* (New York: W. W. Norton, 2021), chap. 3; Thomas Doyle, "What's Wrong with the Comics?," *Catholic World* 156, no. 935 (February 1943): 548–57.

30 Sidonie Gruenberg, "The Comics as a Social Force," *Journal of Educational Psychology* 18, no. 4 (1944): 204–13; Catherine Mackenzie, "Children and the Comics," *New York Times*, July 11, 1943, 23; Laurette Bender, "The Psychology of Children's Reading and the Comics," *Journal of Educational Sociology* 18, no. 4 (December 1944): 223–31; Lauretta Bender and Reginald Lourie, "The Effect of Comic Books on the Ideology of Children," *American Journal of Orthopsychiatry* 11, no. 3 (July 1941), 550.

31 Bart Beaty, *Fredric Wertham and the Critique of Mass Culture* (Jackson: University Press of Mississippi, 2005).

32 Fredric Wertham, "The Psychopathology of Comic Books," *American Journal of Psychotherapy* 50, no. 4 (July 1948): 490, https://doi.org/10.1176/appi.psychotherapy.1996.50.4.417.

33 Fredric Wertham, "The Betrayal of Childhood: Comic Books," Proceedings of the 78th Annual Congress of Correction, American Prison Association, 1948, 71, quoted in Amy Kiste Nyberg, "Seal of Approval: The Origins and History of the Comics Code" (Ph.D. diss, University of Wisconsin–Madison, 1994).

34 Frederic Wertham, *Seduction of the Innocent* (New York: Rinehart & Co., 1954), 34, 189–90. See also Jules Feiffer, *The Great Comic Book Heroes* (Seattle: Fantagraphics Books, 2003), 54; and Mariah Adin, *The Brooklyn Thrill-Kill Gang and the Great Comic Book Scare of the 1950s* (New York: Praeger, 2014).

35 Albert E. Kahn, *The Game of Death: Effects of the Cold War on Our Children* (New York: Cameron & Kahn, 1953), 94.

36 Quoted in John Adcock, "Gershon Legman vs the Crime Comic Books," *Yesterday's Papers*, February 8, 2015.

37 Quoted in Adcock, "Legman vs Crime Comic Books."

38 David Hajdu, *The Ten-Cent Plague*: *The Great Comic-Book Scare and How It Changed America* (New York: Farrar, Straus & Giroux, 2008), 210.

39 James Gilbert, *A Cycle of Outrage: America's Reaction to the Juvenile Delinquent in the 1950s* (New York: Oxford University Press, 1986), 77–78.

40 Hajdu, *Ten-Cent Plague*, 269.

41 Arie Kaplan, "Kings of Comics—How Jews Created the Comic Book Industry, Part I: The Golden Age (1933–1955)," *Reform Judaism*, https://reformjudaism.org/reform-jewish-life/arts-culture-travel/how-jews-created-comic-book-industry-part-i-golden-age-1933-1955.

42 William Gaines, testimony, April 21, 1954, https://www.thecomicbooks.com/gaines.html. See also Peter Kihss, "No Harm in Horror, Comics Issuer Says," *New York Times*, April 22, 1954, 1.

43 Gaines testimony.

44 Amy Kiste Nyberg, *Seal of Approval: The History of the Comics Code* (Oxford: University Press of Mississippi, 1998), 166–69.

45 Arie Kaplan, "King of Comics—How Jews Created the Comic Book Industry, Part II: The Silver Age (1956–1978)," *Reform Judaism*, https://reformjudaism.org/reform-jewish-life/arts-culture-travel/how-jews-transformed-comic-book-industry-part-ii-silver-age-1956-1978.

46 Cass Sunstein, "Marvelous Belief," *Los Angeles Review of Books*, September 21, 2020.

47 See, for example, Randy Duncan and Matthew Smith, *Icons of the American Comic Book*, 2 vols. (Westport, CT: Greenwood/ABC-Clio, 2013).

48 Sunstein, "Marvelous Belief."

49 Danny Fingeroth, *Disguised as Clark Kent: Jews, Comics and the Creation of the Superhero* (New York: Continuum, 2007), 29, 100.

50 Alan Oirich, "Spider-Jew," Aish.com, June 1, 2002; Fingeroth, *Disguised as Clark Kent*, 29.
51 Harry Brod, *Superman Is Jewish? How Comic Book Superheroes Came to Serve Truth, Justice, and the Jewish American Way* (New York: Free Press, 2012), 54.
52 Leibovitz is cited by Sunstein, "Marvelous Belief," A19; Brod, *Superman Is Jewish?*, 9.
53 Liel Leibovitz, *Stan Lee: A Life in Comics* (New Haven, CT: Yale University Press, 2021).
54 Jason Serafino, "The 25 Greatest Comic Book Villains of All Time," Complex .com, September 8, 2013.
55 Curt Schleier, "'Batman v. Superman': Jesse Eisenberg on Lex Luthor's Jewish Qualities," *Times of Israel*, March 25, 2016.
56 Alex Jaffe, "Harley Quinnesday: The Jewish Roots of Harley Quinn," *DC Universe Infinite*, November 21, 2019; Ariel David, "Holy Borscht Belt, Batman! The Jewish Roots of the Joker," *Haaretz*, October 5, 2019.
57 Rebecca Roiphe and Daniel Cooper, "Batman and the Jewish Question," *New York Times*, July 2, 1992.
58 Serafino, "25 Greatest Comic Villains." While Serafino ranks Magneto at number two, Imagine Games Network ranks him number one. See "The Top 100 Comic Book Villains," Imagine Games Network, IGN.com.
59 Arie Kaplan, *From Krakow to Krypton: Jews and Comic Books* (Lincoln: University of Nebraska Press, 2008), 98–99; Eric Greenberg, "A Heimishe Hero," *Jewish Week*, August 9, 2002.
60 Brod, *Superman Is Jewish?* 84, 88.
61 Peter Sanderson, *The Marvel Comics Guide to New York City* (New York: Pocket Books, 2007), 150–52.
62 *Spider-Man: No Way Home* trailer (video), posted by Sony Pictures Entertainment, August 23, 2021, https://www.youtube.com/watch?v=rt-2cxAiPJk.
63 Charles Silberman, *A Certain People: American Jews and Their Lives Today* (New York: Simon & Schuster, 1985), 51.
64 Hajdu, *Ten-Cent Plague*, 194.
65 Wil Forbis, "Al Jaffee," Acid Logic, n.d., Acidlogic.com.
66 See Maria Reidelbach, *Completely Mad: A History of the Comic Book and Magazine* (Boston: Little, Brown, 1991). Steinem is quoted in Brod, *Superman Is Jewish?*, 59.
67 Brod, *Superman Is Jewish?*, 55.
68 Brod, *Superman Is Jewish?*, 76.

8: THE BABY BOOM

1 David Michaelis, *Schulz and Peanuts*, quoted in Maria Popova, "Peanuts and the Quiet Pain of Childhood: How Charles Schulz Made an Art of Difficult Emotions," *Brain Pickings*, January 20, 2015.
2 Amy Ogata, *Designing the Creative Child: Playthings and Places in Midcentury America* (Minneapolis: University of Minnesota Press, 2013), 43.
3 Diana Slavin Forman exhibit at the Weitzman National Museum of American Jewish History, 1991. I am grateful to Claire Pingel for providing the materials from that exhibit.
4 Katharine Seelye, "Dan Robbins, Who Made Painting as Easy as 1-2-3 (and

4-5-6), Dies at 93," *New York Times*, April 5, 2019. See also "Dan Robbins Biography," Paint By Number Museum, PaintbyNumberMuseum.com.

5 Mary Couzin, "All in the Family: The Kohner Family," aNBMedia .com, July 2019. See also "Kohner Toy Company History," Oldwoodtoys.com.

6 Abigail Jones, "Meet Henry Orenstein, the Man who Changed How the World Plays," *Newsweek*, December 21, 2016.

7 Richard Sandomir, "Henry Orenstein, Holocaust Survivor Turned Major Toymaker, Dies at 98," *New York Times*, December 21, 2021.

8 Alan Hassenfeld, interview by the author, March 22, 2022.

9 Niraj Chokshi, "Do Not Pass Go, Hasbro. You're Forgetting Someone," *New York Times*, September 12, 2019; see also Mary Pilon, *The Monopolists: Obsession, Fury and the Scandal Behind the World's Favorite Board Game* (New York: Bloomsbury, 2015).

10 Jeffrey Breslow and Cynthia Beebe, *A Game Maker's Life* (New York: Post Hill Press, 2022); Peter Wyden, "Troubled King of Toys," *Saturday Evening Post*, March 5, 1950; "A Playboy Pad: Swinging in Suburbia," *Playboy*, May 1970.

11 Breslow and Beebe, *Game Maker's Life*, 88.

12 Bill Paxton, *A World Without Reality: Inside Marvin Glass's Toy Vault* (New York: Privately published, 2019), 441.

13 Breslow and Beebe, *Game Maker's Life*, 102. Jeffrey Breslow, interview by the author, February 24, 2024.

14 Eddy Goldfarb, interview by the author, February 15, 2021.

15 John Glionna, "It May Look like Fun and Games . . . ," *Los Angeles Times*, December 23, 1992.

16 Erik Arneson, "Reuben Klamer—The Game of Life," Play and Playground Encyclopedia, PGPedia.com.

17 Alan Hassenfeld remembers many of these distributors and the way they connected the manufacturers with the public. Alan Hassenfeld, interview by the author, March 22, 2021.

18 Richie Monchik, interview by the author, April 9, 2021.

19 Stephen J. Whitfield, "Merchants: The Marrow of the Southern Jewish Experience," Jewish Merchant Project, n.d., Mechants.JHSSC.org.

20 Alan Morrell, "Whatever Happened to . . . Neisner's?," *Rochester Democrat and Chronicle*, May 17, 2014; obituary for Gilbert Fox, *Observer* (Jewish Federation of Nashville) 84, no. 9 (September 2019): 30, 32.

21 Eugene Meyer, "Contrasts of a Private Persona," *Washington Post*, April 25, 1988. See also Tamar Brott, "The Sea Monkeys and the White Supremacist," *Los Angeles Times*, October 1, 2000.

22 Tim Walsh, *Timeless Toys: Classic Toys and the Playmakers Who Created Them* (Kansas City: Andrews McMeel, 2005), 93–98; Andrew N. Wong, "A Brief History of the Magic 8 Ball," Mental Floss, August 24, 2015.

23 Hilde Himmelweit, A. N. Oppenheim, and Pamela Vince, *Television and the Child: An Empirical Study of the Effect of Television and the Young* (Oxford: Oxford University Press, 1961), 25.

24 Jyotsna Kapur, "Out of Control: Television and the Transformation of Childhood in Late Capitalism," in *Kids' Media Culture*, ed. Marsha Kinder (Durham, NC: Duke University Press, 2000), 124.

25 Susan Bordo, *TV* (New York: Bloomsbury, 2021), 30.

26 Sydney Ladensohn Stern and Ted Schoenhaus, *Toyland: The High-Stakes Game of the Toy Industry* (New York: Contemporary Books, 1990), 55.

27 Reid Mitenbuler, *Wild Minds: The Artists and Rivalries That Inspired the Golden Age of Animation* (New York: Atlantic Monthly Press, 2020), 252, 187.
28 You can watch him talk about this at Soupy Sales, "Green Pieces of Paper" (video), posted by Barry Mitchell, January 3, 2009, https://www.youtube.com/watch?v=a-OGy3Kh7yM&list=PLB468BE316B343514.
29 Paul Buhle, *From the Lower East Side to Hollywood: Jews in American Popular Culture* (New York: Verso, 2004), 79.
30 Merry Loomis, interview by the author, February 23, 2021.
31 David Owen, "Where Toys Come From," *Atlantic*, October 1986.
32 Ryan Lambie, "Star Wars: How an Empty Box Became a Must-Have Item in 1977," *Den of Geek*, December 18, 2019.
33 Strawberry Shortcake generated $1.2 billion in retail: 25 million dolls, 10 million accessories, 122 million books, 15 million pieces of children's apparel three gold records, and six animated specials. Ryan Ball, "Strawberry Shortcake Titles Sell 2 Million," *Animation Magazine*, November 24, 2003.
34 Robert H. Mnookin and Susan Bartlett Foote, "The 'Kid Vid' Crusade," *Public Interest*, Spring 1980.

9: THE EXPERTS AND THE STORYTELLERS

1 Nicholas Hammond, *Childhood in the Contemporary World* (Cambridge: Polity Press, 2004), 21.
2 Anne Roark, "Fads, Theories: Parenting: Mother of Invention," *Los Angeles Times*, July 24, 1988.
3 Jyotsna Kapur, "Out of Control: Television and the Transformation of Childhood in Late Capitalism," in *Kids' Media Culture,* ed. M. Kinder (Durham, NC: Duke University Press), 126.
4 "Heidi Murkoff," www.whattoexpect.com.
5 Haim Ginott, *Between Parent and Child* (New York: Three Rivers Press, 1965); see also Henry Jenkins, *Where the Wild Things Were: Boyhood and Permissive Parenting in Postwar America* (New York: NYU Press, 2025).
6 Fanny Goldstein, "The Jewish Child in Bookland," *Jewish Book Annual* 5 (1946–47): 86, 84.
7 Sophie Cederbaum, "American Jewish Juvenile Literature During the Last Twenty-Five Years," *Jewish Book Annual* (1967–68): 194–95.
8 Stephen S. Wise, *Child Versus Parent: Some Chapters on the Irrepressible Conflict in the Home* (New York: Macmillan, 1922), 36–37.
9 Jeanne Lamb, "From the Shelves at NYPL: 100 Great Children's Books 100 Years," New York Public Library, October 3, 2013.
10 "Author Jane Yolen Talks Book Banning and 'Harry Potter,'" *Wired*, January 23, 2013.
11 Margalit Fox, "Maurice Sendak, Author of Splendid Nightmares, Dies at 83," *New York Times*, May 8, 2012.
12 Golan Y. Moskowitz, "Wild Outside in the Night: Maurice Sendak, Queer American Jewishness, and the Child" (Ph.D. diss., Brandeis University, 2018), 49.
13 Katherine Sorensen, "'Where the Wild Things Are' Is a Love Letter to Jewish Children," *Kveller*, February 15, 2022.
14 Moskowitz, "Wild Outside in the Night," 44; Tony Kushner, *The Art of Maurice Sendak: 1980 to the Present* (New York: Abrams, 2003), 190.

15 Moskowitz, "Wild Outside in the Night," 44
16 Nat Hentoff, "Among the Wild Things," *New Yorker*, January 14, 1966.
17 Moskowitz, "Wild Outside in the Night," 158.
18 Moskowitz, "Wild Outside in the Night," 84.
19 Moskowitz, "Wild Outside in the Night," 21.
20 Moskowitz, "Wild Outside in the Night," 351.

10: BEYOND BEN'S "IDEAL" GIRLHOOD: GIRLS AND DOLLS

1 Virginia Lynn Moylan, *Zora Neale Hurston's Final Decade* (Gainesville: University Press of Florida, 2011), 66.
2 Denise Helaine Bond, "Saralee: A Doll Ahead of Its Time," *Doll News*, Fall 2020, 124.
3 "Negro Dolls," *Playthings*, January 1909, 67.
4 "Negro Dolls," *Playthings*, November 1911, 67.
5 Moylan, *Hurston's Final Decade*, 68.
6 "Caricatures of African Americans: The Pickaninny," *History on the Net*, July 20, 2012, http://www.authentichistory.com/diversity/african/3-coon/2.
7 Debbie Behan Garrett, "BDHT: 1947 Sears Catalogue: Noma's Mammy with Charge," BlackDollCollecting.blogspot.com, February 25, 2011.
8 Julian K. Jarboe, "The Racial Symbolism of the Topsy-Turvy Doll," *Atlantic*, November 20, 2015. See also Jan Thalberg, "Topsy-Turvy: The Upside Down Girl, a State of Confusion," *Black Ethnic Collectibles* 5, no. 5 (1993): 16; Wendy Lavitt, *Dolls: The Knopf Collectors' Guides to American Antiques* (New York: Knopf, 1983), 31. Kimberly Wallace-Sanders is not so sure. See her *Mammy: A Century of Race, Gender and Southern Memory* (Ann Arbor: University of Michigan Press, 2008). Correspondence with Wallace-Sanders was especially clarifying.
9 Gordon Patterson, "Color Matters: The Creation of the Sara Lee Doll," *Florida Historical Quarterly* 73, no. 2 (1994): 151.
10 Debbie Behan Garrett's blog on Black doll collecting is a trove of historical information about Black dolls. See Debbie Behan Garrett, "Ideal's Saralee Negro Doll 1951–1953 'An Ambassador of Goodwill,'" BlackDollCollecting.blogspot.com, February 26, 2018.
11 Mel Tapley, "Sun Tan Dolls: Pioneering Effort in Positive Images," *New York Amsterdam News*, December 24, 1988, 23.
12 Rob Goldberg, *Radical Play: Revolutionizing Children's Toys in 1960s and 1970s America* (Durham, NC: Duke University Press, 2023), 88.
13 "Brown v. Board and 'The Doll Test,'" NAACP Legal Defense Fund, n.d., Naacpldf.org.
14 Patterson, "Color Matters," 157.
15 Moylan, *Hurston's Final Decade*, 70.
16 Susan Eastman, "Baby Doll: Sara Lee Creech of Belle Glade Tells a Long-Forgotten Chapter of Civil Rights History." *Broward-Palm Beach New Times*, May 9, 2002. See also Moylan, *Hurston's Final Decade*, 71.
17 Patterson, "Color Matters," 147–65.
18 Patricia Hogan, "The Other Sara Lee: A Doll Story," Strong Museum (Rochester, NY), 2013, MuseumofPlay.org.
19 Patterson, "Color Matters," 161.

20 Sabrina Lynette Thomas, "Sara Lee: The Rise and Fall of the Ultimate Negro Doll," *Transforming Anthropology* 15, no. 1 (April 2007): 43; Eastman, "Baby Doll."
21 Eastman, "Baby Doll."
22 Emily Temple, "How Zora Neale Hurston Helped Create the First Realistic Black Baby Doll," Literaryhub.com, January 7, 2019.
23 "Modern Designs: Manufacturer Find Trends More Realistic," *Ebony*, January 1952, quoted in Patterson, "Color Matters," 149.
24 Eastman, "Baby Doll."
25 Thomas, "Sara Lee," 45.
26 Patterson, "Color Matters," 162.
27 Leonard Sloane, "Ideal Toy's Weintraub Tries to Create Fun Potential," *New York Times*, October 24, 1971.
28 "Monroe's a Doll—But Normal," *Cincinnati Enquirer*, September 20, 1956, 27.
29 Peter Jensen Brown, "Margarete Steiff, Morris Michtom and Teddy Roosevelt—Hunting Down the Origin of 'Teddy Bear,'" Early Sports and Pop Culture History Blog, November 22, 2017.
30 Gary Cross, *Kids' Stuff: Toys and the Changing World of American Childhood* (Cambridge, MA: Harvard University Press, 1999), 172.
31 Messy Nessy Chic, "Meet Lilli, the High-End German Call Girl Who Became Barbie," MessyNessyChic.com, December 19, 2022.
32 Orly Lobel, *You Don't Own Me: How "Mattel v. MGA Entertainment" Exposed Barbie's Dark Side* (New York: W. W. Norton, 2017).
33 Ruth Mosko Handler, *Dream Doll: The Ruth Handler Story* (Stamford, CT: Longmeadow Press, 1994), 12.
34 Jerry Oppenheimer, *Toy Monster: The Big, Bad World of Mattel* (New York: John Wiley, 2009).
35 Maya Salam, "Mattel, Maker of Barbie, Offers Gender-Neutral Dolls," *New York Times*, September 26, 2019.
36 Mary Burt Baldwin, "Toy World Invaded by the Klunk Kin," *New York Times,* August 3, 1962.
37 Nadra Nittle, "Operation Bootstrap: Empowering the African American Community Through Entrepreneurship," KCET.org, November 19, 2019.
38 Rob Goldberg, "Baby Nancy, the First 'Black' Doll, Woke the Toy Industry," *Los Angeles Times*, March 12, 2019.

11: BOYS AND THEIR TOYS

1 Ada Hart Arlitt, "How Separation Affects the Family," *Marriage and Family Living* 5, no. 1 (February 1943), 21.
2 Philip Wylie, *Generation of Vipers* (New York: Rinehart & Co., 1942), 185.
3 "What Is a Balabusta?," Chabad.org.
4 Elaine Tylor May, *Homeward Bound: American Families in the Cold War Era* (New York: Basic Books, 1988), 147.
5 Harvey Levenstein, *Paradoxes of Plenty: A Social History of Eating in Modern America* (New York: Oxford University Press, 1993), 105.
6 "Are You a Dud as a Dad?," *American Home*, August 21, 1950.
7 Donald Hall, *Fathers Playing Catch with Sons* (Berkeley, CA: North Point Press, 1984).

8 "The Best College Basketball Team from Every Decade," NCAA.com, November 27, 2018, https://www.ncaa.com/news/basketball-men/article/2018–10–04/best-college-basketball-team-every-decade. See also Michael Weinrib, "A Team That Chose Principle over Gold Medals," ESPN.com, April 20, 2009, and "Long Island University Basketball Team," International Jewish Sports Hall of Fame, JewishSportsHOF.org.
9 "It Runs in the Family," Topps Archive, April 4, 2011, TheToppsArchives.com. See also Marty Appel, "Memories and Dreams: Sy Berger," Marty Appel, Applepr.com.
10 Chris Olds, "Former Topps Executive Sy Berger Dies at 91," n.d., Beckett.com.
11 "It Runs in the Family," Topps Archive.
12 John Cawelti, *The Six-Gun Mystique* (Bowling Green, OH: Bowling Green University Popular Press, 1971), 2, 83.
13 Kenneth S. Davis, "Coonskin Superman," *New York Times Magazine*, April 24, 1955, 24. See also "The Wild Frontier," *Time*, May 23, 1955, and Sean Griffin, "Kings of the Wild Backyard: Davy Crockett and Children's Space," *Kids' Media Culture*, ed. Marsha Kinder (Durham, NC: Duke University Press,1999), 102–21.
14 Lewis Glaser, "Autobiography of Lewis H. Glaser" January 1, 1955, courtesy of Kim Selbert.
15 Kim Selbert, interview by the author, July 8, 2021.
16 "Models for Millions," *Mechanics Illustrated*, December 1955, 99.
17 "Renwal: A Quick History" (video), Max's Models, https://www.youtube.com/watch?v=Skw2-qbnG8A.
18 "From Secret Weapons to Dollhouse Furniture: Early Renwal History," Collectors Quests, https://ph.pinterest.com/pin/doll-house-484066659963189716/.
19 The popularity of the Visible Man series is suggested by competing claims of creation. In a brief book about Renwal, Charles Donovan suggests it was Lubow who invented it, though Jovine's obituary claims that he did. See Charles F. Donovan, Jr., *Renwal: World's Finest Toys* (Gas City, IN: L-W Book Sales, 1999), and Joanne Isaac, "Obituary: Marcel Jovine 1921–2003," ANS Magazine, Spring, 2003. Neither is true, though both played a large role. The Visible Man's patent from 1961 is in Rosenbloom's name. Adam Rosenbloom to the author, July 6, 2021. See also, "Renwal Classic 'Visible Man' Kit: Invisible Secrets Revealed," *Scale Model News*, March 13, 2014.

12: HOW FIRST-GENERATION JEWS CREATED AMERICAN CHILDHOOD

1 This connection between self-making and anxiety was a centerpiece of my book *Manhood in America: A Cultural History* (New York: Free Press, 1996).
2 Michael Alexander, *Jazz Age Jews* (Princeton, NJ: Princeton University Press, 2001), 60.
3 Paul Buhle, *From the Lower East Side to Hollywood: Jews in American Popular Culture* (New York: Verso, 2004), 124, 85.
4 Harry Brod, *Superman Is Jewish? How Comic Book Superheroes Came to Serve Truth, Justice, and the Jewish American Way* (New York: Free Press, 2012), 192.
5 Stan Lee, foreword to Danny Fingeroth, *Disguised as Clark Kent: Jews, Comics and the Creation of the Superhero* (New York: Continuum, 2007), 10.
6 Rich Cohen, *Tough Jews: Fathers, Sons, and Gangster Dreams* (New York: Vintage, 1998), 77, 26.

7 Robert Bly, *Iron John: A Book for Men* (Reading, MA: Addison Wesley, 1990).
8 Charles Silberman, *A Certain People: American Jews and Their Lives Today* (New York: Simon & Schuster, 1985), 147.
9 Silberman, *Certain People*, 154.
10 W.E.B. Du Bois, "Strivings of the Negro People," *Atlantic*, August 1897; W.E.B. Du Bois, *The Souls of Black Folk* (1903; reprint New York: Dover, 1994), 2.
11 Noel Ignatiev, *How the Irish Became White* (New York: Routledge, 1995).
12 Michael Rogin, *Blackface, White Noise: Jewish Immigrants in the Hollywood Melting Pot* (Berkeley: University of California Press, 1996).
13 Eric L. Goldstein, *The Price of Whiteness: Jews, Race, and American Identity* (Princeton: Princeton University Press, 2006), 53, 54.
14 J. Hoberman and Jeffrey Shandler, *Entertaining America: Jews, Movies and Broadcasting* (Princeton, NJ: Princeton University Press, 2003).
15 James R. Barrett and David Roediger, "Inbetween Peoples: Race, Nationality and the 'New Immigrant' Working Class," *Journal of Ethnic History* 16, no. 3 (Spring 1997): 4.
16 See David Roediger, *Working Toward Whiteness: How America's Immigrants Became White* (New York: Basic Books, 2005), 133. The authorship of this particular line is disputed.
17 Karen Brodkin, *How Jews Became White Folk, and What That Says About Race in America* (New Brunswick, NJ: Rutgers University Press, 1998), 1–2.
18 Roediger, *Working Toward Whiteness*,107–8.
19 Thorstein Veblen, "The Intellectual Pre-Eminence of Jews in Modern Europe," *Political Science Quarterly* 34, no. 1 (March 1919): 33–42.
20 Veblen, "Intellectual Pre-Eminence."
21 Matthew Arnold, "Stanzas from the Grande Chartreuse" (1855).
22 David Biale, "The Melting Pot and Beyond: Jews and the Politics of American Identity," in *Insider/Outsider: American Jews and Multiculturalism*, ed. David Biale, Michael Galchinsky, and Susannah Heschel (Berkeley: University of California Press, 1998), 31.
23 Alfred Kazin, *A Walker in the City* (New York: Harcourt Brace & Co., 1951), 11.
24 Ted Merwin, *In Their Own Image: New York Jews in Jazz Age Popular Culture* (New Brunswick, NJ: Rutgers University Press, 2006), 165.
25 Tim Walsh, interview by the author, October 20, 2020.
26 Neal Gabler, *An Empire of their Own: How the Jews Invented Hollywood* (1988; reprint New York: Anchor, 1989), 119, 5–6.
27 Gabler, *Empire of their Own*, 5.
28 Aben Kandel, *Rabbi Burns* (New York: Covici-Freide, 1931), 256.
29 Brod, *Superman Is Jewish?*, 76.
30 J. Hoberman and Jeffrey Shandler, *Entertaining America: Jews, Movies and Broadcasting* (Princeton, NJ: Princeton University Press, 2003), 274.
31 Paula Michtom, interview by the author, April 23, 2019.
32 *Hearings on S. 1689 Before the Consumer Subcommittee of the Senate Committee on Commerce,* 91st Cong., 1st Sess., ser. 91–11, at 50–51 (1969), testimony of Jerome M. Fryer, president of Toy Manufacturers of America.
33 Gerald Lesser, *Children and Television: Lessons from Sesame Street* (New York: Vintage Books, 1974), 65. See also David Kamp, *Sunny Days: The Children's Revolution That Changed America* (New York: Simon & Schuster, 2020), chap. 13.
34 Kamp, *Sunny Days*, chap. 13.
35 Amy Ogata, *Designing the Creative Child: Playthings and Places in Midcentury America* (Minneapolis: University of Minnesota Press, 2013), 1.

Index

Page numbers in italics refer to illustrations.